Inflation Policy and Unemployment Theory

The Cost-Benefit Approach to Monetary Planning

By the same author

Fiscal Neutrality Toward Economic Growth
Golden Rules of Economic Growth
Microeconomic Foundations of Employment and Inflation
Theory (with others)
The Goal of Economic Growth (editor)
Private Wants and Public Needs (editor)

INFLATION POLICY AND UNEMPLOYMENT THEORY

The Cost-Benefit Approach to Monetary Planning

EDMUND S. PHELPS
Columbia University

W. W. NORTON & COMPANY, INC.
New York

Library of Congress Cataloging in Publication Data

Phelps, Edmund S.
  Inflation Policy and Unemployment Theory.

  Includes Bibliographical References.

  1. Employment (Economic theory) 2. Inflation
(Finance) I. Title.
HB301.P45   339.5   77–174159
ISBN 0–393–09395–6

1 2 3 4 5 6 7 8 9 0

TO EMILY

Contents

List of Figures and Tables

Preface

THIS book is a study in both economic policy and economic theory. As an essay in theory it is directed to the welfare side of macro-economics. It integrates, and in places reformulates, the welfare-economics of money and anticipated inflation. And it resumes the construction, temporarily stymied, of the welfare-economics of un-employment and inflation. The latter analysis, besides reviewing the sociological considerations, attempts to draw some welfare implications from the newer micro-macro models begun in *Micro-economic Foundations of Employment and Inflation Theory* (Norton, 1970).

The other concern of this book is with economic policy, and this has usually taken precedence. My aim has been to argue for what I call the cost-benefit approach to inflation planning. This approach is not radically different from the one originally outlined in my paper, 'Phillips Curves, Expectations of Inflation, and Optimal Unemployment Over Time' (1967). But the argument is now modified in some significant respects, and I have tried to give careful attention to the international ramifications, and the con-sequences for economic stability, that moderate American inflation, anticipated and unanticipated, might probably have.

In focusing on policy I have probably traded off the interests of some theorists. Algebraic formulations have been omitted (except in some footnotes) and diagrammatics minimized in the hope, how-ever unwarranted, of having an early policy impact. Yet much or all of the book's value for economic policy in the long run will depend upon the evaluation of its argument by economic theorists. So I hope that they will try to decipher it.

The new economic policies announced by the American govern-ment in August 1971 came too late to be discussed specifically in the text. Fortunately they do not seem to require any important revisions. The adjustments of exchange rates and the widening of their bands raise my expectations that the international monetary system would be adaptable to increased American inflation. The significance of the recent experiment with wage and price restraints will probably be disputed. I am still inclined to believe that temporary restraints can retard the rise of prices both directly, by blocking desired price and wage increases, and indirectly through their announcement effects and subsequent demonstration effects upon expectations of the inflation rate, provided that monetary forces are not pushing expectations in the opposite direction. Temporary restraints, then, are a cost-saving invention in inflation-fighting, but they are not cost-eliminating. As for permanent controls, I would guess that suitably differentiated wage-price restraints of limited scope could reduce the equilibrium unemployment rate, though I am skeptical that much of a dent would be made in practice. In any case, the problem of inflation planning and the associated costs and benefits do not thereby seem fundamentally to be altered.

This study got under way in 1968–69 during a leave of absence paid by the Brookings Institution. Most of the writing was done the next year at the Center for Advanced Study in the Behavioral Sciences in Stanford, California. A grant from the Fels Institute for Policy Analysis at the University of Pennsylvania helped me to complete the manuscript the following year.

I should have kept a log of the names of those who answered my SOS calls for guidance and comment over those three years. I still recall discussions and correspondence with Robert Hall, Donald Nichols, John Palmer, David Pritchett, Karl Shell, Harry Johnson, Alan Meltzer, Eytan Sheshinski, David Levhari, Kenneth Arrow, Peter Diamond, Alvin Marty, Ronald McKinnon, and Robert Aliber. At the Center, John Rawls and Amelie Rorty were especially helpful.

The Index to Subjects was prepared by Stephen Salant, the crucial Index to Names by Nancy Newcomb. The manuscript was typed and retyped by Susan Thomas, Irene Bickenbach, and Bobbi Granger.

I am deeply grateful for this economic and intellectual assistance.

                                                                              E. S. P.

New York
February 1972

Introduction

THIS is a study of the principles of optimum inflation policy. An inflation policy is like a manual that specifies which aggregate demand target is to be aimed at next in each potential economic situation. Choosing an inflation policy, of course, requires the use of some criterion. The one used here takes the train of social costs and benefits associable with each feasible inflation policy, given the economic situation we initially find ourselves in, and evaluates it in relation to our agreed preferences for early benefits as against late and for smooth as against bunched. The net benefits of the employment effects over time (vanishing or not) of a shift in inflation policy are one component in this stream of costs and benefits.

A great deal of attention has been directed at how to 'stabilize' the unemployment rate (or other indicator) around some predesignated target value. Little attention has been devoted to how the appropriate target at any time depends upon the opportunities and disadvantages presented by the current economic situation. Men in policy-making authority have to make do nonetheless. We often find the economy in a contrived slump, experiencing a shift of the official target, all in the pursuit of some inflation policy. It seems important, therefore, that our inflation policy be subjected to a systematic appraisal. As I write, we are in the midst of another purge of inflation. The considerable loss of jobs and loss of output that have resulted make it highly doubtful that the purge has been in the interests of very many. Those few who would have lost through official acquiescence in the inflation could easily have been compensated from the benefits to the gainers; in all probability most of them would have been. Nevertheless the policy goes unchallenged, at least in its strategic objectives. Critics have sought only to outsmart the officials with cheaper ways to accomplish the same ultimate inflation objective.

A contribution of this study, I believe, is that some late developments in the microeconomic theory of employment decisions are brought to bear on the choice of inflation policy. Neo-neoclassical unemployment theory, both positive and welfare-analytic, occupies much of the volume. According to this theory, there is no immaculate connection running from the rate of growth of the money supply to the rate of inflation, nor from any fiscal control to the inflation rate. The 'frictions' in an advanced economy create a linkage between the path of the unemployment rate over time and the path of the inflation rate generated by the course of aggregate demand. Forces from the demand side which produce an unexpected fall of the inflation rate – a fall-off of price increases in relation to what was planned and expected – tend also to produce at least a temporary bulge of the unemployment rate.

There are also microeconomic and psychological reasons for guessing that a sustained reduction of the inflation rate would permanently enlarge somewhat the average unemployment rate over the future. Those reasons are bound to be somewhat controversial, and the data are reluctant to speak, but never mind: in either case, permanent or temporary, unemployment is a profoundly important desideratum, though not the only one, in the selection of inflation policy. The two lengthy chapters on the economic and social impacts of a recession of employment from its maintainable equilibrium level, plus the reasons for discounting future benefits relative to present ones, argue this persuasively.

Let me not leave the impression that this volume carves out unprecedented subject-matter for economic thought. Learned opinion on inflation there has always been. Quarrels over budgets and interest rates have sometimes concealed disagreements over inflation policy. Few are the greats of the present age, and those past, who have not felt the need to share with us their ideas on the subject. The grand theme of optimum *steady* inflation has, in fact, one of the longest histories in economics. The scholarly clerics who did economics in Renaissance times understood a thing or two about the merits of steady inflation. In the early part of this century, Francis A. Walker in this country and Sir Dennis Robertson in England took prominent inflationist positions. Following their own genetic destiny, some continental economists later argued for a constant money supply with its implications for continuous deflation under conditions of economic growth. A contemporary 'classic' in applied welfare economics calculates the 'optimum' annual rate of steady inflation – finding it to be 18 percent in a hypothetical Latin-style economy.

Many of these contributors have scored individual points, some just recording attitudes, but no architectonics. There has not yet emerged a normal doctrine on optimum inflation (let alone the dynamic aspects), nor a graduated series of handbooks to test the knowledge of and to measure mavericks against. Why? Perhaps it has taken a few decades of immersion in statistics and decision theory, a baptism by random disturbance, in order that economists be able to handle the difficult conceptual problems involving money and unemployment which are at the heart. Whatever the reason, my hope is that the present volume will begin to fill the void. In drawing together various ideas and analytical methods that are sometimes thought dissonant, I hope that I have synthesized something that most contemporary economists will regard as the normal approach to inflation policy.

At least those contemporary economists who are in the philosophical mainstream of their discipline! In the chapters that follow there is little space given to the positions of some who want to make radical departures in the assumptions of the analysis. Nor do I dwell on any popular fears and fallacies about inflation. It may help to throw my own approach to inflation planning into sharper relief if, at this convenient point, I acknowledge the existence of other ways of looking (or not looking) at inflation planning.

0.0. *Approaches to Inflation Planning*

In considering the attitudes of various economic schools toward inflation it is important to consider the background of public opinion (and vice-versa).

As for the public, it believes that the injection of an inflationary policy into the economy, however well meant, would be like loosing Dr. Frankenstein's monster to play with their children. The public has got it into its head that 'reasonable price stability', meaning an approximately zero rate of inflation on the average, is essential for a prosperous and just economy. Fiscal and monetary policies are to be confined to those promising little or no sustained inflation. Only the occasional short-lived price rise can be countenanced, and then only for some temporarily redeeming purpose.

The mystique seems to depend upon the popular misunderstanding of the price level as the cost of 'living'. It is a breakdown in the teaching of general equilibrium theory. The public sees in a price rise only an increase in the money cost of living and not the simultaneous rise in the money means of living. When a bout of unanticipated inflation arrives, it is held guilty by association of many accompanying, yet unrelated, misfortunes – not excluding the increased taxes to limit it. People tend to blame their every loss of real wages on the unaccustomed price rise while asymmetrically crediting their every real income gain to individual prowess.

The same confusion besets the idea of a planned rate of inflation which becomes expected and counted on. The man in the street is frightened by the prospect of a continuing rise of prices, feeling that he will not have the 'market power' to raise his money income compensatorily. He cannot believe that the market will take care of his problem, that the threadworn principles by which real incomes are distributed will be unaltered by prospective inflation, that inflation will not enhance 'their' market power to earn real income at his expense. The force of this mystique should not be underestimated. Without it, it is doubtful that the public would, beginning in 1958 and again in 1970, have accepted the sacrifice of employment and income intended to purge the inflationary spirits.

By contrast, economists are liberated from these myths, even though reticent to expose them. 'For every extra dollar that a buyer must pay as a result of inflation, an extra dollar's worth of income is generated somewhere for sellers.' This arithmetic identity, as trivial to the economist as it is elusive to the layman, makes the theoretician free. Why not inflation? Or why less of it? The dollar will not know. It is the satisfactions of people, and their just distribution, that economic policy must serve, and these objectives are unlikely to require a constant price level.

What stands do economists take on inflation? The profession in this country has in recent years maintained an almost unbroken silence on the mystique. On the whole, it has tended, rather, to give some support to the mystique. Compared with the honor list of free trade defenders, say, the roll-call of economists who have spoken out for inflation – or for positive deflation – is pretty short. The entrenched mystique may have been reason itself: all the troops have been needed in the battle against the business cycle. The absence of normal economic doctrine on inflation objectives may also account for the willingness of most economists to go along with the mystique. The secret inflationist is not sure he will have comrades in battle. The academic inflationist fears that others' inflationism is for the wrong reasons, and academicians abhor strange bedfellows.

From the journals, however, and especially from the oral tradition, one discerns the inflation question within the economics profession. Quite a few economists hold that it would be wise to limit our enthusiasm for rationalism to a few corners of social policy. If the lid is taken off the inflation question, the public will not have the maturity to cope with the responsibility. The reasons for this position vary. One theme is that, whether or not the public succeeded finally in achieving an inflation policy technically superior to rigid price stability, it would not be worth the cost in public nervousness and social strife. A variant of this is that the great beast, with his short attention span, had better not be distracted from greater demands on him.

Having written an overlong book on rational inflation policy, I am oversensitive to this counter-approach. It is all too easy to regard inflation as the solution to every economic problem, from unemployment to scarcity. But this I do not do. So perhaps I can object should someone want to minimize the importance of the choice of inflation policy. If we could have stayed the planned slump of 1970–71 in favor of a reprieve of the current inflation rate, that would have been worth quite a lot of turmoil.

There is also the moral issue to raise. And this should be striking to libertarians among the monetary conservatives. What is the point of political liberty if the voters are ridden with myths? And what committee is to decide which myths to dispel and which to promulgate? I would think that the freedom to decide intelligently, to live by our wits, is a desirable end as well as a means to other ends.

A second theme of public immaturity declares that the public will simply bungle its inflation decisions. These advocates of the price stability mystique will cheerfully admit that zero inflation is unlikely to be optimal, long run or short. But they contend that voters will not be able to demostrate the necessary resoluteness or sophistication or whatever, so that public determination of the inflation policy without benefit of the mystique would produce worse results than does the mystique.

The most dreadful outcome, feared by some, is the development of an ever-mounting runaway inflation. Such a prognostication is, of course, beyond economics. Economic theory offers no obstacles to our manipulating the inflation rate as we like: if the presses that print our money cannot be speeded up, let the government buy more of them; and if they cannot be run more slowly, shut down some of them. The notion that there is a simple choice between the goal of price stability and runaway inflation over the abyss is dime-store political science. It is a *non sequitur* to conclude that because some economic policies aiming for pie in the sky will indeed produce runaway inflation, realistic political decisions that favor some positive inflation rate over a level price trend will somehow lead to the same debacle. Nor is history on the side of this simplistic worry. The famous hyperinflationary take-offs of the past do not appear to have followed a conscious disavowal of price stability; those inflations were in some sense the involuntary response to an underlying social disequilibrium. Moreover, as noted by one inflation historian, ' . . . there are many examples in history when you have had several decades of generally rising prices or of generally falling prices without the prise rise accelerating or the price decline turning into a collapse.'[1]

The less extreme contention heard from this school is that, if left to democratic determination instead of committee, the inflation rate will come to rest all right, but at a grossly excessive rate. A level price trend has the advantage that it more easily enlists the spirit of sacrifice necessary for the maintenance of that trend than does some abstractly optimal inflation rate. Compare 'Price Stability, Right or Wrong', which has a nice ring to it, with 'If I have but one job to give to my economy, let me give it for 5.5 percent inflation as against higher numbers', which is absurd. The danger, it is held, is that voters will be insufficiently disciplined to vote their long-run interests. The analogy to the man who oversmokes or overeats is often drawn – he is not revealing his real preference.

I discuss addiction theories and the heroic approach elsewhere in this book, so I will be brief here. To my mind, it is the disutility of too much inflation that should be left to limit our appetite for it, not a taboo. I see no basis for the supposition that inflation policy, democratically arrived at and unleashed from disfunctional conventions, would be insufficiently farsighted. If the inflation rate is widely regarded as excessive, what reason is there to think that its reduction would not summon a majority of voters? Besides, getting hold of our democratic policy-making potentialities is as much the point as the modest though valuable economic gain that can be expected to result. Conceivably the inflation taboo played a useful role when the political and financial systems were far younger and more fragile than now. In modern times, however, I believe there would be a significant gain from adopting a less ritualistic, more 'calculating' approach to inflation policy.

The mission of this book is to outline a *rational* approach – one

---

[1] M. Friedman, *Inflation: Causes and Consequences* (New York: Asia Publishing House, 1963), p. 20. Reprinted in M. Friedman, *The Optimum Supply of Money and Other Essays* (Chicago: Aldine Publishing Company, 1968).

might say a cost-benefit or *econometric* approach (ah!) – to finding the best management of certain governmental powers and operations that impinge importantly on the rate of inflation and thus on the path of unemployment. The focus is on the stabilization tools already in the hands of the federal government in its steering of aggregate monetary demand. Roughly, it is about choosing a monetary policy, though the uses of fiscal instruments also receive attention.

The emphasis in the words above should be on the word *approach*. The goal of this volume is largely an intermediate one: understanding the nature and influence of the determinants of the socially optimal monetary-fiscal policy toward unemployment and inflation – identifying the kind of empirical knowledge (or assumption) and ethical postulates that shape the character of optimal inflation policy. The aim, at least, is to be able to describe in a qualitative way how the optimal use of the stabilization instrument – say the control over the money supply – depends upon the intersection of weighted individual preferences on the one hand and technically feasible choices on the other. Still, one wishes to have a substantive inkling of what is optimal in the way of inflation.

One hurdle in the way of quantifying the optimal inflation policy – in particular, the monetary policy which is determined to be optimal on this approach – is its dependence on the weights assigned to each individual's preferences: The weights to be given those yet unborn relative to individuals now living, the weights assigned to the poorly endowed and socially disadvantaged relative to those who are better off, these all must be decided. On these weighty matters it is hard to say what every man's feelings are, or would be on re-examination. Equally perplexing is the matter of guessing what, in respect to these distributional aspects, the parallel economic policies to be pursued will be like. But the individual economist need not be neutral *qua* citizen, need not wait for an ever-clearer view. Nor is it necessarily to be supposed that the optimum inflation policy, while conditional on the weights, is terribly sensitive to change in the weights.

What most stand in the way of quantifying the optimal monetary policy (in the above conditional sense) are the extraordinary difficulties of estimating costs and benefits. This is because it is necessary to reckon not just the old stand-bys, consumption and leisure, but the less measurable (though more real) feelings of self-respect, esteem in the community, the sense of economic independence, the degree of security, and job satisfactions. It is perfectly clear that variations in the rates of unemployment and inflation can and do produce emotional effects that are hard for the poor economist to gauge or to describe. The subject needs the eye of an Orwell, the ear of a Pinter – but let me do the book anyway.

As a result of these problems of dimensionality and measurement, we find ourselves in a not uncharacteristic situation: As elsewhere in economics, the statistically practicable models lack theoretical credibility while the realistic theories cannot easily be fitted *in toto* to obtainable data. Yet much of the model can be estimated. The analytical framework usually indicates the kinds of empirical information it would be useful to collect. In the less measurable sphere of the model, the analysis reminds us that the sphere is there and that hunches in these areas must be used if the decision reached is going to be made intelligently. With these caveats in mind, I would venture to say that the model developed here does provide a reasonably persuasive case for moderate inflationism.

The nine chapters that follow may need some introduction to acquaint the reader with the motives of each chapter and the links between them. The notes ahead are more a preview of the book than a description or summary.

0.1. *Inflation and Unemployment Theory*

The effects of a particular monetary policy or fiscal policy are commonly described in terms of aggregates and averages: the unemployment rate, aggregate output, the rate of inflation, certain interest rates, and so on. When the monetary and fiscal authorities assess the 'economic situation' or the 'state' of the economy, in order to ascertain what actions their policy requires, they commonly describe that state in the same macroeconomic terms. These macroeconomic variables are highly convenient for keeping the month-to-month charting of the economic system within manageable proportions. Even a highly compact macroeconomic description can be quite informative to experts because the underlying microeconomic structure does not change quickly.

Yet the utility of these macrovariables in characterizing and formulating monetary and fiscal policies depends ultimately upon the microeconomic meaning behind them. How do such variables as the unemployment rate and the inflation rate signal, if they do, the degree of attainment of the basic individual satisfactions from consumption, leisure, career, and the rest? It is necessary for a welfare analysis to interpret the behavior of the various aggregates in terms of the motivations and choices of the individuals whose behavior comprises the aggregates. Why do some unemployed individuals willingly forgo wage income for a while when, usually, there is some kind of paid employment available? What are the effects of such a decision upon the individual himself? Upon others? And if not all unemployed persons always are giving up current wage income willingly, why is it that some firms seem willing to pass up the opportunity to take advantage of the wish of those individuals to add to their present wage income at going rates? What are the effects of these decisions?

A satisfyingly 'micro' theory of macroeconomic behavior is needed for another reason. There are other macrovariables than the unemployment rate – such as the rate of inflation and money rates of interest – that impinge on the stuff of basic individual preferences. Hence we have to know how these macrovariables fit together and jointly respond to the monetary policy selected. Without a microeconomic theory of job, wage, and price decisions in hand, we are not in a position to hypothesize coherently and consistently about the short-term and long-term relationships that prevail among the macrovariables. One is then in danger, or in greater danger, of extrapolating from limited past experience that does not test for the consequences of the monetary policy being contemplated. The risk is increased that one will award the best marks to some policy whose promised benefits will prove to be infeasible.

Part I of this volume runs the gamut of micro-theory about employment decision by household and firm and the associated theory of wage and price decisions. It begins with the customarily 'economic' kind of theorizing that keeps at arm's length the possibilities of interpersonal and more general externalities (spill-over and neighborhood effects). Here reliance is placed on the economists' model of individual behavior as the outcome of 'expected utility maximization', as the best the individual can do for himself in his circumstances, when acting alone without thought for or pressure from others.

It is natural to start that way. Most of the persons reported unemployed in any month are not jobless as the result of some mental defect or cultural difference or social pathology (though social mores have their effect). In periods of normal or average business conditions, most of the unemployment observed is the 'heat' produced when unpredictable changes in technology and in tastes encounter certain economic frictions. The most notable of these frictions is the costliness to individual households and firms of acquiring infor-

mation about wages, prices, supplies, and demands around the
economy, in the present and in the future. If there were complete
information about the present and the future, we could hardly speak
of unemployment or of inflation, and they would not exist as matters
for public decision. The poorly endowed and the socially disadvantaged would still raise problems for economic policy, but their plight
would be evidenced wholly by their low rates of pay and their low
participation in the labor force.

Saying that unemployment is essentially frictional does not banish
sociological influence. Nor does it rule out monetary influences. In
fact, it is the economic frictions that give the monetary and fiscal
authorities the leverage they have – the traction, as it were – to vary
the rate of unemployment. Without frictions, a change in aggregate
demand brought about by the monetary or fiscal authorities would
instantaneously alter the price level without necessarily affecting the
use of real resources. Moreover, the point that unemployment depends upon frictions reminds us that the unemployment rate of every
social class or economic sub-group has that root in common. It is no
longer surprising therefore that when business conditions affect the
overall unemployment rate, all unemployment rates tend to move in
the same direction, even, very roughly, in the same proportion.

Chapter 1 presents a typology of frictional unemployment, classi-
fied according to the nature of the friction or uncertainty and the
motivations and mechanisms it gives rise to. There is search unemployment of two sorts – negotiable wages in the one case, and job
rationing and vacancies in the other extreme case. There is precautionary unemployment – staying ready for the unpredictable
arrival of the next offer. And there is the speculative ebb and flow
of persons who take jobs (or additional jobs) for rewards expected to
be temporarily exceptional. To each 'model' of unemployment there
corresponds a set of considerations affecting wage and price setting.
In each model there is a concept of macroeconomic equilibrium and
the equilibrium quantity of unemployment. In each model we study
the disequilibrium response of the unemployment rate and of wage
and price behavior when aggregate demand is perturbed from macroequilibrium.

Any particular macroeconomic equilibrium of the economy can
be characterized, measured, or labeled in terms, *inter alia*, of the unemployment rate it displays and the trend rate of change of average
money wage rates and prices that people (firms and households) generally expect in that equilibrium. For short, we will refer to the latter

as the 'expected rate of inflation'. Whether the various feasible macro-economic equilibria cover a substantial range of unemployment rates is a big question that will receive close attention. In any case, there is a feasible macroequilibrium corresponding to each expected inflation rate (positive and negative) within certain limits. Neither 'wage stability', with its accompaniment of falling unit costs and prices, nor 'price stability', with its accompaniment of rising money-wage rates, has any monopoly on macroeconomic equilibrium.

The essential hallmark of macroequilibrium is that the actual inflation rate is turning out equal to the (average) expected inflation rate. Things are working out, upon appropriate averaging, as people thought they would. The actions of the various economic agents are not, on the average, being predicated on misapprehensions of the experiences and actions of others. If these expectations of what firms and workers are doing elsewhere are to be borne out—if the price and wage changes they are expected to make are in fact to be made—then the level of aggregate demand, and hence the amounts that customers are buying from their suppliers, must be of appropriate size. Corresponding to each macroequilibrium is a certain level or path of aggregate demand necessary to 'ratify' the expectations that mark that equilibrium. In the same way, there is associated with each macroequilibrium a certain quantity of unemployment that reflects the ratifying level of aggregate demand.

A typical disequilibrium process, this one on the downside, can be fleetingly sketched. If aggregate demand falls short of the ratifying equilibrating path, the representative producer, believing his demand-experience to be local rather than global, random rather than systematic, prices his products above what he would do with full information. Even if producers 'shade' their prices, it is only *relative* to what each expects his competitors (close and remote) to be doing with their prices; so if they are expected to be raising prices at five percent per annum, each may actually raise his price – but very likely not at the full five percent in a situation of below-equilibrium. Each producer will at first be ignorant of his competitor's softening of their normal price changes, so that mark-ups tend to be set higher than would have been chosen with full information. In the labor market, the same misapprehensions are occurring: Some persons become unemployed or stay unemployed longer, looking or waiting for a better offer than they would hold out for if they knew the generality of the weakness in demand. Instead of an immediate restoration of equilibrium at lower wage and price levels all around, there results some above-equilibrium unemployment and spare capacity.

As experience and new information accumulate, there ensues a learning process in which the reservation wage of the representative job-seeker and the prices set by the representative producer, if rising at all, are increased at a diminished rate – in an attempt to gain or to regain a competitive advantage which will be repeatedly frustrated as long as aggregate demand behaves so as to maintain the disequilibrium. Thus the actual inflation rate will be less than the expected inflation rate. Gradually, as long as the disequilibrium holds, the general expectation of the trend rate of increase of prices and wages – the expected rate of inflation – will itself come to be revised downwards as it is realized that competitors are consistently inflating their prices and wage demands at slower rates than was believed.

It is equally possible that the monetary and fiscal authorities, by luck or by design, will produce a disequilibrium on the upside. Then the actual rate of inflation will tend to exceed the expected rate. Producers and households will then be underestimating rather than overestimating their competitiveness. As they keep learning this, they keep raising their prices and reservation wages by more than the amount consistent with expectations of the general inflation rate. Gradually the expected inflation rate will itself come to be revised upwards as a result.

It is imaginable, and a plausible first approximation perhaps, that every macroeconomic equilibrium, each one corresponding to a different expected inflation rate, is marked by the identical rate of unemployment. This is the 'natural rate' hypothesis: that the unemployment rate is independent of the inflation rate when, as in equilibrium, that inflation rate is already expected. The macroequilibrium unemployment rate is then invariant to the expected inflation rate.

This 'natural' unemployment rate is a razor's edge: If aggregate demand keeps unemployment steadily below the natural rate, the actual inflation rate must continually stay ahead of the expected inflation rate; if expectations are continually revised upwards in response, the actual inflation rate will increase indefinitely – until the inflationary limit of the economy is reached. (This does not mean that the natural rate must never consciously be deviated from: A disequilibrium path leading ultimately to macroequilibrium at a different (expected and actual) inflation rate may well be preferable to living indefinitely with the particular macroequilibrium, and its inflation rate, that happens to be directly attainable – despite the fact that there is no permanent difference in the unemployment rates the two courses provide.) Chapter 2 discusses the merits and defects of this hypothesis from the viewpoint of the neo-neoclassical analysis introduced to that point.

This analysis of unemployment and price-wage dynamics postulates atomistic and largely unregulated labor markets and product markets. Its conclusions are not necessarily affected, at least in many crucial aspects, by the admittance into the setting of more realistic institutional features, including features of a somewhat sociological character. But it is desirable to consider this question in each individual instance. Chapter 3 examines the role of several social factors: racial discrimination, minimum wage laws, social pressures and motivations influencing aspirations for relative wages, labor unions, and the technological and personal effects of certain kinds of job experience. At least these factors alter the volume of unemployment that the econometrician would estimate to be 'natural' – even if they do not destroy the hypothesized invariance of the macroequilibrium unemployment rate to the expected inflation rate. For example, the striving for a wage or salary as good as or better than one's neighbors' would tend to increase the macroequilibrium unemployment rate (at any inflation level) beyond what would be predicted by 'expected utility maximization' without external influences.

Further, the transforming effects of certain kinds of job experience upon people's habits and skills, and possibly too the *modus operandi* of labor unions, suggest that a course of disequilibrium at a higher inflation rate would tend over time to reduce the equilibrium unemployment rate. The transition from one equilibrium to the other tends to have long-lingering effects on the labor force, and these effects may be discernible in the equilibrium unemployment rate for a long time. The natural unemployment rate at any future date will depend upon the course of history in the interim. Such a property is sometimes called *hysteresis*.

0.2. *Welfare Effects of Unexpected and Expected Inflation*

Starting from some macroequilibrium (for simplicity of exposition), the economy would at first respond with unexpected inflation and, later, with a rise of the expected rate of inflation if there were to be a step-up of the growth rate of aggregate demand – engineered, say, by faster increases of the money supply. Correspondingly, there are two categories of welfare effects from such a policy variation: first, the welfare consequences stemming from the unexpected quantity of inflation and the associated dip of unemployment below the equilibrium level; and, second, the welfare consequences of a rise in inflation expectations, with its implication that future equilibrium (if and when achieved) will consequently occur at a higher actual inflation rate.

Accordingly, Chapter 4 begins the study of the benefits and costs of a departure of the unemployment rate from the equilibrium level (roughly the natural rate). Astonishingly, this appears to be the first systematic inquiry into the question: If expectations of inflation are frozen, is the natural unemployment rate then inferior in the familiar efficiency sense to some lower unemployment rate that could be attained by a disequilibrating dose of aggregate demand? In the consideration of this question, the redistributive aspects of reduced unemployment and unexpected inflation are put off to the next chapter.

On this question there exists a couple of schools of thought. One of these schools says that were it not for the tendency of inflation expectations to rise at below-equilibrium rates of unemployment, which rises would eventually have debilitating consequences for the efficiency of the monetary system, less unemployment would indeed be always preferable to more; an output gain will be produced by greater employment as long as the whole of the additional man-hours are not merely diverted to personnel offices for recruitment in the tighter labor market. The other school of thought would extend the classical efficiency theorem *a propos* of competitive equilibrium *sans* uncertainty and externalities to the Keynesian world of frictions: If some lower unemployment rate were superior to the equilibrium level, the Invisible Hand would have created equilibrium at that lower rate.

Certainly there is no presumption that the natural unemployment rate is superior in its allocation of resources to alternative unemployment rates, greater or smaller. Neither is it possible to prove beyond a shadow of a doubt that a reduction of the unemployment rate below the natural level would present an efficiency gain. Not all the arguments fall on just one side. But of the few arguments for holding that *supra*-natural unemployment would be allocatively superior to the natural rate of unemployment, nearly every one would seem to be of minor empirical importance. Contrariwise, there seem to be several strong arguments for believing that, up to some point, a demand-induced reduction of the unemployment rate would bring a more efficient allocation of resources—between marketed labor activities and nonmarketed activities (leisure, for example), between job search and job holding, and so on. The case is virtually sewed up by appeal to evidence on the psychosocial aspects of the level of business activity. (Some fine old literature is saved from oblivion here.)

The second aspect of this same question about unemployment reduction and unexpected inflation is the distributional side, which is covered in Chapter 5. The distributive feature taken to be of prime interest is the share of economic benefits (in the widest sense) going to the poor – measured, for practical purposes, as the bottom fifth (by income) of the populace. The evidence that a rise of employment tends to raise individual real wage rates available to the representative worker, especially to the poor worker, and tends also to produce upgrading and more promising kinds of jobs, is introduced and discussed at length. Of course, a dose of unexpected inflation also redistributes income shares directly by reducing the real purchasing value of fixed money obligations of debtors to creditors. This is a murkier area, but it does not appear that the poor have much to lose from unexpected inflation through that avenue, certainly nothing that would offset their benefits from the associated rise of employment. All things considered, it would appear that the poor have the biggest relative stake in unexpected inflation.

It may be objected that this is some Robin Hood style of distributive justice that only economists would think to accept. Are not the wishes of the electorate to keep the poor impoverished to be respected? Are not freely contracted monetary obligations to be held sacred, or was Burke right in believing that chivalry is dead? These questions are faced and answered at least to my satisfaction.

These benefits and costs from the step-up of the rate of inflation are largely, if not wholly, temporary. As the rates of expected and actual inflation come together, unemployment settles into equilibrium again – at the same level according to the natural rate hypothesis, at a lower rate if the various hysteresis factors operated during the boom. In either case the benefits and costs of the higher expected rate of inflation, matched by a higher actual inflation rate in equilibrium, are continuing – provided the step-up of aggregate demand is not reversed by a subsequent disequilibrium on the disinflationary side. These 'long-run' benefits and costs are the subject of Chapter 6, which is, for the most part, an analysis of 'anticipated' inflation.

By appeal to various types of models of the monetary and fiscal mechanism, the case is built up for the following proposition: A higher anticipated inflation rate is of net benefit up to some point after which the costs of a still higher rate would outweigh the benefits. Charged with deciding where that point is, I would place it at some positive moderate rate of inflation. In many countries abroad that point might be higher, something immoderate by conventional standards.

A sampling of the arguments involved, especially the more readily expressed ones, follows: The expectation of inflation serves as a kind of tax on holding money. Like other taxes, it has its deleterious effects upon incentives. As the income tax discourages working for pay, the inflation tax discourages staying liquid. An optimal package of taxes, whatever the precise quantity of resources intended to be freed for capital formation or public use, would include some 'inflation tax' so as not to place extra burdens on other kinds of taxes. A second argument is that when the economy is geared to moderate inflation, it would actually be less prone to stubborn slumps and runaway increases of the inflation rate. With liquidity less abundant, there would be less tinder around with which to spark a strong boom; and in a slump money markets would be less sloppy, hence more susceptible to central bank influence. A third line of argument makes the point that the transition to a regime of equilibrium at a higher expected inflation rate may leave long-lasting benefits for those workers who gain better opportunities for training and incentives for advancement from their job experiences.

0.3. *Inflation Policy*

Part 3 begins with a discussion of the 'derivation', as it were, of an optimum inflation policy – that is, a manual to cope with every imaginable current state of the economy – out of the elements built up in previous chapters. Later in this material the significance of uncertainty and the relevance of international interests are brought into the discussion.

The principal message of Chapter 7 is simple to state. If the train of future benefits from any permanent economic improvement is considered to be endless and they are not 'discounted' according to their remoteness, then the best aggregate-demand policy would aim the inflation rate on a course heading for the 'optimum' anticipated inflation rate. This means that if the current expected inflation rate is less than that optimum, reduction of unemployment below the equilibrium is indicated by the optimal inflation policy; the dark side is that in the contrary event, an episode of above-equilibrium unemployment is indicated – unless some economic magician can find another way to shrink expectations of the inflation rate.

It is more reasonable, however, to require that future benefits be discounted relative to present ones. Hence any proposal for getting the inflation rate 'down' to the level considered to be the optimum from a static viewpoint ought to be subjected to an interest-rate or 'discount' test just as any other project of social investment. Only if the costs of a planned slump or the benefits lost by a boom foregone promise to 'pay off' in terms of suitably discounted future benefits is it good policy to make such an 'investment' in a lower rate of inflation over the long run.

Of the many qualifications and complications that have needed to be made, those involving the risks and uncertainties surrounding aggregate-demand policy have been grouped together in Chapter 8. For purposes of month-to-month implementation of any inflation strategy, the authorities must deal with the fact that the future effects of each policy action are not completely predictable. Worse than that, the state of the economy at any moment of decision is usually not entirely certain at that time. The statistical problem of estimating the current state of the economy, much as a forecast of the future, is involved in the formulation of monetary and fiscal policy. An effort is made to distinguish between the problem policy of adjustment, in which deliberate disequilibration and a revision of expectations are indicated, and the policy problem of routine stabilization, in which a full adjustment of expectations to the right level has at first been made. Different treatments of expectations would appear to be appropriate to these two policy contexts.

Chapter 9 takes up the qualifications required by international considerations. The main theme here, perhaps, is that a faster rate of inflation in America would not make a world of difference to the international economy. Many countries, notably many of the poorer ones, would probably have reason to welcome such an increase in the rate of inflation of world goods in terms of dollars. Certainly many countries would choose to follow suit, and what is good for the goose is presumably good for ganders.

Yet there may be system effects. A country that desires to march to its own drummer will have to appreciate its currency more often, or depreciate it less often, in terms of the dollar should the American inflation rate be increased. If countries of the first kind were to predominate, greater instability of exchange rates and greater incentives for multinational exchange-rate ties would arise. The price of gold may attract more interest. In the event of faster world inflation, this price, over the long run, might have to become more like the price of steel, being increased at regular and frequent intervals with the general price level.

PART I

Modern Unemployment Theory

the 'stickiness', in a certain sense, of money wage rates. The theory in no way requires that price and wage quotations by the firm be rigid, as if the decision-making bodies in the corporate economy were in a state of *rigor mortis*. Indeed, in the neoclassic speculative labor supply model, some fall of money wage rates and some corresponding fall of prices, both relative to expectations of the normal wage and price levels, are the normal accompaniment of a decline in aggregate demand. But the model leads us to expect that a decline of aggregate demand would produce rather little reduction in money wage rates in the first instance, that is to say, on impact, before disappointment, discovery, and learning. In the limiting case, we can imagine the managers of firms saying that they did not cut many wage rates at all because they knew that had they done so every worker would have gone fishing. There could be a large corps of workers who are at the margin of indifference between working and leisure.

The theory of the speculative responses in labor supply to changes in aggregate demand is capable of illuminating the behavior of prices and wages in a continuing disequilibrium. If aggregate demand were manipulated by the government in such a way as to keep the price level constant at its new and lower level, it is natural to hypothesize that households would gradually adapt downwards their expectations of the future cost of living, as well as their expectations of future money wage rates. These revisions would gradually increase labor supply (at every constellation of real wage rates), thus driving down money wage rates and driving up employment back toward their respective equilibrium levels. If contrariwise the government were to desire to maintain the gap between the present depressed level of employment and the equilibrium level of employment, what must the government do? It must exploit the belief, as long as people hold it, that what goes down must come up. To keep employment down, aggregate demand must be managed so as to generate a continuing surprising decline of the price level, thus keeping alive the expectation that some substantial restoration of prices and of the cost of living is just around the corner. As long as each fresh decline of prices is expected for the most part to be temporary, the government can keep households betting on some future rise of the price level by manipulating aggregate demand so as to produce a succession of unexpected price declines. It should be remarked at this juncture, though we shall have to return to the point in a more general framework later on, that we have been assuming in this exercise that

1 Informational Unemployment and Wage-Price Dynamics

IT will be convenient to categorize unemployment by cause or motive, much as economists are used to classify people's motives for holding money. I shall distinguish speculative unemployment (or, more accurately, speculative underemployment and speculative overemployment), precautionary or 'wait' unemployment, search unemployment, and queue unemployment.

Speculative unemployment (or speculative underemployment) is illustrated by the family that withholds a full-time or part-time worker from paid employment (in either a primary or secondary job) on the speculation that the money wage rates now available are temporarily depressed in terms of their prospective over-life purchasing power. Precautionary or 'wait' unemployment is illustrated by the idleness of a person who regards himself as 'between jobs', who is waiting for the unpredictable arrival of the next contract for his services. Search unemployment is illustrated by the individual who elects unemployment, rejecting some job, in order to facilitate searching for a job that is superior to those he knows to be available to him. Queue unemployment, which is a close relative to wait unemployment in that they both reflect the nonmarket clearing behavior of wage rates and fees in many areas of the labor market, is illustrated by the idleness of the worker who believes he is in line for a job not yet vacant, which he cannot secure for himself by offering his services at a lower wage.[1] These categories, it may be noted, have counterparts in the idleness or underutilization of plant and equipment.

These types of unemployment will be seen to be essentially informational in origin. In a rapidly changing and highly articulated

---

[1] These types of unemployment are not all mutually exclusive. A person who is between jobs, waiting for his money wage opportunities to return to normal or hoping to be recalled to a job at his former company, could spend some spare time searching for a different kind of job or for the same kind of job in a different firm or different area. A person who has rejected employment in order to search for a better job may at the same time take more leisure – shorter days, or longer weekends – and in that way resemble partially those who are engaged in speculative idleness

(developed) economy there is overwhelming heterogeneity of people and of jobs – across space and across time – with the result that there is not the perfect information postulated to prevail in the classic style Walrasian economy. The future is unpredictable and even vast parts of the present are unknown. Three of these unemployment types, at least, are instances of what is customarily called frictional unemployment. Though some quantity of frictional unemployment is normal – and some residue could not be eliminated by monetary measures – the amount of frictional unemployment depends very much upon the level of 'aggregate demand'. Indeed, without these frictions it is doubtful that we would ever observe unemployment at all; aggregate demand could not get the traction to pull unemployment if it wanted to. Consequently, I shall examine, for each type, the mechanism by which aggregate demand influences the quantity of that unemployment and the corresponding process of price and wage adjustment. This leads to the related concept of the Momentary Phillips Curve and of equilibrium unemployment.[2]

1.1. *Speculative Changes in Employment*

By far the most neoclassical type of unemployment – if it can be called unemployment – is the kind we have labeled 'speculative'. In its rigorous elaborations, there is usually supposed to be some means whereby money wage rates for the various kinds of workers and jobs clear the market, leaving no frustrated excess supply of workers nor any unsatisfied excess demand for workers on the part of firms.[3]

The theory of speculative fluctuations over the business cycle in the level of employment is basically a very simple one. Imagine that a decline of aggregate demand, brought about perhaps by higher

[2] The most comprehensive single reference in the existing literature on informational unemployment theory is the multiauthored volume, E. S. Phelps *et al.*, *Microeconomic Foundations of Employment and Inflation Theory* (New York: W. W. Norton, 1970). A revisionist interpretation of Keynes along similar lines is presented in A. Leijonhufvud, *On Keynesian Economics and the Economics of Keynes* (London: Oxford University Press, 1968). For a number of references to the pre-Keynesian literature on unemployment, see the congenial paper by M. W. Reder, 'The Theory of Frictional Unemployment', *Economica*, February 1969.

[3] The speculative theory of employment fluctuations has received a rigorous treatment in a paper by R. E. Lucas, Jr., and L. A. Rapping, 'Employment, Real Wages, and Inflation' in Phelps *et al.*, *Microeconomic Foundations*. A complementary paper in the same vein is E. S. Phelps, 'A Note on Short-Run Employment and Real Wage Rate Under Competitive Commodity Markets', *International Economic Review*, June 1969.

taxes or by a contraction of the money supply, causes a fall in market clearing levels of the various money wage rates. If we sume, for simplicity, that the economy was previously in equ rium – there will be a good deal more about equilibrium in the of this chapter – the new unaccustomed money wage rates wil regarded as abnormal and therefore in all probability tempor When available money wage rates are regarded as being tempora low, it is quite natural (though not logically inescapable) that m families will respond with a reduction in the amount of hour work they choose to do in the market economy. That response c be no more than a change in the timing of an unchanged numb man-hours that the family plans to work over its lifetime – like ta one's next vacation now rather than later.

The theory becomes a little more sophisticated when one supp that the present cost of living falls in response to the declin aggregate demand in the same proportion as the fall of money v rates. Then, in the normal sense of the term, real wage rates ar lower than they were before in equilibrium. Is there then any rea why we should expect employment to fall in response to the ded of aggregate demand? The answer is that there still is such a rea if one of the objectives of the household engaged in employmer the market economy is saving some of the money to be earned the purposes of making future consumer expenditures. Then depressed money wage rates available to the household must judged to some extent in relation to the expected future cost of li as well as in relation to the present cost of living. Let us supp symmetrically with our treatment of money wage expectations, the cost of living, too, is expected to return soon to its normal le Then households will regard the present money wage rates as offe reduced purchasing power over *future* goods at an unchanged a of 'nominal' or 'money' rates of interest available to savers. On money rates of interest were to increase by an amount correspond to the expected rate of recovery of the price level would the depres money wage rates have the same attractiveness in terms of futur well as present purchasing power. To put the matter another v there has been an implicit fall of the 'real interest' which the ho hold can expect to earn on saving from current wage income. implicit fall of the 'expected real rate of interest' presents an incen for the household to take more present leisure at the expense future consumption or future leisure or both.

This view of unemployment, for all its limitations, helps to exp

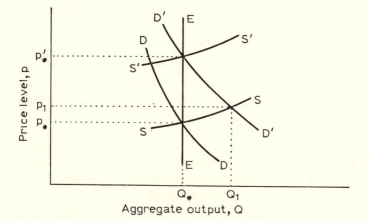

Figure 1.1. The concept of Aggregate Demand is represented by the downward sloping schedule labeled *DD*. It gives the output level toward which aggregate output demanded will tend, in the manner of the multiplier process, provided that the intervening real output levels are actually produced. Behind any aggregate demand curve is a particular money supply, initial level of government indebtedness, some indicator of fiscal policy such as the average tax rate or the 'high-employment budgetary deficit' – as well as such state variables describing the underlying economic situation as the capital stock of the moment and the expected rate of inflation of the moment. References in the text to an increase of aggregate demand mean a uniformly rightward shift of this curve (never a rightward movement along a given curve). The curve's slope, which may be conjectured as due to the liquidity and wealth effects of a change of the price level, is insignificant here given the curve's shiftability by monetary and fiscal policy.

The concept of Long-Run Aggregate Supply is representable, in the simplest case, by the vertical schedule labeled *EE*. It reflects the demand for leisure and the accompanying volume of frictional unemployment that corresponds to it. This schedule depends prominently upon the real wage, hence upon the capital stock and the technology, and so on. The attainment of macroequilibrium requires that monetary and fiscal policy, operating on the demand curve, place the economy somewhere – anywhere – on the long-run supply curve. It will often be assumed, as a satisfactory approximation in the context, that the supply curve does not shift with a change in the fiscal-monetary mix. In general, an easing of monetary or fiscal policy (or both) might still affect the equilibrium output level, at a given expected inflation rate and capital stock, via some slope in the supply curve that demand could slide along. Except where noted, the ultra-neoclassic assumption of a vertical supply curve, hence no liquidity nor wealth effects (save offsetting ones), will be adopted as an approximation. Hence the intercept of the Momentary Phillips Curve in Figure 1.2, below, is independent of monetary and fiscal policy – given the expected inflation rate and the capital stock.

The speculative employment model, though not most models, postulates a Short-Run Aggregate Supply Curve family, such as *SS* and *S'S'*. The curve that prevails at any moment is the one intersecting *EE* at the price level which is believed by households to be the normal level (after de-trending).

expectations, while adaptable, are 'static' in character: households
expect the cost of living and money wage rates to move gradually to
some future level and thus to stay at that level thereafter. The
expected, long-run *trend* rates of change are not themselves being
regarded here as adaptable. In the same vein, let us assume that
households do not become more proficient at adapting downward
(or upward) their expectations of the long-run price level with repeated experience in doing so.

By changing up to down and increase to decrease, *mutatis mutandis*
in the inspired phrase, we can see that a process of unexpected
inflation, brought about by fiscal and monetary policies to produce
rising aggregate demand, induces a level of employment in excess
of the equilibrium level. Households are busy making hay while the
sun shines and the boom is still on the economic flower.

A lesson that emerges from these exercises is that a process of
unexpected inflation brings with it above-equilibrium employment
and the process of unexpected deflation brings with it below-
equilibrium employment. It is easy to show that the level of employment exceeds the equilibrium level by a larger amount the greater
is the rate of unexpected inflation. Symmetrically, employment is
farther below its equilibrium level the greater is the rate of unexpected
deflation. In a mathematical turn of mind, we can say that the level
of employment is greater the larger is the 'rate of unexpected inflation' – where by that term we intend an algebraic quantity which
can be negative, zero, or positive. This relationship has come to be
known as the Phillips Curve (Fig. 1.2) and it is used pretty much
interchangeably to refer to a connection between price inflation and
output, price inflation and employment, the rate of wage increase
and output, and the rate of wage increase and employment.

Notice that the level of employment is being related by the Phillips
Curve not to the level of prices or the level of wage rates, but to the
rate of change of these variables. When we embrace the Phillips
Curve as a useful empirical generalization, if properly understood,
we can still be eclectic enough to recognize at the same time a relationship coexisting between the level of employment and the level
of prices. Indeed, at the beginning of our discussion of the speculative supply model, we noticed that associated with the fall of employment was a one-time fall of the level of prices and a corresponding
one-time fall of the level of money wage rates.

So our findings about the rate of inflation from the point of view
of the theory of speculative labor behavior can be summarized in the

1 Informational Unemployment and Wage-Price Dynamics

I T will be convenient to categorize unemployment by cause or motive, much as economists are used to classify people's motives for holding money. I shall distinguish speculative unemployment (or, more accurately, speculative underemployment and speculative over-employment), precautionary or 'wait' unemployment, search unemployment, and queue unemployment.

Speculative unemployment (or speculative underemployment) is illustrated by the family that withholds a full-time or part-time worker from paid employment (in either a primary or secondary job) on the speculation that the money wage rates now available are temporarily depressed in terms of their prospective over-life purchasing power. Precautionary or 'wait' unemployment is illustrated by the idleness of a person who regards himself as 'between jobs', who is waiting for the unpredictable arrival of the next contract for his services. Search unemployment is illustrated by the individual who elects unemployment, rejecting some job, in order to facilitate searching for a job that is superior to those he knows to be available to him. Queue unemployment, which is a close relative to wait unemployment in that they both reflect the nonmarket clearing behavior of wage rates and fees in many areas of the labor market, is illustrated by the idleness of the worker who believes he is in line for a job not yet vacant, which he cannot secure for himself by offering his services at a lower wage.[1] These categories, it may be noted, have counterparts in the idleness or underutilization of plant and equipment.

These types of unemployment will be seen to be essentially informational in origin. In a rapidly changing and highly articulated

---

[1] These types of unemployment are not all mutually exclusive. A person who is between jobs, waiting for his money wage opportunities to return to normal or hoping to be recalled to a job at his former company, could spend some spare time searching for a different kind of job or for the same kind of job in a different firm or different area. A person who has rejected employment in order to search for a better job may at the same time take more leisure – shorter days, or longer weekends – and in that way resemble partially those who are engaged in speculative idleness

(developed) economy there is overwhelming heterogeneity of people and of jobs – across space and across time – with the result that there is not the perfect information postulated to prevail in the classic style Walrasian economy. The future is unpredictable and even vast parts of the present are unknown. Three of these unemployment types, at least, are instances of what is customarily called frictional unemployment. Though some quantity of frictional unemployment is normal – and some residue could not be eliminated by monetary measures – the amount of frictional unemployment depends very much upon the level of 'aggregate demand'. Indeed, without these frictions it is doubtful that we would ever observe unemployment at all; aggregate demand could not get the traction to pull unemployment if it wanted to. Consequently, I shall examine, for each type, the mechanism by which aggregate demand influences the quantity of that unemployment and the corresponding process of price and wage adjustment. This leads to the related concept of the Momentary Phillips Curve and of equilibrium unemployment.[2]

1.1. *Speculative Changes in Employment*

By far the most neoclassical type of unemployment – if it can be called unemployment – is the kind we have labeled 'speculative'. In its rigorous elaborations, there is usually supposed to be some means whereby money wage rates for the various kinds of workers and jobs clear the market, leaving no frustrated excess supply of workers nor any unsatisfied excess demand for workers on the part of firms.[3]

The theory of speculative fluctuations over the business cycle in the level of employment is basically a very simple one. Imagine that a decline of aggregate demand, brought about perhaps by higher

[2] The most comprehensive single reference in the existing literature on informational unemployment theory is the multiauthored volume, E. S. Phelps *et al.*, *Microeconomic Foundations of Employment and Inflation Theory* (New York: W. W. Norton, 1970). A revisionist interpretation of Keynes along similar lines is presented in A. Leijonhufvud, *On Keynesian Economics and the Economics of Keynes* (London: Oxford University Press, 1968). For a number of references to the pre-Keynesian literature on unemployment, see the congenial paper by M. W. Reder, 'The Theory of Frictional Unemployment', *Economica*, February 1969.

[3] The speculative theory of employment fluctuations has received a rigorous treatment in a paper by R. E. Lucas, Jr., and L. A. Rapping, 'Employment, Real Wages, and Inflation' in Phelps *et al.*, *Microeconomic Foundations*. A complementary paper in the same vein is E. S. Phelps, 'A Note on Short-Run Employment and Real Wage Rate Under Competitive Commodity Markets', *International Economic Review*, June 1969.

taxes or by a contraction of the money supply, causes a fall in the
market clearing levels of the various money wage rates. If we assume, for simplicity, that the economy was previously in equilibrium – there will be a good deal more about equilibrium in the rest
of this chapter – the new unaccustomed money wage rates will be
regarded as abnormal and therefore in all probability temporary.
When available money wage rates are regarded as being temporarily
low, it is quite natural (though not logically inescapable) that many
families will respond with a reduction in the amount of hours of
work they choose to do in the market economy. That response could
be no more than a change in the timing of an unchanged number of
man-hours that the family plans to work over its lifetime – like taking
one's next vacation now rather than later.

The theory becomes a little more sophisticated when one supposes
that the present cost of living falls in response to the decline of
aggregate demand in the same proportion as the fall of money wage
rates. Then, in the normal sense of the term, real wage rates are no
lower than they were before in equilibrium. Is there then any reason
why we should expect employment to fall in response to the decline
of aggregate demand? The answer is that there still is such a reason
if one of the objectives of the household engaged in employment in
the market economy is saving some of the money to be earned for
the purposes of making future consumer expenditures. Then the
depressed money wage rates available to the household must be
judged to some extent in relation to the expected future cost of living
as well as in relation to the present cost of living. Let us suppose,
symmetrically with our treatment of money wage expectations, that
the cost of living, too, is expected to return soon to its normal level.
Then households will regard the present money wage rates as offering
reduced purchasing power over *future* goods at an unchanged array
of 'nominal' or 'money' rates of interest available to savers. Only if
money rates of interest were to increase by an amount corresponding
to the expected rate of recovery of the price level would the depressed
money wage rates have the same attractiveness in terms of future as
well as present purchasing power. To put the matter another way,
there has been an implicit fall of the 'real interest' which the household can expect to earn on saving from current wage income. This
implicit fall of the 'expected real rate of interest' presents an incentive
for the household to take more present leisure at the expense of
future consumption or future leisure or both.

This view of unemployment, for all its limitations, helps to explain

the 'stickiness', in a certain sense, of money wage rates. The theory in no way requires that price and wage quotations by the firm be rigid, as if the decision-making bodies in the corporate economy were in a state of *rigor mortis*. Indeed, in the neoclassic speculative labor supply model, some fall of money wage rates and some corresponding fall of prices, both relative to expectations of the normal wage and price levels, are the normal accompaniment of a decline in aggregate demand. But the model leads us to expect that a decline of aggregate demand would produce rather little reduction in money wage rates in the first instance, that is to say, on impact, before disappointment, discovery, and learning. In the limiting case, we can imagine the managers of firms saying that they did not cut many wage rates at all because they knew that had they done so every worker would have gone fishing. There could be a large corps of workers who are at the margin of indifference between working and leisure.

The theory of the speculative responses in labor supply to changes in aggregate demand is capable of illuminating the behavior of prices and wages in a continuing disequilibrium. If aggregate demand were manipulated by the government in such a way as to keep the price level constant at its new and lower level, it is natural to hypothesize that households would gradually adapt downwards their expectations of the future cost of living, as well as their expectations of future money wage rates. These revisions would gradually increase labor supply (at every constellation of real wage rates), thus driving down money wage rates and driving up employment back toward their respective equilibrium levels. If contrariwise the government were to desire to maintain the gap between the present depressed level of employment and the equilibrium level of employment, what must the government do? It must exploit the belief, as long as people hold it, that what goes down must come up. To keep employment down, aggregate demand must be managed so as to generate a continuing surprising decline of the price level, thus keeping alive the expectation that some substantial restoration of prices and of the cost of living is just around the corner. As long as each fresh decline of prices is expected for the most part to be temporary, the government can keep households betting on some future rise of the price level by manipulating aggregate demand so as to produce a succession of unexpected price declines. It should be remarked at this juncture, though we shall have to return to the point in a more general framework later on, that we have been assuming in this exercise that taxes or by a contraction of the money supply, causes a fall in the market clearing levels of the various money wage rates. If we assume, for simplicity, that the economy was previously in equilibrium – there will be a good deal more about equilibrium in the rest of this chapter – the new unaccustomed money wage rates will be regarded as abnormal and therefore in all probability temporary. When available money wage rates are regarded as being temporarily low, it is quite natural (though not logically inescapable) that many families will respond with a reduction in the amount of hours of work they choose to do in the market economy. That response could be no more than a change in the timing of an unchanged number of man-hours that the family plans to work over its lifetime – like taking one's next vacation now rather than later.

The theory becomes a little more sophisticated when one supposes that the present cost of living falls in response to the decline of aggregate demand in the same proportion as the fall of money wage rates. Then, in the normal sense of the term, real wage rates are no lower than they were before in equilibrium. Is there then any reason why we should expect employment to fall in response to the decline of aggregate demand? The answer is that there still is such a reason if one of the objectives of the household engaged in employment in the market economy is saving some of the money to be earned for the purposes of making future consumer expenditures. Then the depressed money wage rates available to the household must be judged to some extent in relation to the expected future cost of living as well as in relation to the present cost of living. Let us suppose, symmetrically with our treatment of money wage expectations, that the cost of living, too, is expected to return soon to its normal level. Then households will regard the present money wage rates as offering reduced purchasing power over *future* goods at an unchanged array of 'nominal' or 'money' rates of interest available to savers. Only if money rates of interest were to increase by an amount corresponding to the expected rate of recovery of the price level would the depressed money wage rates have the same attractiveness in terms of future as well as present purchasing power. To put the matter another way, there has been an implicit fall of the 'real interest' which the household can expect to earn on saving from current wage income. This implicit fall of the 'expected real rate of interest' presents an incentive for the household to take more present leisure at the expense of future consumption or future leisure or both.

This view of unemployment, for all its limitations, helps to explain

the 'stickiness', in a certain sense, of money wage rates. The theory in no way requires that price and wage quotations by the firm be rigid, as if the decision-making bodies in the corporate economy were in a state of *rigor mortis*. Indeed, in the neoclassic speculative labor supply model, some fall of money wage rates and some corresponding fall of prices, both relative to expectations of the normal wage and price levels, are the normal accompaniment of a decline in aggregate demand. But the model leads us to expect that a decline of aggregate demand would produce rather little reduction in money wage rates in the first instance, that is to say, on impact, before disappointment, discovery, and learning. In the limiting case, we can imagine the managers of firms saying that they did not cut many wage rates at all because they knew that had they done so every worker would have gone fishing. There could be a large corps of workers who are at the margin of indifference between working and leisure.

The theory of the speculative responses in labor supply to changes in aggregate demand is capable of illuminating the behavior of prices and wages in a continuing disequilibrium. If aggregate demand were manipulated by the government in such a way as to keep the price level constant at its new and lower level, it is natural to hypothesize that households would gradually adapt downwards their expectations of the future cost of living, as well as their expectations of future money wage rates. These revisions would gradually increase labor supply (at every constellation of real wage rates), thus driving down money wage rates and driving up employment back toward their respective equilibrium levels. If contrariwise the government were to desire to maintain the gap between the present depressed level of employment and the equilibrium level of employment, what must the government do? It must exploit the belief, as long as people hold it, that what goes down must come up. To keep employment down, aggregate demand must be managed so as to generate a continuing surprising decline of the price level, thus keeping alive the expectation that some substantial restoration of prices and of the cost of living is just around the corner. As long as each fresh decline of prices is expected for the most part to be temporary, the government can keep households betting on some future rise of the price level by manipulating aggregate demand so as to produce a succession of unexpected price declines. It should be remarked at this juncture, though we shall have to return to the point in a more general framework later on, that we have been assuming in this exercise that

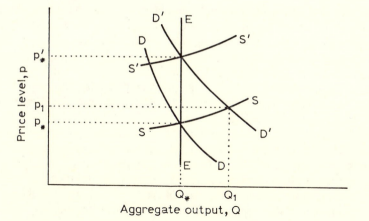

Aggregate output, Q

Figure 1.1. The concept of Aggregate Demand is represented by the downward sloping schedule labeled *DD*. It gives the output level toward which aggregate output demanded will tend, in the manner of the multiplier process, provided that the intervening real output levels are actually produced. Behind any aggregate demand curve is a particular money supply, initial level of government indebtedness, some indicator of fiscal policy such as the average tax rate or the 'high-employment budgetary deficit' – as well as such state variables describing the underlying economic situation as the capital stock of the moment and the expected rate of inflation of the moment. References in the text to an increase of aggregate demand mean a uniformly rightward shift of this curve (never a rightward movement along a given curve). The curve's slope, which may be conjectured as due to the liquidity and wealth effects of a change of the price level, is insignificant here given the curve's shiftability by monetary and fiscal policy.

The concept of Long-Run Aggregate Supply is representable, in the simplest case, by the vertical schedule labeled *EE*. It reflects the demand for leisure and the accompanying volume of frictional unemployment that corresponds to it. This schedule depends prominently upon the real wage, hence upon the capital stock and the technology, and so on. The attainment of macroequilibrium requires that monetary and fiscal policy, operating on the demand curve, place the economy somewhere – anywhere – on the long-run supply curve. It will often be assumed, as a satisfactory approximation in the context, that the supply curve does not shift with a change in the fiscal-monetary mix. In general, an easing of monetary or fiscal policy (or both) might still affect the equilibrium output level, at a given expected inflation rate and capital stock, via some slope in the supply curve that demand could slide along. Except where noted, the ultra-neoclassic assumption of a vertical supply curve, hence no liquidity nor wealth effects (save offsetting ones), will be adopted as an approximation. Hence the intercept of the Momentary Phillips Curve in Figure 1.2, below, is independent of monetary and fiscal policy – given the expected inflation rate and the capital stock.

The speculative employment model, though not most models, postulates a Short-Run Aggregate Supply Curve family, such as *SS* and *S'S'*. The curve that prevails at any moment is the one intersecting *EE* at the price level which is believed by households to be the normal level (after de-trending).

expectations, while adaptable, are 'static' in character: households expect the cost of living and money wage rates to move gradually to some future level and thus to stay at that level thereafter. The expected, long-run *trend* rates of change are not themselves being regarded here as adaptable. In the same vein, let us assume that households do not become more proficient at adapting downward (or upward) their expectations of the long-run price level with repeated experience in doing so.

By changing up to down and increase to decrease, *mutatis mutandis* in the inspired phrase, we can see that a process of unexpected inflation, brought about by fiscal and monetary policies to produce rising aggregate demand, induces a level of employment in excess of the equilibrium level. Households are busy making hay while the sun shines and the boom is still on the economic flower.

A lesson that emerges from these exercises is that a process of unexpected inflation brings with it above-equilibrium employment and the process of unexpected deflation brings with it below-equilibrium employment. It is easy to show that the level of employment exceeds the equilibrium level by a larger amount the greater is the rate of unexpected inflation. Symmetrically, employment is farther below its equilibrium level the greater is the rate of unexpected deflation. In a mathematical turn of mind, we can say that the level of employment is greater the larger is the 'rate of unexpected inflation' – where by that term we intend an algebraic quantity which can be negative, zero, or positive. This relationship has come to be known as the Phillips Curve (Fig. 1.2) and it is used pretty much interchangeably to refer to a connection between price inflation and output, price inflation and employment, the rate of wage increase and output, and the rate of wage increase and employment.

Notice that the level of employment is being related by the Phillips Curve not to the level of prices or the level of wage rates, but to the rate of change of these variables. When we embrace the Phillips Curve as a useful empirical generalization, if properly understood, we can still be eclectic enough to recognize at the same time a relationship coexisting between the level of employment and the level of prices. Indeed, at the beginning of our discussion of the speculative supply model, we noticed that associated with the fall of employment was a one-time fall of the level of prices and a corresponding one-time fall of the level of money wage rates.

So our findings about the rate of inflation from the point of view of the theory of speculative labor behavior can be summarized in the

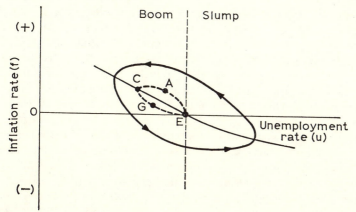

Figure 1.2. A momentary Phillips Curve. It gives a stylized depiction of the 'steady-state' relation between the unemployment rate and the rate of change of the price level. The rate of change of the general money wage level is related in the same way. The expected general future trend of prices and money wages is implicitly postulated to be zero. These expectations are borne out when aggregate demand maintains the economy at *E*, the equilibrium steady-state.

A disequilibrating increase of aggregate demand that leads to *C* could produce a path like *EAC* if prices and wages respond sooner than unemployment. Then a typical business cycle could produce a counterclockwise Lipsey loop between slump and boom. But a trajectory like *EGC* is likely if prices are stickier than quantities.

conclusion that, given static expectations, the rate of inflation is an increasing function of the level of employment (given the size of the working-age population) and also an increasing function of the rate of increase of employment. Since the rate of change of employment cannot diverge for very long from the rate of increase of the working-age population we will not go far wrong in largely neglecting the one-time changes in the level of prices and wages that result from a one-time change of the employment rate – placing our emphasis upon the continuing rates of price and wage change that are associated with the level of the employment rate.

1.2. *Wait-Unemployment*

There is another kind of unemployment which hinges upon the necessity of some workers to choose between getting a job at the present time and getting a different job in the near future. When an actor or a housepainter accepts a job, he knows that he will be tied up in that job for weeks. If every time he was 'between jobs' he slashed his wage, he would be like the man whose normal pay was $100 a day but who never got that much. If a man who finds his service not in demand at his normal wage elects to reduce his wage in order to hasten the expected arrival of the next job offer, he increases the risk that he will have to reject during that new job an offer of employment at his normal wage. It is clear that artisans, lawyers, architects, consultants, politicians, and to one degree or another all self-employed people are in a position of the seller who has to price his goods in the face of a stochastically fluctuating demand. The concept of wait-unemployment has even wider applicability in view of the feelings of some people that it is unethical to leave a job before the employer has had a decent chance to recoup the capital costs of hiring him and in view of the felt self-interest of workers in not acquiring a reputation for being unreliable.

Of course, the notion of precautionary unemployment existed in neoclassical economics and one can unquestionably find a fine passage about it somewhere in Pigou. It was one of several varieties of unemployment that came to be called 'structural' or 'frictional'. Keynes did not forget such structural unemployment in his *General Theory* where he referred to 'frictional' unemployment which is 'due to a temporary want of balance between the relative quantities of specialized resources as a result of miscalculation or intermittent demand; or to time-lags consequent on unforeseen changes; or to the fact that the change-over from one employment to another cannot be effected without a certain delay, so that there will always exist in a non-static society a proportion of resources unemployed "between jobs"'.[4] Keynes characterized this frictional unemployment as voluntary, and he excluded it from the kind of unemployment which he regarded as attributable to or susceptible to the level of aggregate demand. Succeeding Keynesians likewise made a counterproductive distinction between structural unemployment and unemployment due to a deficiency of aggregate demand. The truth is that a great deal of cyclical unemployment is voluntary in every reasonable sense of the term – which is not to say that it is necessarily individually or socially optimal in the circumstance – while some structural unemployment may be involuntary in certain familiar senses of that term.

The quantity of wait-unemployment is very likely to be dependent

---

[4] J. M. Keynes, *The General Theory of Employment, Interest, and Money* (London: Macmillan, 1936), p. 6.

upon aggregate demand in the following way. If aggregate demand declines, there will be a reduction in the frequency of demands for the services of the workers in question at their previous money fees. Equivalently, there will be a decline in the money fees that users of these services would be willing to pay for the normal frequency of service. Now if all workers perceived the altered aggregate monetary situation, they would after some recalculation settle on those new money fees which would restore to them the frequency of employment that they desire over time. Armed with *Economic Indicators* in the one hand and *Variety* (or whatever the appropriate trade paper) in the other, these very models of classical *homo oeconomicus* would always be in equilibrium. It is more realistic to assume, however, that most workers will mistake the systematic decline in the mean of the probability distribution of the demands for their respective services for a transient disturbance not calling at the present moment for a revision of fee schedules. In this situation the typical worker is in disequilibrium in a sense that he is acting on an erroneous estimate of the mean demands for his services.[5]

Just as there can be disequilibrium underemployment, there can be disequilibrium overemployment, where we intend by those terms simply to denote the direction of the discrepancy from the equilibrium employment rate and not to connote necessarily any alleged superiority of the equilibrium employment rate. An increase of aggregate demand, to the extent that it catches suppliers of labor services unaware of the corresponding rise in the mean demands for their services at prevailing money fees, will bring about a decrease of intermittent unemployment. Suppliers of services who happen to have been idle will respond to the demands for their services by accepting employment at their standard rates.

The operational significance of the disequilibrium lies in the response of the prices set by the suppliers of the services. With the accumulated experience of a systematic change in the frequency of demands, workers will begin gradually to revise in the appropriate direction their estimates of the mean of the probability distribution of demands and accordingly to revise in an appropriate direction their standard fees. To maintain the same disequilibrium, and the corresponding amount of overemployment therefore, the government would have continuously to jack up aggregate demand at such a speed as to keep steadily ahead of the rise of fees for labor services.

[5] An important reference is D. F. Gordon and A. Hynes, 'On the Theory of Price Dynamics', in Phelps *et al.*, *Microeconomic Foundations*.

At some strain of the imagination, we can imagine that workers never learn that they must jog just to stay even and run to get ahead. In that case there will exist some steady rate of inflation that can sustain a disequilibrium at the specified level of overemployment. And analogously, there will exist some steady rate of deflation that will sustain a given amount of underemployment. Once again, therefore, the concept of a Momentary Phillips Curve relating levels of employment to the rate of inflation emerges. But again this relation assumes the absence of adaptation to a change in the trends of money-wage rates and money prices.

1.3. *Search-Unemployment*

Speculative response of employment to a change in aggregate demand has its roots in ignorance of future prices, wage rates, and interest rates. Changes in aggregate demand produce changes in the quantity of wait-unemployment because suppliers of services lack correct knowledge of the frequency of demands for their services over the future at given prices. There is another deficiency of information that is important for the theory of unemployment. When workers can substitute among heterogeneous jobs and when firms can substitute among heterogeneous workers, there is a scarcity of information available to workers about wages (including fringes and non-pecuniary rewards) paid at other firms for the same line of work or paid in different kinds of jobs having comparable requirements. When confronted by a reduction in the money wage offered him in relation to his expectations or when he is laid off, the worker may decide to spend his time looking for a better job rather than taking leisure or taking his old job at a reduced wage (if that is possible).

There would be search-unemployment, and the quantity of search unemployment would respond to variations of aggregate demand, even if all money-wage rates continuously 'cleared' the market in the sense that no worker of identical skills would ever be unable to underbid an employed worker for the latter's job. This assumption is a far cry from the overall description of the American economy, as most of us would describe it. But it may describe some parts of the labor market tolerably well; it could be, too, that some wage rates are continuously in a process of approaching their market-clearing levels even if a close approximation is never achieved. It is quite instructive therefore to look at search-unemployment in these terms before moving on to analyze the behavior of unemployment under conditions of job rationing.[6]

1.3.1. *The Market-clearing Case*. The source of the incompleteness of wage-rate information is the enormous variation in jobs most workers can fill and the equally dizzying variety of workers whom employers might consider to fill these jobs. If new people were not always entering the economic system, if technological discoveries and capital investments were not continually creating and destroying jobs, and if people were not restlessly modifying their preferences, we could imagine that human intelligence would eventually overcome this vast heterogeneity and there would be no evidence any longer of the difficulty of acquiring this great amount of information. But this is not the case, and the economy in the aggregate spends millions of man-hours keeping abreast of the continuous accretion of data. In acquiring information many a worker will find it convenient to do so intensively at the expense of having to give up wage income. One can imagine a salesman shining shoes or washing dishes for wage income while he feels out the market for salesmen only gradually. But it is more likely that he will be in a hurry to find an acceptable job at something like his normal wage.

A considerable volume of search-unemployment is the normal (normal, not necessarily optimal) accompaniment of a dynamic economy, even when the labor market is in equilibrium, when aggregate demand is neither high nor low. Firms obsolesce or relocate, industries decline, and workers become discontented or disappointed with their existing jobs. It is an always astonishing fact about the American labor force that approximately 2 percent of jobs are quit by their holders each month. The worker who quits in dissatisfaction with his job and its pay or who refuses the offer of new employment, sees no connection between, on the one hand, the size of this wage offer to him and, on the other hand, the level of aggregate demand and hence the universe of money wage offers that he might instead have sampled. The worker sees trees, mostly one at a time, not the whole forest at a glance.

This suggests a way in which a level of aggregate demand can

---

[6] Notable papers that operate on the assumption of market-clearing wage-setting are those by A. A. Alchian, 'Information Costs, Pricing, and Resource Unemployment', and D. T. Mortensen, 'A Theory of Wage and Employment Dynamics', both in Phelps *et al.*, *Microeconomic Foundations*. The reader is also referred to relevant portions in E. S. Phelps, 'The New Microeconomics in Inflation and Employment Theory', *idem*.

influence the quantity of search unemployment. Let us consider, as a respite from the hypothetical recessions we have been inducing in the past pages, an increase of aggregate demand above its equilibrium level. On our momentary assumption that money wage rates are market-clearing, this increase of demand will stimulate firms to raise their money wage rates; this is one of several means, including additional advertising and other nonwage recruitment outlays, by which they can hope to attract workers from other firms or to attract them away from continued search. The general rise of money wage rates in excess of normal expectations will indeed reduce the quantity of search unemployment. The unemployed workers engaged in sampling money wage offers, not knowing that all money wage rates have tended to rise, will tend to mistake their individual observations of high money wage rates as specific to the firm or job that they have investigated rather than a general tendency of money wage rates to be higher. Unemployment will go on falling until it has reached such a level that the net 'seepage' into jobs of workers who have been holding out for better wages just balances (no longer exceeds) the flow of new entrants into the unemployment pool. Money wage rates thus rise ultimately by just enough to induce the increase in the employment rate induced by the increase of aggregate demand. In

TABLE 1.1.   *UNEMPLOYMENT RATES, AS PERCENT OF CIVILIAN LABOR FORCE, BY AGE AND SEX IN YEARS OF 'AVERAGE' UNEMPLOYMENT*

Age	1957			1965			1970		
	Men	Women	Both	Men	Women	Both	Men	Women	Both
16 to 19	12.4	10.6	11.6	14.1	15.7	14.8	15.0	15.6	15.2
20 and over	3.6	4.1	3.8	3.2	4.5	3.6	3.5	4.8	4.0
Total	4.1	4.7	4.3	4.0	5.5	4.5	4.4	5.9	4.9

the new 'steady-state' a feeling of euphoria will prevail in which most workers feel that they are enjoying a money wage increase not generally given to the rest of the population.

As in our examination of speculative employment changes in response to variations in aggregate demand, there is a one-shot change of money wage rates and prices associated with the change of the employment rate, both being responses to the same increase of aggregate demand. But subsequently there will be a continuing rate of increase of money wage rates and prices, given expectations of the general average level of money wage rates, if the unemployment rate is sustained below its equilibrium level. By the equilibrium

TABLE 1.2. *SELECTED CHARACTERISTICS OF THE UNEMPLOYMENT*

Proportion of Monthly Unemployment having attained Duration Specified, Annual Averages, Percent

	4 weeks or less	5 to 6	7 to 10	11 to 14	15 to 26	27 or more
1957	49.2	9.0	13.7	8.4	11.2	8.4
1965	48.4	8.5	12.5	8.2	12.0	10.4
1970	52.3	9.6	13.8	8.1	10.4	5.7

Monthly Turnover Rates, Employees on Manufacturing Payrolls Only

	Quits	Layoffs	Other	All Separations
1957	1.6	2.1	0.5	4.2
1965	1.9	1.4	0.8	4.1
1970	2.1	1.8	0.9	4.8

Reasons given for becoming Unemployed, as Percent of Civilian Labor Force, Annual Average

	Newly Entering Labor Force	Re-entering Labor Force	Left Job	Lost Job	Total
Nov. 1965	0.6	1.0	0.7	1.6	3.9
Average in 1967	0.5	1.2	0.6	1.6	3.9
1970	0.6	1.5	0.7	2.2	4.9

Source: U.S. Department of Labor, *Handbook of Labor Statistics.*

rate of unemployment we mean that rate whose maintenance by the suitable behavior of aggregate demand would cause, on an appropriate averaging over workers, actual money wage rates being offered to workers to move proportionally to their expectations or beliefs about the probability distribution of potential wage offers. In disequilibrium, expectations are out of line with statistical actuality.

Consider the disequilibrium state of 'overemployment' that the aforediscussed increase of aggregate demand brought about: Average money wage rates have risen beyond expectations and it is this discrepancy that accounts for the reduction of unemployment. (Moreover, firms might not have sought to expand had they not underestimated the bidding for labor by their competitors; but they may be mollified by the unexpected prices they soon find their competitors, like themselves, are charging.) This discrepancy between 'actual' and 'expected' must be preserved if the unemployment rate is to be sustained at its below-equilibrium level. If we hypothesize that information about the equally high money wage rate being paid elsewhere gradually comes to be suffused over employees, then, if the unemployment rate is to be maintained, aggregate demand must steadily be increased so as to keep newly acquired information about money wage rates elsewhere as out-moded currently as previously held wage information was then. For the continuation of the process in which workers on the whole have more employment, or earlier employment or worse employment than each individually would knowingly have selected, there must be cooperation by the monetary authorities. The continuing rise of product prices and the rise of money wage rates would put a strain on money markets, driving up rates of interest and thus reducing aggregate demand, unless the money supply is steadily increased so as to keep aggregate demand moving up *pari passu* with the price level. For a time, the fiscal authorities could substitute in this task by steadily decreasing tax rates.

A decline of aggregate demand from its equilibrium level can be seen to produce a rise of unemployment and a process in which prices and money wage rates rise, if at all, less quickly than is the average expectation. Briefly, a decline of demand drives money wage rate increases below the expected amounts, causing workers to reject employment offers, to search longer for a wage demand acceptable, or to quit existing jobs to search for better ones.[7] Because, unknownst to each firm, other firms are doing the same thing, each firm is happily surprised to find that it can acquire the reduced flow of new workers that it wants at lower and lower money wage rates. At the same time, firms are sadly having to shade prices in order to meet the unexpected price cuts of their competitors. If there is not to be a tendency toward restoration of employment toward its equilibrium level by reason (in the usual analysis) of the associated decline of money rates of interest and the increase of the real value of given nominal cash balances, aggregate demand must be steadily decreased by means of tax increases or money contraction. Then money wage rates will tend steadily to fall as the reservation money wage rates below which workers refuse employment in order to search for an alternative job receive gradual downward revisions as disappointed searchers lower their expectations of the average level of prevailing money wage rates. We see that the responses of employment deci-

[7] The behavior of quit rates under job rationing contrasts with their behavior under market-clearing wage rates.

sions and the response of price and wage decisions to the behavior of aggregate demand combine to trace out a Phillips Curve relation between the steady rate of inflation and the unemployment rate. In this connection, however, we should recall that we have been supposing consistently with the discussion of the foregoing types of unemployment that expectations of the trend rate of change of the price level and of the average money wage are not subject to adaptation despite consistent inflation or deflation.

1.3.2. *Job Rationing and Search-Unemployment.* We have been trying to discuss search-unemployment and the nature of the wage and price decisions on what is largely a somewhat unrealistic assumption, namely, that the firm at each moment chooses the cheaper of two workers for a given job, after making appropriate allowance for differences in the efficiency, reliability, and other cost advantages of the two workers; households then play the game accordingly. The trouble with this classical law of economy is that, in a setting of incomplete information, very often it is not an expected-cost-minimizing practice for the firm to adopt.

The heterogeneity of workers makes it uneconomical for any firm to acquire all the information about a job applicant that would be relevant to it. In the absence of complete information about workers, the wage at which a person says he will accept a job itself becomes an informational datum of interest to the firm about that person. Often the firm will appraise a job applicant by the wage he demands, partially or wholly, in the same way that the household judges fresh fruits by their prices. If a man, believing that his alternatives are grim, tells a firm that he will work for peanuts, the firm may surmise, 'This offer tells us more about him than about the world. There must be something wrong with him.'[8]

Another obstacle in the way of immediate market clearance of money wage rates arises when certain jobs are closely complementary with one another in the production of some final output. A job applicant or job holder may well ask what good it will do him to offer his services for less, in prompt response to a fall in the demand for the product, if there are going to be some rotten apples in the

---

[8] The same phenomenon can operate in an economy in which wage rates are standardized with each job classification, as noted below. The point about appraisal of worker quality by wage is made in G. A. Akerlof, 'The Market for "Lemons": Qualitative Uncertainty and the Market Mechanism', *Quarterly Journal of Economics*, August 1970.

barrel who will not oblige with timely cuts, more or less equiproportionately, in the wages they ask in remuneration for the performance of their complementary tasks. If it is a case of sink or swim
together right now, often it will be sink.

Of course, few workers have the option to negotiate individually
their wage. The very heterogeneity of workers which is an important
aspect of the scarcity of information about jobs makes it too costly
in a good many cases to negotiate man by man over the money wage
rate to be paid to each worker. It is a great deal more convenient
administratively to set a common wage rate to be paid to holders of
jobs of a given description and to proceed to make wage-rate distinctions according to the average characteristics expectable in
workers most likely to occupy those jobs. Moreover, it is certainly
possible that wage rate differences for workers doing identical work
can be detrimental to employee morale when the employees find
those differences to be discriminatory or too abstractly based to be
comprehensible. Let us then consider the phenomena of job rationing
and unemployment on the assumption of impersonal or standard
money wage rates within broad job categories.

It should be recognized that despite the restriction of uniform wage
rates within job categories there could nevertheless be a kind of
modified or constrained market clearance through the continuous
adjustment of the wage rates by category. One can imagine a company in which the application of a new secretary who meets the
requirements of the job category would be the occasion for a Dutch
auction to locate the smallest wage at which the required number of
secretaries could be retained for that day. Of course, the thought
would be repugnant to most secretaries but in fact many of them
submit routinely to a different risk, that of being discharged. It is
typically the employer's convenience that prevents them from ex-
pressing a preference between these two risks, I should think, not
some foregone consensus that the one risk is preferable over the
other to employer and employees alike.

One reason we do not usually observe such nice determinations of
the wage scale is that the employer faces a stochastically fluctuating
supply of services, much as the film actor faces a stochastically
fluctuating demand. As a consequence the employer is not sure, at
each wage, how many workers and which workers will quit tomorrow and how many unemployed workers in the various categories will seek and accept jobs at the firm. To reduce the risk of
losing critical workers through occasional undersetting of wage

scales, the firm may be willing in normal times to pay wage rates in the various categories which are, intermittently and perhaps most of the time, unnecessarily high for generating the average employment levels that the firm likes to have. This consideration is surely most important when there is considerable technical complementarity among jobs in many production processes. At the same time, such a firm may very well have what it aptly calls job vacancies in a significant number of its job categories.

A second reason why we do not find that wage scales by job category tend to be instantly responsive to the vicissitudes of supply and demand goes back to the problems of the employer's appraisal of workers by their wage demands. Some people, while demonstrably qualified, may find they are unable to capture job vacancies in low-rung jobs, or be unable to unseat employees currently occupying those jobs, because employers figure that they are overqualified. 'The applicant must be crazy. If he isn't, then he'll leave soon. It won't pay to hire him in either case.'

In the world of job rationing, a rise of aggregate demand above its equilibrium level succeeds in raising the employment rate without any necessary help from the concomitant rise of money wage rates. Imagine that, in equilibrium, a representative assortment of workers is going from firm to firm, sampling from a representative assortment of vacant jobs. When aggregate demand increases, a larger number of firms will make openings for workers in each job description. Consequently, the unemployed workers tend to find openings of the type they were looking for earlier on average than when aggregate demand and hence vacancies were lower. If the aggregate demand succeeds in maintaining a steady-state of higher employment, the fall of the unemployment rate expresses this shortened search time, not a reduction in the number of people who become unemployed. In fact, the data we have on the American economy support strongly the hypothesis that a larger proportion of the working-age population experience unemployment in prosperous times than do so in depressed times. This paradox is due to the very inducement to quit one's job and enter the unemployment pool to search for a better job that is provided by indications that job vacancies are easier to find.

In the labor markets so described, such rises in money wage scales as occur are inessential in bringing about the increase of employment. Indeed, they can have little or no effect upon the aggregate unemployment rate in labor markets where the relevant firms are few and the wage rates they pay well known. Then an individual firm can gain workers by raising its money wage rates, given other firms' money wage rates, but it is impossible for all firms in the aggregate to gain workers from a rise of money wage rates, except possibly new entrants speculating on temporariness of the money wage increase, the phenomenon we discussed in the first section of this chapter. This is almost to be presumed, at least approximately, where money wage rates are adjusted by each firm only infrequently, partly for reasons of uncertainty alluded to earlier, or additionally for reasons of administrative convenience such as releasing decision-making time for other uses. In that case, the shortage of information affecting workers is primarily about the presence or absence of openings and the nonpecuniary properties of the jobs available at the various accessible firms.

1.3.3. *The 'Wage-wage' Spiral.* While the general round of money wage rate increases which will occur in the disequilibrium situation under discussion is unlikely to be of causal importance for the rise in employment that results from the increase in the level of aggregate demand, each individual firm, when it reaches the point for wage-scale decisions, will naturally regard these wage scales as being of paramount importance for the success it can expect to have in recruiting workers from the unemployment pool and from other firms to fill its job vacancies. In many submarkets for labor, wage scales are revised seriatim, firm by firm, and even, within the same firm, job by job. In some firms wage scales may be reviewed periodically, usually with annual regularity, and at some firms wage scales may be reviewed opportunistically, when the attention of the management is being directed anyway toward certain personnel or manpower problems.

If aggregate demand is high (above equilibrium), the process of rising wages is therefore slow, but nonetheless sure. Firms which are at the stage of revising wage rates will respond to the bulge of demand by raising their wage scales as a part of their plans to attract more labor. In the case of annual review, within a year all firms will have had an opportunity to respond to the increase in demand. Because the firm whose 'turn' to raise wage rates later in the 12-month period will have the opportunity to observe the rise of the average wage up to that moment, the firm which sets wage rates early in the year will actually find, at the onset of the next round, that it has suffered a decline in its relative wage scales. If it is to attempt again to raise its relative wage scales, it will have to raise its money wage rates in proportion to the average money wage drift over the past 12 months. So the wage-setting firms have a lot of catching up to do. The desire of the typical firm for a 3-percent advantage in its relative wage, if maintained by the required management of aggregate demand, could easily produce a general rate of money wage increase of, say, 6 percent per annum – even though each firm optimistically figures that wage stability is just around the corner, that all the other firms setting wage rates will be content with their present wage rates.

Another way to describe the wage disequilibrium inflation process is to say that there are a variety of factors which the typical firm mispredicts in this disequilibrium – the paucity of callers for vacant jobs, the extraordinary quit rate it is experiencing among its existing employees, as well as the unexpected wage increases going on at other firms – with the result that the firm's efforts to close the additional vacancies created by the aggregate demand increase must fail, leaving vacancies higher while the unemployment rate, and accordingly the average daily flow supply of workers available to the firm, are both smaller. Hence, the excess demand for labor of the various descriptions is on the average higher. This loose and simple indicator of the degree of frustration and disappointment that employers (and workers) are finding in the labor market can be regarded as the explanatory variable for the rate of wage inflation – given, as throughout our discussion, static expectations about future wage rates and prices.[9]

The consequences of a fall of aggregate demand to a level below its equilibrium value are quite symmetrical. A decrease of aggregate demand extinguishes vacancies in many job categories – in all job categories in the event of a fall of demand of major proportions – with the result that unemployed workers searching for suitable job openings take longer to get placed, and frequently settle for a job in a category inferior to what they had hoped for. The duration of

---

[9] Such a model is the subject of E. S. Phelps, 'Money-Wage Dynamics and Labormarket Equilibrium', *Journal of Political Economy*, August 1968, Part II. A clearer exposition of the same model can be found in the paper of the same title in Phelps *et al.*, *Microeconomic Foundations*. In that version, there is a mathematical appendix on a continuous-time model of leap-frogging that may be of particular interest. An earlier discussion of leap-frogging and the wage-wage spiral can be found in W. J. Fellner *et al.*, *The Problem of Rising Prices* (Paris: Organization for Economic Cooperation and Development, 1960). Another recent contribution in the same vein is G. A. Akerloff, 'Relative Wages and the Rate of Inflation', *Quarterly Journal of Economics*, August 1969.

unemployment lengthens while at the same time there is a tendency for the quit rate to fall and therefore fewer people voluntarily to jump into the unemployment pool. On the other hand firms become more exacting and are quicker to discharge unsatisfactory workers. If a firm operates on statical assumptions about other firms' future money wage rates, then it will take advantage of the reduction in vacancies forced on it and of the increased flow-supply of unemployed workers seeking jobs to lower their money wage costs a little by reducing its money wage scales, hoping that the decline in its relative wage which it expects to result will produce enough savings to offset the greater difficulty it may also anticipate in attracting workers at its lower relative scale. Its surprise at the similar wage reductions being made by other firms leads to a recurring process of unexpected wage deflation.

We arrive at a familiar proposition, one that seems to be the outcome of nearly every theory of unemployment and wage-price behavior so far invented: Under static expectations of future trends in general wage rates and prices, there exists a relation between the rate of change of money wage rates and of prices, on the one hand, and the rate of employment on the other. Our analysis has led us to the conclusion that when the disequilibrium in the labor market brings unhappy surprises to firms and happy ones to workers, when it is a sellers' market, then money wage rates are unexpectedly rising; when the shoe is on the other foot, when it is a buyers' market and it is the workers who are frustrated, then money wage rates are unexpectedly declining.

It might seem at this point that the analysis has somehow lost sight of and contradicted the familiar observation that money wage rates have long been rising on the average for jobs of almost every description. Why is this so and how can this fact be accommodated into the analysis? It is sometimes said that money wage rates rise because of the growth of labor productivity. This gets the grade of 'C', even if the word *marginal* is properly inserted. A better answer is that money wage rates are typically going up because firms and workers generally expect that money wage rates will be going up. If rising money wages is the normal expectation, firms that wish to maintain their respective capacity to produce, and hence their number of employees, must raise their money wage rates just to maintain their expected relative wage in the labor market. But for an 'A' answer one would want to add that only if firms expect to be able to pay these higher wages without consequently finding it appropriate at the same time to raise prices relative to those of competitors – thus having to face the prospect of a shrinkage of customers – would each firm actually decide to plan on maintaining its employment force; thus there must ultimately be the expectation of technological cost reductions or of inflation or both.

As a consequence, when we speak of 'underemployment' (employment below the equilibrium level) and associate these conditions with unexpected wage decreases, this point must always be recalled: if the prevailing expectation is one of 4 percent money wage rate increases, such a disequilibrium is evidenced by average rates of money wage increase of 3 percent just as much as by – 1 percent in the case of static ('flat') expectations. In either case, the essential point is that money wage rates are rising, if at all, less quickly than people have been expecting them to.

This permits us to clarify a little the concept of the equilibrium employment rate. One can say that the equilibrium employment rate is characterized by equality between the average rate of increase of money wage rates and the *expected* average rate of increase of money wage rates. This equality results when (and only when) firms on the average are having roughly the success (or difficulty) they were expecting to have in recruiting and retaining employees, and workers are having roughly the success (or difficulty) on the average that they were expecting in finding jobs of the type and pay that they were hoping for.[10]

---

[10] What does this theory do, one may ask, about a man who is holding out to be Archbishop of Canterbury or its equivalent? (The Samuelson-style question is from the master himself.) A man like that is in 'disequilibrium' in the present sense of the term. When a psychotic is termed *unbalanced*, there is the same thought in mind: things are never going to work out for him as he expects they will. But the thrust of the question is toward the exact meaning of our concept of equilibrium in the large when, in that state, it is not to be expected that there is a comprehensive equilibrium in the small. The answer must be that in calculating the macroequilibrium we have to assign a weight to each individual's expectations in proportion to this quickness to perceive his error and his adaptability in revising those expectations and accordingly in modifying his behavior. It follows, therefore, that macroeconomic equilibrium does not require that we rev up the economy to near-maximum employment in order that the disappointment of madmen be balanced by the surprises of realistic and responsive participants in the labor market. In this connection we should add that if there are psychological biases operating in such a way that, for equal 'objective' surprise, the reluctance of people to believe that job opportunities are fewer and worse than expected is, say, smaller than their eagerness to conclude that jobs are more plentiful and better than they expected – if there is this asymmetry in the speed of learning – the equilibrium unemployment rate must be large enough so that those who are quickly boosting their money wage demand in response to excess

1.4. *Discrimination, Seniority, Regrading, and Queue-Unemployment*

It is appropriate at this point to take notice of certain likely features of the composition of search-unemployment. Reflections on these features will lead us to discern yet another type of unemployment, one that is subtly interwoven with search-unemployment.

1.4.1. *Seniority*. When a firm is operating with established wage scales for the various job categories, it is natural to ask who gets hired and who does not in any category. In a general way, the firm rejects an application when there is a sufficiently good chance of finding a sufficiently better worker to fill the open job. The question then becomes, whom does the firm regard as better? One attribute that may help to make a man a better candidate for a job than another man is experience, especially experience in the very firm itself. It is quite impossible to become informed as to the exact abilities and reliability of a worker without actually trying him out. It is even rather costly to acquire personal data from the individual from which some predictions of the worker's ability can be made. As a consequence, the firm will often prefer to take the employee with whom it has had actual experience over the worker with whom it has had no experience. Folk wisdom tells us this in a thousand ways: don't buy a pig in a poke; old friends are the best friends; and a bird in the hand is worth two in the bush.

This consideration obviously works disadvantageously for those members of the labor force who are looking for their first adult job. It also helps to explain certain preferences that are often given to senior employees. Each year of experience that the firm has with an employee reduces a little the firm's uncertainty about his capability and reliability. Even if there are no systematic forces tending to correlate ability with age, we should expect, therefore, that the younger an employed worker is the more likely he will be laid off or discharged. On the other hand, when a veteran worker is discharged it may be taken by other firms as evidence that he has been found to be inadequate after a long opportunity for a careful observation of his performance. It would not be totally surprising, therefore, to find that the average duration of unemployment by age is distributed bimodally, though there are so many other factors operating on

---

demand for their services are sufficiently outnumbered by those who are lethargically reducing their reservation wage rates in response to the excess supply of their services. Some of these matters are reviewed in Chapter 4.

this variable that the absence of such a distribution would not be telling.

Another way of stating the above is to say that the veteran worker has some firm-specific human capital invested in him – namely, a confidence factor. This reminds us that there are many other investments that a firm makes in a new employee. The typical new hire may do little new work at the beginning while he is being shown the ropes. These investments will have similar implications for the incidence of unemployment.

1.4.2. *Statistical Discrimination.* Hiring biases may also be displayed in the choice between two workers with whom there is equal inexperience. Then the expected-cost-minimizing decision can only be based on readily obtainable data that the firm believes to be useful in predicting worker performance. The firm will likely latch on to such data as age, sex, height and weight, years of schooling, diplomas and degrees, birthplace, previous job held, number of months held – going on down a list that is dictated by the beliefs of the personnel decision-maker about how performance in the job in question tends to be correlated with observations on such variables. The firm is thus doing statistics, the art of choosing among scarce data and comparing them to other data in order to come to an intelligent decision. 'Errors' may be made, therefore, even with the application of the optimal decision rules. A bank might choose for its economist a man who has a Ph.D. in the expectation that this achievement reflects his superior stamina and ambition, though the rival candidate may in fact be better endowed with both of these qualities and greater ability too.

A traveler might be said to be 'discriminating' if, in the absence of local information, he makes it a rule to dine outside rather than at the hotel – though inevitably the restaurant selected will sometimes be inferior to the hotel.[11] Similarly, a cost-minimizing firm may 'discriminate' on the basis of a few data which it uses as proxies for some detailed description of the individuals that it does not believe economical or maybe even feasible to secure. To take a safe example, the firm might be wise – social scientists would be needed to test the hypothesis – to discriminate in favor of married men over divorced ones. Some amount of statistical 'prejudice' is 'economical' for the firm in a range of decisions because it is too costly to get at all the

[11] Yet he should go outside every time he lacks information about a hotel, not mix his strategy, if he feels the hotel is inferior on the average.

facts or to wait for all the facts to come in, let alone to test formally the behavioral hypotheses being relied upon.

Accordingly, what has been called racism – similar remarks apply to 'sexism' – can be hypothesized to be the consequence of 'scientific management' in the impersonal pursuit of maximum profit, not racial hostility or intolerance. Much of this sort of racial discrimination is unscientific, notoriously so. Statistical discrimination in hiring is often based (though one does not know how prevalently) upon stereotypes that are in scientific disrepute. There is, for example, no substantial empirical evidence that black people labor under genetic disadvantages compared to whites and other races; the presumption of most ethnologists and geneticists and other experts is certainly against such hypotheses. Where blacks encounter employers operating on false stereotypes, their grievance is indisputable.

But the sad fact is that there are harmful generalizations about racial groups that would be assented to by disinterested social observers. These are essentially accepted hypotheses about group behavior that originate in the group's experiences in the particular society. Such damaging information about the group is used against every individual in it no matter how talented. Symmetrically, the commendatory truths about the socially advantaged groups serves to boost every person in those groups no matter how untalented he may be. This might occur even though no one cared a hoot about skin color when it comes to personal relations.

The statistical accuracy of such 'prejudices' does not mean that the resulting group-based racial discrimination is ethically satisfactory. Far from it. Society would be justified in refusing to condemn men to dead-end jobs on the basis of skin color merely because, in view of the costs of acquiring more information, that was the way to maximize the net national product. Social critics are asking whether we do not require, in the labor market and elsewhere in our society, something more than blind justice and statistical fairness. It may be that the liberal principle of impersonal buying and selling, of cruelly equal opportunity, has to be alloyed with some principle of personal concern.

Discrimination against nonwhites and against women tends to reduce their wage earnings relative to whites and to men, respectively. General intolerance toward having nonwhites or women in the firm would do the same.[12] Whether such racial and sex biases tend to pro-

[12] The neoclassical theory of racial bias as 'taste' is developed in G. S. Becker, *The Economics of Discrimination* (New York: Columbia University Press, 1959).

TABLE 1.3. *UNEMPLOYMENT RATES BY RACE AND SEX, PERCENT OF CIVILIAN LABOR FORCE*

| | 1957 | | | 1965 | | | 1970 | | |
Race	Men	Women	All	Men	Women	All	Men	Women	All
White	3.6	4.3	3.8	3.6	5.0	4.1	4.0	5.4	4.5
Nonwhite	8.3	7.3	7.9	7.4	9.2	8.1	7.3	9.3	8.2
All	4.1	4.7	4.3	4.0	5.5	4.5	4.4	5.9	4.9

Source: U.S. Department of Labor, *Handbook of Labor Statistics.*

TABLE 1.4. *UNEMPLOYMENT RATES BY NEIGHBORHOOD AND RACE (PERCENT)*

| | 1967 | | | 1970 | | |
| | Urban Areas | | All Areas | Urban Areas | | All Areas |
Race	Poverty Areas	Other Urban	Urban and Nonurban	Poverty Areas	Other Urban	Urban and Nonurban
White	5.3	3.2	3.4	6.3	4.5	4.5
Nonwhite	8.9	6.1	7.4	9.5	6.5	8.2
All	6.8	3.4	3.8	7.6	4.6	4.9

Source: U.S. Department of Labor, *Handbook of Labor Statistics.*

duce a major disparity in unemployment rates as well is hard to say. In Chapter 3 I shall be discussing unemployment behavior that is due to a variety of sociological and psychological factors. Discrimination against blacks may very well increase *that* kind of unemployment. But I confine attention here to the frictional kinds of unemployment that we are concerned with in this chapter.

1.4.3. *Regrading and Queue-Unemployment.* Where blacks and women succeed in being hired in the higher job categories, it may often be the case that they find themselves the first to be fired and the last to be hired because the employer assumes that they are less steady, less reliable, more casual, and therefore have less investment value to the firm. This example, by the way, perhaps illustrates the shaky sort of stereotype that could gain currency, for the data show that the quit rate among middle-aged black males is below that of whites of the same age and sex. Another way by which such discrimination can produce an incidence in unemployment is through

---

Note that the neo-neoclassical theory of discrimination based on statistical prejudice, rather than psychic intolerance or hostile bigotry, does not depend upon the existence of racial tastes.

the tendency that may result for these workers to be placed in low-skilled jobs that are not long bearable or are subject to frequent hiring and firing. In short, those afflicted by these biases might not want to accept wage-rate differentials of the magnitude that would be required to achieve the same unemployment rate, the same frequency of joblessness, that they would have if they were white males.

The elaboration of this point brings us to the subject of regrading labor. Up until now we have been talking about a segmented and imperfect labor market in which musicians, actors, electricians, and so on, are all highly specialized and, most recently in our discussion, possibly quite individual in their talent, yet there is no hierarchy of skills within the firm. We have been neglecting the fact that, in some areas of technology, certain skills in a worker enable him to carry on in his present job or to work with equal success in a myriad of jobs which are 'lower' in the hierarchy.

Within the firm that is subject to such a hierarchical structure of tasks, a fall of demand for its products may precipitate a domino effect in which some of those holding the most skill-demanding jobs are downgraded (formally or not) to less skill-intensive assignments, some of the workers in those jobs are in turn downgraded to assignments in the next level, and so on, with the end result being the layoff of the least skilled workers. The reason for this is that the firm has typically its largest 'investments' in the most skilled workers. Being the most versatile and complex, their ilk are the most difficult to acquire detailed information about and hence the riskiest to try to replace. It will frequently be more economical to retain high-skilled versatile workers in less useful employments, especially if the low level of demand for the firm's product is expected to be temporary, than it is to discharge such workers and then laboriously and gradually rebuild the team of highly skilled workers. When the depression in demand is thought to be only fleeting, the firm may very well elect to retain its entire labor force, putting workers onto postponable chores such as bringing records up to date which are best accomplished when the opportunity presents itself.

As a result of this bumping process we can expect that, at firms displaying this hierarchical character, discharges and new hires will tend to concentrate at the least skilled job levels. If there should be a doubling of the number of high-skilled workers who are unemployed, we would expect to see that the number of low-skilled workers who are unemployed would more than double. This is because the number of unskilled jobs that are vacant decreases not just in proportion to the decline in product demand according to the input-output coefficient; it drops further with the avalanche of overskilled workers who are dropped (temporarily it is hoped) into those low-skilled job categories. Therefore, low-skilled workers would find it even harder to find alternative jobs at other firms than would high-skilled workers.[13]

In such times, as a consequence, it is likely that low-skilled workers will be discouraged from making efforts to find similar work at other firms. As long as the unemployed low-skilled worker feels he will be re-employed within the tolerably near future, his inclination is to wait his turn in the expected future call-up of veteran employees when business picks up. This sort of unemployment has been called queue-unemployment – thus calling to mind the assumption that the individual is prevented from buying himself a better place in line by means of the offer of money, i.e., the offer to fill a job at a lower money wage. Clearly, queue-unemployment does not depend upon speculation of a decline in the marginal opportunity cost of leisure. It is not like search-unemployment because there is no active search necessarily being conducted. It is most like the type of unemployment that we called precautionary; but it is not identical to it because the period of waiting for resumption of one's normal employment is not a voluntary decision based upon the calculations of the seller of the labor service.

There is some question of whether queue-unemployment can stand for long as a distinct type of unemployment. It tends to blend into the other types if we acknowledge that most workers of however little skill could, perhaps only after lengthy and arduous search, reasonably expect to find employment somewhere, in some kind of paying job, at some wage not beneath consideration (barring the observance everywhere of minimum wage laws). Once desperation begins to set in, many of these jobs are flushed out (the word seems appropriate) and to our distress we find that labor markets are less imperfect than we thought. The chronicles of wage rates and working conditions in the market for farm labor in the 1930s offer us an appalling demonstration of that. Nevertheless, in short recessions

---

[13] For tests of this and some other hypotheses under discussion, see L. C. Thurow, *Poverty and Discrimination* (Washington, D.C.: The Brookings Institution, 1970). The term *queue-unemployment*, introduced above, is used in that work.

and, at one time or another, in almost every part of the economy where structural changes are reducing the profitability of production, it does seem possible to identify queue unemployment as an entity separate from the other types.

The existence of a disequilibrium quantity of unemployment has consequences, in a hierarchical model, for the relation among wage rates and skill categories. When the level of aggregate demand is below equilibrium, the initial bunching of excess supplies of labor at the low-skill job categories will produce a faster rate of decline of wage scales in these low-skill categories compared to the higher-skilled categories, at least at first. It seems unlikely, however, that this uneven response would continue indefinitely (in conditions of otherwise steady disequilibrium), for it is unlikely that the relative wage paid to low-skilled workers would go to zero. It is more likely that a kind of steady-state would tend to result in which the relative wage paid on low-skilled jobs would have fallen to such a level that enough low-skilled workers would have recaptured jobs from expensive high-skilled workers who refused to be downgraded.

1.5. *The Idleness of Nonhuman Resources, Price Dynamics, and Underdemand for Labor*

The reader might well ask whether the types of unemployment we have been discussing correspond, wholly or at least partially, to the 'involuntary unemployment' discussed by Keynes. He identified 'involuntary' unemployment as that idleness of workers which is attributable to an insufficiency of the money bids ('demand prices') for goods in relation to the reservation money wage rates of workers. Accordingly, the elimination of such idleness would not require a rise of real wage rates. Thus Keynes writes, 'Although a reduction of the existing money-wage would lead to a withdrawal of labor, it does not follow that a fall in the value of the existing money-wage in terms of wage-goods would do so if it were due to a rise in the price of the latter.'[14] There are differences between the interpretation of the inelasticity of money wage rates hinted by Keynes on the one hand and the various reasons for money wage stickiness given in the modern theories discussed here. Keynes had his own sociological theory, it appears, of the causes of money wage stickiness and its potentialities for unemployment.

However, the types of unemployment discussed here all have the

[14] Keynes, *General Theory*, p. 8.

essential operational property that Keynes wrote of: An increase of aggregate demand brings about an increase of employment, and quite possibly a coincident rise of the money wage level, without any necessity of a rise of real wage rates. The foregoing types of unemployment (as much as Keynes's own sociological type of unemployment) would probably pass his test for the existence of 'involuntary' unemployment: 'Men are involuntarily unemployed if, in the event of a small rise in the price of wage-goods (i.e., consumption goods) relatively to the money wage, both the aggregate supply of labor willing to work for the current money wage and the aggregate demand for it at that wage would be greater than the existing volume of employment.'[15] Only workers who are rationed out of a job, queueing for a hoped-for increase of the ration, would fail to be detected by Keynes's test, and certainly their idleness is 'involuntary' in the accepted sense of the term.[16] What is most significantly different about the modern theories herein from the concepts of the Keynesians is the former's treatment of 'unemployment' as frictional and greatly subject to the influence of aggregate demand *because* of the frictions; Keynesians had treated frictional unemployment as irreducible whatever the pressure of demand.

It might seem odd at first that Keynes's test involves a more-than-proportional rise of goods prices relative to money wage rates. This reflects his belief at the time of the *General Theory* that, starting from settled conditions either prosperous or depressed, business firms always have to have an improvement of goods prices relative to labor prices if they are to calculate that their profit-maximizing output has gone up. He believed that prices clear goods markets just as he believed that money wage rates tend to clear (but not equilibrate in our sense) labor markets. He went even farther, postulating that product prices were determined through pure competition in commodity markets or by a process that converged quickly enough to pure competition. Accordingly, he believed that in the depression, with so few employees luxuriating in an undiminished capital stock,

---

[15] Keynes, *General Theory*, p. 15.

[16] In applying Keynes's text, one has to suppose that firms are price-takers and workers are wage-takers. So it is difficult also to fit precautionary wait unemployment into Keynes's scheme. Let me also remark that the test appears to be somewhat overstrong in the event that there are discontinuities in the relationship between the supply of labor and real wage rates of such a nature that any decline of real-wage rates, such as Keynes constructs for the purpose of his test, would lead to a discrete reduction of the labor supply (through retirements and so on) that swamps the reduction in the number of workers who are demanding higher money wage rates.

the marginal productivity of labor would be abnormally high and hence, too, real wage rates.

Subsequent empirical analysis has cast great doubt upon the assumption that real wage rates measure marginal productivities with equal precision (or bias) over the business cycle. Keynes thus necessarily excluded the possibility of another kind of unemployment which may coexist with the types of unemployment we have been considering and which, like these types, falls under the influence of aggregate demand behavior. It is fairly well agreed (and well supported) that real wage rates rise, if at all, much less than the estimated marginal productivity of labor when a reduction of aggregate demand brings about a reduction of employment. The larger the size of the depression, the greater the shortfall between real wage and marginal product is. If the total supply of labor is an increasing function of real wage rates, there is a much smaller increase in the total supply of labor (some of whom would find jobs) on account of the 'depression' of real wage rates in depressions and there may even be a decline in the total amount of labor supplied if real wage rates actually fall (relative to expected secular trends). This underdemand for labor that we are now positing is the idleness attributable to the aggregate-demand-associated shortfall between real wage rates and marginal labor productivities. In terms of prices, the shortfall develops this way: At given money-wage rates, the reduction of the employment of labor on given capital facilities reduces the money marginal costs of production at the industry level (and perhaps even within each firm); but commodity prices, according to the theory, fail to fall in proportion to this induced reduction in the level of marginal costs. What fun a Berle or Galbraith might have with the contrast between this remarkable increase in markups which corporations thus contrive in slumps and the asceticism with which competitive producers are imagined in the textbooks to drive prices down to marginal costs. Who knows but that evil spirits are uncapped in a depression, that the larger economic aggregates, heretofore benign, exercise their monopoly powers more severely in times of business distress.[17] Yet it is significant that the implied behavior of prices relative to money costs can be explained in the neoclassic

---

[17] It was the hypothesis of M. Kalecki that in a slump businesses collude and combine more vigorously, thus protecting capital's relative share of income and in so doing reducing real wage rates. The most accessible reference is his *Theory of Economic Dynamics* (London: George Allen & Unwin, 1954). Apparently this is essentially an augmented edition of his book from the 1930s.

microeconomic terms of the foregoing analysis of labor idleness. In periods of abnormally low aggregate demand, machinery may be idled or left to run at below-normal speed on the speculation that it is economical to save them for future use. Consequently, addition or subtraction of employed labor to existing capital may produce a smaller effect on output than would be expected from the marginal productivity of labor when calculated at 'full' utilization of capital. Second, in some instances a firm may elect to hold a capital asset idle for precautionary purposes in order that it be uncontracted for and available for use in the hoped-for event that its services are soon demanded at its regular standard rental. Third, capital assets are sometimes idle when they have to be diverted from production in the course of finding a user for them. New automobiles are not auctioned off on the instant of their arrival at the dealer's showroom, but rather remain idle on display until buyers can be found who like them. The idleness of store properties, apartments, and a host of other capital assets tends to depress available real wage rates. When demands for the products of these capital assets are depressed, their idleness is intensified. There may be instances of a fourth type of excess capacity, one of the queueing type. If a producer is confronted with buyers of his product who ration their suppliers, the supplying firm may frequently be in the position of holding its capital equipment idle, awaiting the opportunity to meet an order when the buyers find it appropriate to reach down to its position in the queue in order to satisfy their needs for supplies.

It is important, too, that even if there were no transactions costs or uncertainties affecting the hiring of the services of heterogeneous labor and capital goods, there would be a tendency for the 'underuse' of all factors of production arising from the costliness of the search by the firm for customers for its final products. This costliness results in the 'goodwill' item that is essentially the discrepancy between the reproduction costs of the firm's capital facility and the market value of the claims to the firm. This wedge between cost and value also results in a shortfall both of real wage rates from marginal productivities of labor and of the rentals (under a proper accounting) from the marginal productivities of capital goods.[18]

Because product markets and capital goods markets are thus afflicted with uncertainty arising from the scarcity or unavailability of information, it is not to be supposed that these markets are

[18] E. S. Phelps and S. G. Winter, Jr., 'Optimal Price Policy under Atomistic Competition', in *Microeconomic Foundations*.

necessarily in equilibrium anymore than the labor markets. Equilibrium in the product market requires that producers be experiencing the frequency of orders, the finding of customers, and the discovery of competitors' prices that conform in the large with their expectations. If, to take the simplest case, expectations are 'static' and no trend rate of change of prices and wage rates over the future is built into those static expectations, a disequilibrium in the direction of overutilization of capital will be marked by rising goods prices, and underutilization by falling goods prices.

When a depression of aggregate demand throws both the labor market and the product market into disequilibrium, firms will be setting money wage rates at depressed levels, as with prices. The product prices need not be reduced proportionally to the decline in unit variable costs that result from the reduced operating level and lower wage rates. It turns on firms' expectations of the frictions in customer flow relative to employee flow and upon the relative speeds of learning (or strengths of equilibration) in the labor and goods markets. As a result, we do not observe the tendency for a rise in the level of real wage rates that a diminishing-returns technology and perfectly frictionless competitive pricing would lead us to predict.

The same is true on the other side of equilibrium. A boom involving overemployment and overutilization of capacity does not require that real wage rates (or, more accurately, product wage rates) be depressed. Capital goods fall into uses, and additional labor is hired to assist, which they would not be assigned to if each firm manager appreciated the systematic and global character of the change in the demand he is experiencing and correctly conjectured how his competitors would respond to the same parametric change.

There is nothing wholly new under the sun. There is an adumbral anticipation of the notion of overutilization (and, by implication, underutilization) by Dennis Robertson, who described the phenomenon with characteristic flair. Referring to a rise of prices in excess of the expected or customary trend, if any, he wrote:

> . . . the stimulus of rising prices is partly founded in illusion . . . [The business leader] is spurred on . . . by imaginary gains at the expense of his fellow businessmen. It is so hard to believe at first that other people will really have the effrontery or the good fortune to raise their charges as much as he has raised his own.[19]

[19] D. H. Robertson, *Money* (Cambridge: Cambridge University Press, 1929).

2 Macroequilibrium, Inflation Expectations, and the 'Natural' Unemployment Rate

THE previous chapter has introduced, from at least three angles, the concept of equilibrium in the labor market and in the product market. Following a quick summary of these equilibrium notions, there is a discussion of the requirements for equilibrium to prevail in both markets – overall macroeconomic equilibrium.

We move from there to the role played in equilibrium and disequilibrium by expectations of price and wage inflation. There is the matter of the determinants of these expectations and there is the question of their effects on the character of macroequilibrium. A question of considerable interest for inflation policy is whether the size of the unemployment rate *in overall macroequilibrium* depends appreciably upon the size of the expected inflation rate associated with that equilibrium.

According to the essentially classical concept of the natural rate of unemployment (with its corollaries of natural employment and natural output levels), the answer to this question is no. We will address ourselves to this concept and also to the kind of assumption about the behavior of expectations of the inflation rate that is usually found to be a companion of the natural-rate assumption. Taken together, these two assumptions comprise what will be called here the *natural-rate hypothesis*. This hypothesis has implications for disequilibrium: A change of inflation policy can bring 'only' a temporary variation of output and employment, and, further, the prolonged maintenance of an unemployment rate away from the natural level must eventually bring either rising inflation or growing deflation in an explosive fashion. The argument for this hypothesis, and some ways in which this hypothesis needs to be qualified, purely from the standpoint of standard economic theory, will be discussed at length. We shall also consider the bearing of certain kinds of evidence on the tenability of the hypothesis.

2.1. *Macroeconomic Equilibrium in General*

When there is equilibrium in the product market, and only then, the representative producer finds that customers are buying the amount of goods he expected them to demand, and he is having the experience of finding and losing customers that was assumed in his pricing decisions. This means that on the average each producer has correctly guessed the implications of his pricing decision for his competitiveness *vis-à-vis* his rival firms and the makers of substitutable products. He has guessed the trend in the average price being set by his competitors.[1] Analogously, households are finding the prices and availabilities of goods from suppliers to be consistent with their assumptions. Therefore, when the product market is in equilibrium, the prices that producers on average actually charge over time, relative to expectations of general prices over time, will not need to be revised. If, for example, households and firms are expecting the trend in competitors' prices to be flat, then in equilibrium it is implied that producers as a whole are not raising or lowering their prices.

When there is equilibrium in the labor market, and only then, households on the whole find their sampling of wage rates, their experience with job openings, and the mean frequency of demands for their services to be consistent with their expectations.[2] And analogously for firms. When the labor market is in equilibrium, therefore, there is no general tendency for a wage-setter to revise that wage relative to his current expectations of average money wages being set by competitors. If, for example, households and firms expected no trend in average money wage rates set elsewhere over the economy, labor market equilibrium will be marked by a zero rate of change of actual money wage rates on average.

The dual fulfillment of these two conditions determines the equilibrium average real wage rate and the equilibrium size of the labor force, given technological, demographic, and factor-endowment parameters. On the demand-for-labor side, in full macroequilibrium, the money wage that the representative firm expects to have to pay to maintain its competitiveness in the labor market *relative* to the price it believes it can charge for its product without erosion of its customers is just high enough that the firm is willing at the moment to employ just its current work force, neither more nor less; we may

---

[1] Furthermore, the producer's capital utilization decision is predicated on a correct forecast of the future rise of the general price level in relation to available money interest rates.

[2] Furthermore, households' labor force participation decisions are based on correct forecasts of the prospective purchasing power of current money wage earning possibilities, i.e., on correct forecasts of the future price-level rise in relation to the money rate of interest.

take this 'demand price' to be smaller the larger the work force at the representative firm is. On the supply-of-labor side, the aggregate work force (total employment) is at the level consistent with the average money wage that households expect to get relative to the average money price they expect to have to pay for consumer products. We may assume that these two relationships jointly determine some solution for the equilibrium value of the average expected real wage.[3]

There is accordingly a 'supply-side requirement' for the realization of full macroequilibrium: Expectations of going real wage rates must be at such a level as to allow equilibrium in the labor market when the product market is simultaneously in equilibrium. If the expected real wage were below equilibrium, firms would bid up money-wage rates beyond the wage increases expected elsewhere in an effort to obtain larger work forces. Expectations of the trend in money wage rates would hence be disappointed, and some current decisions would be regretted. The expected rate of increase of money-wage rates would be revised upward. If it is assumed that real wages tend to increase over time with the rise of productivity, it follows that, if macroequilibrium is to be realized, the real wage level must be expected to show a trend that is consistent with the improvement over time in productivity.

There is also a 'demand-side requirement'. It is that fiscal and monetary incentives induce the typical customer to buy the amount of goods at the equilibrium prices that is consistent with producers' expectations, expectations on which they have in part been basing their current pricing and wage-setting decisions. If the labor market is in equilibrium, this demand requirement is that there not be a deficiency or excess of 'aggregate demand.'[4] There is frequent reference in this volume to the 'level' of aggregate demand. This can be thought of as the highest price that customers are willing to pay for the currently producible output by current employees (considered as a function of employment) or as the amount of product that customers are willing to buy (considered as a function of the product

---

[3] Technological opportunities for substituting capital-goods production for consumer-goods production will determine a condition on the level of expected money prices on capital goods in relation to expected money-wage rates. I believe it will be safe to ignore this aspect here.

[4] Really, one should require, in view of the frictions in moving labor from one employer to another and the product specialization of firms, that customers make the demands that they have been expected to in *both* the consumption-goods industries and in the investment-goods industries.

prices set by producers).[5] Macroeconomic equilibrium, then, requires that aggregate demand be at such a level as to equilibrate the
product market.

To any macroequilibrium path there corresponds a certain time
path of the quantities of unemployed labor and idle capital. When we
say that the quantity of unemployment *and* the quantity of spare
capacity are currently 'at their macroequilibrium values,' we mean
that expectations about money wage rates and expectations about
money prices (and hence the ratio of these) are, at the moment,
logically consistent 'in the large' and hence they are sustainable, and
will be sustained, *if* and only if aggregate demand follows the
appropriate time path by luck or government intent (or both). It is
'up to aggregate demand' to determine in that situation whether
macroequilibrium will be realized. If aggregate demand behaves in
such a way that the representative customer demands from his
respective suppliers the quantity of product that he was generally
expected to, expectations of the money wage rate trend elsewhere
and of the trend of money prices elsewhere in the economy will be
broadly confirmed. Then households will not exhibit any systematic
tendency to regret their job acceptance/rejection decisions or wish
that they had found different product suppliers on whom to bestow
their patronage. Likewise, firms on the whole will not feel any
systematic regret or surprise at the results of their price and wage
setting for the attraction of new customers and employees. Plans are,
in a suitable statistical sense, working out as people hoped and
feared they would. In overall macroequilibrium, therefore, plans are
not being subject to revision in the aggregate.

2.1.1. *Further Definitions and Conventions.* As already implied, there
is the fine point to be acknowledged that the attainment of the unemployment rate path necessary for equilibrium may conflict with
the realization of the rate of idle capacity necessary for equilibrium.
Keeping separate track of two 'quantity' variables, the rate of capital
utilization and the unemployment rate, would be important for
analyzing the movement of money wage rates and money prices in
those cases where there has been a significant disturbance in either
the supply of labor or the stock of capital. Then implicit expectations of real wage rates may prevent equilibrium whatever aggregate

---

[5] There will be no ambiguity if we do not bother to specify whether the demand
quantity or demand price is 'before' or 'after' the completion of hypothetical
multiplier effects.

demand does. There could then be opposite disequilibrium motions of the average money wage and the average money price level (relative to expectations of their changes in the labor and product markets).[6] Barring upheavals from the supply side, however, a major departure of aggregate demand from the path required for macro-equilibrium will normally produce a like kind of disequilibrium in both the labor and product markets. Except where expressly indicated to the contrary, it will always be assumed in the present volume that 'running the economy' at the equilibrium unemployment rate will simultaneously yield the equilibrium rate of idle capacity and hence satisfy overall macroequilibrium. In the same spirit we shall normally use the term *expected inflation rate* to cover both the expected wage and expected price trends.

There are a couple of remaining points about the above concepts that need to be clarified. Are we to think of the unemployment rate that prevails in the macroequilibrium of a particular moment as unique – if you have macroequilibrium today, this is the exact unemployment rate that will surely go with it – or is the existence of macroequilibrium consistent with the occurrence of any unemployment rate from a certain range of values? Ultra-Keynesians believed, at least before postwar government bites out of the inflationary apple cost them their innocence, that there was a whole range of unemployment rates whose maintenance was consistent with the realization of flat trendless price and wage expectations; equilibrium might occur as easily in a state of underemployment as 'full' employment.[7] If for no other reason than the simplification of the exposition, I choose the modern assumption. I shall suppose that at any moment of time there is available just one macroequilibrium state in terms of the unemployment rate. Only one trajectory of the unemployment rate will permit equality between the actual and expected inflation rates, as suggested by the negative slope of the momentary Phillips Curve.

[6] To illustrate, a substantial lowering of the average age of worker retirement might put the labor market in an excess-demand disequilibrium, with wages rising relative to expectations and the unemployment rate low while, at the same time, for smaller levels of aggregate demand, there could be an excess-supply disequilibrium in the product market, with prices falling relative to expectations and the rate (proportion) of idle capital high.

[7] Their position is usually depicted in terms of a flat momentary Phillips Curve coinciding with the horizontal axis over an extensive range. They make no allowance, however, for underemployment equilibrium at a positive rate of anticipated inflation. In this respect their concept of macroequilibrium was not completely articulated.

But this question of range versus point reappears in a different guise in section 2.4 below.

The other question is this: Are we to conceive the unemployment rate which corresponds to macroequilibrium to be like the equilibrium corn output in a static model of competitive equilibrium? Or is it to be conceived more broadly as a transition path of the unemployment rate, if such exists, that starts from the current unemployment rate level, whatever that happens to be, and (presumably) threads its way along some hairline path to its steady-state resting value? I shall use the term 'equilibrium unemployment rate' in the first sense only, in the sense of a kind of *steady-state* equilibrium unemployment rate.[8]

When we speak of 'the' equilibrium rate of unemployment, therefore, we mean an equilibrium unemployment rate that is independent of the actual unemployment rate prevailing at the moment. But it is not intended that the numerical value of the equilibrium rate is independent of the underlying economic structure, nor that it is invariant to *all* aspects of the current state of the economy. To take an example of the influence of the economic structure, the rate of growth of the working-age population will certainly have an effect upon the size of the equilibrium unemployment rate. So too will the rate of technical progress going on in the economy. The equilibrium unemployment rate, therefore, is certainly not constant over time.

Neither is the equilibrium unemployment rate entirely independent of the state of the economy. It may be conceded, without much certainty as to the direction of the relationship, that the size of the equilibrium unemployment rate depends upon the trend which producers and households expect to be prevailing in the average of money prices and money wages being set by firms in the economy at large. We have stressed before that the implications of equilibrium and disequilibrium for the actual rate of price and wage change are *relative* to such expected trends, which is to say, relative (essentially) to the 'expected rate of inflation' over the near future. When expectations generally are for 5 percent inflation, equilibrium causes actual prices to be rising at 5 percent by definition. But it does not follow that the same value of the unemployment rate is equilibrating when

---

[8] In terms of the earlier Figure 1.2, this implies that a time path which coincides with the horizontal axis, so that actual and expected inflation rates are kept equal, at zero in the case illustrated there, will not be described as an equilibrium. Nonsteady-state equilibrium trajectories are implicit, however, in the discussion of routine stabilization policy contained in section 8.2.

expectations are for 5 per cent inflation as when they are for zero inflation. We turn to this subject now.

2.2. *The Natural-Rate Hypothesis*

We have been trying to discuss some consequences of macroeconomic *dis*equilibrium basically on the artificial assumption of 'static' expectations. An example, but only an example really, of static expectations is the case in which the rate of change of prices and wage rates that people expect to see over the future is zero and remains zero despite deviations of the current rates of price and wage change from zero. It is only a modest generalization, though an elusive one, to introduce expectations of a nonzero rate of price and wage change. Then expectations are essentially static if the expected rates of change of prices and wage rates are invariant to deviations of the actual rates of change of prices and wage rates from their expected rates of change. The notion of macroequilibrium as a state in which expectations of the frequency of orders, of the behavior of competitors' prices, of average wage rates elsewhere, and so on, are being borne out remains in force. But if expectations are that prices and wage rates will typically rise at, say 2 percent, a disequilibrium on the 'overemployment' side will then be marked by an excess of the rate of price and wage change over 2 percent, not zero. A disequilibrium state with underemployment of labor and underutilization of capital will then be marked by rates of price and wage increase that may be positive or negative, the only deduction possible being that they are less than 2 percent.

Economists are regularly charged with holding an obsolete theory of price and wage behavior whenever, following a lengthy boom, labor and product markets are no longer demonstrably tight and yet prices are still rising. People begin to fear that somewhere greed or treachery, hitherto held somehow in check, have gotten loose, and they suspect economists of having naively left these factors out of account. But this charge against the adequacy of normal economic analysis is utterly incompetent: It neglects the tendency, allowed for in the theory, for expectations of regular price and wage increases to become instilled into the calculations of firms and households in the course of a prolonged boom. Whatever the merit of modern inflation theory, its content does not identify disequilibrium necessarily with inflation or deflation – only with an excess of inflation or of deflation from the expected trends in money wages and prices.

We turn now to a controversy, that surrounding the hypothesis of the so-called 'natural' rate of unemployment. This controversy turns on two empirical questions in connection with the concept of macro-economic equilibrium. One of these questions is: What is the functional dependence, if any, of the *equilibrium* quantity of unemployment upon the expected rate of inflation (or the expected rate of change of money wage rates)?

2.2.1. *The Natural Rate of Unemployment Assumption.* Consider these provisos, the 'terrible ifs,' of neoclassical theory: Money is merely a veil, taxation is accomplishable without deadweight efficiency loss, prices are resettable continuously without administrative cost, and people are effortless and errorless calculating machines. On those provisos it would be natural to assume that there is no causal relationship going from the expected rate of inflation to the equilibrium unemployment rate. If expectations were for regular price increases at 4 percent per annum and aggregate demand happened to sustain an inflation at 4 percent per annum, why should the associated unemployment rate be any smaller or any larger than the unemployment rate that would prevail if expectations were generally for price stability over the future and aggregate demand behaved so as to produce stable average prices? This case is depicted, as in Figure 2.1a, by a family of parallel Momentary Phillips Curves which display a one-percentage point displacement from one another corresponding to each one-percentage point difference in the expected rate of inflation (this latter variable being taken, remember, as a satisfactory proxy, in steady-states at least, for expectations of both price and wage change).

The intuitive defense for this assumption, a defense which could be elaborated in terms of any one specific model of manageable proportions, is the assertion that the microeconomic decisions of firms and households depend only upon expectations and probability distributions of what are essentially relative prices, present and future, including the real rate of interest expected to be earned on current investments; these relative prices do not intrinsically involve rates of change of 'nominal' or 'money' prices, so the latter do not influence the *quantities* decided upon (given the expectations of relative prices), only the setting of the money wages and prices required to effectuate the individual price-setter's desires for certain relative prices at each moment.

The assumption that the quantities of employment and production are invariant to the rate of inflation *when that inflation is expected* and thus already properly 'discounted' can be traced to continental writers in the 1920s, and perhaps farther back on a between-the-lines reading of classical contributions.[9] In our own day this doctrine is associated with the tag, 'the natural rate of unemployment'. This is the designation that Milton Friedman has given to us for the equilibrium unemployment rate in the singular case in which the *equilibrium* unemployment rate is independent of the expected inflation rate.

This unemployment rate is 'natural' in the sense that it emerges from inescapable economic frictions and is thus not the artifact of some convention in monetary management. However, the actual unemployment rate is not implied to be bound to the natural level: Disequilibrating policies are always open to the fiscal and monetary authorities. Furthermore, the natural rate may vary over time and may be altered by governmental measures to change the structure of labor markets.

2.2.2. *Adaptation of the Expected Inflation Rate.* The other question that arises about macroeconomic equilibrium is the responsiveness of the expected inflation rate on which people base their decisions to a discrepancy between the actual and expected rates. Nothing said so far strictly implies that expected trend rates of change of money wages and prices respond at all to discoveries of error in these forecasts. One could imagine that people would never revise their expectations of the inflation rate because they feel that it is too complicated to figure out what went wrong in the model underlying their

---

[9] One reference is L. von Mises, *The Theory of Money and Credit* (New Haven: Yale University Press, 1953), an English translation of the 1924 *Theorie des Geldes*. In the United States the doctrine was most associated with the names of William Fellner, Abba Lerner, and Henry Wallich. Its current revival and formalization were begun by Milton Friedman and by the present author. These references are M. Friedman, 'Comments', in G. P. Schultz and R. Z. Aliber, eds., *Guidelines, Informed Controls and the Market Place* (Chicago: University of Chicago Press, pp. 55–61) and M. Friedman, 'The Role of Monetary Policy', *American Economic Review*, March 1968; E. S. Phelps, 'Phillips Curves, Expectations of Inflation and Optimal Unemployment over Time', *Economica*, August 1967, and E. S. Phelps, 'Money-Wage Dynamics and Labor-Market Equilibrium', *op. cit.*

For further statements of this position in terms of explicit economic models like those in the previous chapter the reader is referred to E. S. Phelps *et al.*, *Microeconomic Foundations of Employment and Inflation Theory* (New York: W. W. Norton, 1970), especially the papers by D. F. Gordon and A. Hynes, R. E. Lucas and L. A. Rapping, and D. T. Mortensen.

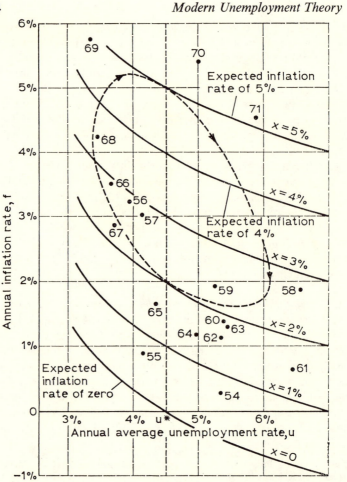

Figure 2.1a. A family of Momentary Phillips Curves on the Natural-Rate Assumption. Each one-point increase of the expected inflation rate (x) is hypothesized to displace upward by one point the Phillips Curve of the moment. The locus of equilibrium unemployment rates along which the actual and expected inflation rates are equal is therefore a vertical line whose abscissa (u^*) is the natural rate of unemployment. When aggregate demand is such as to make the unemployment rate (u) smaller or larger, respectively, than the natural rate, the actual inflation rate (f) will be greater than or less than the expected inflation rate, respectively.

If we add the Adaptive Expectations Assumption, when the unemployment rate (f) will be greater than or less than the expected inflation rate, respectively. (falling). In a regular cycle, therefore, the expected inflation rate reaches its peak and trough when it passes by the natural rate, while the actual inflation rate reaches its peak and trough earlier, as illustrated by the dashed clockwise loop. A Lipsey loop around each Phillips Curve would complicate the picture.

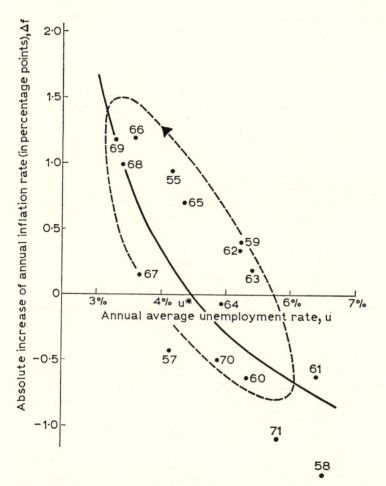

Figure 2.1b. The inflation adjustment relation under steady disequilibrium. This relation is the rigorous implication of the Linear Adaptive Expectations Assumption together with the Natural-Rate Assumption. The curve depicts the time-rate of increase of the inflation rate as a function of the unemployment rate when aggregate demand is holding the latter steady *pro tem*. Equivalently, the curve gives the (disequilibrium) steady-state level to which the unemployment rate tends if aggregate demand keeps the actual inflation rate rising at a constant pace per unit of time.

Outside the steady-states, points will be observed above or below the curve. When the unemployment rate is falling (rising), the increase of the inflation rate is greater than (less than) the amount given by the steady-state curve. The discrepancy reflects the movement along the Phillips Curve of the moment.

previous forecasts. As a purely logical matter, it is perfectly possible that the foregoing apparatus could stand while only one Momentary Phillips Curve would ever have any empirical relevance! That durable Phillips Curve would describe a 'trade-off' for monetary policy between unemployment and inflation. But it is more likely (compared to that extreme) that expectations of the trend in average money wages and prices do respond to systematic errors in their forecast.

One treatment of the adjustment speed is the linear adaptive expectations model which stipulates that a certain fraction of the discrepancy between 'actual' and 'expected' is added to what was previously expected to form the new expectation.[10] A typical value for this fraction in diverse empirical studies that use this construct is two-fifths. If people expect no inflation over the next 12 months and they get 5 percent inflation, 12 months from now people will expect 2 per cent inflation. If in the next year they get 7 percent inflation, the following year they will expect 4 percent, and so on. If the gap between expected and actual inflation is only half as large, the expected rate of inflation will be revised only half as fast. To maintain that smaller gap, the actual rate of inflation would have to be increased at the same rate, that is, at 1 percent per year.

To understand the characteristics of this model, consider the inflation adjustment curve in Figure 2.1b. The logic of this curve rests on (1) the natural-rate assumption that it is the *discrepancy* between the actual and expected inflation rate that is functionally related (in Phillips Curve fashion) to the steady-state unemployment rate, not the actual rate of inflation independently of expectations; and (2) the linear adaptive expectations assumption, just discussed, according to which the change in the expected inflation rate is proportional to that same discrepancy. This leads to the prediction that, in steady-states, there is a connection between the *time-rate of change* of the inflation rate and the level of the unemployment rate.[11] The

[10] P. H. Cagan, 'The Monetary Dynamics of Hyperinflation', in M. Friedman, ed., *Studies in the Quantity Theory of Money* (Chicago: University of Chicago Press, 1956).

[11] This is the simple system introduced in E. S. Phelps, 'Phillips Curves, Expectations of Inflation and Optimal Unemployment over Time', *Economica*, August 1967. The natural-rate Phillips family is described by (1) $f = \phi(u) + x$, where f is the inflation rate, x is the *expected* inflation rate, u the unemployment, $\phi'(u) < 0$, and $\phi(u^*) = 0$, $u^* > 0$ being the natural unemployment rate. This is conjoined to (2) $x' = \beta(f - x)$, $\beta = \text{const.} > 0$ and x' the time derivative. These imply (3) $f' = \beta\phi(u) + \phi'(u)u'$. For steady u (i.e., $u' = 0$) we have the *single* curve in Figure 2.1b.

hypothesis is that this curve is stable, though this curve too is vulnerable to the charge that it could shift with accumulating economic experience.

The curve forecasts the steady-state value to which the unemployment rate will tend corresponding to a given advance over time (increase per unit of time) of the inflation rate. Even in the absence of stochastic disturbances which might produce deviations of this advance on either side of the steady-state curve, we will tend to observe deviations around the curve on account of movements over time of aggregate demand. If the level of aggregate demand is rising sufficiently to cause the unemployment rate to be falling over time, the economy will be moving up the Momentary Phillips Curve (that pertains to the moment) so that the rate of inflation will be rising on this account alone. In addition to this rise, there is the change in the rate of inflation attributable to the discrepancy of the actual and expected rate of inflation, which is to say, the discrepancy between the unemployment rate at the moment and the natural rate of unemployment. Hence, points above the curve are predicted to correspond to time periods in which the unemployment rate is smaller than in the preceding time period. A regular boom-bust cycle is therefore predicted to trace out a scatter of points on the dashed counterclockwise loop in Figure 2.1b.

Note the corresponding implication of a *clockwise* loop in terms of the *level* of the inflation rate as illustrated in Figure 2.1a. The explanation of this clockwise loop is that the expected rate of inflation 'remembers' the inflation rate of the recent past. In the present model, the expected inflation rate reaches its peak when the unemployment rate has subsided just to the natural level and the expected inflation rate reaches its minimum at the point the natural rate is reached coming out of the slump.[12]

[12] It may occur to the reader who is versed in the early literature of the Phillips Curve to ask whether the implication of this clockwise loop in Figure 2.1a does not contradict the sometime findings by several investigators (notably Lipsey and Phillips) of a counterclockwise motion in the same plane. Indeed, some of the analyses in Chapter 1 suggested that, associated with a demand-induced increase of employment, there would be a one-time increase of money wage rates and money prices as a prelude to the continuing drift of money wages and prices in the event aggregate demand is made to behave in such a way as to maintain employment at an above-equilibrium level. It would hardly surprise us therefore to see instances of counter-clockwise loops.

A full analysis would show that this counterclockwise cycle is at war with the clockwise motion of the expected inflation rates, and that the outcome depends upon the amplitude and the period of the cycle (confining ourselves to regular

The assumption that expectations of the inflation rate are proportional to the discrepancy between actual and expected inflation is overly restrictive. A nonlinear adaptive mechanism will do as well.

2.2.3. *Rational Expectations in a Stationary Setting.*

Expectations are said to be rational if they are predictions based upon some intelligent model of the relevant economic behavior, typically the best model available (it being customary to abstract from the costs of acquiring the knowledge embodied in the model). Commonly the analyst employing the rational expectations assumption posits that the expectations are none other than the predictions of the analyst's own model. Hence he assumes that expectations are unbiased predictions.[13]

This treatment of the behavior of expectations has little appeal when the economic world, and hence the policy decisions made in that world, are nonstationary. Then you cannot say, 'this looks like 19— all over again,' for calendar time matters and it makes each year presumably different from any other. It would be uncanny for anyone to be able to make unbiased predictions of the future in such a world as there can never be enough observations for him, nor for the economic analyst, to get the hang of things. Hence if new men take over the conduct of the nation's monetary policy who have unheard-of objectives for the path of the inflation rate, one cannot plausibly assume that their moves will be correctly anticipated on the average by the population at large. In this sort of situation, where a new policy is introduced, the notion of adaptive expectations seems to be the order of the day almost by default.

In stationary economies, where the rational-expectations assumption should be seriously entertained, it may turn out that the dynamics of the underlying stochastic structure are such as to make adaptive expectations non-rational. Adaptive expectations are not rational when economic policy tends recurrently to drive the inflation rate toward some target. In such a policy regime, how does the expected

---

cycles). The 'sharper' the cycle – the smaller its period or the larger its amplitude – the more likely it is that a counterclockwise cycle will be evident. But the slow alternation of great depressions and the great booms will tend to produce a clockwise loop. The interval spanned by the data in Figure 2.1, which witnessed two considerable and rather prolonged expansions at either end of a long period of stagnation and smaller fluctuations, gives pretty good evidence of such a clockwise loop though there is, of course, an occasional short jog in a counterclockwise movement.

[13] J. F. Muth, 'Rational Expectations and the Theory of Price Movements', *Econometrica*, July 1961.

inflation rate respond differently to the ups and downs of the actual inflation rate when it is rational rather than adaptive? As long as people have the idea that the monetary and fiscal authorities are constantly shooting for some unchanging long-run inflation rate target, expectations of the inflation rate will gravitate toward the long-run target unless the actual inflation rate lies sufficiently above the previously expected inflation rate to offset the gravitational pull.[14] In the extreme case, people take each period's deviant inflation rate as completely transitory, with no tendency to persist whatsoever, so that each period's expected inflation rate is simply the expectation of the ordinary policy objective. Such a theory of expectations requires modifying the predictions in Figure 2.1 of the inflation cycle that goes with a given cycle of unemployment. The modifications may be slight to the eye but can throw off the econometrician in testing for the validity of the natural-rate hypothesis.

2.3. *Testing the Natural-Rate Hypothesis*

One can regard the natural-rate hypothesis as a striking operational implication of standard economic theory, even if the restrictiveness of the neoclassical provisos makes it clear that the hypothesis is only an approximation to more realistic formulations. For that reason alone, there is great interest in whether econometric analysis of the evidence from time series will support the hypothesis. The other reason for interest in testing the hypothesis is the relevance for the choice of inflation policy of the effect, if any, of an increase in the inflation rate upon the corresponding equilibrium unemployment rate.

If the federal government of this country were to adopt an inflation rate target of 5 percent annual rather than 2 percent, and if it were to achieve this target with the same dispersion and time profile of deviations around this target as would have been achieved around the old, would the corresponding equilibrium unemployment rate (around which the actual unemployment rate would likewise fluctuate) be no lower or higher than under the other target? Until the

---

[14] Two very recent papers that postulate rational expectations of the inflation rate are R. E. Lucas, 'Econometric Testing of the Natural Rate Hypothesis', presented at the FRB-SSRC Conference on Prices, November 1970, and T. J. Sargent, 'The $\alpha = 1$ Controversy', manuscript, February 1971. The latter paper derives the formula: $x' = \beta(f - x) - \delta(x - x^*)$, where $\delta > 0$ and x^* is the long-run policy target.

government actually carries out the experiment, we shall never know for sure. Econometricians have sought to judge the plausibility of the natural-rate hypothesis by estimating the parameters of some hypothesized model of inflation behavior and then checking to see whether those estimates come close enough to meeting the restrictions on them implied by conjoining the natural-rate hypothesis to the hypothesized model. If the estimates of the parameters do not satisfy these restrictions, the remaining question is: What went wrong, the natural-rate hypothesis or the overall model in which it was imbedded?

The most hopeful case for the empirical investigator is that in which he has data from time periods over which the monetary and fiscal authorities have varied their inflation objectives. But even in that case the investigator must carefully attend to the lag structure if he is not erroneously to reject the natural rate hypothesis when it is in fact true. For example some economists have carelessly presented the downward slope of a line fitted to the inflation-unemployment data points, such as in Figure 2.1a, as evidence against the natural-rate hypothesis. Actually this evidence is worthless because the assumption regarding the behavior of the expected inflation rate in the total econometric model is unacceptable. If one adopts the more plausible assumption of adaptive adjustment of the expected inflation rate, as discussed in section 2.2.2, the natural-rate hypothesis leads us to predict just such a tendency for the scatter of points to cluster around some downward sloping *'statistical* Phillips Curve.' This pattern is due to the implication of the simple adaptive model that the inflation rate reaches its peak over the course of a regular cycle at an unemployment rate below the natural rate; for only at such a rate can the upward push on the inflation rate coming from the disequilibrium and its upward effect on the expected inflation rate be strong enough to offset the downward pull on the inflation rate that is felt when aggregate demand is in the stage of receding from its maximum; at the point where the economy is passing by the natural rate, only the downward pull is being felt – the excess of actual over expected inflation having vanished – with the result that the inflation rate must then be falling.[15] As a consequence of this tilting of the axis between inflation-rate peak and trough, we may say that, on the whole, when the inflation rate is above average, it is higher than the expected inflation rate and when the inflation rate is below average, it is lower than the expected inflation rate. This means that the statistical relationship between unemployment rate and measured or actual inflation rate is biased away from the relevant relationship between unemployment rate and expected inflation rate – biased in the negatively sloped manner.

A more sophisticated econometric model of inflation behavior will leave room for 'errors' in the expected inflation rate. If the econometrician chooses to adopt the adaptive expectations assumption as the appropriate way to make allowance for errors, he will be led to use, in one way or another, the past values of the inflation rate in order to have a proxy for the current expected inflation rate. Then the behavior of the current inflation rate and unemployment rate will have significance only in relation to the lagged values of these variables. Unfortunately the econometrician is dogged by many estimation problems in carrying out such a test of the natural-rate hypothesis. One of these problems is that the presence of an endogenous monetary policy that aims at the gradual achievement of some inflation objective may lead to the misspecification of the lag structures: parameters are then likely to be misestimated in a way that is unfavorable to the natural-rate hypothesis.[16]

As was suggested in the previous section, the assumption of adaptive expectations makes sense when, at the initiation of policymakers or due to influences beyond their control, the underlying structure of the macroeconomic variables appears to be evolving in an as-yet-unknown way. But the adaptation of the expected inflation rate to the actual rate seems a less plausible assumption when it comes to the ups and downs that are consistent with an unchanged structure. If the econometrician uses the adaptive-expectation assumption when, over much of the sample space, expectations are rational and *not* adaptive, once again he is apt to reject erroneously the natural-rate hypotheses.

The simplest case to see is that in which there is no expected persistence in the deviation of the inflation rate around the anticipated

---

[15] This stylized history of the business cycle omits the potential influence of stickiness in the unemployment rate, so that the rate of change of unemployment figures in the dynamics of inflation, and the possibility that long-term wage contracts will defer some catch-up wage increases over to the slump side of the natural unemployment rate. The charting in terms of inflation and unemployment rate of every boom and bust will undoubtedly reveal marked differences among them, including occasional abnormalities.

[16] There is an algebraic example in my paper 'Inflation, Expectations and Economic Theory', in N. Swan and D. Wilton, eds., *Inflation and the Canadian Experience* (Kingston, Ontario: Industrial Relations Center, Queen's University, 1971).

long-term trend. Each year, whatever the recent past, the best guess of the inflation rate is the long-term average. Then we will observe years in which aggregate demand sends the inflation rate above the expected rate, with output and employment sent above their natural levels, and years of inflation rate below the expected rate and consequently output and employment below their natural levels. These observations will tend to lie on (or around) a sloping curve in the inflation-unemployment plane. They will be misinterpreted as evidence against the natural rate. It will be inferred either that the expected inflation rate does not adjust to discrepancies between actual and expected or that such adjustments as do occur do not have the effect of displacing the Momentary Phillips Curve.[17]

A more complex case of rational expectations is that in which a deviation of the actual inflation rate above the norm establishes the expectation of a continuing, but transient, deviation in the same direction. Unlike the adaptive-expectations assumption, not even a portion of such a deviation is expected to be permanent or perfectly durable; but unlike the simplest case of rational expectations just discussed, a deviation from the inflation norm is not expected to be wholly momentary or fleeting. Some persistence is expected, though of the vanishing kind. Suffice it to say here that the econometrician who, analyzing data from that world, misspecifies his model to be one with adaptive expectations will be led probably to reject the natural-rate hypothesis even when it is true; the reason is essentially the same as in the simpler case just examined.[18]

2.4. *Approximative Character of Natural-Rate Hypothesis*

The natural-rate hypothesis makes the bold assumption that the equilibrium unemployment rate is independent of the expected inflation rate: Equilibrium at a high inflation rate will occur at the same unemployment rate, and same level of employment, as would be observed in a low-inflation equilibrium. As a purely mathematical or geometrical point, it is clear that there are countless logical possi-

---

[17] The irrelevance of the adaptive-expectations econometric models for the acceptance of the natural-rate hypothesis when expectations are in fact rational is the theme of Lucas, 'Econometric Testing',

[18] Sargent, 'The $\alpha = 1$ Controversy'. In this hybrid model between ordinary adaptive expectations and the simplest rational case, the sum of the coefficients of the lagged inflation rates in the weighted sum that provides the best forecast of the next inflation rate is less than one. If the econometrician construes it to be equal to one, the influence of this variable on the equilibrium unemployment will be biased against the natural-rate hypothesis.

bilities open for the relationship between the equilibrium unemployment rate and the expected inflation rate. Figure 2.2 illustrates one of these possibilities with no particular economic motivation or justification.

If the sky is the limit on the sorts of economic theories we are willing to admit, we can all identify plenty of factors, perhaps each one quite small by itself, many of somewhat ambiguous influence, which will make us doubt the precise invariance of the equilibrium unemployment rate to the expected inflation rate. One ponders the fundamental determinants of the equilibrium quantity of unemployment (at any specified inflation rate) and then considers how these determinants themselves vary with the equilibrium inflation rate. Attention is restricted in this chapter to qualifications of the natural-rate hypothesis which are entirely in the spirit of standard contemporary monetary theory – one might say, the neoneoclassical theory that recognizes and emphasizes frictions and transactions costs (unlike neoclassical theory) and which has been slowly developing since Keynes. Thus the qualifications to which attention is confined here are those that arise upon lifting the neoclassical provisos mentioned in motivating the natural-rate hypothesis (section 2.2). Chapter 3 will bring in externalities and social factors generally as they bear on the size of the equilibrium unemployment rate at any moment and the accuracy of the natural-rate hypothesis. That later discussion raises some doubts as to whether normal economic theory, with its deemphasis of historical factors (especially recent history), is not itself in need of important revisions.

The slippage between the exact implications of contemporary monetary economics on the one hand and the natural-rate hypothesis on the other arises from the fact that, as the latter ignores, the monetary, fiscal, and calculational efficiencies of actual economies are a good deal less than '100 percent' – contrary to the neoclassical provisos. Just how much less than 100 percent depends (in not necessarily simple ways) upon the equilibrium rate of inflation.

Consider the matter of monetary efficiency.[19] Full monetary efficiency requires that the various kinds of money each bear a certain rate of interest. That some kinds of money, like currency, do not bear appropriate interest and typically bear no interest is one of the observations that has led some economists to the conclusion that a one-time step increase in the rate of inflation stimulates capital deepening – even when, and in particular when, it is matched by an equal increase in expected rate of inflation following the restoration

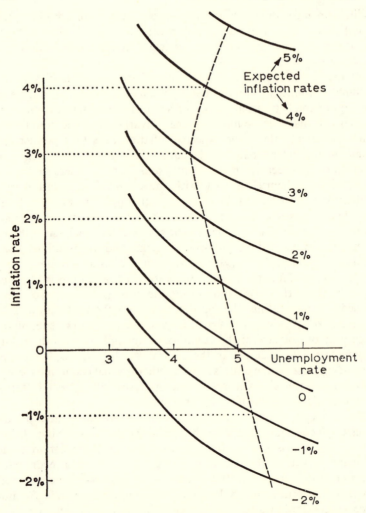

Figure 2.2. A family of momentary Phillips Curves yielding bowed equilibrium locus. At small or negative expected inflation rates, a one-point increase of the rate of expected inflation displaces upward the momentary Phillips Curve by less than one point (in terms of the actual percentage inflation rate). But there is reached an expected inflation rate beyond which each further increase by one point in the expected inflation rate produces a more than one-point upward displacement. Consequently the locus of macroequilibrium points, where (at each) the unemployment rate is such as to equate the actual to the expected inflation rate, is bowed in toward the vertical axis – instead of being the vertical line under the natural-rate hypothesis.

of macroequilibrium at the natural rate. The flight from money reduces the real value of liquidity which in turn enhances thrift (shifts downward the consumption function). Saving and thus investment are affected by the expectation of inflation via its taxlike effect upon the consumer's 'net' income. When he anticipates having to set aside a portion of his real income for the purpose of replenishing the real quantity (purchasing power) of money balances being drained by inflation, he will consume less out of a given disposable income. This effect upon thrift is one entry point, then, by which inflation, even in macroequilibrium, can penetrate (over walls of false dichotomies) into the harem of the 'real sector'.

The consequent fall of the expected real rate of interest (the prospective real yields on capital) would very likely produce an effect on the size of the equilibrium unemployment rate. There might be more investment in tangible capital, in human skill, and industrial technique. Present resources (or real income) would stand at less of a premium in relation to future resources (or future income). Hence some people would be willing to wait longer or to search longer for work at better wage rates than those known to be available at the moment. On the other hand, by employing more intensive recruitment efforts via advertising and remote-location interviewing, firms might be more active in facilitating the efforts of workers to find job vacancies and to find better wages.

Because an expected inflation lessens consumption, other things being equal, it can be used to relieve ordinary methods of taxation for the purpose of achieving a certain rate of consumption. If the government were to maintain the rate of consumption in the face of a shift to a faster-inflation equilibrium, it would then have to reduce one or more tax rates, such as the income tax rates. What if this option were selected?

The careful exchange of ordinary tax revenues for an 'inflation tax' such that consumption expenditure is left unchanged would replace to some degree the substitution effects of the former upon leisure and unemployment for the substitution effects of the inflation tax. The reduction of tax rates on wage income, by itself, would provide greater incentive to sacrifice leisure for extra paid employment to earn extra income. As for the unemployment rate, it might be reduced for the same reason: there is less of a tax saving available

[19] Chapter 6 contains a fairly comprehensive review of this subject. The present discussion intended only to be suggestive is of some of the possible effects of inflation on unemployment in macroequilibrium.

from idleness. Search unemployment is discouraged through the increase in the real interest rate after-tax.

Then there are liquidity effects. With consumption being maintained, and hence expected *real* rates of interest being maintained approximately, the higher expected inflation rate will make equilibrium money rates of interest that much higher. After a point, the higher households calculate the opportunity costs of holding money to be, the greater the amount of time they will tend to spend managing their transactions so as to economize more intensively on cash. This would have the effect of reducing the incentive to take paid employment. If unemployment tends to produce as a joint product an increase in the time available for engaging in that kind of household management, it could be that the unemployment rate would be marginally higher at a very much higher equilibrium inflation rate; with liquidity in shorter supply, the household welcomes more frequent idleness to help make it stretch. More likely, perhaps, the increase in the costs of keeping liquid will discourage a little the willingness to risk idleness and the cash drain it imposes.

If we remove the proviso that prices and wages can be continuously reset without administrative cost, when rapid wage and price increases are expected, we might see some increase of the equilibrium unemployment rate attributable to the willingness of some workers to arbitrage between low-wage and high-wage firms, the differential between which is due to their wage-setting dates in the year being out of phase.

The inability of people to make perfect and effortless logarithmic extrapolations of past observations in their heads, as would be ideal for each individual acting alone if he possessed the correct economic model of the world, would lead to a negative relationship between the equilibrium unemployment rate and the expected inflation rate – at least in the range of inflation rates such that money wage rates are rising. Then a tendency, when money wages are rising, to under-extrapolate, to underestimate the trend of money wage rates generally, through sheer algebraic error, would tend to produce a smaller equilibrium unemployment rate the larger the expected inflation rate, up to some rather large figure at which people begin to resort to calculational aids, such as an alternative unit of account.

A circumspect view of the natural-rate hypothesis – the natural-rate assumption and error-correcting or error-avoiding expectations – will consider the likelihood that small errors of forecast may be so costly for people, especially households, to ascertain that they go unnoticed. As a simple step in that direction we could suppose that a discrepancy between the actual and expected inflation rates would fail to produce a revision of the expected inflation rate if and only if it is less than some positive constant (which is, say, independent of the expected rate). Then there is a *band*, all points within which are behaviorally like a genuine macroequilibrium. It is centered around the natural rate or its equilibrium-locus generalization. It causes the inflation adjustment curve to have a flat stretch along the horizontal axis within that band. Because expectations of trend are not revised in the large, it would be hard in practice to detect a disequilibrium inside the band. Remembering that the reward to inframarginal units is sometimes entirely pure rent, we note the possibility that there are enough sharp operators in labor and product markets to prevent any long maintenance of inert or benign disequilibriums. Little reliance will be placed on the band hypothesis in this volume. But probably it deserves consideration as an important feature in the portrait of the connections between unemployment and inflation dynamics.

Despite all these disclaimers of accuracy on behalf of the natural-rate hypothesis, I suspect that if the natural rate, interpreted as a band and subject to change like everything else under the sun, is seriously misleading as a model – I am not venturing that it is – the reasons for that must be found in some quite different theories of unemployment. To such different theories we now turn. Chapter 3 opens the door to broader doubts about the natural-rate hypothesis (and occasionally a lot of other economics besides).

3 Social Factors in Unemployment Determination

THE informational theories of wage and job decisions tell us to expect unemployment as a common occurrence in an economy as developed, dynamic, and income-minded as is the American economy. This body of theory also predicts that the incidence of unemployment will fall disproportionately among groups relatively high in new entrants, hence the young, and relatively high in re-entrants, hence adult women. Moreover, these economic notions suggest that disadvantaged workers and victims of discrimination will also suffer above-average unemployment rates insofar as the inferior jobs to which they are shunted tend to offer less steady work.

While these insights offered by the informational theories are of fundamental importance, the question nevertheless arises of whether this body of theory is a tolerably accurate and complete description of unemployment determination, even for the single case of the present-day American economy. There are some points at which the economic models thus far considered misspecify prevailing social institutions and perhaps individual behavior too. The existence of minimum wage laws and trade unions, for example, runs counter to the assumption that labor markets are unregulated and atomistic. The issue then becomes whether the misspecification in question makes much difference to the behavior under study.

Some facts of unemployment in this country, when set against our analytical framework so far, rather suggest that a substantial widening of that framework is needed. Consider that the rate of black unemployment is approximately twice that of the rate of white unemployment, adults and teen-agers alike. The teen-age unemployment rate was 5 times the adult rate in 1969. The female unemployment rate might also be judged surprising, nearly twice the male unemployment rate in 1969. International comparisons raise questions too. Estimates of the equilibrium unemployment rate in America, on the average over the past two decades, are at least as high as 4.5 percent. Britain and Sweden, despite a similar industrial structure, apparently can have unemployment rates of less than 3 percent – even if rough allowance is made for national differences in unemployment definitions – without any disequilibrium aggregate-demand pressure that would escalate the inflation rate.

Some of the surprise in these figures, if there is any surprise left in them, may be due to a tendency of economists to think of the labor force as consisting wholly of clear-headed, bright-eyed, well-educated people who are versatile and adept at coping with change, uncertainty, and imperfect information. A full accounting of the various handicaps that many people have in finding and holding long-term jobs, even with the most favorable institutions and motivations – handicaps like illiteracy, ignorance, and poor health – might make these figures less surprising. The more favorable position in respect to these factors of the most developed European countries, where somehow the problem of severe poverty is not widespread, helps to explain the lower unemployment rates in those countries. Yet a wider body of theory, one appealing to the mores and mentality of the society, is necessary for a satisfying understanding of the size and composition of unemployment in this country.

The crucial limitation of the foregoing informational theories of unemployment, I would argue, is their omission of certain externalities. Notable in this respect is the neglect by the informational theories of motivation of an individual beyond the wish to maximize over the feasible set of probability distributions of his own lifetime consumption stream. That very private kind of motivation is perhaps an adequate postulate for analyzing Crusoe without Friday but it probably is not enough for analyzing much choice behavior in a social context.

A person's job, its wage and tasks and advancement opportunities, are sufficiently central to him as to be likely sometimes to involve his feelings of self-respect, group prestige, resentment, sense of fraternity, loyalty, decency, and so on. These feelings have economic-behavioral effects insofar as they inject 'externalities' into the individual's utility function. They even help to explain certain institutional discrepancies from unregulated atomistic markets. And certainly they are relevant for a rounded welfare analysis.

So while the informational theories of unemployment make a significant breakaway from classic economics, it may be that a full analysis of employment and wage behavior must also depart from the classical model on the matter of what it is that the individuals are maximizing. It should be noted that the two departures tend to go hand in hand. Where substantial economic frictions occur, such as the informational frictions in labor markers, economic transactions

become interpersonal and are hence apt to be influenced by interpersonal and group considerations. Causality tends to run in the
other direction too, so the market for spouses is imperfect.

This chapter collects a number of theories of unemployment, in
some cases little more than remarks, which have in common the
theme of externalities. Many of these theories hypothesize that an
individual's utility function contains more than own-consumption –
that it contains some external variable such as his relative wage or the
income of some group to which he is allied. These observations
increase the proportion of unemployment one would expect to be
borne by people who are poor and discriminated against. These
notions also increase somewhat the rate of overall unemployment
that one would expect the American economy to exhibit at any stable
rate of inflation. They enlarge the unemployment that is 'natural'.
Some of them put the invariance property of the equilibrium unemployment rate in doubt.

3.1. *Discrimination, Relative and Real Wages*

One of the significant theorems of classical economics is that there
can never truly be technological unemployment. There can be too
little capital to support life, too little for a living wage. But there
cannot be so much capital, or capital of such awesome productivity,
that there is no productive work for some workers to do. Every
person must have a comparative advantage over other workers and
over machines in some kind of work. Individuals who cannot be
economically employed on capital goods can produce services that
do not require plant and equipment. It cannot be, consequently, that
for some workers, there is no work in a competitive economy that
would pay positive wage rates.[1]

In explaining why the victims of social disadvantage and discrimination suffer from above-average rates of unemployment, it is
inaccurate technologically to say that there do not exist enough
productive jobs. There may, however, be a shortage of legally per-
missible jobs; the next section will discuss the minimum wage laws.
There may also be a shortage of acceptable jobs, jobs deemed worth-

[1] H. A. Simon, *The Shape of Automation* (New York: Harper & Row, 1965);
or Simon, 'The Corporation: Will It Be Managed by Machine?' in M. Anshen
and G. L. Bach, eds., *Management and Corporations, 1965* (New York: McGraw-
Hill, 1960), pp. 17–55. I do not believe that externalities and joint products, like
a smelly worker, upset the theorem although they will affect the size of wage
rates.

TABLE 3.1. *UNEMPLOYMENT RATES BY RACE, AGE, AND SEX, AS PERCENT OF CIVILIAN LABOR FORCE MEMBERS*

1957

Race	Men 16–17	18–19	20+	Women 16–17	18–19	20+
White	11.9	11.2	3.2	11.9	7.9	3.8
Nonwhite	16.3	20.0	7.6	18.3	21.3	6.4
All	12.4	12.3	3.6	12.6	9.4	4.1

1965

Race	Men 16–17	18–19	20+	Women 16–17	18–19	20+
White	14.7	11.4	2.9	15.0	13.4	4.0
Nonwhite	27.1	20.2	6.0	37.8	27.8	7.5
All	16.1	12.4	3.2	17.2	14.8	4.5

1970

Race	Men 16–17	18–19	20+	Women 16–17	18–19	20+
White	15.7	12.0	3.2	16.3	11.9	4.4
Nonwhite	27.8	23.1	5.6	36.9	32.9	6.9
All	16.9	13.4	3.5	17.4	14.4	4.8

Source: U.S. Department of Labor, *Handbook of Labor Statistics.*

while. Both are routes which, in conjunction with the facts of economic friction, lead to explanations or hypotheses about the size and character of unemployment in underprivileged minority populations. Here I shall suggest some ways in which discrimination aggravates unemployment.

It is increasingly recognized that job discrimination and simple intolerance are practiced to varying degrees against a spectrum of skin colors, a variety of ethnic groups, against certain life styles, and against women. To some extent the people burdened by discrimination are the victims of the aggregation of individual discriminations by firms and labor unions in *favor* of persons of particular social, ethnic, or religious backgrounds. In this country, discrimination is probably heaviest against the black population, and this is a macroeconomically significant proportion of the population, more than 10 percent. While the discussion here will be directed to the influence of discrimination upon Negro unemployment, 'black' could be considered a metaphor for all nonwhites (of whom 92 percent are Negro) and to some extent for victims of discrimination generally.

The disadvantages experienced by the majority of the black population in this country, owing to past and present racial bias, are roughly measured by the fact that average black male wage earnings in this country are roughly 60 percent of average white male earnings. The background of economic and social deprivation dating from slavery makes it difficult, even in the present day among the urban population, for the majority of blacks to acquire the education, skills, commercial orientation, and cultural assimilation necessary to earn something like a median wage income. The reported breakdown of the institution of the family in the most disadvantaged stratum of the black population is undoubtedly worsening the problem. In addition, there is mounting evidence that current racial prejudice continues to be an important cause of income inequality between whites and blacks of equal education. This prejudice consists of the bias among whites in favor of having whites as neighbors and fellow employees as well as statistical discrimination.[2]

A black person who is confined to inferior jobs because he is socially disadvantaged and discriminated against might well be expected frequently to 'drop out' of the labor market, to reject employment in the market sector for a while in favor of leisure activities.[3] At least this hypothesis can be maintained to apply to workers who are not assuming the responsibility of supporting a family. There are two sorts of reasons for this expectation of above-average unemployment in the black population. One of them involves a familiar point about the alternative uses of time.

It is known that low-skilled blacks and young blacks commonly accept low-wage jobs. Most of them do not lack chances for employment. But they will often quit such a job as soon as enough money has been saved to go another spell without wages; or they will quit out of the cumulative dreariness of the job. In the neighborhood of macroequilibrium at least, there is no great shortage of very low-wage jobs, so there is little risk in leaving them.[4] When there is little satisfaction in most of the available jobs, when they are no fun,

[2] See Chapter 1. The books by G. S. Becker, *The Economics of Discrimination* (New York: Columbia University Press, 1959), and by L. C. Thurow, *Poverty and Discrimination* (Washington, D.C.: The Brookings Institution, 1970), are the most recent full-length economic analyses.

[3] It should be noted that during intervals of nonemployment there are increased opportunities for engaging in domestic work, charitable work, and criminal work.

[4] A study of applicants at manpower training centers in Boston found that most of the unemployed workers had previous work experience and had left employment voluntarily. P. H. Feldman, D. M. Gordon, and M. Perch, 'Low Income Labor Markets and Urban Manpower Problems', Institute of Economic Research, Harvard University, Discussion Paper No. 66, February 1969.

dead ends, and when they pay poorly, one may decide to take one's pleasures in other ways (the 'tune in, turn on' side of dropping out).

The willingness to enjoy less wage income in return for more leisure may sometimes be expressed by favoring part-time jobs, some of which are as steady as any job but simply offer a shorter workday or shorter workweek. But often this preference will be revealed instead by more frequent exits from the full-time labor force or by a greater willingness to hold out for the exceptional temporary job. Because with each re-entry into the labor force there is typically a period of time of looking or waiting for employment, these two sorts of diminution in labor-participation rates will duly be reflected in a higher unemployment rate. Thus the dearth of *good* jobs paying *good* wages relative to the value of leisure time available to young blacks and blacks without heavy family responsibilities presumably shows up to some degree in a higher unemployment rate for these groups.

The welfare economist can properly regard the reduction of employment that is due to current racial discrimination and the resulting artificial reduction of real wage rates available to blacks as an instance of 'undersupply of labor'. This is not to say, however, that it is irrational or pathological for an individual to respond to the specified discriminatory situation by reducing the frequency of his employment. Without a future of college and career to think about, and aware of not being fully assimilated into such institutions as the school and business, some black youths have been forced to develop different patterns for obtaining the essential satisfactions and prestige that would otherwise be available in industry or in school. The fact that urban blacks can find other blacks to hang around with on the street corner, to jive with on the set, makes leisure intervals all the more attractive to them. Yet one can welcome public policies that widen the opportunity set confronting black people, so that other life styles can be chosen.

There is a second reason for expecting a higher unemployment rate among blacks than whites, though perhaps a reason less widely applicable. When a person feels unjustly disadvantaged and discriminated against, it may be that even the best of the jobs available to him are hard for him to take (or to take for very long). These empty and demeaning jobs, if not shunned altogether, are apt to be endured for only short times, depending upon the degree of economic need, because the opportunity costs of those jobs include some loss of self-esteem as well as a loss of leisure time. The victim of discrimination and oppression may insist on a reservation wage that is higher than is required merely by maximization of the mathematical expectation of the present discounted value of wage over life. This boosting of the asking wage entails a reduction in the average frequency and duration of employment.

Such a phenomenon, in principle, could be observed at high income levels as well as low. But it is presumably the low-income black or middle-income black who would be apt to have the greatest difficulty maintaining his sense of pride in the face of discrimination. A black person who has aspirations for economic success may in some instances have to economize on his self-esteem more than his white counterpart, husbanding the short ration of it by holding out, as often as he can afford, for jobs that offer uncommon satisfactions and status. There must be some normal range over which a response of this kind to discrimination can be regarded as healthy.[5]

The presence of psychological and attitudinal parameters in the determination of the unemployment rates among disadvantaged groups does not erase the influence of aggregate demand. It is quite clear in fact that the unemployment rate of nonwhite youth is just as responsive to aggregate demand as is the white teen-age unemployment rate. Furthermore, it is not evident that these factors in any way should be assumed to jeopardize the macro-accuracy of the natural-rate model.

3.2. *Minimum Wage Laws*

We noted the theorem from classic economics that there is potentially work for everyone in the sense of a positive marginal productivity for all. Yet unbridled perfect competition might assign some severely disadvantaged persons to jobs that are below the 'dignity line'. Some jobs might pay demeaning wages or entail degrading work. The physical or mental limitations of the workers who had to take them would be manifest.

The minimum wage laws tend to eliminate instances of grossly low wages. While the exact motivations of these laws need not detain us, it may be noted that they are explicable in terms of certain externalities. They reflect the understandable concern and embarrassment about low pay and, possibly, subhuman work tasks. Society bars employment paying less than a certain wage with the thought that

---

[5] For a mine of first-hand insights into the urban street corner people's attitude toward their job opportunities, see Chapter 2 of E. Liebow, *Tally's Corner* (Boston: Little, Brown, 1967).

it is beneath the dignity of human beings, or ought to be. Perhaps the basis is not so much altruistic as it is a matter of not wishing to see or read about people who are badly handicapped. The objective is probably not primarily to raise the incomes of the very poor, though some benevolent intent may be present.[6]

One effect of the minimum wage is to raise the pay of very low-wage workers who are able to stay employed. But it is a fair assumption that in many areas of the economy, perhaps most areas, the introduction of minimum wage laws has tended also to increase the equilibrium quantity of unemployment. This seems especially to be likely for those school-age people interested only in part-time work, typically poorly paid. A noticeable rise of teen-age unemployment in 1957 is sometimes attributed to a rise of the minimum wage. Some commentators have urged that the minimum wage regulations be lifted or at least eased to help teen-agers looking for temporary casual jobs.

Some full-time workers, those severely handicapped, may simply be unable to obtain employment in any job paying a wage better than or equal to the legal minimum. These workers become permanently unemployed, though one supposes it is unlikely that these workers would then be included in the unemployment statistics. Other full-time workers affected by the legislation will be driven to employment activities less well-liked than the activities that the wage legislation makes illegal. In many cases they will have to accept infrequent and temporary work (at various jobs paying the minimum wage or better). The reduced steadiness of work is one likely effect. This is one 'dimension' in which the 'utility loss' will be 'taken out'. Some workers may opt for dangerous or extremely onerous or even criminal occupations where the disutility of the work limits the supply. Those sorts of jobs also tend to be less steady. (There may grow up institutions to effect an equitable sharing of the work at

---

[6] The minimum wage laws may be intended also to counteract the exploitive power attributed to those large firms that operate in a highly isolated labor market. The one-company rural town offers a model of the static monopsonist who pays a wage less than the worth to him of having one more employee at that wage because to bid for a larger number of workers would necessitate paying high wage rates to all workers including those he has already in his employ. By interposing a minimum wage between the worth of the marginal worker, it is possible to raise the wages paid to all the employees while leaving undiminished (or even increasing) the firm's profit-maximizing employment level. Insofar as new workers are in fact brought into the firm as a consequence of the elimination of this monopsony power, it may be that the normal unemployment rate in the economy is actually reduced by the minimum wage.

legal wages.) The presumption, then, is that minimum wage laws have some tendency to reduce the frequency of (legal) employment.

It is perhaps a little naive of the economic theorist, however, to suppose that the nation's minimum wage laws have the effectiveness that the laws intend. There are known cases of evasion of these laws by employer and employee. There are also cases of circumvention of these laws by the payment of a fee to some intermediary alleged to have been helpful in finding the employment and in other ways assisting in the continued contractual arrangement. The incompleteness of their coverage also weakens their effect. Moreover, the fraction of equilibrium unemployment which should be attributed to the national minimum wage legislation is clearly hard to estimate. It is not surprising that appraisals of the quantitative importance of this legislation by economists and by other observers of the economy range extremely widely.

The influence of aggregate demand upon minimum wage induced unemployment depends upon its effect on the real value of the minimum wage rates established in the current legislation. If it is assumed that the legislation adds to unemployment, an unexpected inflation that catches legislators as well as private firms and households off balance will reduce the minimum *real* wage and thereby reduce this quantity for unemployment. One can imagine that if the legislators do not adapt their expectations of the trend rate of change of general money wage rates over time, a steady inflation will succeed in maintaining a continuing relaxation of the minimum wage rates in real terms. But if the legislators do in fact learn to adjust their expectations of the trend rate of change of the general money wage level to the actual trend, it will take an indefinitely increasing inflation rate to maintain unemployment below its 'natural' level – which now includes whatever 'unnatural' unemployment is due to the incidence of the minimum (real) wage legislation. There is some evidence that legislators are capable of anticipating normal trends when they have been normal long enough. So it seems unlikely that the behavior of the minimum wage laws is such as to make seriously misleading in a qualitative way the natural-rate hypothesis.

3.3. *Social Frictions in the Dynamics of Individual Wage and Price Adjustments*

The fashion these days is to bring hardboiled applied microeconomics (frequently of the stochastic operations-research type) to bear on a range of behavior (and social problems arising therefrom) that was once treated as mainly sociological, traditional, moral, and so on. The area of job decisions and wage behavior has been now invaded by the microeconomists, as Chapter 1 illustrates, or re-invaded, to give Pigou his due. Keynes's *General Theory* is currently being reread for neglected evidence of its cybernetic limited-information foundations,[7] as if to legitimize the new paradigm.

In the American classroom interpretation at least, Keynesian economics is normally presented as assuming that the actual economy behaves 'as if' there were pure competition, there being no con-spicuous shortage of information. We start from some macro-equilibrium and suppose that stable product prices and stable money wages have been the norm. Should there occur a sudden fall of aggregate demand, market-clearing product prices drop as necessary to clear the day's bread off the shelves. Now if workers will immedi-ately accept money wage cuts in proportion to the fall of the cost of living, it will be business as usual (merely at lower nominal wages and prices) tomorrow. But they do not accept money wage cuts, not at first, anyway. In that fatal hesitation, that first moment of resistance, real unit labor costs are up and profit-maximizing output and em-ployment are thereby decreased.

Why the reluctance to accept a money wage cut? Partly social pressure from the working community. Only a fink would want to be the first one on the block to accept the cut (especially as wage information spreads so far and fast). No one wants to 'scab' on his fellow workers, especially if it will topple money wage rates all around. Even if their wage rates are assumed independent, a worker's prestige may be thought by him to be tied to his money wage. Why is he suddenly 'worth' less than before? If production costs have to be cut, let others less deserving take wage cuts, or let the costs be absorbed by the firm. He would rather work where he is more appreciated. Conceivably the same effect could be produced by an inhibition on the supply side. It has been remarked that one of the worst things you can do to a man is to reduce his money wage (though firing him leaps to mind as a close second). The upshot of all this is that some men have to be laid off. The multiplier process begins.[8]

---

[7] See A. Leijonhufvud, *On Keynesian Economics and the Economics of Keynes* (London: Oxford University Press, 1968), especially pp. 91–102.

[8] For two papers partially representative of the oral tradition being described, see J. Tobin, 'Unemployment and Inflation: The Cruel Dilemma', in A. Phillips

The General Theory holds that when employment has settled down, there will correspond to the new employment level a certain *level* of the average money wage; it refers provocatively to underemployment equilibrium. If literally no wage earner will swallow his pride, there can indeed be little accommodation by the average money wage to the decline of demand – save for some tendency for overpaid workers to be laid off first. But there may be some tendency for a lower wage *level*, since overall household income is generally down, the worsened financial margin makes the worker less ready to run risks, and, after all, groceries are a bargain if you can earn the money wages to buy them with.[9] So pride goeth before a wage fall, but with too long a leadtime to avert the unemployment.

Keynesians have often flirted with symmetrical formulations of behavior in the product market.[10] No one wants to be known at the club as a chiseler. (And from the demand side, perhaps one can imagine a customer of such sensitivity that he would rather not buy at all than take advantage of his supplier's distress.)

Probably there would be some willingness to give ground on the point about money wages and prices finding steady levels. As the average duration of unemployment lengthens, realistic reappraisals of prestige and real income are going to be made. There is bound to result a jockeying for jobs and a downward spiral of money wage rates and prices in the process. The slowness of the process arises here, not from lags in feedback but from the time it takes to make these reappraisals, to decide what one really wants. (This point, that prices will fall, in no way implies the presence of an automatic stabilization property within some completed version of the model.)

But even if a degree of money wage flexibility is granted, the psycho-sociological approach to wage behavior certainly requires us to examine in its light the natural-rate hypothesis. Some exponents of this approach reach the conclusion that the equilibrium unemployment rate will be larger (after a point) the faster the rate of decrease

---

and O. E. Williamson, eds., *Prices: Issues in Theory, Practice and Public Policy* (Philadelphia: University of Pennsylvania Press, 1968), pp. 101–107, and the same author's earlier classic, 'Money Wage Rates and Unemployment', in S. E. Harris, ed. *The New Economics* (New York: Alfred A. Knopf, 1957).

[9] J. M. Keynes, *The General Theory of Employment, Interest, and Money* (London: Macmillan, pp. 252–253.

[10] R. H. Strotz elegantly so in his 'The Keynesian Model with a Generalized Money Illusion' in T. Bagiotti, ed., *Essays in Honor of Marco Fanno: Investigations in Economic Theory and Methodology*, Vol. 2 (Padua: CEDAM, 1966), pp. 636–652.

of money wage rates that the behavior of aggregate demand brings about. If so, then in this range, exit the natural rate!

Their argument against the natural-rate hypothesis asserts that, as in the little scenario above, the psychological resistance to the acceptance of money wage cuts creates a friction that would generate permanently higher unemployment when aggregate demand is made to take a strongly deflationary path. As long as there are a few workers who would otherwise be faced with wage offers all less desirable than their respective last-earned wages, each decrease of the steady *de*flation rate (each increase of the steady *in*flation rate) will be associated with some decrease of the corresponding *equilibrium* unemployment rate.

A defender of the natural-rate hypothesis might shrewdly concede that there may well be important social frictions adding to the equilibrium unemployment rate at *any* steady expected inflation rate. But he will argue that it is not maintaining a person's money wage up to its previous peak that matters; what matters is maintaining it relative to some norm. Being required to take a money wage cut in times of general money-wage stability is not any more face-losing or wounding than being deprived of a normal expectable pay raise of 5 percent; it need not be more discomforting than being required to go without the normal pay increase in times when all your fellow workers have been counting on normal wage increases for themselves, and up until now all have been getting theirs. The amount of emotional friction on which the equilibrium rate of unemployment partly depends, it can be argued, revolves around the painfulness of the adjustment of one's money wage *relative* to some norm; this norm may be steadily rising or steadily falling – it matters not to the pain, given the relative wage. The defense rests.

What shall be our verdict? Would the monetary engineering of a steady decline in the average money wage rates, if accompanied by expectations of the same decline of average money wage rates, necessarily exacerbate the frictions raised by omnipresent relative wage adjustments and thus lead to a higher equilibrium unemployment rate (as in a range of the curve in Fig. 2.2)? We shall not be able to decide by introspection. The necessary mental extrapolation seems too great. But we can be pretty sure that it would take a long time for expectations of money wage cuts to become entrenched. Even the establishment of a Robertsonian world of stable money wage rates – thus a world of price deflation at the rate of productivity growth, some 3 percent per annum – would take several years of heavy deflation to accomplish, and in those years the informational and societal frictions would entail a *temporary* rise of the unemployment rate to a considerable height. It will be an implication of the welfare analysis to follow that the gains (if any) realizable from such a move could not likely justify the accompanying costs. So we need not fret much over the exact sensitivity of the equilibrium unemployment rate to positive expected *de*flation rates.

3.4. *Mobility and Space*

Traditions in worker mobility and (relatedly) in job stability make a difference to quit rates and to discharge rates in an economy and hence to the average unemployment rate.

Casual reflections on American development, its early settlement, and the movements across the country, suggest that (among most groups) even today it is not remarkable in this country to pick up and move on or move back. Connected perhaps is the American's demand to do the best he can, not content (except maybe in local replicas of the old country) with staying in the neighborhood or sticking to the parental model. The relatively high incomes in America make it easier to afford that tradition of restless ambitious mobility.

A reciprocal ambition to maximize profits (at all human cost) stimulates a rate of (employer-originated) employee separations not found correspondingly abroad. The sporting traditions of mobility encourage employers to discontinue inessential employees in slack times. Middle- and low-level management have been alleged to maintain a store of 'layoff fodder' to satisfy occasional or periodic orders from the top for salary economies.[11] Compare this to Continental and Japanese overhead traditions that verge on lifetime guaranteed wages. High layoff rates operate, by feeding the flow-supply of unemployed labor to firms, to reinforce layoffs, it being generally easy as a result to hire replacements. The consequence of these high quit and discharge rates is a higher unemployment rate (proportionally high if the representative time spent in the unemployment pool is invariant, the extreme case).

No doubt the natural setting of the American economy also plays a part. The physical and the climatic diversity, which its spacious-

---

[11] A frightened report on American firing practices in what must be an unrepresentative professional field, electronics engineering, may be found in I. Catt, 'The New Reality in U.S. Management', *New Society*, November 20, 1969, pp. 814–815.

ness permits, probably increase the attractions of long-distance moves. Even if the setting were physically homogeneous, the greater space to roam in, for equal population and job densities, would alone present a greater expected reward from an unconfined search for a new job and from making a fresh start in a new place. We know about the huge migrations (and re-migrations) of labor from Italy and elsewhere in Europe into Switzerland, Germany, Sweden, and other countries. (Perfect immobility is not really practiced.) If the unemployment of resident foreigners and of nonresident nationals were fully included in an all-Europe unemployment rate, it might be that this figure would be higher than the average of the official unemployment rates reported by those countries.

3.5. *Unemployment and Trade Union Theory*

The controversy over the influences, if any, of trade unions upon the equilibrium quantity of unemployment can no longer be put off. Nearly 22 percent of persons in the total labor force in America belonged to labor unions in the 1960s. The percentage is somewhat greater if one excludes the armed forces and greater still if one excludes government workers generally. (By further excisions it is possible to get the percentage to any desired level short of 100.)

A thorough analysis must therefore reckon with this institution. During that reckoning, one can keep in mind that the trade unions are not the whole story or even the major part of the story. And in casting about for dis-similarities between organized and unorganized labor markets one should never lose sight of the similarities: labor unions make wage demands much as individuals calculate their reservation wages, both on the basis of certain preferences and perceived opportunities of the sort described in the foregoing survey.

The absence of a widely accepted etiology of trade unions has fortunately not deterred a number of investigators from empirical studies into the question of how the presence of a union affects wage behavior and unemployment in its own labor market and in the surrounding labor markets. The tendency has been to judge that trade unions increase the equilibrium volume of unemployment, pushing up wages in excess of expected gains elsewhere 'earlier' in an expansion than would be the case if the market were unorganized (where 'earlier' conceals difficulties noted below). Some have held that, at the same time, the presence of unions flattens the Momentary Phillips Curve (as it raises it), while others have seen some steepening.

These cross-section studies are bedeviled, as their practitioners would be the first to say, by the arbitrariness or tenuousness of their underlying postulates as to the characteristics of a labor market that cause it to be unionized. Their findings would be more conclusive if we could accept that, from an economic point of view, labor unions are sprinkled over the economy in a wholly random fashion or by intelligent statistical design as if in some agronomic experiment. Many of these studies also suffer from the limitations of their partial-equilibrium single-market approach. It might be true that the organization of labor into unions in those industries which are unionized has increased the average unemployment rate *in those industries* when the economy is in macroeconomic equilibrium; it might simultaneously be true that this unionization has decreased the average unemployment rate, occurring at a time of macroequilibrium in the unorganized industries.

The hypothetico-deductive method has its own difficulties even before confrontation with the data. In the perfect-information world of Walras, it is a tricky business even to postulate the existence of labor unions. Without coalitions, each individual bids with imperceptible effect against an impersonal mass of countless buyers and sellers. If in market activities individual preferences are felt and expressed only for impersonal economic goods like food and drink and leisure, i.e., no externalities, it is virtually impossible that a coalition of workers could prevent some countercoalition from outbidding it. As the number of buyers and sellers is indefinitely increased, the possible unblockable coalitions shrink to nothing. It is each man by himself (and may the poorly endowed receive large government transfers).

Yet one need not be puristic: one could stipulate fraternal feelings, threats of violence, ethnic traditions of skill, and so on in order to arrive at a logically valid, maybe worthwhile (even if not satisfactory) theory of unions of a 'noneconomic', 'purely sociological' character. Holding to that notion provisionally, we can say a few things about the consequences of trade unions for macroequilibrium unemployment in a general-equilibrium context.

In a perfect-information setting, Walrasian but for the presence of labor unions here and there in the economy, the effects of these unions is fairly clear: The after-union situation will continue to be, like the pre-union situation, one of zero unemployment in any strict sense. Certainly the unions affect relative wages, pushing some real wage rates up and some down. If substitution effects prevail over income effects, there is some presumption that the deadweight efficiency loss from the distortion of real wage rates would reduce the total labor supply; but if unions make working more congenial for those who belong to them, this is not so presumable.

Upon the introduction of economic frictions due to imperfect information and uncertainty, the macroequilibrium unemployment rate becomes a number greater than zero. How will the selective introduction of labor unions into the economy (according to the over-brief sociological suggestions above) affect the equilibrium unemployment rate in this case? Without an economic theory of what unions do and how they arise, the answer does not seem very clear. Why should the workers who are organized (or who organize themselves) into trade unions want to any degree to exercise their possibilities for economic gain in the form of more frequent unemployment, especially if a shorter work week or longer vacations were available?[12]

First, a short week or short year may increase unit costs of production for the same wage income achieved by other means. It may be attractive, from the standpoint of costs and thus the wages employers can be made to pay to a given number of employees, to take vacations 'opportunistically' – when aggregate demand is seen to be temporarily low. Further, a higher wage would be a compensation to workers for greater irregularity of employment. It may be, therefore, that the union can retain workers who, without union organization, would choose to be more steadily employed either in the same trade (at lower wages) or in other occupations. But one would expect that, for unions which are able to secure a relative wage

---

[12] It may be useful to contend with the sometime impression left by Milton Friedman (whether or not it is his exact intent) that the introduction of unions *cannot* increase the macroequilibrium unemployment rate and *can only* influence relative wage rates. For simplicity, assume the qualitative validity of the natural-rate description of macroequilibrium and disequilibrium wage behavior. Friedman appears to say that it is a schoolboy error, one confounding nominal wages with relative wage and real wages, to believe that the advent of unions to a sector will send money wage rates upward indefinitely. But whether it is or not depends entirely upon what is being held constant. If aggregate demand is being controlled in such a way as to maintain the aggregate unemployment rate constant, making the assumption that money wage rates in the unionized sector will go up only a finite amount is to assume (or preconceive) the answer to the question, namely an answer (in the negative) that the natural rate is not increased. If instead the money supply and tax rates are held constant, money wage rates will of course go up in the unionized sector by only a finite amount whether the natural rate is thereby pushed up or down. M. Friedman, 'Comment', in G. P. Shultz and R. Z. Aliber, eds., *Guidelines, Informal Controls and the Marketplace* (Chicago: University of Chicago Press, 1966).

improvement in the neighborhood of only 15 percent or less, say, the union could not survive if it could not promise a frequency of unemployment for its workers (over life anyway) no more than a point or two beyond the prospective unemployment rate (over life) outside the union. It is no wonder therefore that unions seek to make a reasonable amount of job security, via seniority arrangements and guaranteed wages, one of the economic gains they obtain alongside a higher relative wage.[13]

Economists at least will be happier when we can see our way to an economic theory of trade unions. The dim outlines of such a theory begin to appear when we look beyond Walras: The non-Walrasian economy of imperfect information and uncertainty, of searching and hoping, is a veritable spawning ground for labor union activity. The survival of a union against competing coalitions is aided by the frictions to which those imperfections give rise – and is required if we exclude threats and social pressures. Further, these frictions give the trade union a certain *raison d'être*: The labor union, from an informational point of view, may be said to exist in order to collect and diffuse information to its members.

Labor unions perform many functions of an essentially informational character, activities of no purpose in perfect markets, that may well reduce the macroequilibrium rate of unemployment in the world of frictions. A union can advance its members' safety from industrial accident nearer to their preferred level, the free market being incapable of producing the proper incentives in this respect by reason of insufficient information possessed by each individual supplier of labor. A union, by imposing uniform wage rates for like work across firms in an industry, or in wider aggregates, can reduce the wage uncertainty of its members, eliminating the likelihood of a worker's having to canvass many firms until finding a wage offer above the mean wage or above whatever his reservation wage rate would be[14] A union can serve too as an employment agency, telling members

[13] My paper 'Money Wage Dynamics and Labor Market Equilibrium', *Journal of Political Economy*, August 1968, especially the first section, expressed the belief that the presence of unions may increase a little the macroeconomic equilibrium unemployment rate (without altering the qualitative features of the friction-based model of disequilibrium wage behavior, including the natural rate). The remainder of this section shows some change of mind. The economic theory of labor unions that I have been trying subsequently to develop lends some additional support, but it adduces new considerations suggesting that unions may reduce the macroequilibrium quantity of unemployment.

[14] But it may be noted that if there are possibilities of work-sharing, hence risk-pooling, the union may dare to set a higher wage for the given members

where there are vacancies in the various job categories. In the bargain, a union provides the warning camaraderie that workers need in the often cold and cruel non-Walrasian world.

By far the most important function of the union, however, is researching (gathering and processing of information on) the wage rates, working conditions, and strength of demand in closely competing types of jobs in other industries or geographical areas, and the estimation of the demand for the services of its members in the near future in the jobs within the union jurisdiction, all in order to reach an informed decision on the money wage scales that it should demand for its members. In short, the labor union acts as an economist for its members, ascertaining opportunity costs and demand, in order to set a collective reservation wage. In its wage decision, as Keynes observed, the rational union acts very much like the rational individual: 'Every trade union will put up some resistance to a cut in money wages (since such reductions 'are seldom or never of an all-round character'). But no trade union would dream of striking on every occasion of a rise in the cost of living . . .'[15]

To the degree that the informational imperfections in the labor market are lessened by the activities of labor unions, the unions tend probably to reduce the quantity of unemployment that, in equilibrium, would otherwise be experienced by their members on account of the frictions in unorganized markets.

As intimated in Section 3.1, however, the existence of labor unions may operate to increase unemployment outside the union membership. Wherever a union is successful in establishing a wage for its members that exceeds the wage that its members or similarly skilled workers could earn elsewhere, it produces workers who are on the lookout for such union jobs as may arise when there happens somewhere to develop an unexpected excess demand for workers in those jobs. And where the unions practice discrimination against ethnic groups already disadvantaged, additional unemployment may occur among those discriminated against via the feelings of resentment and alienation thereby produced. These may be important effects of some labor unions. They operate to increase the equilibrium rate of unemployment.

Let us suppose that, to a wide extent, a union aims to establish a money wage that (waving aside its appreciation of probabilistic

---

than they would set individually. Then between-job unemployment may be increased by the union.

[15] Keynes, *General Theory*, pp. 14–15.

factors) will be low enough to employ all its members and, subject
to that constraint, as high as it can extract from employers (confining
ourselves to the many-employer case). Let us also assume a union
shop: If there are no union personnel available, a firm can hire
workers from outside the union provided the workers are willing to
join the union and pay their dues. An increase of aggregate demand
large enough to cause an unexpected increase of the demand for the
products of these firms will increase the number of workers that these
firms want to employ at the wage established by the union. Thus,
when there is an abnormal increase in aggregate demand, it becomes
easier for workers not previously belonging to the union to find
union jobs, in the process becoming members of the union. As a
result, there tends to be a reduction in the aforementioned kind of
unemployment experienced by excluded members (and, if there
should be some excess supply of union workers at the moment, owing
to a previous miscalculation, a reduction also of unemployment on
the part of union members). There are two reasons for this: Fewer
people are now among the unemployed who are waiting for or
looking for an opportunity for a union job. If the union is to maintain the employment of its enlarged membership, it cannot afford to
raise wage rates – certainly not to the extent of the one-time increase
in the average money-wage rate outside the union sector which
results from the increase of aggregate demand.[16] As a consequence,
the relative size of union wage rates is reduced, thus lessening somewhat the aforementioned unemployment attributable to the relative
size of union wages.[17]

[16] Reference is made here to the counterclockwise Lipsey loop toward the
high point on the pertinent momentary Phillips Curve, discussed in Sections 1.1
and 1.3, and pictured in Figure 1.2.
  Of course, the union will be able, within its constraint of establishing wage
rates low enough to provide jobs for its members, to keep up with the subsequent upward drift of money wage rates in the rest of the economy that will
occur if aggregate demand is managed so as to keep the nonunion sector in such
a disequilibrium.
  Note that, at union headquarters, there will be official deploring of the associated one-time rise in the cost of living relative to union wage scales. There
will be grumbling at the failure to predict the bulge in demand when the current
wage contracts were drawn up. A major boom presents difficulties for the union
management nearly as serious as a major slump.
[17] I owe this important idea to a conversation with Robert E. Hall, who has
developed this analysis himself. My discussion has not benefited from his subsequent manuscript on this subject, 'Unionism and the Inflationary Bias of
Labor Markets', January 1970.

What bearing has this phenomenon on the concepts of the family of Phillips Curves, equilibrium unemployment, and the natural rate of unemployment? The single round of unexpected inflation just analyzed is going to have effects that will survive into the future. This feature has ramifications for the Phillips Curve and for the concept of the natural rate. If the unions take as their first responsibility

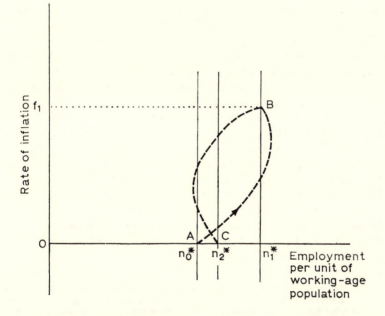

Figure 3.1. Starting from macroequilibrium at the natural employment level n^*, expressed as a ratio to the working-age population, a boom can produce hysteresis factors that might increase the natural employment level to n_1^*. In the illustration, the trajectory AB makes possible a new sustainable equilibrium state at point B. In this latter state, the steady inflation rate is f_1. If it should be desired to return the inflation rate to its original value, a contraction would accomplish that. That would produce the same reverse hysteresis factors that had operated to increase the natural employment level in the previous boom. But, it would appear, there is no likelihood that the same old natural employment level will be experienced.

Instead the downhill trajectory is likely to lead to point C, where the new natural employment level is left higher than it was originally. In this case, one cannot speak of an *ahistorical* Equilibrium Locus as was done in Chapter 2. There exists no ahistorical 'long-run Phillips Curve' vertical or sloping. The equilibrium employment level that corresponds to any steady inflation rate depends upon the recent history of the economy.

the employment of their members, new and old alike, the bulge in the union roster will for a long time reduce the relative wage that the union can establish. As a result there will be a long-lasting reduction in that component of the overall unemployment rate attributable to the disparity in available wage rates between union and nonunion work. If the inflation rate is stabilized at the higher (positive) level, the equilibrium unemployment rate that corresponds to the (equally) higher expected inflation rate will be found smaller than the old equilibrium unemployment rate that prevailed before the boom, when zero inflation was expected and the union had not yet grown. Thus we lose the natural-rate hypothesis that the equilibrium unemployment rate is invariant to the expected inflation rate; neither is it an invariant function of the expected inflation rate. The *live* hand of history produces a hysteresis effect: The time path to equilibrium partially shapes that equilibrium.[18]

The hysteresis effect upon the equilibrium rate of unemployment, and accordingly upon the family of Phillips Curve, would be really permanent if the members of the union have the custom of automatically admitting their children to memberships in the union when they become of working age. In that case, the proportion of persons in the labor force belonging to unions, hence the relative wage rates that are set by unions, and thus the part of the unemployment rate attributable to the responses on the part of nonunion members to union wages will all be permanently affected by a transitional period of unexpected inflation.[19]

[18] If the fiscal and monetary authorities should adopt policies which in time restore the expectation of zero inflation, the corresponding equilibrium unemployment rate may also be smaller than before the increase of union membership. Thus there may be some resulting looseness in the correspondence between the equilibrium unemployment rate and the expected inflation rate. But the unexpected deflation necessary to restore expectations of zero inflation, by causing some union members to be laid off, may produce a reverse hysteresis effect insofar as some of the disemployed union members despair of resuming union employment, hence cease to pay union dues, give up their union associations, and establish themselves firmly in some nonunion occupation or employment activity. See Figure 3.1.

[19] By contrast, Robert Hall has examined the case in which union membership is not transferable to one's children. Then there is a tendency for union membership to shrink and, accordingly, for the union's relative wage to rise in the process. That unemployment which is a function of the wage disparity consequently tends to grow (short of the point where the unions cease to be economically significant in the labor force). This implies that only by the repetition of episodes of unexpected inflation, can the equilibrium unemployment rate be prevented (in that case) from rising over time.

3.6. *The Role of Job Experience*

There are, however, a number of other hysteresis effects from any period of unexpected inflation. Every boom may have permanent effects upon the attitudes of the workers. A boom may draw young workers from school sooner than would otherwise occur, and that could result in an irreversible rise in the equilibrium quantity of un-employment in the future (for every expected inflation rate). After a boom, the economy is typically left richer in material capital, in government debt, in job experience, and charge accounts as well as union memberships.

Of these, job experience, with its opportunities for learning by doing and on-the-job training, is possibly the most important. When people are engaged in sustained work of a kind with which they have not had any similar experience, they become different for it in a number of ways that are relevant for the equilibrium unemployment rate. Getting to work on time is just about the most important habit a worker can have in nearly every kind of job (or so my mother has always maintained). Being in the army is said to have a permanent effect upon some habits such as early rising. For many of the people who comprise the hard-core, most frequently unemployed group, getting to be 'reliable' and learning to work with other people are necessary attributes for continuation in the job. Also, the more advantaged middle-class workers and managers need time to learn to work with or supervise the guy in the orange suit.[20] In these simple ways, it may happen that the initial increase of employment from an increase of aggregate demand beyond the equilibrium level leads finally to some shrinkage of the equilibrium unemployment rate itself – at least if the increased inflation rate is sustained, and perhaps even if the same old expected inflation rate is eventually restored.

For other people, the opportunity to acquire skills at more demanding jobs in the skill hierarchy than they could ordinarily qualify for under normal always-equilibrium aggregate demand behavior may be the more important aspect. This can occur at all job levels. The upgrading of many workers that results from a dis-equilibrating rise of aggregate demand may gradually lead to a true upgrading in the average quality of the labor force. But for the

---

[20] For a couple of newspaper accounts of employer experiences in giving jobs and training to young people from black ghettos in Detroit and New York, see *The New York Times*, Sunday, March 24, 1968, p. 1, and *The Wall Street Journal*, February 4, 1970, p. 1.

behavior of the macroequilibrium unemployment rate, what is crucial is the differential effect upon the skills of the least skilled. A magic wand that makes us all uniformly more productive – making it 1990 technologically speaking – would not promise any reduction of the equilibrium unemployment rate if the history of the past decades is any guide. Since it is the unemployment rates of the least skilled and most disadvantaged that fall by the largest number of points when the general unemployment rate falls a given amount, these people do get a chance to catch up somewhat with the already more skilled when aggregate demand drives down the overall unemployment rate.

There is a closely related point. Equipment and procedures tend to get designed for clear-eyed, steely-nerved supermen. In those cases where the workers brought into jobs for which they were not previously hired never succeed in matching the skills possessed by the previous occupants of those jobs, the sustained employment of these new workers may lead to the design and introduction of new techniques, production methods, and complementary capital equipment in order that the firm can utilize the less-skilled personnel at lower unit costs. The experience with above-equilibrium employment transforms management techniques and equipment, not only the workers.

It is clear that every departure from equilibrium produces irreversible effects of many kinds. The problem for the analyst of inflation and unemployment is the judgmental one of deciding which, if any, of these effects is of importance in the overall policy decisions. In this volume, the strategy will be to keep our analysis open to the possibility of hysteresis effects as well as to the sources (discussed in Chapter 2) of a relationship between the equilibrium unemployment rate and the expected inflation rate. These possibilities will be treated as contingencies. But we shall not build the whole analysis in such a way as to emphasize, and from the outset seem to depend upon, those possibilities, however likely they may be.

This completes our introduction to the motives and mechanisms that lie behind the existence of unemployment in the economy and behind the relationship between unemployment and unexpected inflation, on the one hand, and the level of aggregate demand on the other. The following chapters seek to use this theory, along with other economics introduced as needed, to evaluate the cost and benefits of alternative aggregate demand policies with reference to unemployment, unexpected inflation, and expected inflation.

PART II

Costs and Benefits from Unemployment and Inflation

4 Divergences between Social and Private Benefits from Employment

THE purpose of this chapter is to look at the consequences for 'allocative' efficiency of altering the employment level by monetary and fiscal means. Analysis of the distributional effects from the employment change and from the accompanying inflation (or deflation) is discussed in Chapter 5.

The discussion begins on the hypothesis of the natural unemployment rate. Later in the chapter some departures from this hypothesis are accommodated. In terms of the natural rate, we are inquiring: Is the natural employment level efficient with respect to its allocative consequences for leisure, consumption, and other benefits over time, or is some smaller or perhaps larger rate superior – given the tastes of the populace, a specification of the distribution of relative benefits between rich and poor, and holding constant also the expectations of inflation?

4.1. *The Nature of the Efficiency Question*

There has long been a debate among economists and businessmen about the advantage of high employment for economic productivity.[1] The businessman's view has been that whenever employment rises to an abnormally high level, firms experience difficulties in finding and keeping appropriate workers for skilled jobs, with the result that economic efficiency begins to suffer.

Economists, taking the opposite side, have often answered with a rhetorical question: The increase of employment raised aggregate output, did it not? It is well known that at unemployment rates of 4 per cent or more small increases of the employment rate are statistically associated with increases in output as well. It may be, of course, that output per employee or output per man-hour declines with the

---

[1] Some of the standard references are: W. H. Beveridge, *Full Employment in a Free Society* (London: George Allen & Unwin, 1944); B. G. Ohlin, *The Problem of Employment Stabilization* (New York: Columbia University Press, 1949); A. P. Lerner, *The Economics of Employment* (New York: McGraw-Hill, 1951); M. F. Millikan, ed., *Income Stabilization for a Developing Democracy* (New Haven: Yale University Press, 1953). See also the later references in this chapter.

rise of total output, especially once reserve labor is rehoarded; but, in any case, there seems definitely to be a positive association between employment and output.[2] This is hardly surprising. External dis-economies would have to be more severe than we are accustomed to believe in order that the decision of the individual firm to hire another man, while increasing his own current real revenue, would actually reduce the current national product.

Focusing on total output rather than output per man-hour is a step forward. But it does not adequately meet the question of whether the natural employment rate is efficient. It seems to impute no eco-nomic value to unemployment. Implicit in the rhetorical question is the thought that, when output is increased, the unemployment and leisure foregone was 'involuntary', that there is 'revealed' by their freely taken decision to take jobs a preference of households for more immediate income and employment at the expense of less job search and less leisure. But no such preference is unambiguously displayed insofar as the reduction of the unemployment rate is a disequilibrium phenomenon based upon a widespread mistaking of global for local, permanent for temporary, systematic for random. Such an efficiency argument for 'maximum output' is defective.

A reexamination of the welfare costs of unemployment requires us to remember that most unemployment decisions and labor force participation decisions have an investment aspect. From that point of view, the rhetorical question misleads in that it looks only at the *current* effects on output of a reduction of unemployment, not also at any output effects in the future of the current unemployment reduction. There is also the question of the degree to which the additional goods produced go to the people who most want them when they want them. At the same time, one should keep in mind that man does not live by output and leisure alone: The externalities and related societal parameters are equally important.

The three types of unemployment models expounded in Chapter 1 are intertemporal so that insofar as these purely economic models are apt descriptions, one has to evaluate a discrepancy of the unemploy-ment rate from the natural level from their intertemporal point of view. In each case unemployment is viewed as a private investment. The models of search unemployment view unemployment as a sacrifice of present wage earnings in return for the expectation of an

[2] The classic investigation of the short-term confluence is A. M. Okun, 'Potential GNP: Its Measurement and Significance', in *Proceedings of the Business and Economic Statistics Section*, American Statistical Association, 1962.

improvement of future wage earnings. Precautionary unemployment is interpreted as an investment, an act of waiting in order to be available for a better use. The speculative labor supply model views employment as an intended intertemporal trade of present leisure in response to a supposed improvement in the leisure cost of future consumption and future leisure.

Looked at in an intertemporal perspective, it is also clear that an individual's unemployment may constitute an act of *social* investment. Consider a shift of aggregate demand that permanently reduces the amount of unemployment per year. Gross national product immediately goes up, roughly by the amount of the marginal product of the affected types of labor. But what will happen to future output?

According to search models of unemployment, the resulting shortening of search unemployment reduces the average amount of wage improvement achieved by the representative worker in the time he spends in the search-unemployment pool. If the wage rate paid for each job is proportional to (at least, is an increasing function of) the marginal productivity of a man filling that job, there is corresponding reduction in the average amount of marginal productivity improvement that workers achieve by their dips into the search-unemployment pool. Output per worker (as well as per man-hour) could ultimately be reduced as a result. There should be nothing surprising in this point. If the question were whether a single man shall always be employed or always be unemployed throughout his life, certainly output at each point in time would be larger in the former case. But that question is not pertinent for workers who may legally accept current employment opportunities at any time. The proper exercise consists of comparing the average output *gain* from more frequent or more regular employment throughout life with the output *loss* that is associated with the widening dispersion in the distribution of wage rates and hence corresponding marginal productivities across workers.

Precautionary unemployment can be regarded as a social investment. They also serve who only sit and wait. By refusing to cut fees so as to acquire employment, a man who is currently accepting wait-unemployment reduces the national product in the present but achieves some increase of future national product, provided that his expected productivity in his future job is higher than in jobs obtainable at present only by cutting his fee.

In the neoclassical labor supply model, it is employment that is essentially an investment. You eat out of your existing wealth, you work for the future. The neoclassical household withholds feasible labor services on the intertemporal calculation that the real rate of interest that it expects to receive on the extra wage income earned would not buy enough future consumption goods (or hasten retirement enough) to justify the loss of present leisure.

It is therefore not immediately apparent, in terms of these models, that the natural unemployment rate exceeds the 'efficient' rate. Yet these remarks go only as far as to show that, at least for low enough rates of social discount, some unemployment is allocatively better than none. They do not show that the natural unemployment rate is allocatively the best rate, that it constitutes an allocation between employment and search or leisure that is unimprovable by some disequilibrating aggregate demand policy.

The concern of this chapter and of Chapter 5 is with the 'optimality' of the natural rate of unemployment – holding, until Chapter 6, the expectations of money wage increases and price increases in a state of suspended animation. The matter of 'optimality' may be broken down into two familiar components: 'distribution' and (given the distribution) 'efficiency'. This chapter inquires into the question of whether or not the natural rate of unemployment is 'efficient'. Chapter 5 will survey the distributional consequences of a departure from the natural rate.

What do we mean by the term *efficient*? A particular unemployment rate will be said to be inefficient if (and only if) the engineering of some different unemployment rate by monetary or fiscal means makes it possible, for a given relative share of after-tax-and-transfer economic benefits enjoyed by the poor, to improve the discounted overlife disposable incomes or economic benefits of both groups, the advantaged and disadvantaged.

Some clarifications may be useful at this point. The relative shares of after-tax-and-transfer economic benefits received by the poor and the non-poor are imagined to be held constant only for the sake of the thought experiment, the hypothetical test for the efficiency of some unemployment rate, in particular the natural rate. It is not implied that the after-tax-and-transfer distribution of economic benefits would actually remain unchanged as the unemployment rate is hypothetically altered by changes in aggregate demand. Chapter 5 will analyze the distributional effects of unemployment reductions. It will be brought out there that 'the' efficient unemployment rate is apt to depend somewhat on the size of the relative share going to the poor that we take as given. In this chapter we are taking as given the relative share that would currently prevail (at the natural unemployment rate) by reason of the currently prevailing tax and transfer system in the interests of relevance.

In performing a cost-benefit analysis of hypothetical variations in the level of employment, it is necessary, in view of the intertemporal aspects, to specify the 'social rate of discount' by which one compares future benefits to present ones. For this purpose I have in mind the use of the average real rate of interest at which, in macro-equilibrium, firms are able to borrow in order to finance investments of average risk.[3] I shall postpone a lengthier discussion of the appropriate discount rate until later in this chapter. The conclusion to be reached is that the problem is murky but probably not critical to the answer to the qualitative question addressed in this chapter.

In asking whether an unemployment rate is efficient, we are taking 'as is' the information structure in markets, indeed the whole web of socioeconomic institutions and their objectives. This does not mean, of course, that we could not contemplate testing the efficiency of the natural unemployment rate after some (actual or hypothetical) improvement of this environment.

When we take the underlying features of environment as they are, it is clear that the efficient unemployment rate (for a given distribution) is greater than zero, as already argued. It is no strike against a positive unemployment rate in the economy as it is that, in a world of perfect information and certainty, the efficient unemployment rate would be zero (for every distribution). It would be fallacious to say that imposing upon our economy the efficient allocative solution of some perfectly certain and frictionless version of that economy – or even moving in that direction – would necessarily be an improvement.

But it is equally true that there is no presumption that the natural rate of unemployment is efficient for this imperfect world – the best rate of a bad lot, as it were. Certain externalities are intrinsic to economies characterized by imperfect information and uncertainty. There is the possibility too of systematically biased forecasts of the future by households and firms. Consequently invisible hand theorems are likely to be the exception rather than the rule. And if the invisible hand were to triumph over these obstacles in a no-government

---

[3] The income tax drives a wedge between after-tax and before-tax real rates and the consequences of this for the subject at hand are dealt with in Section 4.2.1 and could be applied again to the other models discussed in subsequent sections.

economy, it would then not do so in an economy greatly permeated
by the incentive distortion of the necessarily imperfect taxes by which
the wisest of governments must largely finance its business. The question for us is really 'Is the natural unemployment rate too large or
too small for efficiency?'

Thinking about the myriad of different taxes, subsidies, and
expenditure programs that finance ministers and politicians have
ingeniously devised might lead one to ask: What gain possibly could
be accomplished by a monetary move to set the unemployment rate
(however temporarily) at a level away from the natural rate that
could not be equally well achieved through use of some of the other
policy tools at the public disposal, especially the power to tax, subsidize, and otherwise encourage various kinds of economic activities
by households and firms?

One answer is that every existing policy tool in use has deadweight
side effects, and monetary policy and budgetary policy are no excep-
tions. But each of these tools is a little different in its imprint, no tool
being a (linear-dependent) scale replica of some other tool. So the
more policy tools the merrier. The availability of monetary policy –
and fiscal (budgetary) policy too, if one is willing to take his eye off
the growth target – expands a little the 'opportunity set' of choices
open to the government. It is quite unlikely that the *optimal* use of the
nonmonetary policy tools would have the property of making the
natural rate of unemployment exactly efficient, thus removing any
efficiency case for the use of monetary policy to produce a deviation
of the unemployment rate from the natural level.[4] If, for example,
the natural rate of unemployment is inefficient, the use of monetary
policy to bring about a change of the unemployment rate in the
efficient direction, weighing in the other costs of that action and the
costs of bringing alternative policy tools to bear, may very well
increase welfare.

The efficiency question posed here has needed some elucidation

[4] There may exist some incredibly ingenious system of taxes and subsidies,
linked perhaps in some way to load factors, unemployment rates, and whatnot,
which is capable of improving the allocation of resources. But it is only in a
rather hypothetical sense that such subsidies and taxes could be calculated and
administered. After all, firms are capable, as capable as government officials, of
finding sensible sliding scales of prices and wage rates according to the availability of labor, the frequency of patrons, and so on. Don't tear down the fences
until you have found out why they were put up, goes a New England saying.
We must remember the various reasons, discussed in Chapter 1. for such seeming
rigidities of price: and wage rates. Ideal tax and subsidy arrangements would face
the same difficulties.

because it is a novel one. Investigation of the possible inefficient biases in an economy of imperfect information brings us into waters still pretty much uncharted by the economics profession. The analysis here may leave one feeling that there are some central insights still to come. Yet, on the basis of the understanding achieved so far, it is my belief that, if a decision must be made, one could only come to this provisional conclusion: Some limited reduction of the unemployment rate below the natural level would bring a net efficiency gain, while no increase of the unemployment rate above the natural rate would do so. This proposition would seem to be a better-than-even bet when looking just at the conventionally economic kinds of frictions. Enlarging one's view to include contemporary social factors in this country seems to be to reduce any residual doubt to a tolerable level.

4.2. *Inefficiencies of the Natural Rate*

In considering likely sources of inefficiency in the natural level of the unemployment rate, it will be convenient to organize the discussion by models, proceeding in the order of the various models of unemployment presented in Chapters 1 and 3.

4.2.1. *The Neoclassical Model of Speculative Labor Supply.* Even from the neoclassic standpoint, the sagacious viewer of the economy would not presume the equilibrium volume of employment in our economy to be efficient any more than he would presume the output of timber or the volume of saving to be efficient. Many of those valid arguments to the effect that there is too much timber produced or too little saving (when the government is following some specified tax policy) can be transported to the question of whether the 'competitive' supply of labor in a mixed enterprise economy is too small or too large for economic efficiency.[5]

[5] Note that in every case the question of whether the supply of labor or the supply of saving or whatever is too large or too small must be relative to the tax policy being pursued. One standard that is convenient for use as a 'reference policy' is the policy of fiscal neutrality. Very roughly this means a balanced budget (so as not to favor high total private consumption and leisure or low total consumption and leisure) plus some sort of evenhandedness in the incidence of taxes upon the individual goods in the consumption bundle.

There is a rather thorough application of this approach (for its day anyway) to the question of the adequacy of private saving in my book, *Fiscal Neutrality toward Economic Growth* (New York: McGraw-Hill, 1965). The arguments of the present sub-section 4.2.1 regarding the 'supply of effort' have counterparts in that book's analysis of the 'supply of saving'.

Here I shall offer some neoclassical reasons for thinking the natural level of employment to be too small – the natural *un*employment rate too large – though diligence could doubtless produce some countervailing factors of an equally neoclassical character.

The taxes that the government in this country uses discriminate in favor of leisure-taking and nonmarket-produced consumption and thus against the consumption of market-made goods (both in the present and in the future). This is the inevitable consequence of avoiding any element of lump-sum taxation which puts an individual behind the 8-ball even before he has earned his first dollar. If an individual is not to be taxed when he earns no income and thus enjoys only the goods of leisure and maybe some home-produced goods, and if at the same time he is to be offered through the tax system an incentive to sacrifice leisure that is equal to the incentive created by taxes to give up market-produced consumption goods, all revenue the government collects from the latter taxes would have to go for the subsidies to employment necessary to discourage the leisure. There would then be no proceeds left for the government with which it could make expenditures or loans.

The income tax, on which the federal government, and increasingly the state governments, place heavy reliance (including the corporate income tax), produces a substitution effect which encourages leisure at the expense of wage income and market-made goods. (The income effect may work the opposite way, thus concealing the incentive effect from casual empirical inquiry, but the point is that the same income effect would be produced under any efficient tax arrangement, like lump sum taxes, while a substitution effect would not be.) The extra buying power a household obtains from taking an additional job or of working more frequently is the extra wage income obtained less the additional taxes that must therefore be paid. On the assumption that the social marginal productivity of employment (i.e., of 'labor') is at least as large as the wage paid, the resulting discrepancy between after-tax and marginal product must lead to an inefficiently small equilibrium employment level.[6]

The same bias is likely to result from the taxation of interest income and of profits. If the social rate of return to investment is at

[6] Some students of the American scene report that many lower-class women in the labor force are working to satisfy an addiction to consumer goods. Perhaps, though, we should seek to change the culture rather than spiting it by engineering reduced labor-force participation. Yet, if a temporary recession below the natural employment level were certain to break the habit, not increase the craving, this factor would deserve some consideration.

least as high as before-tax rates of profit, the taxation of interest and dividend income drives a wedge between the after-tax private rates of return available to household savers and the real interest rate at which firms may borrow to make investments. The latter is our social rate of discount. The substitution effect of this fall in the after-tax rate (relative to the discount rate) is again a reduction of the level of employment; for as the speculative theory of disequilibrium labor supply behavior emphasizes, an increase of the real rate of interest that a household expects to earn (after tax) from additional saving adds to the attractiveness of working to the extent that the additional wages earned would be saved for future expenditure.

From this point of view, on these counts alone, a disequilibrating increase of aggregate demand which drives employment above its equilibrium level does a service for economic efficiency. It reduces leisure and home-produced consumption of which, from an efficiency point of view, there is too much in macroeconomic equilibrium. Of course, this is not an argument for an indefinitely large increase of employment (relative to the working-age population); at some point of 'overemployment' relative to the natural rate of employment there is reached the efficient level.

4.2.2. *Precautionary Unemployment and Overpricing.* Let us consider sellers of heterogeneous labor services who face a randomly fluctuating demand for their respective services. Typically, when the mean frequency of demand (at each fee which might be set) is guessed correctly, each supplier of the service accepts the risk of some idleness from time to time; for to increase the frequency of his being engaged, while worth the additional cost in terms of leisure, would entail a cut of his fee all the time, even for those engagements that he would have gotten anyway at a higher fee. If the supplier of labor services could enjoy the higher frequency of employment without a sacrifice of real remuneration per job performed, he would (up to a point) gladly opt for the increase in frequency of employment.

Quite often, firms are in a like situation. Each one acting alone does not find it worth it, in view of the reduction of price it must offer relative to its wage and other factor outlays, to solicit an increased frequency of orders from its existing customers or to try to bid away customers from competitors. But if the same small increase in the frequency of product demands is served up on a silver platter, without need to charge customers less or to offer factors of production more, the firm will cheerfully increase its employment to service the more frequent demands.

In this world of uncertain demands, the heterogeneity of each supplier puts him somewhat in the position of a monopolist, at least in the short run, who fears to spoil his market by price-cutting to increase the amount he sells. An increase of aggregate demand generates an increase in the amounts supplied by taking advantage of the inability of sellers (at least at first) to appreciate that a systematic shift of the distribution of demands has occurred rather than a chance sampling of deviations above an unchanged mean. Thus an increase of aggregate demand which drives unemployment below the macroequilibrium level is a way of eliciting an increase of labor and product supplies that each supplier welcomes but is unwilling to undertake unilaterally knowing that it would entail a sacrifice of the mathematical expectation of real income over life.[7]

It may be remarked, in passing, that the presence of ordinary monopoly, unilateral or bilateral, permits one to make the same line of argument. Also, the taxation of interest income in this model, like the previous one, adds to the excessive incentive to hold off one's supply because it reduces the after-tax rate of return on the investment of revenues from present sales.

The general argument for *some* occasional idleness of heterogeneous resources (or rather of policies that make occasional idleness likely) is, of course, that a seller who holds off his service from low bidders will thereby be saving it for some other future buyer for whom the service will be socially as well as privately more productive (or profitable). We have given one reason for expecting that uncoordinated private markets tend (in equilibrium) to produce an excessive amount of idle resources – vacant apartments, inventories, self-employed contractors between jobs, and so on. There is clearly another argument, though one a little less pure.

Some buyers may not know the market well, either through perfectly rational ignorance in view of the costs of acquiring information or owing to the novelty of the market for the buyer. As a result,

---

[7] This proposition lends some justification to an optimally operated system of rent control in order to nullify the monopoly power that each apartment's heterogeneity from others confers upon it. One also sees one advantage for economic efficiency of collusive agreements whereby a collection of buyers agree not to pay more than a certain price for certain services. Where such arrangements are operative, the efficiency gain from disequilibrating increase of aggregate demand is vitiated, the excessive idleness having already been largely corrected (or maybe even overcorrected) by other means.

some sellers may hold off their supplies, waiting for a chance to charge an exorbitant price to kids, tourists, and newcomers. A market sometimes contains a seller or two who are specialists in selling to ignorant or gullible buyers. An increase of aggregate demand, by stimulating an increase in the quantity of services provided, helps to reduce overcharging and undersupply.

4.2.3. *Search Unemployment.* The question of whether, from the point of view of economic efficiency, there is too much or too little search unemployment in macroequilibrium is at its most difficult when it is postulated that money-wage rates at each firm are fully responsive to changes in local flow supplies of labor – that they are in a sense market-clearing, so that no man is rationed (even momentarily) out of a job. I shall start by analyzing factors which can be fitted into market-clearing models. But the influence of job rationing is nevertheless relevant in some instances for the implications that can be drawn.

Even without job rationing it will frequently be the case that the money wage offers to some unemployed workers, at least the best of the money wage rates known to some persons who are at any moment searching for a job, are more than high enough to compensate for the disutility of the respective employments entailed, even though jobs at these wage rates are not accepted because of the expectation that further search for still better wage rates will be rewarded. If firms are wage-setters, it will also be true, even in an atomistic situation, that in macroeconomic equilibrium employers will generally be offering money wage rates that are short of the marginal productivities of workers because of their calculation that waiting or searching for additional average-wage workers is cheaper than recruiting or accepting high-wage workers. In the normal case, therefore, there is a discrepancy between the marginal disutility of working in the currently known jobs and the marginal utility of the social marginal productivity of current work.

Yet one cannot immediately deduce any conclusion for the efficiency of the natural rate of search unemployment from this single observation about a discrepancy between marginal utility and marginal disutility. The existence of search unemployment entails the aforementioned discrepancy. Certainly some investment of 'foregone wages' in the search for better wages is socially productive, for without any search-unemployment it seems likely that marginal productivities of labor in different employments would get more out of line with one another. The question is whether there tends to be overinvestment or underinvestment in search activity at the natural rate of unemployment.

4.2.3.1. *Optimism and Pessimism.* The 'high road' of analysis to that question makes the assumption that every participant, in macro-equilibrium, has realistic expectations about the probability distributions of the unknown data – in the sense that he will do as well for himself as 'some bureaucrat' or some academic scribbler could do for him. Before following just that approach, it may be worthwhile to explore contrary assumptions.

The natural rate of search unemployment may be influenced by the balance of optimists and pessimists. The natural rate of unemployment was described as the unemployment rate corresponding to an economic state in which matters are, averaging suitably over participants, working out consistently with expectations so as not to entail any systematic aggregate net revision of those average expectations. But a lot of mistaken beliefs can survive in macroequilibrium. It need not be generally the case that only correct expectations are never revised.

It could be that some or all persons are chronic pessimists about the average money wage that they could obtain elsewhere: Each man believes that the mean wage from the population as a whole is lower than it actually is. The average expected mean wage is smaller than the actual mean wage – though, in macroequilibrium, the actual trend of wage rates is equal to the expected trend in mean wage rates. Why do the pessimists not learn that things are not as bleak as they believe? As long as there is little or no word-of-mouth information passed about wage rates, the facts can remain undiscovered. Every man could go through life believing that he is being paid more than the average wage owing to his special good luck in his past search effort.[8] This is an argument to the effect that people, in particular the

---

[8] Note that each individual may very well calculate his optimal reservation or acceptance wage to be greater than his expectation of the mean wage of the distribution of wages from which he expects to sample. Even if future wage income is discounted relative to present wage income by reason of the availability of lending and borrowing opportunities at a positive market rate of interest or for some other reason involving limited access to credit, the probability that the maximum wage to be offered him will exceed the mean wage can be sufficient to justify on expected utility maximization grounds his holding out for a wage offer better than his expectation of the mean wage. This is definitely optimal in one case, that of the risk-indifferent infinitely lived individual with indefinite access to credit.

pessimists, are insufficiently choosey that the reservation wage rates they hold out for are too small in relation to the objective mean wage actually available, with the result that quitting is too infrequent and search, when it does occur, is terminated prematurely on the average from the point of view of efficiency.

Optimism is likely to be less hardy. The prolonged unemployment to which it leads will tend on the average to teach people to revise downward their rosy expectations of mean wages. But there is a fool born every minute and thus a possibility that the supply of optimism will be continuously replenished. If optimism holds sway over pessimism, unemployment is typically too prolonged, especially for inexperienced workers and perennial optimists, from an efficiency viewpoint.

Suppose that pessimism predominates. How could aggregate demand be managed so as to produce an efficiency gain via departure from the natural rate of unemployment? One's first answer is that more unemployment is wanted on this account. A disequilibrating decrease of aggregate demand will lengthen job search as it increases the unemployment rate. But this answer is no longer obvious once one brings job rationing into the picture. Then the reduction of aggregate demand can be anticipated to reduce the quit rate. Fewer people then experience unemployment, while those who do experience it do so longer on average. Man-hours of search are increased, but it is possible that the inefficiencies in the allocation of labor over jobs are thereby calcified a little more rather than dissolved. Looked at this way, perhaps an increase of aggregate demand which reduces the unemployment rate below the natural level is indicated. Older and pessimistic workers who tended in equilibrium conditions to stay put, believing that conditions elsewhere were insufficiently favorable to moving, will thereby be encouraged to search for better jobs, thus making likely an allocative improvement. At the same time there would be a gain from drawing the younger and optimistic workers earlier into jobs. Only the foreshortening of the already too-short search of the pessimistic persons among the unemployed would be an efficiency loss.

Considerations of this sort could be important. But clearly one can only conjecture about them in the present state of knowledge. Let us therefore assume henceforth that people are neither optimists nor pessimists, at least not on the whole. It is still true in that case, as mentioned in the previous footnote, that the relatively long-lived workers will tend to hold out for an above-average wage (relative to their expected mean wage) if the dispersion in the probability distribution of their wage offers is believed by them to be great enough. But these persons will tend to be balanced by people who will accept below-average wage offers. In equilibrium, consequently, it is even conceivable that every employed worker has correctly guessed the mean wage being paid for people of his skills and ability.[9]

4.2.3.2. *Information Spillovers.* There is an externality aspect to search unemployment that is displayed by an analogy between technological research and searching for a job. Economists have long been familiar with the point that when inventors lack the power of perfectly discriminating monopolists who can charge each user with the appropriate fee, there tends to be a smaller production of technical knowledge than would be produced under efficient institutional arrangements. It is imaginable that competitive markets subject to the shortage of information that we have been discussing here also produce less knowledge of job opportunities and wage opportunities than would be produced, with due recognition of the social costs of producing that knowledge, under the best feasible institutional arrangements.

The analogy to technological research is suggested by the fact that the worker cannot usually be expected to 'appropriate' entirely to himself the knowledge about wage rates and job openings that he acquires in the course of his search. The unemployed worker can be viewed as an intelligence agent who each evening returns to report to family members and the boys at the bowling alley. If we assume that wage offers are roughly proportional to marginal products, there is a tendency on this account for the representative individual to curtail his search before the socially efficient time. Part of the social reward from extra search is the value of the information to others that the individual would report back after his additional search.

Sometimes this general point is thrown into reverse. It is sometimes said that a neighborhood is served by the employed worker who is able each day to report to his friends on a variety of wage data and job openings. The unemployed worker is comparatively efficient at accumulating and spreading around the neighborhood much eco-

---

[9] The macroequilibrium quantity of search unemployment has the property that it is just large enough to reduce the variance of the subjective distribution of wage offers held by the 'representative' worker to the point where he is content to accept a wage offer at or above the mean.

nomic information of special interest to himself and to those having like technical skills; the employed worker is more likely to accumulate general information about a particular firm. Obviously it is very difficult to mediate with any empirical sureness between these two conflicting views of the informational by-products arising from the employment status of an individual.

Another likely source of the discrepancy between the efficient unemployment rate and the natural unemployment rate is the distinction between social risks and private risks. Whenever an individual decides to quit or elects not to accept his latest wage offer, he takes the chance that it will be a long time before a wage offer as high is available to him again. This means that if the individual is averse to risk, his acceptance wage will be a little lower than if the individual were willing to maximize the mathematical expectation of his discounted lifetime wage earnings. Now, for the country as a whole, the law of large numbers will pretty well insure against any appreciable risk that the entire nation will lose out from a spell of bad luck in the hunt for better allocations of labor. Thus, from the point of view of national efficiency, the unemployed are too timid.

Here, too, there is some analogy to the risk-shy firm which is unwilling to gamble on technological research of uncertain payoff.

Individuals might buy some kind of insurance that would compensate them to a degree if they should run into an unlucky run of insufficiently attractive job offers. But there would be a moral hazard here, a temptation of the insuree to search less actively (though longer) once his insurance benefits are rolling in. Search might not be encouraged much, and the resulting expense of the premiums makes it unlikely that private industry would find it profitable to provide this kind of unemployment insurance to any great degree.

We do have a system of *public* insurance for the unemployed. It offers substantial benefits for periods of unemployment and frequencies of unemployment that are within the normal range; it offers little or no insurance for workers who are running into a string of unattractive wage offers and who are, just from an efficiency point of view, deserving of insurance benefits to encourage them to carry on appropriate efforts at wage improvement. It is like hospital insurance schemes that pay minor benefits for routine operations while offering too little protection for medical catastrophes. This system probably encourages job search, but it also encourages shortening the duration of job-holding.[10]

[10] I return to the subject of unemployment insurance below.

These considerations argue that, in terms of expected lifetime income, there tends to be too infrequent quitting and premature job acceptance by those who are unemployed. Once again, an aggregate demand shift that produces less unemployment will increase the number of employed workers who quit in order to search; but it will shorten average search time even more. The lesson is, therefore, not completely clear.

4.2.3.3. *High Demand as Real Wage Insurance.* While the previous section reached no striking conclusion, for some time after drafting it I felt there was something disturbing about it. Workers are pictured as dragging down economic efficiency by their timidity or risk-aversion, unemployment insurance being inadequate to overcome it. Certainly there is some lack of perspective here. If someone asked you and others to bear risks of occasional yet serious real income cuts throughout your working life, all for the sake of a small increase of the gross national product and even a small increase in the mathematical expectation of your own lifetime income, you would probably ask to be counted out.

Changes in the technology, in tastes, and in demographic features routinely expose people to the risk of losing their jobs or of having to accept serious real wage cuts in order to remain employed – even when the economy is coasting along in statistical macroequilibrium at the natural rate of unemployment. The occasional unemployment or real wage cuts to which structural change in the economy gives rise strike capriciously, visiting private economic losses on some individuals and not on others with no particular justice. It is hardly surprising therefore that unemployment has a bad name in every country and that a rise in the unemployment rate is regarded by people as bad news and a personal ill omen.

The economist will note that insofar as individuals dislike to bear the risks of losing their jobs or of searching for better jobs, they will be averse to quitting and to long job search and in this way tend to reduce the quantity of unemployment normally observed in macroeconomic equilibrium. The natural rate of unemployment is thus smaller the less willing individuals are to go a period without holding a job (as already cited above). But in a labor market exhibiting frictions from incomplete information and the rest, each individual will sense, and suffer from, some of the costs to him of ending or averting his unemployment when the occasions to pay those costs arise. He will be aware of the necessary reduction in real wage or the step down the job ladder that he must accept on such occasions. Another tactic to reduce the uncertainty about one's real income is to favor jobs offering greater employment security. Yet, each individual has to pay something for additional job security and real income certainty, other things equal. While the frequency with which you are unemployed or suffer real income losses over life may reflect your preferences and an admirable capacity to optimize under uncertainty, this does not imply that you are pleased with the treacherous environment in which you have to optimize.

The same aversion to the risks of real wage cuts or the loss of a job – certainly most people would prefer more security to less for the same average expectation of real income over life – causes people to be willing to accept the costs of a certain amount of 'social insurance' against the temporary income loss when a job is extinguished by structural changes. Presumably the proper theory of public unemployment insurance in this country is that it is intended to provide such insurance against real income losses (rather than to provide incentives to search or to work in high job-risk lines). In return for a small portion of every individual's wage income, the government stands ready to share in the real income losses to an individual who loses or finds it best to leave his job. But social insurance is not a perfect solution to the problem of the risks of individual real income losses from structural change. It creates the 'moral hazard' that it will diminish the incentive of a person to keep a job or to find a new one as quickly as he otherwise would; this adds to the costs of the insurance. While the present levels of unemployment insurance benefits may well be less than is socially desirable, even the setting of benefits at the best level would, in view of the disincentive effects, leave each employee uncomfortably at risk if structural change should reduce his earning power at the firm in which he is presently employed.

I maintain therefore that the ways by which people, individually and through social insurance, can improve their job security or real income certainty have been perceived by them to be sufficiently costly that the problem of real income security for members in the labor force remains a serious one. The risk of having to take a cut in real wages or of having to search long for another job with the same real wage is a not uncommon source of worry among white collar and blue collar workers alike in this country. In addition, it may be that many people tend irrationally to underestimate their risks and the hardships that structural change can bring, so that wage differentials between secure and insecure jobs may be an insufficient measure of what the risks are deemed to be worth to avoid. We all know that a structural change, whether ultimately a temporary shift in fashion or some irreversible obsolescence, may leave some careers broken or risk doing so. The loss of a job may cause a man as much psychic damage as economic loss.[11] Even if an increase of unemployment somehow cost society no loss of real output, therefore, it would still be costly in terms of people's sense of well-being. Note too that this is not a distributional effect, for there is no offsetting psychic gain for those who manage to keep their jobs or who would get the real income lost by those who became unemployed if indeed national output were mysteriously invariant. Indeed, if the higher rate of unemployment increased the worry of those still employed that they would lose their jobs in time – the unemployed will compete for the jobs remaining – there might be a very general reduction in well-being.

Some increase of aggregate demand which reduced unemployment below the natural level would be beneficial in this respect. It would diminish the frequency with which people would have to accept real wage cuts or experience unemployment to find new jobs. Of course, its tightening of the labor market would not eliminate the shake-out of obsolescing firms and jobs; but it would improve the chances that people would be able to reach retirement age without need for a severe adjustment of their real incomes or the interruption of having to find another job elsewhere. This consideration is particularly important to older workers whose earlier education, despite their long job experience, may make their skills less adaptable to the requirements of other firms and more specific to the firms in which they are employed. Older workers would have a better chance in a tight labor market of finishing their careers without a break and hence without a major reduction in real income earning opportunities. If workers were infinitely lived, the effect of the tightening of the labor market could perhaps be viewed simply as a postponement of the dates at which each of the various jobs in the economy would cease to be economical for firms to fill; the same interpretation might be possible if we viewed the sons or grandsons as reincarnations of the father. But as long as time is money, this observation does not depreciate the utility of improving the duration with which today's jobs can be held with security against a major adjustment of real income.

[11] This is discussed in Section 4.3.2.

Of course, the analysis is symmetrical. If aggregate demand pushes the unemployment rate above the natural level, some jobs are extinguished earlier than otherwise and workers who remain in their jobs then have to fear a somewhat greater chance of having to move to another job before any specified date in the future.

Is this case for above natural employment neglectful of the costs? It could be that average lifetime real incomes would ultimately suffer a little with the reduction of job search and waiting. But, as suggested earlier and as argued further below, this is far from certain. Any such reduction is probably a small price to pay. In Continental Europe and Japan entire institutional practices have been altered to provide greater job security.

4.2.4. Search-Unemployment Under Job Rationing. Many of the important arguments for the excessiveness of the natural unemployment rate from the point of view of economic efficiency depend upon a characteristic of many submarkets for labor that has been admitted to the analysis only peripherally thus far, namely the feature of non-wage job rationing.

4.2.4.1. The Lemon Problem. Just as the seller of a used car dare not price it too low, however eager he is for cash, for fear that potential buyers will judge its quality by its price and conclude it is a 'lemon', the seller of complex and hard-to-evaluate skills and talents may find that his attempts to underbid workers holding jobs at wages above what he would accept and possessing abilities no greater than his own are to no avail. For many kinds of workers, therefore, finding a job is a matter of finding an opening at some rather well-agreed estimate of what is the going wage in the kind of work they seek.

A consequence of this statistical decision phenomenon is that the real wage rates paid to many workers exceed the acceptance real wage rates at which many unemployed labor force members would be willing to take those same jobs. While some or all of the unemployed workers of a given moment may voluntarily shun some inferior employments in the expectation of finding more accustomed work at better wages eventually, there is definitely an involuntary aspect to their prolonged unemployment in search of a job opening at the normal wage – even in macroequilibrium at the natural unemployment rate, and *a fortiori* at above-natural unemployment levels. In macroequilibrium, the average real wage in the market-clearing sectors of the labor market is depressed by the job-rationing practice while employment in that same sector is correspondingly increased; the reverse is true in the nonclearing sector where the job rationing is going on.

It seems fairly clear, fixing our eyes on the labor market alone, that there is an efficiency gain available to us by adjusting aggregate demand so as to reduce the unemployment rate below the natural level. Individuals temporarily in the unemployment pool and some individuals in the market-clearing sector of the labor market where real wage rates just cover acceptance wage rates for the kinds of work there will both be drawn to some extent into the sector with rationed jobs where real wage rates tend to exceed the acceptance real wage rates of many qualified workers.

Even if the quality appraisal problem were the sole kind of argument against the efficiency of the natural unemployment rate, I doubt that the ideal unemployment rate would be far enough below the natural rate to eliminate all 'involuntary' unemployment – so low that there would be not a single worker for whom there would be a gap between the average real wage paid in various jobs in which he would perform at least 'average' and his acceptance wage. An employer too may on occasion have to hold down his wage offers lest potential recruits infer that there must be something wrong with his firm. Firms also face the lemon problem from time to time. A tightening of the labor market makes it harder for such firms to attract the kinds of workers they want and, indeed, the kinds of workers who might most want employment with them insofar as there is, as there must be in a market of heterogeneous jobs and workers, imperfect information about the quantity and quality of job openings at the various firms. It is likely, therefore, that the most efficient unemployment rate is not so low as to remove all involuntary unemployment in the sense of the above 'gap' of paid wage and acceptance wage. It is conceivable that the ideal unemployment rate, from the viewpoint of efficiency, occurs where there is equality with the vacancy rate (itself a decreasing function of the former rate in steady-states).[12] This leaves some involuntary unemployment presumably, though that unemployment rate is well below the natural unemployment rate in all likelihood. But I know of no persuasive argument for that particular unemployment rate. Nor do I anticipate any in view of the difference between firms and workers with respect to information held and sought – to mention just one factor.

[12] Beveridge, *Full Employment*.

4.2.4.2. *Job Rationing and Congestion Phenomena.* I believe that another argument can be made for the proposition that job rationing itself drives a wedge between the private contribution of unemployment to future individual earnings and its social contribution to future productivity. This argument is based on a different theory of job rationing. The underlying idea is the analogy between the search for jobs, many of which are already occupied, and various operations research models of congestion and queueing processes.

Let us imagine that, without any change in the objective situation, each firm overnight becomes aware of the administrative costs of 'pricing' heterogeneous workers and, more importantly, becomes aware of the randomness in the flow supply of workers of each type that makes it uneconomic to recalculate the optimal wage in a job category in response to every arrival and every departure of a worker in that category. Accordingly, each firm switches to the establishment of normal pay scales in each job category. As a consequence, in the neighborhood of macroequilibrium, it will generally be the case that in some job categories at some firms there will be workers who find themselves 'rationed' out of a job. Additionally, some workers who were earning extraordinarily high money wage rates occasioned by a momentary shortage in their job categories will lose that windfall and elect to look elsewhere, though firms may yet manage to retain some of these workers by establishing enticing overtime rates.

Under the new wage-setting arrangement, no worker who is driven into the unemployment pool can persuade the firm to retain him, even though the new wage scale is more than sufficient to compensate him for the fruits of leisure and of search for better jobs that he must forego if he accepts employment there. But unless there existed factors the net effect of which was to make the macroequilibrium unemployment rate too small efficiency wise before the shift to the new wage-setting arrangement, this expulsion of workers into the search unemployment pool makes the new macroequilibrium unemployment (now a larger figure) definitely too large from the point of view of social efficiency. A disequilibrating increase of aggregate demand that reduces the unemployment rate below its (new) natural level operates in the direction of reducing excessively long and excessively widespread search activity created by the rationing of jobs.

A rigorous defense of this contention is considerably beyond the scope of this work. But perhaps an analogy will lend it credence. Consider the behavior of a continuous string of tourists to the site of a great falls or canyon. The population of sightseers is stationary (at least stochastically so) with the mean number of new visitors each hour a constant. There are many heterogeneous vantage points and most people would find more than one lookout worth some viewing time. But there is congestion at the site and much jockeying for positions, there being no calculated program available for threading people through in an efficient way – i.e., in a way of which it could be said that no one could have enjoyed a better assignment of views without someone else having had to suffer a worse assignment. The inefficiency is clear: When (and if) a person gets a good spot, he overstays in it, for he does not have to compensate the others whom he will keep waiting for the extra time he spends in his position. As a result, most of the visitors are driven to spending too much time searching for a satisfactory spot, or are frozen into a position early for fear of doing so. There may be a few really unlucky ones who give up before ever finding a vantage point worth staying at if congestion is sufficiently heavy.

Visiting the falls can be likened to participating in the labor market, the new arrivals being the new entrants and the current stock of visitors being the current labor force. Holding a position with a view of the falls, of course, corresponds to holding a job with pay. ('Every job with a view of the falls, folks.') Time spent in unemployment is the time spent looking for or waiting for a vacant vantage point.

To the extent the analogy is useful, it suggests that, in macro-equilibrium, employed workers are induced to hold onto their jobs too long by the risks entailed in finding better ones and the inability of the unemployed to create incentives to bear that risk. As a result, at one time or another, most labor force participants are driven to spend too much time searching for a satisfactory job at such times as they do find themselves unemployed. The search process is inefficiently strung out and quitting is inefficiently dampened. If efficient assignments could somehow be programmed, a better variety of jobs would on the whole be made available to each worker over his life and a given amount of lifetime income could be earned by an earlier age.

A tax or subsidy on unemployment, quitting, hiring, and the rest, at variable rates governed by the economic situation, is no more sensible than the gyrations of wage rates that would occur if each firm, in response to stochastic fluctuations in the flow-supplies of the various kinds of labor, were to attempt to find the minimum wage that would retain the desired number of workers in each category. But an increase of aggregate demand works in a doubly right direction: it reduces expected search time, thereby reducing unemployment, and at the same time thereby encouraging poorly allocated employees to quit in search of a better job. With reference to our analogy, it is as if the government were to install guide posts to previously unperceived viewpoints, thus reducing the congestion.

The proposition being advanced here ramifies over a wider area of economic policy. Consider the matter of inventories held by a variety of heterogeneous stores in a small geographical market. Just as the neoclassical economist is instinctively averse to the presence of positive unemployment, his first reaction is one of unease at those positive inventories. On deeper reflection he recognizes that those inventories do not lack a social purpose. But is their total amount efficient or wasteful? If the suppliers were to band together, agreeing to reduce their inventory holdings across the board by 1 percent, for example, the quantity of inventory reduced could be consumed, one would think, without impairing the flow of production and consumption in the future. But one must set against this the additional frequency with which customers would find their customary suppliers short of a product.[13] The calculation thus reduces to a comparison of, on one hand, the benefits of the diversity of sellers against the costs of carrying the additional inventory necessitated by the actual market arrangement. It seems plausible that the reduction of average inventory at each store would produce an external economy by stimulating the rate of sales and inventory rundown at other stores.[14]

[13] It is true that if one feels no nuisance cost to going to the next nearest seller there is no social cost entailed. But there must be some sort of cost; otherwise the individual sellers could not coexist, each earning a normal rate of return on an inventory that exceeds the amount that would be held under pure competition for speculative purposes.

[14] One may be reminded of the old discussion of Chamberlain equilibrium and the contention that the number of firms in the Chamberlainian industry is excessive from a social point of view. There is a *prima facie* case that each Chamberlainian firm deserves to survive because the area under its cost curve is smaller (and substantially so) than the area under its demand curve (and compensated demand curve). But that counterargument to the traditional contention is inadequate because what matters is the hypothetical compensated demand curve confronting the firm in question when all other firms are pricing at marginal social cost rather than pricing at their respective marginal revenue levels. But there are informational economies that would result if small decentralized firms were brought under more centralized management. Such economies might also result in significantly smaller unemployment in such industries.

4.2.4.3. *Queueing and Upgrading.* Another efficiency objection to the natural rate of unemployment arises from the fact of wage-setting by class of job rather than strictly according to characteristics of the worker.[15] In view of the heterogeneity of workers, both in skills and preferences and in expectations, it will frequently be the case that a worker is offered a wage in excess of his acceptance wage. The fact is that many firms define certain grades of jobs and the wage is uniform within each grade. The wage in each grade must be high enough to hold the best worker in that grade. Those workers at the firm whose skills are least in their respective grades generally receive a wage in excess of their acceptance wage. When the government increases aggregate demand, thus creating more jobs at top grades, firms may upgrade their work forces by transferring the best men in each grade to the low end of the next grade. To the extent that this is the means by which a firm increases its output and employment, i.e., by upgrading together with additional hiring at the bottom grade, it appears that the social costs of the firm's increasing its output and employment are smaller than the private costs of doing so. The social costs of this increase in output by the firm consists only of the diversion of a worker from the unemployed pool who would have otherwise found work elsewhere or the diversion of another employed worker from a firm. But in figuring the private costs of the additional output, the firm will naturally include the wage increases it must pay to those workers whom it moves up a grade. There arises thus a discrepancy between the private marginal revenue from hiring relatively unskilled workers at the end of the queue and the social revenue from the additional employment. It seems therefore that the government, in increasing aggregate demand, can effect that higher level of output and employment that would be desirable for firms to produce and that firms would choose to produce if their marginal private costs of additional output and employment were as low as the true marginal social costs of additional output.[16]

4.2.5. *Effects of Disequilibrium in Product Markets.* Some economists will concede that an increase of aggregate demand that drives

[15] I owe the point made in this section to Max D. Steuer. He mentions an unfinished manuscript on upgrading, authored by M. Godfrey and himself.

[16] It is true that the same results could be obtained in principle by a sophisticated system of taxes and subsidies which would correct in a suitable way the wage rates paid to the various workers in each grade according to their own particular abilities and skills. But the recommendation of any such scheme ignores the practical computational costs of finding the appropriate wage corrections and the administrative costs of implementing them.

unemployment below the natural rate seems worthwhile when focusing on the labor market alone. Corresponding to 'fixed-wage' job rationing in the labor market is 'fixed-price' product rationing in the product market, including notably the capital goods market. Delivery times are longer and the allocation of output to capital goods buyers and consumer durables purchasers is more arbitrary the smaller is the rate of spare capacity. These effects, it is sometimes implied, substantially vitiate or even nullify the gain in economic efficiency which would otherwise be available from a (small) push of the unemployment rate below the natural rate.[17]

Certainly product markets can be excessively tight, as can labor markets. High-income consumers, whose time is more valuable, may be particularly vulnerable to lengthening queues for goods and services. But we can rest assured that there is no set of efficiency arguments which demonstrate that there are efficiency losses from more taut product markets that precisely cancel the efficiency gains from more taut labor markets. Most of the objections raised against the efficiency of the labor market in macroequilibrium are only reinforced when applied to the product market as well. The presumption is that the natural rate of spare capacity is too high, like the natural rate of unemployment. I give two examples:

It was argued above that the taxation of interest income operates in the direction of causing an undersupply of labor. A disequilibrating increase of the level of aggregate demand stimulates additional labor force participation and thus helps to rectify the undersupply. In a similar way, it can be argued that the taxation of interest income causes an overlengthening of the operating lifetimes of capital goods possessing a variable user-cost characteristic; there is, if I am right, a tendency on this account for underutilization of some capital goods. A disequilibrating increase of aggregate demand operates to correct this by stimulating more intensive use of these capital goods.

Consider, as the second example, precautionary idleness. It was argued that the independent wage-setting contractor would welcome fewer intervals of idleness at his normal price, but not at the lower price that, if he were acting alone, would be necessary to secure more frequent work when aggregate demand places the economy in

---

[17] Much of this is oral tradition and written analytical treatments are scarce. Though their criticisms of 'high-pressure' aggregate demand policy are wider than the couple of points raised in the above paragraph, see, for example, F. W. Paish, *Studies in an Inflationary Economy* (London: Macmillan, 1962), and H. C. Wallich, *Mainsprings of the German Revival* (New Haven: Yale University Press, 1955).

macroequilibrium. This opens the door for an efficiency gain by increasing the level of aggregate demand. In the same way, there is likely to be an efficiency gain, up to a point, from the reduction of vacant apartments, reserve capacity, and inventories via a disequilibrating increase of aggregate demand.

On the other hand, it is useful to recognize that corresponding to each rate of unemployment is a certain rate of spare capacity. Hence the 'efficient' unemployment rate must be regarded as just balancing the efficiency gains and losses in both labor and product markets. It is logically possible that, if we think of the unemployment rate being reduced by successive amounts via increasing aggregate demand levels, an efficiency loss on the product side would eventually develop and become high enough to counterbalance the efficiency gain on the labor side before the latter gain had peaked out. The efficient rate of unemployment would then still be less than the natural rate – but not so much less. Whether this is in actual fact the case is quite uncertain.

The main thrust of observations about the consequences of overtight product markets may be readily agreed to: Operating rates can be too high, and employment rates also too high, for economic efficiency. Efficiency requires a positive unemployment rate and a positive rate of spare capacity in an economy beset by incomplete information and uncertainty.

4.2.6. *Aspects of Monetary-Fiscal Efficiency and Credit Allocation.* We have been discussing aggregate demand methods of engineering a departure of the employment level from the natural level. The monetary or fiscal technique (or techniques) employed will have consequences for what may be called 'monetary efficiency' and fiscal efficiency. Thus the ends (a more efficient allocation of resources) are not independent of the means. All the same, I do not regard the considerations introduced here to be of critical importance under normal circumstances for the existence of some efficiency gain from a departure from the natural rate.

Suppose that the disequilibrium rise of the employment rate above the natural level is engineered 'purely' by a reduction of tax rates to stimulate consumer-good spending and output. We are stipulating then, only for simplicity, that monetary policy is used to counteract any inducement to greater investment spending from the resulting rise of consumer-good production and profits. I shall examine only the attractive case in which it is assumed that society had originally been operating with the best fiscal-monetary mix in macroequili-brium at the natural rate. Then a small fiscal easing – if it were accompanied by sufficiently strong monetary tightening to reduce investment demand enough to accommodate the increased consump-tion demand so as to leave employment at the natural level – could not be counted as a gain in efficiency. The gain in efficiency from the reduction of deadweight substitution effects from tax rates would be just offset by the various costs imputable to the tighter monetary policy – namely, the additional liquidity costs from the higher money rates of interest (plus any algebraic gain from the change in the consumption-investment division of the national product).

If monetary policy is not tightened by so much, so that output and employment are allowed to rise above their natural levels, the gain in fiscal efficiency may then not be fully offset.[18] The usual textbook assumption is that if investment is not to be choked off to accommo-date the increased consumption demand within the confines of macroequilibrium aggregate output, interest rates need not be raised by so much. But there might be a pump-priming phenomenon at work: The higher the level of aggregate output is the higher the requirement for money interest rates for the maintenance of the same investment demand level might be. Then the conclusion could be reversed: The small gain in fiscal efficiency could be more than offset by a sizeable rise in the costs of liquidity and by congestion in credit markets.

It should be noted that insofar as the monetary tightening is un-anticipated and regarded as abnormal, it may have especially dis-ruptive effects upon the efficiency with which credit is allocated to borrowers. As the screws of job rationing and so on are loosened, the screws of credit rationing are tightened; the household suffering the lemon problem in the labor market may now suffer the lemon problem in the market for funds. Yet one should not confuse the consequences for money markets and the allocation of investment funds of a planned and orderly disequilibrium of fiscal origin with the consequences of a sudden and major fiscal expansion as in time of war.

Suppose now that the disequilibrium rise of the employment rate is engineered by monetary easing. And, again to take the pure case, suppose that tax rates are raised to maintain consumption demand

[18] Tax rates might return a part of the way back to their original levels as the government found it necessary to service a large public debt (relative to a larger taxable income) while maintaining the same enlarged deficit.

unchanged. In the textbook case, interest rates are lowered and credit rationing is eased. Tax rates are increased but, symmetrically with the previous supposition, not so much as to nullify the gain in monetary efficiency. But the pump-priming phenomenon could operate strongly enough to leave interest rates higher rather than lower (at least before capital deepening had proceeded very far).

In short, the fiscal and monetary techniques that would be necessary to stimulate employment above the natural level would themselves be a source of some efficiency gain in the textbook case and some efficiency loss in the pump-priming case. But the efficiency case that has been developed up to this point for an employment level above this natural rate is probably sufficiently strong that these money market considerations are unlikely to be decisive for the desirability of such an employment expansion – in the carefully limited sense in which we are discussing that issue in this chapter. It is true, on the other hand, that money market consideration, the costs of liquidity, and the severity of credit rationing could become important enough in a severe disequilibrium.[19] This argues that if a managed disequilibration to bring about above-natural employment were optimal in the circumstances at hand, it would strive to keep the disequilibrium to reasonable proportions with a view to all markets, not only the labor market.

4.2.7. *The Appropriate Social Rate of Discount.* One emerges from this 'narrowly economic' analysis of the possible inefficiencies of the natural rate of unemployment with the substantial presumption that it is too large for economic efficiency. It should be acknowledged that not every argument was resolved this way and not every point resolvable at all. But the balance of the arguments pro and con tend definitely in this direction.

There is a subtlety remaining however. We viewed searching and waiting as investment, and in those terms the conclusion we have reached is that unemployment is a poor investment. In investment counseling terms, this means that unemployment is an item which

[19] The acute reader may have noticed that the seriousness of any addition to the cost of liquidity depends upon the level of money interest rates with which the economy starts in macroequilibrium before the expansion of employment. Hence it depends upon the level of the expected rate of inflation that we are taking as frozen in this chapter. The latter cannot be critically high, however, in the neighborhood of the optimal long-run expected inflation rate and *a fortiori* at lower expected inflation rates. Both points are properly reflected in the locations of the respective short-run utility peaks in Figure 7.1.

recurs too frequently in the representative or composite man's port-folio so that its performance in achieving his objectives is not as good as it could be. But what if his objectives are wrong? Then his technical error may be just the second mistake needed to set right the first, thus to serve his proper objectives.

Concretely, what if people are led on the whole to overdiscount future goods? Then, in their own 'objective functions' they are placing too little emphasis upon future consumption, future security, and other future goods. I do not imply here a willingness to second-guess the way people run their own private affairs. Rather, the point goes to the issue of the appropriateness of the market rates of interest that individuals use to discount future income. Whatever the individual's *pure* 'time preference' or 'impatience' (as measured by the price he would pay in diminished future consumption for some small increase in present consumption when his consumptions would otherwise be equal in every period), if he can earn 7 percent real after-tax interest on current income that is saved, he will not find it rational to give up ·current income (e.g., in order to search for a better job, or in order to get additional schooling) for an after-tax rate of return of less than 7. Consequently some people will be taking jobs more frequently or earlier than they would do if market interest rates were lower. In macroequilibrium at the natural rate, some leisure is being sacrificed and some search is being foregone because the discount rate indivi-duals are using is so high. On this account, *taken by itself*, the natural employment level would be too high. At least it would be if search has a positive social rate of return at the natural employment level.

Some upward bias to the market real rates of interest available may be imparted by the private sector. When the government is pursuing a more or less neutral fiscal-budgetary policy, there may exist a tendency for undersaving for much the same reasons as those adduced here for expecting a tendency for excessive unemployment in macroequilibrium.[20] Yet it is true that the government could take nonneutral fiscal and monetary steps to lower interest rates (expected real rates, to be precise) and to create additional public saving. If one interprets government budgetary policy as knowing and instrumental, at least on an intuitive level, to take the position that market interest rates are too high implies a disagreement with the decision-making bodies in government over their selection of a budgetary policy and

---

[20] For a catalog of possible defects in saving decisions see Phelps, *Fiscal Neutrality*. The pertinent chapter is reprinted in A. K. Sen, ed., *Readings in Economic Growth Theory* (London: Penguin Books, 1970).

its results for market rates of interest (in macroequilibrium). One may very well do so, feeling that the citizenry and its representatives are typically too present-minded or careless of the well-being of future generations. But it is at least clear in such a case that one's criticism of the natural employment level as too high on this account – whatever one's net overall judgment – is based upon one's own far-out position on the optimal-social-discount limb.

The alternative interpretation of the hypothesis that market rates of interest confronting individuals are too high is that the executive and legislative branches of the federal government are preoccupied with more pressing and less opaque matters than the optimal level of market interest rates and the fiscal-monetary mix. In that case, the welfare economist should evaluate the efficiency of the natural employment level according to a social discount rate that need not equal any real rate of interest in the marketplace.

One view is that the appropriate discount rate to use is people's rate of marginal time preference – or even a lower figure if people do not make morally acceptable provisions for future generations. But in that approach one seems to disregard any tendency for the increased investment that results from it – say, increased job search and greater willingness to wait for relatively good job offers – to displace other investment such as private capital formation which are earning the relatively high market rate of return.

In any second-best problem of 'suboptimization' by a single branch of government (here, the Federal Reserve System is a natural example of such a branch), one has to watch for such displacement effects. If the displacement is dollar for dollar, we are back to the before-tax rate of interest as the shadow discount rate appropriate for public investment tests. There is little way of telling at this stage of economic knowledge, however, whether disinvestment in search and waiting of one dollar would tend, given the fiscal-monetary mix, to encourage a dollar of investment in capital formation.

Fortunately, the discount rate need not be supposed to be critical here. Searching and waiting may even have negative social rates of return at the natural employment level so that the choice of the social discount rate can only affect the extent to which the efficient employment level exceeds the natural level. And the sensitivity of the efficient level to the discount rate need not be large. While it has been necessary to acknowledge the shaky foundations of the discount choice – insofar as searching and waiting are productive of some future social benefits – it seems doubtful that a reconsideration of the choice of the social rate of discount would overturn the presumption reached in the previous sections that the natural employment level is excessive from the viewpoint of allocative efficiency over time.

4.3. *Efficient Unemployment in View of Societal Externalities*

The previous section may be looked at as having brought out the several externalities which are intrinsic to any economy operating under uncertainty, incomplete information, and imperfect fiscal tools and public administration. Because of the external effects upon others from individual employment and job decisions, the conditions for efficiency are not satisfied in macroeconomic equilibrium. But these rather traditional sorts of externalities are not the only ones with which we must be concerned in our inquiry into efficient unemployment.[21]

This section will discuss the bearing of other externalities, most of them already introduced in Chapter 3, upon the question of efficient unemployment. Naturally the economist feels uneasy and diffident in dealing with the more psychosociological externalities, but there is no avoiding them if we aspire to a well-rounded assessment of unemployment.

4.3.1. *Value of Financial Independence and Self-respect from Good Jobs.* Economists should remember that the labor market is different from most other markets in that it involves people in very central ways. Participation in the labor market is the principal source of livelihood for most people, it consumes vast amounts of time and energy, and it greatly influences a person's functions and effectiveness within family and community. Consequently there are a lot of psychic incomes and costs to be considered in this connection alongside cash income and real net national product. In a way these psychic aspects are externalities because they arise from the social context of working, from comparing oneself to others and possibly from concern with the judgment of others. A person's real earnings involve more than his consumption.

---

[21] I should elaborate upon my use of the term *externality*. I restrict it to interdependencies that the market fails adequately to handle without public intervention. It is true that a man's purchase of any good sends ripples throughout the economy. But this interdependence is not an external effect if he pays the marginal social cost (net of social pleasure) of his taking the good.

HUNT LIBRARY
CARNEGIE-MELLON UNIVERSITY

A decrease of the unemployment rate below the natural rate gives greater opportunities for good jobs to workers whose natural endowments and social disadvantages place them at the low end of the job hierarchy. The creation of better job opportunities is likely to produce a gain in the dignity and self-respect of those workers who catch these opportunities (as well as a gain in their real before-tax incomes).[22]

It would seem likely that this point would have special applicability to workers from the impoverished and underprivileged minorities who bear emotional problems engendered by racial discrimination in a variety of ways. Some sociologists are firmly of the opinion that the institution of the family is breaking down in the black ghettos. This phenomenon is in part attributed to scarcity of opportunity for the unskilled adult man in the ghetto to play the role of the major breadwinner in his family. The father is unable to compete effectively with the income from welfare and sometimes with the income earned by his wife.

The conclusion to be drawn is that, on this account, the efficient unemployment rate is lower than it would be calculated to be on the narrow economic considerations addressed in the previous section. This is true whatever the distribution of income that is specified in advance. This conclusion strengthens the presumption left by the earlier discussion to the effect that the natural rate of unemployment is too large for economic efficiency.[23] Conceivably, it will also prove to be too large for the survival of the lower-class urban black family unless other ameliorative steps are taken.

There is, however, the qualification of uncertain importance. In this chapter we have been engaging in thought experiments in which the unemployment rate is driven away from the natural rate and held there for an arbitrary interval of time. But it is in the nature of the natural rate that the monetary managers literally could not maintain

[22] This subject is discussed at length in Chapter 5.

[23] It might be objected that the author promised in this chapter to keep to the alpine road of Paretian efficiency, along which no one need cast a glance back at worrisome distributional effects; and now he asserts a social gain from a move that helps the poor but (at some point) hinders the rest. What I have in mind, however, is that the beneficiaries of the psychic gain from better employment opportunities would be able to compensate the losers, so that relative 'benefits' would show the same distribution and both rich and poor would be left better off. It is true that aggregate consumption in the national income accounts (from a suitable intertemporal viewpoint) would not show a gain from this last extreme push of the unemployment rate, but the point is that employment has income dimensions beyond cash earnings.

a nonnegligible discrepancy from the natural level forever without there eventually developing a rate of inflation or deflation so large as to be utterly inconsistent with the monetary system as we now know it; these monetary aspects will be considered fully in Chapter 6. Therefore, we really have in mind a finite interval of time over which the natural rate is deviated from. This is of no consequence for the answers to our efficiency inquiry if there exist no asymmetrical effects from *increases* and from *decreases* of the level of the unemployment rate in the transition phases being contemplated. But there might be just such irreversibilities: A short slump in employment opportunities might be so scarring that the eventual recovery to the natural employment level would not end the damage. One can also imagine that the eventual return to the natural rate after a boom, 'back to reality' in one economist's phrase, would be so disillusioning that the withdrawal pains of that transition would outweigh the temporary gains in the period of subnatural unemployment; but this would not be so if there were a matching exhilaration in the transition to subnormal unemployment, or if there are in fact no significant transition effects at all.

4.3.2. *Economic Status and the Pursuit of Relative Wages.* In Chapter 3 note was made of the hypothesis that there exists a competition for economic status and that, in some quarters, there is a lot of self-esteem tied to a person's relative wage rate and the other attributes of his job. When people hold out for a better job than any known one available because they want to have a better job than (or as good a job as) their neighbors, average search time is lengthened and the macroequilibrium unemployment rate is thereby increased.[24] Roughly speaking, the equilibrium unemployment rate has to be large enough that the corresponding search times people estimate to be necessary to find better jobs are so long that most people grudgingly accept the relative wage that nature and society have ordained them to receive in macroequilibrium.

This competition for relative position is not constructive in the aggregate. The average man does not improve his relative wage and his position on the job ladder if all men try equally to do so. The extended periods of job search and job waiting may bring people some gain in their overlife real earnings, though even this is not certain; but they will not bring people the improvement in relative position that was their motive, so they will not compensate people for the

[24] Hence, job search as ego trip.

present income they forego. This undue sacrifice of present earnings opens the way for a welfare gain through an expansion of demand policy that stimulates employment above the natural level. Insofar as it is just relative income that people want, such a disequilibrating demand policy would gratify people's wishes for the perception of a higher relative wage without the need for protracted job search on their part. It is true that it would only be an illusion of people as a whole to believe their *relative* incomes have improved; but it is certainly right to fool people with such a policy if, without that policy, people end up only fooling themselves.

The above argument for this welfare gain from an expansion of demand does not require that we regard the competition for status as irrational on the individual level. No doubt the symbolic significance that a high relative income has for some people is irrational to a degree. If you pointed out to them that they are primarily valued by their friends and associates for quite different qualities than their economic achievements, they might alter their behavior. From this viewpoint, the expansion of aggregate demand is a great deal cheaper than individual counseling, abstracting, as always, from its consequences for inflation expectations, a topic reserved for Chapter 6.

But it would be unrealistic to view the quest for economic status as an individual disorder of curious generality in this country. Our society does in fact award prestige according to the attributes of men's jobs. So it is hard to see how, in the American setting, a little aspiration for economic success as the system defines it, some wish to do relatively well in the game, can be regarded as abnormal. This is especially true of those groups in our society that have been deprived of equal chances to achieve. From this standpoint it remains true that the competition for relative achievement may, from the standpoint of the labor market at least, exact some social cost in foregone present income. An expansion of aggregate demand was credited with forestalling that social cost, not with catering to the achievement ethic. Nevertheless the symbolic significance of jobs should be reckoned with as well.

In a society where the ethic of economic achievement has been so dominant, the psychic costs of losing a job may exceed the economic costs. Even if a man finds a job that is better than his previous one, he may feel injured by his unemployment. The psychic damage from becoming unemployed is likely to become especially serious, one study notes, 'in a country where idleness carries a strong social and moral stigma . . . A further cost to the unemployed is feeling useless and unwanted by society . . .'[25]

There is direct and indirect evidence with which to document these psychic costs. Even during the Great Depression when unemployment was general enough, many people who lost their jobs felt ashamed, personally guilty and defeated.[26] It is said that corporation executives today sometimes keep their unemployment secret from friends or even family until they have found satisfactory reemployment. A study of New York State data 1910 to 1960 showed that the behavior of the State unemployment rate index explains most of the variations in the admissions to mental hospitals.[27] It is evident that the loss of a job often triggers mental illness in the victim or in members of his family.

It would seem fair to suggest therefore that, in this country where the 'aspiration' for an appropriate job status is almost a compulsion, a tightening of the labor market beyond the point where narrowly defined economic benefits just outweigh economic costs might bring an additional gain. Those who are saved the anguish of being unemployed might be willing to pay the others; what they cannot give up is their aspiration for economic status.

4.3.3. *Group Pride, Powerlessness, Strikes and Protest.* It is sometimes contended, in a spirit opposite to the foregoing, that maintenance of the employment rate above the natural level produces an unhealthy mood of frustration over relative shares. When people believe, for a while, that they have gotten even or gotten ahead of other groups, only to be disappointed to see that the other groups get ahead or get even again, they come to feel tricked and angered. The accompanying strikes, wildcat stoppages, or threats of same, are said to manifest that ugly mood. It is held by some observers that these occurrences 'tear at the social fabric' and ought not to be encouraged by 'permissive' monetary and fiscal policies. How shall we assess this contrary view?

[25] T. Scitovsky and A. Scitovsky, 'Inflation versus Unemployment: An Examination of their Effects', in Commission on Money and Credit, *Inflation, Growth and Employment* (Englewood Cliffs, N. J.: Prentice-Hall, 1964).

[26] S. Terkel, *Hard Times: An Oral History of the Great Depression* (New York: Pantheon Books, 1970).

[27] The explanatory power of the unemployment rate was greatest for middle-aged men, especially German-Americans. It was least for blacks until after the war. See M. H. Brenner, 'Mental Illness and Unemployment', *Social Psychiatry*, November 1968.

I doubt that, historically, times of abnormally high aggregate demand and employment have been, on the whole, marked by angry frustration and serious social disruption. It is much more common to associate booms with a mood of ebullience and relatively good cheer.[28] If some of the great inflations have been marked by social unrest it may be because they have been occasioned by a war and their potential benefits partially diverted to supporting that war. High-income and middle-income people in particular may have felt no net benefit.

Disequilibrium on *either* side of the natural unemployment rate carries with it a heightened level of disappointment and surprise as compared to macroequilibrium at the natural rate. But there are distinctions to be made. In macroequilibrium, many unemployed workers will find that job vacancies are scarce – some with surprise, some not. The severity of the nonwage job rationing then would seem to be more 'frustrating' than the disappointments of the boom. In a boom, jobs are secure and easy to find though, to one's regret, the extraordinary part of the wage gains one is getting are being matched elsewhere and are being roughly offset by extraordinary and unexpected cost-of-living increases. The evidence of the previous section is pretty clear on this.

It is nevertheless a somewhat cautiously accepted hypothesis among labor economists that the smaller the rate of unemployment is the more numerous the strikes are, judging from observations of the business cycle.[29] It makes sense to believe that when unemployment is abnormally small, there will tend to be a wide dispersion in expectations of what is an 'optimal' wage in any trade or industry, and hence an increased likelihood that negotiations will fail to reach an early agreement. A strike may be necessary to make the rank and file, the union leadership, or the management (or even the stockholders)

[28] I took the opportunity in a survey paper to question the Lucas-Rapping interpretation of 'high employment' as attributable to the substitution effect of a *rise* of the expected real interest rate, pointing out that logically the same result could have been obtained from the income effect of a *fall* of the expected real interest rate. In a subsequent letter, Lucas noted that if the mechanism were the latter rather than the former, the psychology of the boom would be one of depression rather than euphoria. It may be, however, that the sluggishness of employment clouds the picture. Hence the *onset* of the *downturn* may trigger gloom, impatience, and feelings of protest. For another economist's analysis of much the same problem, see A. D. Scott, 'Investing and Protesting', *Journal of Political Economy*, November 1969.

[29] See O. Ashenfelter and G. Johnson, 'Bargaining Theory, Trade Unions, and Industrial Strike Activity', *American Economic Review*, March 1969.

see the 'facts of life'. Strike activity in this country was at its peak in 1919 and 1946, years of very high unexpected inflation and major allocative transitions. Yet, from this primitive theoretical point of view, it is rather puzzling to hear it said that strikes are not equally frequent when unemployment is high, for then employers are apt to overestimate the strength of their hand (and unions the weakness of theirs). It could be that the empirical relationship between unemployment and 'strike activity' needs further examination. One British labor study, in fact, states that in times of slack labor markets, strikes tend to be longer and more damaging.[30] Perhaps one's reading of the 'facts' depends somewhat upon the measure of strike activity that is used.

If it is in fact the case that strikes are more *frequent* when aggregate demand keeps the rate of unemployment low, what then for our analysis of the efficient unemployment?

So far as *ex post* effects upon gross national product are concerned, these are pretty well agreed by economists to be minor at most. The man-hours 'lost' from strikes are always small compared to the man-hours 'lost' from unemployment. The increase of the former tends never to be anywhere nearly as large as the decrease of the latter when the latter is reduced by an increase of aggregate demand. Of course, each strike, being localized and usually a complete stoppage, may do more to reduce the national product if it goes on long enough to create shortages than a balanced and partial reduction of output in all sectors together. Yet expert opinion holds that most strikes do far less widespread economic harm than is generally feared and that even major strikes believed at the time to endanger the nation's health or safety were not demonstrated to have jeopardized the economy upon careful study after the fact. Their worse effects are limited to those on neighborhood business and employment, but the possibilities of advance preparation for the strike and of overtime work after the strike tend to recover these costs.[31]

It has often been pointed out that professional and managerial

---

[30] H. A. Turner, *Is Britain Really Strike-Prone? A Review of the Incidence, Character and Costs of Industrial Conflict* (London: Cambridge University Press [for the University of Cambridge Department of Applied Economics Occasional Papers], 1969). Incidentally, this study locates the principal cost of strikes for Britain in the balance of payments. The effect of higher American strike activity upon this country's export earnings would hardly be as important.

[31] A recent study of three postwar longshore strikes, following an earlier study of the 1959 steel strike, by the U.S. Department of Labor, reaches these conclusions, according to a report in the *New York Times*, Sunday, January 11, 1970.

people enjoy at least occasional moments of excitement and fulfillment in their careers, while the working lives of most industrial workers are exceedingly tedious and soul-destroying. For the latter, belonging to a union may diminish a little their sense of powerlessness,
and the accompanying tradition of an occasional strike may be the
principal means to enjoying comparable drama in their lives.[32] Business managers and union executives may deprive little enough pleasure from a strike. But for the workers, a strike may be living theater,
an adventure and an expression of group (or class) pride.[33] Certainly
there has been no detectable movement among union workers, or
among the socioeconomic classes to which they belong, for outlawing
or limiting strikes despite their occasional inconvenience to every
household.

4.3.4. *Criminal and Other External Diseconomies Imposed by the Unemployed.* In the early part of this century it was common practice
in business cycle studies to emphasize the correlative behavior of
a host of social variables: crime, pauperism, marriage rates, the
divorce rate, the death rate, suicide rate, alcoholism, and so on.
Aftalion devoted two chapters to such social indicators and Tugan-
Baranowsky the greater part of a book. The important American
work of this kind was apparently begun by Dorothy Swaine
Thomas in the early 1920s on through the interwar period.[34]

It is a fair generalization from this early work and the more recent
work up to the mid-1960s to say this: Those social indicators, like
the homicide rate, that are generally thought to be external dis-

[32] See Chapter 7 in *Toward a Social Report*, U.S. Department of Health,
Education, and Welfare, January 1969; A. Neal and M. Seeman, 'Organizations
and Powerlessness', *American Sociological Review*, March 1964.

[33] A congenial newspaper piece along these lines is by P. Worsthorne, 'Strikers:
the Power and the Glory', *Sunday Telegraph*, London, August 10, 1969. To
quote a little: 'The truth is that irrationality, impetuosity, explosiveness on the
shop floor make sense: not money sense but human sense. That blast furnaceman
[pictured after a strike vote with a wide grin and the thumbs-down sign in the
week's papers] was behaving naturally, as to the manner born, true to himself
and his traditions. Perhaps in Germany or the United States some skillful con-
ciliator would have ironed out the differences before they came to the boil. But
in so doing they would have blocked one of the few meaningful moments in his
working life. The balance of payments and economic growth might have been
promoted, but by no means necessarily the sum of human happiness.' Right on,
Peregrine.

[34] See D. S. Thomas, *Social Aspects of the Business Cycle* (New York: E. P.
Dutton, 1925), and the historical review by her of earlier work. See also the
British investigations of E. W. Bakke.

economies on people are inversely correlated with the business cycle, reaching their trough at or shortly after the employment peak. The opposite tends to be true of the other social indicators. In particular, the data have tended to support the hypothesis that homicide, suicide, and various other crimes are smallest when the labor market is at its tightest. This does not mean, of course, that literally every type of criminal activity follows the same pattern in every socioeconomic setting or that business cycle variables do an adequate job of explaining the fluctuations in criminal activities over time. The past 5 years have witnessed a doubling of the suicide rate among blacks age 15 to 24, for example, while there was no rise of the general unemployment rate or of the black unemployment rate; nor has there been a comparable increase of the white suicide rate.[35]

It might be objected that these correlations do not confirm any steady-state relationship. It is not known with any precision to what extent these correlations reflect a sustaining relationship with the unemployment rate rather than the short-lived consequences of the *change* of the unemployment rate from one level to another. If the effect of a reduction of the unemployment rate upon the social indicators were entirely transitory, the temporary reduction of that rate would still move some of this year's crime to a later date – postponing the evil day.

The upshot for socioeconomic welfare of this hardly needs stating: Because the victim or victims of homicide, suicide, theft, arson, and the like would be willing to pay something for these crimes to be prevented but do not usually have that opportunity, crime insurance and crime prevention methods being so imperfect – we have here a spectacular and rather beautiful case of 'market failure' – society tends to gain a little on this account from aggregate demand measures that push down the rate of unemployment.

We have been speaking about the variety of highly overt, even violent, external diseconomies that an increase of the unemployment level may cause to be committed against others, most often the employed. There is, I think, a much more subtle class of external diseconomies that unemployment brings upon the employed. Hearing about the unemployment of a friend is apt to worry people, or

[35] The following literature may be consulted: A. Henry, Jr., and J. F. Short, Jr., *Suicide and Homicide* (Glencoe, N.Y.: The Free Press, 1954); D. Glaser and K. Rice, 'Crime, Age and Employment', *American Sociological Review*, October 1959; B. F. Fleisher, *The Economics of Delinquency* (Chicago: Quadrangle Books, 1966). Work on black suicide behavior is being done by R. H. Seiden of the University of California School of Public Health.

make them uncomfortable. It is natural to feel concern when our neighbor is discontent with his economic opportunities, and we may feel some embarrassment if we are satisfied with our own. These feelings may be exaggerated by some association in our minds of unemployment with being poor. So, to some degree, it may be possible to reduce the anxieties of some employed people by faster injections of money and public debt into the economy to reduce the rate of unemployment (more geld, less guilt).

4.3.5. *External Effects From Better Job Experience.* When aggregate demand drives unemployment below its natural level, unskilled and alienated workers who are hyperfrequently unemployed receive opportunities and inducements to take and to stay in jobs that are more attractive (and some that only seem more attractive) than those they are likely to fill ordinarily. As a result of their experience in holding more stimulating, dignified, demanding jobs, these workers gradually acquire greater zeal, self-confidence, and on-the-job training.

There are two external effects of this process. For the workers themselves, they come to enjoy working more, to fear and hate it less, thus experiencing non-pecuniary rewards out of which, in principle, they could compensate their employers and still be left better off; they might be willing to make compensations, working at first for less money, were it not that job rationing makes it difficult or impossible to get the chance to do so. For rival employers other than the workers' own employer, there is the effect of a resulting enlargement of the pool of workers having the desired skills and orientation; under institutional arrangements superior to those in actuality, these beneficiaries of the fallout would subsidize one another to hire these workers.

Government training programs and government-subsidized on-the-job training programs can be used, and are being used, to achieve these two external benefits specifically. But insofar as these programs are insufficiently intensive or insufficiently comprehensive, there is room for an increase of aggregate demand to stimulate on-the-job training via market institutions as they exist. Appropriate government job training, moreover, may very well enhance the external benefits obtained from the reduction of the general unemployment rate. Note also that these external benefits do not all evaporate with a return to the natural rate, though the degree of transformation and the opportunity to advance a notch increase with the duration of the job experience. Indeed, there may occur a hysteresis effect that makes the 'natural' employment level higher than it was originally; see Chapter 3.

It is sometimes argued, by the way, that all the job training in the world for members of groups that are disadvantaged and discriminated against and, perhaps, for those who are underprivileged for some other reason will do no good unless aggregate demand drives the unemployment rate substantially below the natural rate. This cannot literally be true. It is not the case that no white man is unemployed as long as there is a black man available to stand in his place.

It would be somewhat more accurate to say that the black population is clustered toward the end of a queue, yet with whites (and other races) interspersed to a diminishing degree up to the head of the queue. The farther one is placed up the queue, the better is one's chance of getting a 'good' job. Presumably, a significant amount of job training can effect the position in the queue of the person receiving the training. Whatever the level of aggregate demand therefore – one thinks of this as the capacity of the football stadium people are queueing up to get into – there is presumably some gain from job training directed at the right 'level' in the queue, viz., at those workers who are not hopelessly far from the prospect of being able to use the training. Moreover, the potential usefulness of job training really extends over more than one level of abilities, one would think; for surely people of different endowments differ in what they believe they can reasonably hope to achieve and to take pride in. (There are many queues into the stadium of fulfillment.) Yet it is true that a given dollar expenditure on job training can be spent with greater payoff, and spent over a wider class of trainees, and thus with less risk of misguessing the areas of greatest payoff, the greater the level of aggregate demand is. The level of aggregate demand maintained and the level of expenditures on job training programs can be said to reciprocally enhance the payoff to an increase in the level of each – like 'land' and 'labor'. But extracting a payoff from the increase of one does not require a complementary increase of the other. It would be more accurate technically to characterize them as substitutes, best when mixed.

4.3.6. *Getting Into Labor Unions.* Just as a lasting transformation is wrought upon breaking into the world of decent jobs, there are lasting effects from breaking into a labor union. As suggested in

Chapter 3, an increase of aggregate demand which decreases the unemployment rate below the natural level improves the chances that persons who might otherwise not be likely to get membership in a union would find themselves able to get union employment. Even with an eventual return to the previous unemployment, some important consequences for economic efficiency would have ensued. The wage differential between union employment and nonunion employment would tend as a result to be narrowed to the extent that the unions made wage demands consistent with employment of their membership.

The reduction of that wage discrepancy is another strike for greater economic efficiency. There is a familiar economic effect of improved resource allocation wherever the differential between union wages and nonunion wages is causing an uneconomic scarcity of labor input in some activities relative to other activities. The psychological effects of the increased union membership are comparable in magnitude, if not much greater. The workers who gain access to the unions during the contrived boom will no longer feel so much on the outside and so deprived of their just life chances. Of course, this works in reverse when unemployment is instead increased: the workers who would lose what little chance they would ordinarily have to gain access to union employment will feel more alienated and powerless than before. In addition, when the union wage differential is narrowed, the frustration felt by those still not able to obtain union membership and union employment is dissolved a little, the deprivation lessened. Hence, if there were a return to the previous unemployment rate, the unemployment would be borne more evenly and borne with less distress. Further, as pointed out in Chapter 3, this model of the operation of the labor market, like the model suggested in the previous subsection, opens the door to a limited escape from orbit around the natural rate of unemployment: the historical experience with above-equilibrium employment in time decreases the size of the macroequilibrium unemployment rate that emerges if the higher inflation rate is maintained by suitable demand policies.[36]

[36] Even if the previous inflation rate is sought to be regained via an offsetting (not to say, upsetting) episode of unexpected disinflation via the reduction of aggregate demand, the finally emerging macroequilibrium unemployment rate may not be exactly the original equilibrium unemployment rate corresponding to the original expected inflation rate – or, being more meticulous, the macroequilibrium unemployment rate that would have occurred at the end date had not the whole excursion ever been ventured.

4.4. *The Operative Presumption Henceforth*

At the point, in Chapter 7, of fitting together the pieces of Chapters 4, 5, and 6, it will be a practical expositional necessity to stipulate the direction in which the peak-efficiency unemployment rate lies from the macroequilibrium rate – at least in the neighborhood of the expected inflation rate that would be ideal from the fiscal-monetary viewpoint adopted in Chapter 6. If no strong presumption were allowable, we could and would carry around the three possibilities in this respect. When there is enormous ignorance about the climate, the traveler has to pay the price of carrying around more baggage with which to meet a wider range of contingencies than he would like. But surely for this trip, we have reached a pretty good idea of what the climate is like. I shall specify in Chapter 7 that there is a gain of efficiency, up to a point, in reducing the unemployment rate below the aforementioned macroequilibrium rate. One could say, to put it mildly, that if you are going to have only one assumption in this respect, this is the one to have. But it seems fair to conclude, in view of what has been said above, that any defense of the opposite proposition would have to place heavy stress on one or two factors against quite an array of opposing factors or else be based on as-yet unknown insights.

5 Distributional Effects of Employment and of Unexpected Inflation

I F, despite distributive biases in technological advances and resource discoveries, our legislative system behaved so as to maintain for each economic group a fixed share after taxes and transfers of the total economic benefit produced by the economy, we could justifiably regard each improvement in allocative efficiency as a clear social gain. At least we could as long as it could be presumed that society would not spend the allocative gain in some counterproductive way. It would be inappropriate on almost any description of political decision-making, however, to suppose that economic benefits tend, after redistributions, to be divided up always in the customary proportions. It is conceivable, depending on the theory, that certain allocative improvements would make the poor poorer as they make the rich richer even after the political process has carried out its redistributive tax-and-transfer program.

In judging whether the allocative improvement would be a net social gain in his own estimation, the economist ultimately needs an economic *and* a political theory with which to predict the distributive outcome of the allocative move and he needs then to consult his own moral preferences – his personal 'social welfare function'. If there is a prediction of losers as a result of the allocative improvement, he will want to compare the predicted gains of the gainers against the predicted losses of the losers, giving a weight to each according to his own moral preference.

In the next section I shall discuss the dimensions, parameters, or categories in terms of which I believe the distribution outcome of unemployment reduction ought to be described and our moral preferences expressed. Anticipating the descriptive theories and empirical findings to follow, I note my own moral approval of the distributive outcome predicted here. In the subsequent section the theory used here of political intervention in distributive outcomes is discussed. Finally we come to the economic sources of distributive biases from unemployment reduction on which the distributive outcome ultimately hinges.

5.1. *Characterizing and Judging the Distributive Outcome*

The primary distributive outcome of reducing the unemployment rate by aggregate demand as required for allocative efficiency, it will be argued here, would be substantially to increase the relative share of total socioeconomic benefits received by the poor, by the bottom fifth of households by income.[1] It might be that some identifiable economic groups of persons would systematically suffer an absolute (as well as relative) loss of economic benefits, namely certain income groups among the aged; but it may be predicted that they will receive partial, and in some cases perhaps complete, compensation through reduced taxes or increased transfer payments or both. Those individuals who still experience an absolute loss of economic benefits after transfers and taxes are likely to be holders of amounts of bonds and other credit instruments, either directly or indirectly through certain financial intermediaries, which are exceptionally large in relation to their equity capital holdings and their 'human capital'; comparatively few of these persons will number among the poor.

This distributive outcome, whatever its exact shape, appears to be well within the set of outcomes which I for one, according to my own moral preferences, would be willing to call a net social gain. Those who believe with me that the public, through the legislative process, has redistributed far too little income to the poor, owing perhaps to some incapacity to take an impartial view or to some overestimate of the cost of the nonpoor to increasing the benefits received by the poor, will likewise conclude that the unemployment reduction in question would be a definite net social gain. Most, perhaps all, economists in this country would make the same judgment, I believe. They, like others, have occasionally revealed differences of opinion as to how much income per head they deem to be worth giving up (where it is agreed some output must be sacrificed) in return for a specified reduction in income inequality. Yet most economists have wanted more redistribution to the poor than has so far been instituted in this country, perhaps because of greater sympathy for those in economic need – no doubt there is some self-selection in choice of profession here – and perhaps because they have not estimated the incentive effect of redistribution to be as

[1] Here I am abstracting from the effects upon allocative efficiency and distribution of the results of such a move for the expectation of inflation. Roughly, I am talking about a reduction of the unemployment rate from 4.5 percent or so – the neighborhood of the natural rate – to 4 or 3.5 percent (assuming this last figure is not too small for allocative efficiency in this *ceteris paribus* sense).

deleterious as the general public. There is the possibility that some economists would object to the distributive outcome of unemployment reduction if, alongside the improvement in the relative position of the bottom fifth, there were shown also to be a much greater improvement in the relative position of the top fifth, so that the middle class was squeezed from both ends. But this is only a hypothetical possibility for which there is no evidence. (In any case my own preference is to favor the bottom more than to disfavor the top.)

What needs to be defended most, perhaps, is the description of the distributive outcome, and hence one's moral judgment, in terms of the size distribution of socioeconomic benefits, in terms of the share of such benefits going to low-income persons as against high-income persons. There are other ways, after all, of characterizing the comparative losers and gainers from unemployment reduction (and accompanying unexpected inflation) insofar as we can detect systematic tendencies toward a differential impact upon identifiable demographic, social, and economic categories of the population.

Some observers emphasize that, as we have noted several times, unemployment is disproportionately concentrated at the young end of the age distribution. Over the normal range of unemployment rates, the young also bear a disproportionate share of any increase of the unemployment rate. A few have expressed the view that, when the unemployment rate is low or moderate, it is 'only' teen-agers who are frequently unemployed. Yet the ease with which good jobs can be found by people in their formative years in the labor force ought to be a matter of concern about as much as the career outlook of adults. In hardly any instance is a person's unemployment likely to be a matter of destitution, and each situation has its peculiar strengths and weaknesses. At the other extreme, the overall unemployment rate sometimes raises concern precisely because teenage unemployment rate rises tend to be a multiple of increases in the overall rate. This view also seems a little odd when one thinks of the teen-age years, up to age twenty or so, as a time for coming of age, seeing the country, perhaps a time of casual work between intervals of schooling, in any case, not primarily a period for making steady income to help meet extensive household responsibilities. It is far from clear that a greater equalization of unemployment rates *by age* would be a net social gain.

Another systematic source of an unequal effect from unemployment reduction is that the aged, persons 65 or older, have a comparatively small direct stake in the tightness of the labor market and, possibly, a comparatively larger vulnerability to unexpected inflation. The labor force participation rate of the aged is much smaller than for those under 65, while the aged may own comparatively more monetary assets relative to consumption standard. But age is, again, not a variable of intrinsic interest. The aged poor, it seems to me, do not deserve special emphasis compared to the young and middle-aged poor. Indeed, society may do relatively better by the aged poor than the nonaged poor, because the former are a more socially and radically representative cross section of the population than the latter and because it may estimate that there is less deadweight efficiency loss per unit of benefits transferred to the former than to the latter.

There are other dimensions by which to compare the before-tax incidence, some of them merely journalistic handles for the week's story. One could debate the comparative seriousness of higher unemployment for men and women, for Nebraskans and Pennsylvanians, and so on. But surely the main emphasis should be placed on the comparative effect on relative shares between the poor and the nonpoor.

Certainly there is much economy in focusing on the poor – for example, those who tend usually to occupy the bottom fifth in per capital earnings – irrespective of age, sex, and color. In one attempt we capture those aged people who are having difficulty making ends meet, and working wives in economic difficulty, teen-agers in the labor force whose incomes are low, the whole range of persons who are severely handicapped in the pursuit of income for whatever reason, be it physiological, psychological, sociological, or eco-regional. As the population of this country is predominantly white, it is no surprise that most of the poor are whites, ranging from those in rural Appalachia and the Panhandle to those in impacted urban areas. Yet a disproportionate number of blacks are under the poverty line.

Despite the simplicity and economy of focusing on the bottom fifth, there is a case for taking note of the differential incidence of unemployment upon whites and nonwhites. There is unquestionably a substantial fraction of the black population that, while not below the official poverty line or even in the more numerous bottom fifth, still suffer (in the fullest sense) from unjust discriminatory treatment. So if these people are differentially aided by a reduction of the unemployment rate, it is reasonable to judge that there is on that account a distributional gain in social welfare. Further, some of the bottom fifth and some of the people who fit the measurements of poverty at least momentarily are not really poor from an overlife perspective – medical students, for example, and some retired people who own a home and safe low-yield bonds – while being black is not a transient state.[2]

5.2. *Political Intervention in the Distributive Outcome*

In making his own evaluation, the economist may wonder how others will judge the outcome and whether he will be alone in his judgment. By contrast, one is sometimes given the picture of the policy analyst as an heroic and maybe quixotic figure who from time to time holds out a policy proposal he favors to a clumsy political machine. With each proposal the machine-watchers buzz and quote odds that the machine will swallow it, though it is not believed the machine reads through the proposals. No doubt the political process is beset by ignorance and uncertainty as is the market process. It is conceivable that an allocative shift, be it legislated or decided administratively, will attract no legislative attention then or later to its distributive consequence, so that only the policy experts ever make judgments about the distributive outcome of the allocative move. But the distribution of after-tax-and-transfer economic benefits is not one of those legislative matters to which one would expect the political process to be oblivious, despite sporadic distractions by other issues.

If one interprets the alteration in the distribution of income after taxes and transfers that accompanies an allocative improvement as the result of the intelligent choice behavior of voters or their representatives acting in the democratic political process, it may be argued that the distributive outcome of the allocative change represents the decision of a majority as to how best to take advantage 'socially' of the distributive possibilities raised by the allocative improvement. Political economists and moral philosophers are not, after all, the only persons having a taste for certain amounts of income redistribution under certain conditions. If they were, it would be hard to explain the substantial transfer payments received by the poor, however inadequate you and I may regard them.

From this point of view, it can be argued that if, as I have main-

---

[2] There is another point. Often we lack data on unemployment by income classes, so that the comparative experience of the nonwhite may be useful as a proxy for the comparative experience of the poor.

tained, the reduction (via aggregate demand measures) of unemployment as necessary for allocative efficiency causes the poor to gain disproportionately as a group, it is because the unemployment reduction raises the incentive perceived by the participants in the political process to increase the relative share of income, or more broadly, socioeconomic benefits, going to the poor. This response to this incentive, in leaving the poor with a larger share, is one that increases the politicoeconomic satisfaction of the majority that so act, which is what motivates them so to decide. The change in the distribution of economic benefits, after-tax-and-transfer-adjustments are legislated, is one that is in some sense deemed gainful by the majority that votes it as compared to the dogged restoration by means of an exactly compensatory revision of taxes and transfers, of the original distribution of after-tax-and-transfer income between poor and nonpoor. For a majority, therefore, the unemployment reduction will lead to a two-part gain: an allocative improvement and a distributive improvement. The policy analyst would be missing a trick perhaps not to point this out, as though his favoring the move were due to some eccentricity in his own preferences. Let me now elaborate this economic theory of the political ratification or intervention in the determination of the distribution outcome.

The change in the aforementioned incentive to cause, permit, or ratify a change in the distribution of income after taxes and transfers will be posited here to hinge on what may be called the 'distributive bias' of the unemployment reduction we are discussing. By this bias is meant the direction in which the unemployment reduction alters the 'terms of trade' on which socioeconomic benefits can be redistributed from one group to another – in particular, from the poor to the nonpoor though other identifiable groups will come in for discussion later. If it were practicable on a continuing basis to make income transfers among persons without producing any 'deadweight efficiency loss' in the process, the terms on which socioeconomic benefits could be transferred from nonpoor to poor would be a constant, independent of the unemployment rate and indeed of resource allocations in every respect. But even the best practicable tax and transfer tools, whereby taxes paid and transfers received are graduated according to earnings, definitely engender 'substitution effects' which dull incentives to work and save as compared to the unattainable ideal of lump-sum taxes and transfers. The terms of trade become more and more costly the greater the relative amount of redistribution to be undertaken. If we consider the quantity of redistribution necessary to achieve a given share of economic benefits to the poor *after* taxes and transfers, it is clear therefore that the terms of trade become less costly as a consequence of the unemployment reduction if and only if the unemployment reduction tends to increase the relative share of economic benefits earned by the poor *before* taxes and transfers, for then less of the incentive-dulling redistribution-generating taxes and transfers will be needed relative to total earned income to accomplish the specified after-tax-and-transfer pattern of relative shares.

It will be the finding of this chapter, however inconclusive the data are on a few points, that a demand-induced unemployment reduction has a definite distributive bias toward (in favor of) the poor as a group.[3] It thus improves the aforementioned terms of trade. This is a shorthand way of saying that the unemployment reduction will increase the relative share of socioeconomic benefits before taxes and transfers that are earned by the poor. The politicoeconomic theory sketched here, according to which the relative share received by the poor in economic benefits *after* taxes and transfers would increase with a reduction of unemployment, starts from the assumption that it possesses this distributive bias toward the poor, that it would increase the relative share earned by the poor before taxes and transfers.

Before the rest of this theory of the distributive outcome is elaborated, it may be mentioned that this distributional bias from an unemployment reduction would by itself produce an allocative improvement in efficiency if 'counterredistributions' were made (or redistributions lessened) in such a way as to keep the after-tax-and-transfer shares unchanged. The implied reduction of tax rates on the nonpoor and the reduction of transfer rates (relative to earned income) to the poor would diminish *dis*incentives to work and save and thereby, on the normal presumption, yield an allocative improvement on top of the sorts of allocative efficiency gains discussed in the previous chapter. As a corollary, it follows that the unemployment rate that is allocatively efficient in producing economic benefits is smaller the larger the share of after-tax economic benefits that is specified to go to the poor.[4] But, according to the theory here, the

---

[3] This does not mean that literally every poor person (even if we exclude from the poor those persons with only temporarily low income) has his bread buttered on the side of lower unemployment.

[4] This is confirmed by the geometry of Figure 5.1, where the various unemployment rates each take a turn at being on the 'efficiency frontier'.

political decision will be to seize the more favorable opportunity to increase the realtive after-tax share received by the poor, perhaps cutting back on transfer payments to the poor somewhat but not by so much as to keep the after-tax-and-transfer economic benefits of poor and nonpoor in fixed proportions.

In analyzing the voters' response to the alteration of distribution possibilities occasioned by the unemployment reduction, one may draw an analogy, though it is necessarily a limited one, between the substitution by an economy of resource-endowed agents between food and clothing, say, and the substitution by the 'polity' of vote-endowed agents between economic well-being of the poor and economic well-being of the nonpoor. Hardly any household prefers to consume all of one and nothing of the other and, similarly, most voters would not want the poor to receive nothing or the nonpoor to receive nothing. The extent to which the political process substitutes some benefits to the poor for some benefits to the nonpoor depends upon the afore-discussed terms of trade available and, critically, the preferences that some or all of the nonpoor have regarding such substitutions. The amount of the redistribution decided upon (by majority vote) is determined by the interaction of the terms of trade with people's degree of interest in the relative after-tax share received by the poor.

Given people's distributive preferences, an improvement in the terms of trade arising from an allocative shift will cause the substitution of benefits to the poor for benefits to the nonpoor to be carried somewhat farther by the voters. Because of the 'limited substituta-bility' for voters between economic benefits to the poor and to the nonpoor, the distributive bias of the allocative improvement (here, the unemployment reduction) imparts an additional gain in the opportunity for average voter satisfaction that would not be present if people were to demand that economic benefits be distributed in fixed proportions or were somehow required to do that. Think of the allocative effect of the unemployment reduction as a 'parallel' outward shift in the possibilities for achieving economic bene-fits for poor and nonpoor alike *plus* a tilting of the benefit possi-bilities which leaves the old relative share of after-tax-and-transfer benefits to the poor (the old relative shares distribution) still avail-able – and still desired were it not for the change in the terms of trade. Because this distributive bias or tilting enlarges the gain in economic benefits to the poor obtainable from each extra sacrifice of benefits by the nonpoor (beyond the initial point), this distributive bias or increase in the terms of trade will be broadly welcomed as expanding the voters' relevant choices; for while it is also implied that there would be an increased cost to the poor of achieving any increase in the amount of benefits to go to the nonpoor, this will not be counted as a relevant loss of opportunity, at least not by a majority, as there had not been a majority that wished to vote an increase in the share going to the nonpoor when the opportunity

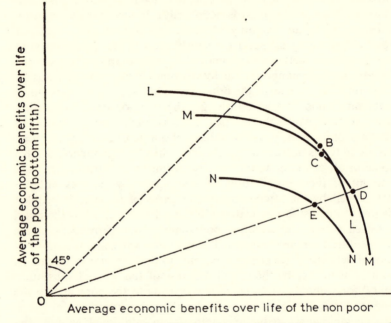

Figure 5.1. The locus of points *NN* gives the possible distributions of economic benefits, after taxes and transfers, between the poor and the nonpoor if aggregate demand maintains the unemployment rate at the 'natural' level. In that event, point *E* is selected by the political process.

The natural-unemployment rate is allocatively inefficient, though, for obtaining distributive shares along the ray *OED*. For that ray, the lower unemployment rate corresponding to *MM* is efficient and permits point *D*. But because of the distributive bias of unemployment reductions, *MM* is steeper than *NN* at the ray. Consequently the political process will 'substitute' along *MM*, choosing a point northwest of *D*, like *C*.

At the new distribution corresponding to *C*, still lower unemployment might be necessary for allocative efficiency. In that case there is a point *B*, north of *C*, for which some lower unemployment rate corresponding to the locus *LL* is efficient. Point *B* is like *D* in that it lies on some outer envelope of the loci, the frontier of 'efficient' points.

As the unemployment rate is successively reduced from the natural level, the expansion path winds through points *E* and *C* to reach the frontier, say at *B*.

cost to the poor was less, as before the distributively biased unemployment reduction.

The nonpoor who cast their vote for the increased share for the
poor might comment along these lines: 'The reduction of the unemployment rate was seen to be in the interest of efficiency, and the
vote was unanimous when it was stipulated that the existing after-
tax relative shares would be maintained through a sort of kickback
from the poor who we knew would otherwise get the lion's share of
the gain. But on later reflection, most of us decided we would feel
even better letting the poor keep most of their disproportionate
before-tax gains, since the cost to us of improving their relative
economic position had been decreased. Some of the better off were
opposed on that vote, but it is not clear that even they are absolutely
worse off than before the unemployment reduction. We are now
asking economists to calculate the efficient unemployment rate for
the new, less unequal distribution.'

As a purely positive description or prediction of the political intervention in the distributive outcome of the unemployment reduction –
and some such prediction is needed to make one's own moral judgment of this outcome, never mind the pleasure of some majority of
citizens – the theory concludes therefore that the group(s) which
loses in relative share before taxes and transfers tends to be compensated (or to compensate itself) only incompletely if (and only if)
the real opportunity costs of doing so are increased as a result of the
unemployment reduction. In truth, there is no guarantee that in
every conceivable case political group decisions will necessarily
satisfy, any more than market behavior in every case will satisfy, the
axioms of rational individual choice. Further, the notion that many
or all the nonpoor will show more sympathy to the poor the smaller
the cost of doing so might cease to be applicable once the nonpoor
(or enough of them) gauged the poor to be above some 'adequate'
income level. Finally, as acknowledged earlier, the political system
is no more informationally frictionless than the economy. This point
is especially pertinent if the unemployment reduction is a temporary
one (owing to the accumulation of offsetting efficiency costs being
created by reduced unemployment). Nevertheless recent analyses of
theoretically frictionless political decision-making processes have
been illuminating in showing that those processes reach a determinate solution in coping with 'externalities in consumption' –
public goods (joint consumptions), shared concerns, and so on
– specifically, that they reach a resource allocation and after-tax

distribution that is not 'inefficient' in the fullest sense on account of externalities of that type.[5] The psychic benefits felt by nonpoor persons from an improvement in the economic well-being of the poor is such an externality, and one may, along these lines, interpret the political redistributions which we observe in our progressive tax-transfer system as necessary for the efficient satisfaction of these interdependent preferences.[6]

As a theory which says that the distributive outcome is one that will please people, there are also some needed qualifications. All I have said is that a distributive bias toward the poor will be a welcome opportunity for most, and that a majority will feel there to be a gain from taking advantage of that opportunity. There is no guarantee that the increase in the relative share received by the poor will be preferred by everyone. Some people may be less altruistic than the majority, or may 'spend' (internalize) their altruisms in other ways. While the 'point' selected by the political process in the distribution of economic benefits between the poor and the nonpoor may be 'Pareto optimal' in the sense that more altruistic people and the poor cannot redistribute farther without frustrating the desires of the less altruistic, there is the empirical possibility that the point chosen will go too far for some. The reduction of the unemployment rate to an efficient level makes it possible for everyone to be better off; if there are feelings of altruistic concern for the poor on the part of some of the nonpoor, the distributive bias of the unemployment reduction would make new distributions feasible which would be capable of making everyone feel still better off. But there may exist a non-altruistic minority that is coerced by the majority. So there is no certainty, or even likelihood, that literally everyone will be made better off by the distributive bias after the political process has done its work.[7] There is only the presumption that most people will feel

[5] One critical assumption is that all possible tax-transfer-expenditure 'proposals' can be voted upon or, in effect, there is an unlimited possibility for vote trading. The 'only' information needed by everyone is the various prices and wage rates corresponding to each proposal. It is not implied that the political process can do the programming necessary to handle perfectly the externalities in production functions and nonconvexities that atomistic markets may fail properly to handle. Without implicating that paper in the above remarks, I should cite my own entry point to this literature, D. K. Foley, 'Resource Allocation and the Public Sector', *Yale Economic Essays*, Spring, 1967.

[6] See H. M. Hochman and J. D. Rogers, 'Pareto Optimal Redistribution', *American Economic Review*, September 1969.

[7] Yet the more-for-all potential in the allocative efficiency improvement from the unemployment reduction could cause everyone to be left better off on balance. I am speaking here only of the distributive bias.

better off as a result of the political decision to increase the relative share to the poor – namely, the poor and the altruistic among the nonpoor who together comprise a majority, however slender.[8]

5.3. *Distributive Biases From Unemployment Reduction and Unexpected Inflation*

We shall be analyzing here the nature and extent of the distributive biases from a demand-induced reduction of the general unemployment rate of a magnitude consistent with achieving allocative efficiency. Such a reduction of the unemployment rate via aggregate demand carries with it at least a temporary increase (or averts a temporary decrease) of unexpected inflation. Under the natural-rate hypothesis, the increase in the quantity of unexpected inflation must be maintained (hence the inflation rate must be continuously raised) if the reduction of the unemployment rate is to be sustained for a given duration.

There are three avenues of potential distributive bias for or against the poor from such unexpected inflation. The unexpected inflation, through its effects on the money-wage rate structure and upon employment rates, might aid the poor as owners of unskilled human capital comparatively more or less than owners of skilled human capital. It might benefit owners of nonhuman capital comparatively more than owners of human capital as a whole and thus benefit the poor comparatively less than the nonpoor in that way. It would benefit owners of nonhuman capital who were comparatively heavily invested in inflation-protected assets and might affect the poor differentially through that route. In any or all these ways the unexpected inflation might be imagined to benefit the poor, if at all, comparatively less than the nonpoor. But it will be argued here that

---

[8] This observation leads one to wonder: Would a distributive bias in the other direction, toward the nonpoor, be 'welcomed' by a majority as an opportunity for an increase of socioeconomic benefits to the nonpoor at terms which, while not costless to the poor, were more favorable than before? Yes, as long as the altruistic voters who swing the voting feel there to be some 'limited substitutability' between the well-being of the poor and the well-being of the nonpoor, they will say that it makes sense to make such a substitution. They will point out that the poor will receive larger transfers and the well-off pay larger taxes in order that the poor be partially compensated for the losses of before-tax economic benefits imputable to the nonpoor, who would be coerced by the majority decision. Unless everyone accepts the same moral principles, there will not be unanimity on distributive justice so that each person can expect to differ from the majority in his own preference.

in none of these ways does there seem to be an *a priori* theory or
direct evidence on which to conclude or presume that the distributive
bias runs significantly against the poor as a group. Indeed, theory
and evidence suggest that, as owners of relatively unskilled capital
and as persons who are comparatively frequently unemployed, the
poor enjoy a distributive bias in their favor from the effect upon the
wage structure and upon employment rates of such unexpected inflation and general unemployment reduction.

As explained above, distributive bias is a matter of before-tax-and-
transfer opportunities for and rewards from actions which earn socioeconomic benefits. For all its limitations, it is natural as a first step
to check the movement of relative shares of before-tax personal income earned by the poor and by nonwhites. The behavior of these
data in certain prominent years in the postwar period certainly casts
doubt on anyone's supposition that the poor and the nonwhites gain
less proportionately than the nonpoor whites from labor market
tightness (Table 5.1).[9]

TABLE 5.1. *INDICATORS OF THE RELATIVE INCOMES OF
POOR AND NONWHITES*

	1968 (%)	1965 (%)	1961 (%)	1950 (%)
Share of lowest fifth in total personal income	5.7	5.3	4.8	4.5
Share of next-lowest fifth in total income	12.4	12.1	11.7	12.0
Share of personal income received by nonwhites	6.9	6.2	5.3	—
Nonwhite median family income as percent of white median income	63.0	55.0	53.0	—
Unemployment rate	3.6	4.5	6.7	5.3
Unemployment rate for married men	1.6	2.4	4.6	4.6

Source: A. F. Brimmer, *Inflation and Income Distribution in the United
States,* before a conference, *Input–Output 1969,* sponsored by the Pittsburgh Commerce Institute and *Business Week,* Pittsburgh, December 2,
1969. All data were made available by the Bureau of the Census.

To test whether the improvement in the relative income of the poor
in the 1960s can be statistically attributed to the decline of the unemployment rate in those years, one wants an econometric analysis

---

[9] It is true that the data in Table 5.1, which give relative shares in total personal
income (before taxes and transfers), give too much stress to changes in the share
of wage income. Much property income, in the form of capital gains and imputa-
tions, is not measured by personal income.

of all the postwar years. One recent study gives strong statistical support to the dependency of the relative share earned by the poor upon the unemployment rate. It finds a significant negative relationship between the relative share of total income received by the lowest-income quintile of households and the unemployment rate – whether or not the inflation rate is 'held constant'. This relationship between relative income and the general unemployment rate is particularly pronounced for nonwhites.[10]

Such evidence on the behavior of personal income shares certainly suggests that the poor and the blacks enjoy a comparative gain in before-tax-and-transfer economic benefits from unemployment reduction and the associated unexpected inflation. Yet personal income does not measure certain kinds of income comprising total income. Equally important, socioeconomic benefits, even narrowly defined economic benefits, are not coextensive with income as ordinarily defined. Economic benefits may be imputed to current leisure (up to a point) as well as to current consumption and to future consumption prospects. And the latter can be enhanced by time invested in improving one's future earnings as well as by saving out of current earnings. Previous chapters remind us that there is some private opportunity cost to job-holding however much, from the standpoint of social efficiency, individuals may be seen to overestimate those costs at the macroequilibrium unemployment rate. An analysis of the behavior of the individual ingredients in an improvement in economic benefits will offer firmer ground for a conclusion on the matter of comparative gain or distributive bias.

5.3.1. *Relative Money-wage Gains.* A reduction of the general unemployment rate in keeping with the achievement of allocative efficiency might, for example, bring a gain in the returns to human capital – to people in their capacities as actual or potential members of the labor force – not just a gain in the returns to owners of tangible

---

[10] See R. G. Hollister and J. L. Palmer, 'The Impact of Inflation on the Poor', Institute for Research on Poverty, University of Wisconsin, April 1969. This chapter has benefited considerably from discussions with Palmer on a range of matters. Note that, on the natural-rate hypothesis, the inflation rate in this study might be interpreted as a proxy for the expected inflation rate, since the unemployment rate is then interpretable as a loose proxy for the quantity of unexpected inflation at least under conditions of steady unemployment. The comparative effects of the overall employment rate upon median incomes of whites and nonwhites have been estimated by L. C. Thurow, *Poverty and Discrimination* (Washington, D.C.: The Brookings Institution, 1970), pp. 58–61, with similar results.

capital or other nonhuman wealth claims. With respect to such a general unemployment reduction, the question we seek to answer in this section is the following: Will the returns earned on the relatively unskilled, untrained human capital characteristically owned by the poor increase proportionately more than the returns on the human capital owned by the nonpoor? Is there, in other words, a 'comparative' or (equivalently) 'disproportionate' gain in before-tax-and-transfer economic benefits for the poor arising from a comparatively greater improvement in the uses of, and rewards to, their time and abilities afforded by the general unemployment rate reduction? Here we are concerned with the comparative behavior, as between poor and nonpoor, of money wage rates and with a careful evaluation of differential employment rate responses; the behavior of real wage rates and their comparison to real rates of return on nonhuman capital will be taken up in section 5.3.3.

For a systematic analysis of the comparative gain in economic benefits to the poor from unemployment reduction we must examine *separately* the comparative behavior of wage rates and of employment for the poor. If it were the case that the observed differential improvement in the share of wage income earned by the poor masked a comparative worsening of the relative wage rate earned by the poor as a group – the average wage paid to poor employees relative to the average wage paid to nonpoor employees – the gain in the personal income share earned by the poor would not be clearly indicative of a distributive bias in economic benefits from unemployment reduction in favor of the poor. Then it would be implied that the poor had to make a disproportionate reduction of job search, leisure, and so on in order just to keep even in relative shares.

Neither wage theory nor the wage rate evidence suggests, however, that such a deterioration in the relative wage occurs with a reduction of the general unemployment rate. Indeed it may be, though there is uncertainty on the point, that the poor obtain a significant portion of the comparative gain in economic benefits from unemployment reduction from an improvement in their wage rates relative to the wage rates available to the nonpoor. We turn now to this theory and evidence.

Considerations of frictionless wage theory lead one to 'bet' on some decline in the relative wage earned by the poor when firms decide to cut production, as in response to some widespread loss of capital equipment. Looking at the demand side we note that the firm often has overhead labor requirements which are less sensitive to its planned rate of production than its overall labor requirements. Probably this overhead labor comprises a disproportionate number of relatively skilled, well-paid workers. So a decline of aggregate demand can be expected to decrease the 'derived demand' for skilled labor proportionately less than that for unskilled workers (at a given configuration of wage rates).[11]

On the supply side, there is perhaps not much reason to suppose that the relatively skilled and the better-paid workers are readier to substitute leisure for income in response to a given proportionate drop in wage rates than are the poor and unskilled. But the skilled workers have been noted to have an advantage over the unskilled, namely a margin of substitution less accessible to the unskilled. When the wage available for doing relatively skilled work falls, the relatively skilled workers can substitute working at lower-skill jobs instead of substituting leisure. The relatively unskilled workers have on average less room to maneuver this way, there being fewer rungs below them on the job hierarchy ladder. One is left with some presumption, though a chancy one, that without any frictions at all we would observe the relative wage of the poor to be less 'sticky' – to move proportionately more – with respect to changes in production – than the wage earned by the relatively skilled.

When the decline in production plans is due to a fall of aggregate demand and there are frictions in the labor market, a proper analysis of the effect on the money wage differential requires some attention to the possibility of the differential frictions. But it would not be surprising, by reason of the above frictionless factors, to find that even in frictional labor markets the relative wage of the poor tends to be higher the smaller the general unemployment rate – especially when the unemployment rate is abnormally large so that the relatively skilled workers are not in substantial excess demand and are occupying less-skilled jobs.

Attention to the role of frictions may actually strengthen the presumption that the relative wage earned by the poor rises with increased labor market tightness. When, starting from normal conditions, aggregate demand slackens, firms may be more cautious about discharging (or allowing the attrition of) their relatively skilled workers, including those not required for overhead. The firm may

---

[11] With respect to the proportionate decline in the 'demand price' for skilled labor compared to that for unskilled labor, there may be some countervailing tendency for the wage elasticity of demand for skilled workers to be smaller than that for unskilled workers.

want to 'hoard' some of its skilled employees in anticipation of eventual return to normal operations or secular growth of the firm in order to save search costs and firm-specific training costs in the future. These initial 'investment costs' of finding relatively unskilled workers are presumably comparatively smaller (even relative to their smaller wage rates), for they are comparatively more homogeneous so that the inducement to hoard unskilled labor is correspondingly smaller. When aggregate demand is high and the labor market abnormally tight, it is the relatively skilled workers who can be 'dishoarded', for it is the skilled workers that firms will tend to have hired 'ahead of demand' as a precautionary reserve. The purpose of the reserve is to use it in just such times.

In addition, the increased labor tightness will have increased the investment costs, searching, and interviewing, that would be required to bring the ratio of skilled to unskilled workers back to the level appropriate for normal operations. So firms will tend to skimp on skilled labor on the whole as long as the labor market tightness continues. At the new employment position, firms' job vacancies for skilled personnel will be reported to be abnormally high, more so than their vacancies for unskilled workers. This presumably signifies that, after the firms have made their limited employment adjustments to the higher output demand, the marginal worth to them of having on the payroll an extra skilled man has increased proportionately more than that of having an extra unskilled man – for frictions have gotten in the way of acquiring the former more than the latter. It does not signify that firms will be offering comparatively larger proportionate pay increases to skilled workers than to unskilled workers. The incidence of the increased frictional transaction cost can be expected to fall partly on the skilled worker, driving a wedge between pay and marginal worth. If firms were to make equal proportionate pay increases to skilled workers, let alone more than proportionate wage increases, job vacancies for skilled personnel would not be found any longer to have increased in larger proportion: At such high wage rates, some of the jobs for skilled personnel that would otherwise be reported as vacant would not in fact be economical any longer to fill at such high wage rates.

There may be a friction operating from the supply side that supports the presumption that the wage rates of skilled workers are stickier than those for unskilled workers. When aggregate demand is low and the labor market slack, it may be that the worth of the worker to the firm to which he applies for employment depends for its credibility upon his maintaining a normal or standard wage demand to a greater extent in the case of a skilled worker than for an unskilled worker whose abilities are more predictable. And when the labor market is tight, it may also be that the skilled worker, in whom the firm would be making the greater investment, will be motivated to fix his price on the basis of long-run prospects to a greater degree than the unskilled worker, lest the firm judge that, if hired, he would be an administrative headache.

The observation that the general unemployment reduction increases the shortage of relatively skilled personnel more than unskilled persons, and the corresponding observation that the money wage rates paid to skilled persons are stickier, leads to the point that the relatively unskilled can secure an additional gain in their average relative wage insofar as some of the relatively unskilled workers can as a consequence be upgraded into higher-skill jobs. If the worth to the firm of having an extra man able to do some high-skill job has gone up more than the wage for skilled personnel ordinarily performing that type of job – the widened gap being due to the increased cost and delays of finding such workers and perhaps the stickiness of their asking prices – relatively low-skilled workers stand a better chance of being hired or upgraded and being given on-the-job training in order to fill some of those high-skill job vacancies. On a similar thought it has been noted that blacks and others who are discriminated against – in the sense that they have a poorer chance of being hired for a certain job, all other things being equal – will fare comparatively better in getting good jobs when the labor market is tightened, for the cost to the employer of discrimination against them, of holding out for workers of the color, sex, or whatever that the firm prefers, is thereby increased. If the money wage of poor workers, relatively unskilled ones, rises comparatively more with an increase in labor market tightness, that fact does not mean that *overall* they have increased in their comparative expensiveness to hire in higher-skill jobs for it then takes longer to acquire more skilled persons than before. The increase in the relative wage of poor persons is partly the result of the upgrading, which proceeds until the overall expensiveness is restored to balance. So in the frictional model of labor markets as well as in the frictionless model, interjob category substitution up the job hierarchy is an important source of a gain in the relative wage earned by unskilled persons on average that accompanies a general increase of production and labor market tightness.

TABLE 5.2. EARNINGS OF SKILLED, UNSKILLED, AND WHITE COLLAR WORKERS (1961 = 100)

Year	Unskilled[a] (Plant) Nominal Index			Real Index			Skilled[b] (Maintenance) Nominal Index			Real Index			White Collar[c] Nominal Index			Real Index		
	Average Hourly Earnings (dollars)	Percent Change (1960–64)	Percent Change (1964–68)	Average Hourly Earnings (dollars)	Percent Change (1960–64)	Percent Change (1964–68)	Average Hourly Earnings (dollars)	Percent Change (1960–64)	Percent Change (1964–68)	Average Hourly Earnings (dollars)	Percent Change (1960–64)	Percent Change (1964–68)	Average Weekly Earnings (dollars)	Percent Change (1960–64)	Percent Change (1964–68)	Average Weekly Earnings (dollars)	Percent Change (1960–64)	Percent Change (1964–68)
1960	96.50			97.57			96.50			97.57			96.80			97.88			
1961	100.00[d]			100.00			100.00[e]			100.00			100.00[f]			100.00			
1962	103.20			101.98			103.10			101.88			103.30			102.08			
1963	106.60			104.10			105.90			103.42			106.20			103.71			
1964	110.00	14.0		106.08	8.7		108.80	12.7		104.92	7.5		109.20	12.8		105.30	7.6	
1965	113.20			107.30			111.40			105.59			112.30			106.45			
1966	116.80			107.65			115.50			106.45			115.90			106.82			
1967	121.80			109.14			120.30			107.80			120.90			108.33			
1968	128.40		16.7	110.40		4.1	126.90		16.6	109.11		4.0	126.80		16.1	109.03		3.5

[a] Includes janitors, porters, cleaners, laborers, and material handling.
[b] Includes carpenters, electricians, machinists, mechanics automotive, painters, pipefitters, and tool and die makers.
[c] Office clerical category which includes a broad range of white collar workers. Included are typists, stenographers, different classes of clerks, keypunch operators, bookkeepers, and office boys and girls.
[d] The dollar figure for 1961 is approximately $1.93.
[e] The dollar figure for 1961 is approximately $2.89.
[f] The dollar figure for 1961 is approximately $77.10.

Source: U.S. Department of Labor, Bureau of Labor Statistics, Handbook of Labor Statistics, 1969, Table 94, pp. 200–201, and A. Burger, 'The Effects of Inflation, 1960–68', St. Louis Federal Reserve Bank Review, November 1969.

The evidence on the cyclical behavior of the median wage rate earned by poor persons as a ratio to the overall median wage rate is rather sparse at this writing. There are some time series data on the average paid for work in unskilled job categories and skilled job categories. While such data does not capture the upgrading of workers into better paying job categories, they are of great interest. The behavior of these data since the war appear to be consistent with the hypothesis argued for here – that the interoccupational proportionate wage differential between skilled and unskilled jobs tends to a narrower figure the lower the general unemployment rate is. An examination of the 1960s shows a very marked narrowing of this (proportionate) interoccupational differential during that part of the decade when the unemployment rate was falling quite fast. The differential showed relatively little tendency, if any, to narrow further in the latter stages of the boom. In those years it may be that upgrading is left as the relatively more important source of the relative wage earned by unskilled and poor persons. In any case, we can say with some confidence that there is no evidence that the relative wage rate paid on the average to holders of low-skill jobs turns down when the labor market tightens over any range of the general unemployment rate.

On the matter of upgrading as a route to higher wage rates, we shall see from evidence to be presented below that upgrading is an important phenomenon for the labor force as a whole. But whether in fact the poor are the beneficiaries of a proportionately greater wage-rate increase than the nonpoor when the labor market tightens is not something that can be gotten at directly from currently existing data. One can hope for sample survey data that will permit analysis of the combined effect of job upgrading with changes in job wage scales as measured by wage income of persons doing an unchanged number of man-hours of work. One might be able plausibly to infer something about the behavior of the relative wage rate earned by the poor by comparing the change in the median income of poor persons to the change in their average numbers of hours at work and contrasting this with the corresponding results for the nonpoor. But there are so many factors to be 'controlled' in such an analysis that cannot be undertaken here.

At the risk of what might appear to be circular reasoning, one could argue that the greatly disproportionate increase of employment by poor persons in response to a reduction of the general unemployment – the facts of which I shall be turning to in a moment –

can only with difficulty be attributed to anything but a strong, presumably comparatively stronger, improvement in the levels of jobs made available to poor persons of relatively little skill when the labor market tightens. For if one assumes that the market for unskilled labor is comparatively less imperfect than the market for skilled and therefore comparatively heterogeneous labor, at least at moderate unemployment rates or lower, – more precisely, if work in the less attractive sorts of jobs can always be found quickly – and if one is not much impressed by the narrowing of the interoccupational wage differential with labor market tightening, especially at low unemployment rates, to what else should the marked increase of employment by poor and unskilled persons accompanying general unemployment reduction be attributed except a major increase, possibly a comparative increase, in the rate of pay and job satisfaction from the jobs thus opened up to them?

Be that as it may, we seem to be quite safe in assuming for the analysis which follows that demand-induced reduction of the general unemployment rate brings no significant adverse movement in the median money wage earned by the poor compared to the median money wage earned by the nonpoor. On that assumption we can proceed to consider the differential behavior of employment by the poor and its significance for the distributive bias in economic benefits of unemployment reduction.

5.3.2. *Comparative Response of Employment Rates.* The stylized facts on the distribution of unemployment by race and poverty class and the behavior of this distribution over the business cycle are broadly agreed upon. The interpretation of this behavior for the question of which group is the comparative gainer in economic benefits has not received a correspondingly wide discussion.

The elasticity of the labor force participation rates of the poor does not appear to differ appreciably from that for the nonpoor. The same is true of comparisons between whites and nonwhites. In each case the improvement in job openings and money wage offers which accompanies the reduction of the general unemployment rate apparently brings out into the labor force some portion of a 'hidden reserve' of workers who had not met the conditions for being reported as unemployed in the government sample survey. An increase of the 'employment rate' of 1 percent age point, therefore, is typically accompanied by a greater than 1 percent increase of employment (as a percent of its initial value, that is). Obviously, the nonpoor have their own hidden reserve.[12]

With respect to the structure of unemployment rate, it is a fair approximation of the normal range to say that the unemployment rates of poor persons and of nonwhites are fixed multiples of the general unemployment rate. A familiar rule of thumb has it that the black unemployment rate is twice the overall unemployment rate. Recent studies have taken a more detailed look at the interrelationships among unemployment rates by color, age, and sex. According to one set of econometric projections from postwar data, a reduction of the white unemployment rate by a third in 1966 would have been accompanied by a reduction of the nonwhite unemployment rate by a third also.[13]

It follows algebraically that employment of poor persons and of nonwhite persons as a percentage of the poor and nonwhite

[12] See J. D. Mooney, 'Urban Poverty and Labor Force Participation', *American Economic Review*, March 1967, and the subsequent comment on it by G. C. Cain and J. Mincer, *American Economic Review*, March 1968. No doubt the proposition in the text is only approximate, subject to survey biases and not necessarily applicable to every constituent age group and sex alike.

[13] Thurow, *Poverty and Discrimination*, pp. 57–58.

TABLE 5.3. *DISTRIBUTION OF UNEMPLOYMENT REDUCTIONS, BY COLOR, SEX, AND POVERTY AREA*

Unemployment Rates	Medium Unemployment Structure		Low Unemployment Structure		Ultra Low Unemployment Structure
	1965	1970	1966	1968	1969
White total	4.1	4.5	3.4	3.2	3.1
Adult men	2.9	3.2	2.2	2.0	1.9
Adult women	4.0	4.4	3.3	3.4	3.4
Teen-agers[a]	13.4	13.5	11.2	11.0	10.7
Nonwhite total	8.1	8.2	7.3	6.7	6.4
Adult men	6.0	5.6	4.9	3.9	3.7
Adult women	7.5	6.9	6.6	6.3	5.8
Teen-agers	26.5	29.1	25.4	24.9	24.1
Urban poverty areas	n.a.	7.6	n.a.	6.0	

[a] Ages 16–19.

Note: n.a. = not available.
Source: U.S. Department of Labor, *Handbook of Labor Statistics*.

populations respectively increases by a greater amount than do the employment rates in the white and nonpoor populations. This is simply because there is a larger fraction of the poor and nonwhite populations who are moved to the employed state when the unemployment rates fall in equal proportions in the various populations. According to one estimate, a 1 percent increase of total employment by adult whites in 1966 would have been accompanied by a more than 3 percent increase of employment of adult nonwhite women.[14]

Does this mean that the poor and the nonwhites gain comparatively more from the general unemployment reduction? What must be assumed by way of a minimum to make such an inference? The assumption that the allocatively efficient unemployment rate for each group in terms of its own self-interest is the same number – for example, 3 percent – would facilitate such an inference. But so stringent an assumption is not necessary for the conclusion that the poor and the nonwhites are the comparative gainers in economic benefits on account of the larger gain in their employment rates when there is a general unemployment reduction.

Let us assume, for the sake of the argument, that the point as measured by the general unemployment rate at which further tightness of the labor and product market would be damaging for their own overlife efficiency in allocating their time between working, job search, leisure, and the rest is the same for the poor and the nonpoor. It is then possible to argue along classical lines that if (according to our conservative assumption) the respective rises in the average money wage offer to poor and to nonpoor accompanying the demand-induced unemployment reduction are in equal proportion while there is a proportionately greater increase in the employment of poor persons than of nonpoor persons, the poor as a group can be said to receive the larger proportionate gain in economic benefit. The reasoning is like that according to which the lifting of a tax on some commodity is said to be more beneficial the more substitutable that commodity is for other commodities; if you have to tax only one commodity, tax housing or meat. One may think of the increase of aggregate demand and the accompanying rise of money wage offers as analogous to the lifting of a tax on present job-holding or the lifting of a pernicious subsidy to leisure-taking and job-searching. Both groups, the poor and the nonpoor, receive an equal 'pure income gain' as measured by the equiproportionate increase in their money wage offers (though we have to attend later to the 'real value'

[14] Thurow, *Poverty and Discrimination*, pp. 57–58.

of such increases). But there is a further gain from reallocation that is the greater for the group that takes fullest advantage of the substitution away from job search and leisure-taking that the lifting of the tax encourages.[15]

The conclusion that the poor and the nonwhites are the comparative gainers with reference to returns on human capital from a reduction of the general unemployment rate is strengthened insofar as it may be agreed that the poor have an interest in achieving a somewhat lower overall unemployment rate from the point of view of allocative efficiency than do the nonpoor. It is at least conceivable that the nonpoor would find a nonpoor unemployment rate of 3 percent in their self-interest and prefer a corresponding overall unemployment rate of 3.5 percent, and the poor would likewise be best served by an unemployment rate among poor persons of 3 percent, and hence an overall unemployment rate of 1.5 percent – to pull some illustrative figures from the air. But, as a guess about the conflict of interest over degrees of labor and product market tightness, that assumption would almost surely go too far. The poor as consumers might suffer from shortages in product markets that would begin to offset completely the additional gain to them in the allocation of their labor time before their own-group unemployment rate had reached 3 percent.

But there can be little doubt that when the general unemployment rate has reached a level that is allocatively ideal for the nonpoor and for whites as a group, the poor and the blacks would still benefit from a further reduction. Some of the poor will have opted for unsteady jobs because their rates of pay are better than the steady work that is available. But the optimality of that selected position on their bed of nails does not mean that those persons would not benefit from the more frequent availability of such better-pay jobs. If precautionary or wait unemployment tends to be excessive in macroequilibrium, it is especially excessive for those who are predominantly exposed to it.

Some of the poor tend to be frequently unemployed because they become discouraged and discontent with jobs lacking any satisfaction or advancement opportunities. Others are unable to perform well enough to keep their jobs for long. From the standpoint of allocative efficiency of the economy as a whole (for given weighting of the benefits to various groups), the presence of these people in the labor force increases somewhat the overall unemployment rate that

[15] The addition to a person's 'producer's surplus' is proportionately greater the more elastic is his (compensated) supply curve.

is efficient. But these poor persons themselves will have more interest in greater labor market tightness than the labor force as a whole, for it is they who will often be searching for jobs.

Some of the comparative gain to poor persons from an extremely tight labor market may take the form of future income. With the disproportionate employment gains to the poor and to the nonwhite from unemployment reduction, there is considerable upgrading. The opportunities created for poor workers to acquire experience in more demanding and more promising jobs may have permanently transforming effects upon them. Some of them may as a result literally achieve an escape from poverty that would carry over to the future even if the general unemployment rate were ultimately to recede to some higher level. (This in no way denies that at the same time there is a hard-core stratum of people who, while they may work more regularly when the labor market is tighter, will never escape from poverty by that means alone, if by any.) It may be that it is substantially the blacks among the total poor who stand to benefit the most from the improved opportunities for attractive jobs because the hurdles for many of them in getting out of poverty are likely to be matters of opportunity and experience, hence surmountable.[16]

Our conclusion that general unemployment reduction offers a comparatively greater advantage to the poor need not be restricted to the economic benefits of income and leisure. The poor and the nonwhites bear a disproportionate share of the 'external' social costs from slackness of the labor market. Individuals in poverty areas and ghetto neighborhoods have to bear the costs of their own occasional unemployment and also a disproportionate share, relative to income, of the social disorganization and crime that is stimulated by high unemployment in the area.

One should not neglect either the psychological effects of the upgrading in level of job occupied that presumably accompany the increase in the employment rates of the poor and the nonwhites. These effects may spill over into the community, affecting children, relatives, and friends. The improvement in opportunities for obtaining jobs that promise better advancement and that offer more satisfying work experience may be as significant as the increase in wage income which steadier employment in better jobs produces. For the poor and for the blacks especially, this upgrading probably makes

---

[16] Some preliminary findings on black mobility are available in J. J. McCall, 'An Analysis of Poverty: Some Preliminary Findings', RM-6133-OEO, The RAND Corporation, Santa Monica, California.

an important contribution to self-respect and to the sense of belonging in the society. For the nonpoor, who already have respectable
jobs and often good career prospects, the upgrading associated with
their employment gains is not typically of such critical importance.

5.3.3. The 'Real Wage' and Employment: The Equilibrium Case.
Decades ago it was quite commonly believed by neoclassical economists that the high employment level achieved by a tight labor
market in an inflationary period was only a fool's paradise for the
'working class'. They believed quite widely that, as a rule, the real
value of the money wage in these conditions would be depressed.
This contention naturally found support among neoclassical economists for it was their theory that the real wage measured the marginal
productivity of labor. Under diminishing marginal productivity, only
by a reduction of real wage rates would employers be induced to
increase their employment rolls.

This 'lag' of money wage rates behind rising or abnormally rising
goods prices was held to nullify the gain that workers might otherwise derive from the higher level of employment – for if workers had
wanted to work more, they could have bid down the real wage rates
themselves. The main beneficiaries then are the owners of capital
who enjoy higher markup on the original volume of business that the
workers previously toiled to produce at better real wages. If there is
a constructive side to the 'profit inflation', it is the larger supply of
saving which the redistribution of real incomes toward the rich and
thrifty will generate. Keynes believed that inflationary episodes were
historically associated with cultural achievements as they brought
'freedom from economic cares' to the governing class.[17]

These early beliefs, despite tough sledding recently among economic historians, are still very much alive as popular prejudices
about current-day relationships between real wage and unemployment or between real wage and unexpected inflation. Some agencies
of the federal government release data inviting the interpretation that
the American factory worker failed to keep up with the cost of living,
let alone with the productivity growth, during the inflation between
1965 and 1969. This impression seems still to be not uncommon in

---

[17] J. M. Keynes, *Treatise on Money*, Vol. II (London: Macmillan, 1934), p. 154.
As mentioned in section 1.5, Keynes's belief in the inverse relation between
employment and real wage rate remained through the *General Theory*, though
his causality was not classical. Others prominently associated with this hypothesis
include Jacques Rueff in France and Earl Hamilton in the United States.

central bank circles where the notions of profit inflation developed and flourished much earlier.[18]

We have to investigate the possibility that the *real* wage earnings of the poor and the blacks actually suffer from the reduced unemployment through a lag of wages behind prices. Is it possible that the poor's relative gain is only relative to a weakened middle class? It could be, in principle, that the gain by blacks and by the poor in their median incomes relative to the overall median, and the gain in the share of income by the poor and by the blacks which accompany a reduction in the level of unemployment, conceal a serious decline in the total *real wage* income as a share of *total* real income to be divided between poor and nonpoor and between white and nonwhite – i.e., an increase in the share of total income going to capital which is even more concentrated among whites and the nonpoor than is labor income.

That this hypothesis has enjoyed so much credence for so long is partially a reflection of the oft-noted historical association between rapidly growing inflation and deep-seated socioeconomic troubles, troubles that were typically hard on owners of machinery and structures as on owners of human capital. (More on this, below.) Certainly modern economic theory would in no way lead us to expect a decline, or at any rate a significant decline, in labor's share in consequence of an aggregate demand policy producing high employment. Some of this material has already been covered, but a brief recollection of it will do no harm.

In this section we consider only the possibility that the reduction of the unemployment rate is a change in the macroequilibrium unemployment rate, corresponding to a higher actual *and expected* inflation rate. Then one has to ask what went wrong with the natural-rate hypothesis to give the faster inflation rate a sustained effect on the unemployment rate. For example, if the mechanism is the acquisition of skills and habits which lead to a greater commitment of some workers to work in the commercial business sector, one would expect *those* workers to enjoy higher real wages in the new situation than they would have in the old. Other inputs that are complementary with this labor input will enjoy an increased remuneration per unit and possibly a higher share, while those other

[18] A. F. Brimmer, 'Inflation and Income Distribution in the United States', before a conference, *Input-Output 1969*, sponsored by the Pittsburgh Commerce Institute and *Business Week*, Pittsburgh, December 2, 1969. Virtually all of Brimmer's data, however, belie the conclusions he apparently took them to support.

inputs that are substitutable will find their remuneration bid down. It is hard to say, and of dubious relevance, what will happen to labor's overall share and the average real wage.

Or take the explanation that the labor unions get caught with enlarged memberships and so have to set lower real wage rates to maintain the employment of their members. Then, while manufacturing real wages may be reduced a little (and a good thing too, the efficiency analyst would say), there is likely to be a rise of real wage rates outside the union sector and a rise of the *average* real wage owing to the movement of workers from low-wage to high-wage employments.

Or take, as the last example, the argument against the natural-rate hypothesis based on the alleged inability of people to make unbiased estimates of the relevant logarithms when prices and wages are rising considerably. Then the increased employment is like an increase in the supply of effort (a reduction of the demand for leisure) in its effects upon real wage and the wage share. Even a major increase of labor supply may make little difference to the mean wage. Consider a Cobb-Douglas description of the economy in which labor receives its marginal product – or a fixed fraction of it. A 2 percent increase of total employment in that world would increase real wage income by 1.5 percent due to a one-half of one percent fall of the average real wage rate; in the first year, owing to technical progress, real wage rates might therefore rise at 2 percent instead of 2.5 percent, thereupon to continue at the normal trend rate of 2.5. The loss in the mean real wage is thus roughly the gain to a worker from being born two months later into the technically progressive economy. This figure of one-half of one percent would be decreased if we recognized the lesser productivity on the whole of marginal workers. On the other hand, it would be increased if capital and labor are, in the aggregate, not so substitutable as the Cobb-Douglas model portrays them to be.

Before considering the alternative interpretation of the unemployment reduction as a disequilibrium phenomenon and finally looking at some data, we should add that the achievement and subsequent maintenance of employment at a higher level immediately raises profit rates and social rates of return to investment. Therefore, unless the government counters the tendency, the increase of employment is likely to evoke a greater proportionate rate of capital growth.[19]

[19] R. Eisner, *Three Lectures on Investment and Growth* (Athens: Institute of Economic Research, 1967).

There is not only the saving out of the original path of income produced by the previous and lower employment level but now there is
to be added some saving out of the additional real income from the
additional employment – up to the point that the efficient employment level is reached. The rate of economic growth corresponding to
the constant unemployment rate – or to any reference unemployment rate or 'potential capacity' notion – is immediately made
higher therefore and recedes only gradually back toward the natural
growth rate given by population expansion and technological progress as capital deepening proceeds. In this process the normal real
rate of return on capital will tend eventually to be restored and the
average real wage will likely tend asymptotically to recover from its
depression to its original level.

A full discussion of the profit inflation hypothesis requires that we
acknowledge an implicit assumption made by at least some of its
proponents, namely, that the reduction of unemployment and the
allegedly concomitant lag of the average money wage behind the
price level are both (at least to an important degree) attributable to
the unexpected character of the inflation. So let us carry on the discussion of the wage lag hypothesis under the heading of unexpected
inflation. Toward the end of that discussion we shall examine some
contemporary American data bearing on the real wage lag hypothesis.

5.3.4. *The Profit Inflation Hypothesis Again: The Disequilibrium Case.*
The early credibility of the profit inflation hypothesis rested heavily
(if not entirely) on the assumption that the reduction of unemployment to inflationary levels is a disequilibrium phenomenon associated
with an excess of actual overexpected inflation, as would be predicted by the natural-rate hypothesis. Yet modern disequilibrium
unemployment theories have cut that ground from under the profit
inflation argument.

According to modern disequilibrium theory, aggregate demand
need not reduce real wage rates in order that it succeed in raising the
employment level. It is true that the abnormal increase of aggregate
demand leads the representative household to accept a smaller real
wage as the terms for undertaking the increased amount than it
would demand if it had wider information about the altered aggregate situation, particularly the situation of similarly placed households. But sellers of products are in the same boat: The abnormal
strength of aggregate demand leads the representative firm to offer

its products at a smaller markup than it would set if it were better informed of the altered aggregate situation, especially the similar experience of its closest competitors. It is perfectly possible, therefore, that real wage rates may tend on balance to be above trend when unexpected inflation is occurring and keeping the employment level.

Perhaps the 'natural presumption' is that the average real wage would vary over the business cycle only in fixed proportion to the average product of labor – for example, gross private product per private man-hour of employment. Both might be expected to fall a little as the levels of output and employment are increased inasmuch as comparatively fewer productive workers and fewer productive machines are brought into play when production is increased. The average real wage earned by a standard bundle of workers according to immutable characteristics of age, sex, and so on, should not be expected to fall on this account, nor should output per 'standardized man-hour' if enough unused machines were found to equip the added workers. If machines tend to be more fully employed than the labor force, the 'average product of standardized labor time' might fall. But if a certain amount of man-hours are as much overhead necessary for producing something as certain machines and buildings – because there are informational and entrepreneurial tasks to be undertaken, the marginal product of standardized labor need not be less than the average product (in the relevant range, despite diminishing marginal returns throughout); hence output per standardized man-hour need not fall, and may even increase, when employment is increased.[20] If output per man-hour is constant or even increasing (as a function of employment), the presumption is then that the real wage paid to a standardized bundle of workers tends to a level that is independent of, or perhaps an increasing function of, the employment rate.

So much for the range of possibilities consistent with modern theory. A casual inspection of some contemporary data pertinent to this issue discloses no support whatever for the profit-inflation or

[20] There is a further point to be made here. The economist is accustomed to think of the 'rising industry supply curve' as attributable not only to rising costs within each firm but to the tendency for additional production to keep alive some high-cost marginal firms that would otherwise have passed the point of economical operation. But when markets are imperfect, the consequences of a drop in aggregate demand can no longer be argued to fall with precision accuracy on the marginal firms. A similar point applies to marginal plants within the decentralized multiplant firm.

lag-of-wage-behind-price hypothesis. In the expansion phase of the two most recent inflationary episodes in this country, employers had to pay a standardized crew of workers sharply higher money wage rates whose real value, measured against the current cost of living, was also noticeably higher than the trend increase of real wage rates. Likewise, labor's relative share of gross product appears to peak at the top of the business cycle. Whether this procyclical behavior of real wage rates and labor's share tends to persist in prolonged disequilibrium (steady-states) is a question beyond these casual investigations. Certainly there is no indication – nor would anyone for a moment dream of thinking – that real wage rates would *grow* faster relative to output per head in a steady-state of higher employment; but whether markups would manage to recapture some of the loss of share going to capital if employment were maintained in its disequilibrium situation is hard to say on the basis of scant evidence and nonpowerful statistical methods.

There have been sporadic efforts at a more systematic and intensive inquiry into the relation, if any, between the level of real wage rates and the level of employment, making use of data accumulated since World War I. The earlier of these studies are not among the glories of modern econometrics: They confuse rates of change with rates of acceleration, fail to detrend variables, and mistake transient relationships among levels for permanent relationships among rates of change. The later and most careful studies, however, are fairly convincing against the wage-lag hypothesis as a description of the American economy in the postwar period and, less surely, in the interwar period as well. And one study of longer-term historical data for this country also finds that real wage rates have tended to peak coincidentally with the employment cycle.[21]

At this point we ought to address a more sophisticated argument that might be advanced toward the contention that owners of capital gain at the expense of owners of human capital when unexpected inflation drives employment above its natural level. It is conceded

[21] An extensive survey of the past literature and a new econometric analysis of American and Canadian data is contained in R. G. Bodkin, 'Real Wages and Cyclical Variations in Employment', *Canadian Journal of Economics*, January 1969. The historical study referred to is C. D. Long, 'The Illusion of Wage Rigidity: Long and Short Cycles in Wages and Labor', *Review of Economics and Statistics*, May 1960. It might be mentioned in this connection that the historical thesis that the 'price revolution' beginning in sixteenth-century Spain helped to depress real wage rates and thus to inaugurate an era of more rapid economic development has undergone some revision by economic historians in the past few years.

TABLE 5.4. *LABOR EARNINGS, PERCENT OF*
GROSS NATIONAL PRODUCT

Year	Gross Compensation of Employees as Percentage of G.N.P.	Unincorporated Enterprise Income as Percentage of G.N.P.
1954	57.0	7.6
1955	56.4	7.6
1956	58.0	7.5
1957	58.0	7.4
1958	57.6	7.4
1959	57.7	7.3
1960	58.4	6.8
1961	58.2	6.8
1962	57.8	6.6
1963	57.7	6.4
1964	57.8	6.4
1965	57.5	6.2
1966	58.1	6.0
1967	58.9	5.9
1968	59.3	5.7

TABLE 5.5. *REAL WAGE AND AVERAGE PRODUCT IN*
PRIVATE BUSINESS SECTOR

Year	Hourly Wage of Standardized Labor Input in Private Business Sector	Consumer Price Index	'Real' Hourly Wage of Standardized Input
1954	2.28	93.6	2.44
1955	2.38	93.3	2.55
1956	2.52	94.7	2.66
1957	2.66	98.0	2.71
1958	2.78	100.7	2.76
1959	2.91	101.5	2.87
1960	3.00	103.1	2.91
1961	3.07	104.2	2.95
1962	3.22	105.4	3.06
1963	3.32	106.7	3.11
1964	3.48	108.1	3.22
1965	3.65	109.9	3.32
1966	3.93	113.1	3.47
1967	4.18	116.3	3.59
1968	4.53	121.2	3.74

that real wage rates are not depressed by above-natural employment. But it is contended that the workers are not fully compensated for the disutility of their additional sacrifice of leisure. As illustrative of such an argument, we may take the theory that workers are duped into working longer hours and in more jobs than they would ordinarily choose at the real wage rates prevailing in the boom because they overestimate the purchasing power over future consumer goods of the portion of their extra wages that they save. Thinking of some normal price trend, they are by implication counting on some offsetting future unexpected *de*flation (the shortfall of actual from expected inflation) to erase the believed temporary effect on the trend of living costs of today's unexpected inflation.

Of course, each household and each firm can do better than it is doing, whatever the public policies followed, if it alone can see into the future and what the government will be doing. The government has to take great pains in many areas to see that information on its intentions are not arbitrarily or discriminatorily given to any individuals or groups for their private gain at the expense of a private loss for others and, most likely if an intelligent policy is being pursued, for a social loss as well. The question is whether households bear any loss from the deception implicit in a controlled policy of greater-than-natural employment.

The essential reply is that owners of capital are similarly deceived. They are led to speed up the utilization of their capital goods having a user-cost fixed-running-time characteristic and exhaustible resource holdings. If capital and labor are equally susceptible to the unexpected inflation – as the real wage data strongly suggest – we are, so far as the functional share issue of profit inflation is concerned, simply back to the question of the efficiency or inefficiency of the macroequilibrium level of resource idleness.[22]

There is, lastly, a popular objection that needs briefly to be considered. If episodes of unexpected inflation and abnormally low unemployment are typically so enjoyable for the poor and even the middle-income wage and salary earners, why do they so frequently bring cries of economic pain? Why don't most people appear to feel better? A partial answer is that oft-times most people do feel better and the indicators of mental health are up. It is usually the high-income people who have the greatest influence upon media of public expression on the issues of inflation and unemployment. The well-

---

[22] Efficiency with reference to intertemporal models of labor force participation and capital utilization are sections 4.1.1 and, somewhat subliminally, 4.1.5.

off certainly are inconvenienced by the increased real costs of labor services, the widened bidding for luxury goods, and generally having to stand in line. The poor and middle-income people are more silent in their small pleasures at having a swell job or a wonderful raise. This observation just reinforces the evidence of the relative gain that high employment confers on the poor.

What is central, however, is that people will not tend to feel as prosperous and gratified by a boom as they might if the lion's share of the additional production is devoted to government expenditures which bring no sense of additional well-being comparable to private expenditures. A boom brought on by a war that uses 2 percent of total resources and which brings no sense of increased national security or gratification is not likely to engender Dickensian good cheer. Time and again, the big boom is given a black eye, fouled as it were before the bell rings in its bouts with lesser contenders.

5.3.5. Differential Effect of Inflationary Wealth Redistribution. What we have been discussing thus far has been the question of redistribution between human capital and tangible capital from unexpected inflation. No doubt much more could be said on this question but enough probably has been said to raise grave doubts that owners of tangible capital would gain at the expense of owners of human capital. There seem to be no reasons for supposing that the under-expectation of inflation works to the disadvantage of labor as against capital. Nor did we find any evidence supporting a contention that it does in this country today. Consequently there is no reason on this account to believe that the unexpected inflation necessary for holding the unemployment rate below the natural level would nullify or vitiate the substantial differential gain to blacks and to the poor from a reduction of the unemployment rate. Hence the improvement in the share of (before-tax) real income going to the poor from a reduction of the unemployment rate does not appear to reduce the share going to middle- and upper-income wage and salary earners by more proportionally than the share going to capital.

Another kind of redistribution is that between wealth owners who hold their wealth predominantly in the form of capital or equity claims on capital and wealth owners who hold most of their wealth in the form of 'monetary assets' whose principal is fixed in the nominal value or whose nominal interest payments, if any, are fixed in advance – money, savings deposits, bonds, and the rest – *net* of those same persons' 'monetary liabilities'. The latter assets suffer a

reduction of their real market value when there is unexpected inflation. Hence, on this account, creditors lose from unexpected inflation
while debtors gain. Several dimensions of this phenomenon have
fascinated monetary economists for a very long time. Here the discussion will be confined for the most part to the stakes that the poor
and the blacks have in these redistributions of the real value of
wealth.

It might be thought at first that the poor can hardly have much
stake in these redistributions one way or the other. In fact that is not
far off the mark. Their wages and transfer payments are their main
sources of income. Yet the poor do have some monetary assets and
liabilities. A dose of unexpected inflation can have a magnified effect
on their real value and contribution therefore to future consumption
possibilities to the extent these holdings are long-term. This is
because the period during which actual inflation exceeds expected
inflation, however finite, must at the end of that period (other things
equal) leave the expected inflation rate higher than at the beginning
if expectations of the future inflation rate have the adaptive property
postulated in Chapter 2. As a consequence, a return to equilibrium
at zero unexpected inflation[23] – whether or not this entails, as on the
natural-rate hypothesis, that the unemployment return to the same
old level – would mean that the actual inflation rate must be correspondingly higher thereafter. Consequently the purchasing power of
these long-term assets will continue to erode over the future. An
equivalent conclusion results if these assets are sold in favor of new
ones. Abstracting from any changes of expected *real* rates of interest
attributable to the (temporarily or permanently) altered unemployment rate and the causes of that alteration – these are paper changes
of very little real consequence anyway – money rates of interest must
at the end of this period be higher by the amount of the increase of
the expected inflation rate (relative to what they otherwise would have
been). Therefore, in terms of the cost of living at the moment the
unexpected inflation ends, these assets must be selling at a greater
discount.[24] So, looked at in these ways, a small finite dose of unexpected inflation can have an effect on the present discounted real
value of a person's consumption possibilities over his remaining life

[23] Or to any specified subsequent path of the quantity of unexpected inflation.
[24] For analytical purposes in the ordinary case, we can charge all of this
period's unexpected inflation to this year (as reflected by asset revaluations)
rather than, for each future period, keep a memory bank of each past period's
expectations.

span that is magnified to the degree the monetary assets held are long-term.

It is repeatedly said that inflation is an arbitrary 'tax' that is 'cruelest' on the poor. This is a somewhat unusual use of the term 'tax'. In Chapter 6 I shall liken the *expectation* of inflation to a tax in that it inhibits consumer spending. Hence, it does a job like, and may substitute for, ordinary taxes that governments commonly levy. But the sense in which an actual rise of prices in excess of expectations is truly like a tax is even more restrictive.

Even if unexpected inflation were properly termed a tax in the fullest sense, it is hard to see why that should condemn it. The payment of taxes is, up to a point, a welcome alternative to government borrowing or conscription. Taxes are not involuntary tributes to a foreign power. In the same way, when a bout of unexpected inflation reduces the real value or purchasing power of the fixed monetary assets, it is not as if these assets were unfortunate loans to foreigners that are now worth less. On the whole these sorts of assets held by Americans are the liabilities of Americans. Primarily, therefore, an unexpected inflation simply redistributes real net worth from people who have a positive net holding of monetary assets, net of monetary liabilities, to persons with a negative holding – from creditors to debtors.

When we come to look at the data we will find, notwithstanding, that nearly all groups manage to have a positive position in these holdings of fixed monetary assets. The most important factor that makes this possible, of course, is the existence of positive government indebtedness, at nearly every level of government but especially at the federal level. This federal indebtedness consists roughly of government interest-earning bonds held by the public and held by the Federal Reserve Bank. The latter is the 'outside quantity of money'; it is transformed into deposits of commercial banks with the Federal Reserve which are not money for the nonbank public, and currency in circulation, most of which is money; its essence is that it equals that part of the government debt which has been monetized by the central bank, so that it is equal to that sum of money outstanding that is not attributable to and hence not matched by the liabilities of privately owned commercial banks. Another factor that adds to the net holdings of fixed monetary assets by households is the failure of the available data to net out from these holdings the monetary liabilities of the corporations in which the various persons hold equity interests.

Let us now consider whether the poor and the blacks are heavier net holders of these monetary assets relative to their respective net worths without waiting to make a variety of interpretive caveats beforehand. The basic studies of American data with which economists have been familiar for more than a decade all show that it is the prosperous, not the poor, who are vulnerable to unexpected inflation on this account. The lowest income bracket of families always displays the smallest net holdings of these fixed monetary assets relative to net worth. The most important explanation is that the poor are frequently in debt. The high-income people are not in debt as a group.[25] Perhaps the low-income persons in a single year are in debt partly because they feel themselves to be only temporarily

TABLE 5.6. *NOMINAL FIXED-VALUE MONETARY ASSET HOLDINGS NET OF LIABILITIES BY FAMILY INCOME CLASS, AS PERCENTAGE OF FAMILY NET WORTH*

Income (dollars)	*Net Monetary Assets[a] (percent)*	*'Real' Assets[a] (percent)*	*Real Assets as Percent of Gross Assets[a] (percent)*
0–999	8	92	88
1,000–2,999	15	85	87
3,000–4,999	13	87	84
5,000–7,449	15	85	88
7,500 or more	15	85	95

[a] From A. Ando and G. L. Bach, 'The Redistributional Effects of Inflation'. See also J. Conard, 'The Causes and Consequences of Inflation'.

low in income and have borrowed more than they would if they believed themselves to be permanently at their current income level. Yet the permanently poor can feasibly go through virtually their whole life financing consumer durable purchases through borrowing. Some of them may very well elect to do so on the calculation that the opportunities foregone by not waiting to buy durables outright,

[25] See G. L. Bach and A. Ando, 'The Redistributional Effects of Inflation', *Review of Economics and Statistics*, February 1957, and J. C. Conard, 'The Causes and Consequences of Inflation', in the Commission on Money and Credit volume, *Inflation, Growth and Employment* (Englewood Cliffs, N.J.: Prentice-Hall, 1964). I understand that these papers rely on 1958 household data on which the most detailed source became R. W. Goldsmith and R. Lipsey, *Studies in the National Balance Sheet* (New York: National Bureau of Economic Research, 1961).

investing the funds in savings accounts, and the like until they amount to enough, are insufficient to justify waiting instead of borrowing; such a calculation is less likely to be made by owners of larger amounts of wealth who can get higher yields on their earning assets.

Another reason possibly, though there is still some controversy on the point, is that money is a 'luxury good' that occupies a larger fraction of the portfolios of high-income people. Certainly the prosperous can better afford the opportunity costs of holding no-yield money than can the poor and middle-income groups, though they can also better afford the risks of high-return equity investments. It may be that because the convenience yield or amenity value of liquidity is not a part of taxable income, there is a stronger incentive for high-income people to avail themselves of the advantages and convenience of money-holding than there is for the poor and middle-income groups. Moderately recent evidence on the financial characteristics of consumers lends some support to the contention that the disposable-income elasticity of demand for highly liquid assets is greater than one.[26]

In examining the comparative 'vulnerability' of the poor to a loss of real market value from an unexpected inflation, one should consider that the nonhuman net worth of the poor is quite small relative to the overlife consumption expenditures (and receipts of income-in-kind from public assistance) of the poor. One reason is the inheritance of a comparatively large amount of nonhuman capital by the nonpoor. Another reason is that the low-income person can expect to receive a comparatively larger fraction of his income from public transfer payments right through the retirement years to death so he need save comparatively less. These features receive the proper weight if we focus on the real capital losses of low-income persons relative to their total income. A recent study of the vulnerability of the poor to unexpected inflation examines the financial data of median families below the official poverty line, both for all ages and for the aged separately. According to these estimates, a 5 percent quantity of

[26] See the regression results and references to earlier literature in J. Crockett and I. Friend, 'Consumer Investment Behavior', in *Determinants of Investment Behavior* (New York: Columbia University Press, for the National Bureau of Economic Research, 1967), pp. 50–52, especially. Using Federal Reserve Board data of household finances in 1962, these authors report a disposable-income elasticity of 1.57 and 1.07, the former figure referring to a sample in which the income distribution at either end has been truncated more sharply than the latter figure.

unexpected inflation would create a real capital loss of only one-sixth per cent of annual income for median poor families with non-aged heads, and one-quarter percent of annual income of median poor families with aged family heads (Table 5.7).[27] The nonpoor would experience much larger capital losses relative to income.

Do these data warrant the conclusion that the nonpoor stand to be the comparative losers in terms of nonhuman capital holdings from unexpected inflation? Two qualifications are important. It makes

TABLE 5.7. *VALUE OF TYPES OF ASSETS FOR FAMILIES WITH INCOME BELOW THE POVERTY LINE (AND NET WORTH BELOW $50,000) IN 1961*

	Median Values			Mean Values		
	Nonaged Head	Aged Head	All Heads	Nonaged Head	Aged Head	All Heads
Net worth	1,823	5,121	2,434	5,539	6,418	5,845
Fixed value assets	790	607	743	2,932	2,224	2,686
Nonfixed value assets	317	2,384	611	3,516	4,570	3,883
Fixed value claims	58	17	23	910	376	724
Amount vulnerable to inflation	366	501	422	2,023	1,849	1,962
Income	1,336	1,059	1,164	1,660	1,149	1,482

Source: R. G. Hollister and J. L. Palmer, 'The Impact of Inflation on the Poor', Institute for Research on Poverty, University of Wisconsin, April 1969, p. 42, Table 12.

little sense, in speaking of the *nonpoor* as a group to regard their holdings of corporate debt as a source of their vulnerability to inflation. For it is the nonpoor families that own the common stock of the corporations who owe the corporate debt. In calculating a family's true net monetary asset position there ought to be added to its monetary liabilities (if any) the sum of its indirect indebtedness which takes the form of the *pro rata* corporate debt of the companies in which it owns shares. Then it becomes less clear that the nonpoor are deeper into net monetary assets than the poor.

[27] Hollister and Palmer, 'The Impact of Inflation', p. 42. See Table 5.7 here. The qualification may be mentioned that future real declines of the real value of the monetary assets await insofar as they are long term. But the poor do not hold bonds to speak of. Indeed, it is their monetary debts that are likely to be long term. So these calculations may conceal a definite gain.

For obtaining the true comparative net monetary position of the poor, we may also consolidate the commercial banks (as well as the other private financial institutions) with the corporate business sector. We do this on the assumption that nearly all bank stock, like corporate business shares, is owned by the nonpoor. Then we do not add to the monetary liabilities of the nonpoor families (who own the corporate shares) that portion of corporate indebtedness which consists of debts to the banks – only the corporate debt held by households. And we add as an addition to the nonpoor families' monetary liabilities the bank deposits held by all households – but not that held by corporate business. When we take the latter step, we see that the nonpoor are significantly less liquid than we might first have concluded from the foregoing data; much of their holdings of money constitute their own liabilities as owners of banks.

The standard conceptual basis for disentangling these various elements starts with the proposition that the corporations, banks, and other financial intermediaries owned by the nonpoor do not add to the value of the net monetary assets of the private sector in the aggregate.[28] This aggregate value remains equal to that part of the federal, state, and local government debt held by the public and that part held indirectly and embodied in debt monetized by the Federal Reserve System. To determine whether the poor have a larger share of their net worth in the form of net monetary assets than do the nonpoor, we simply need to compare the former share with the share of aggregate net monetary assets in aggregate private net worth.

The previous figures state that median monetary assets of poor persons, after subtraction of median monetary liabilities of poor persons, amounts to $422, or about 17 percent of the $2,434 median net worth of poor persons. (It would have been useful to obtain a consistent picture of the balance sheet of the median income-earner

[28] This does not mean that the creation of these financial institutions does not make a contribution to the efficiency of the economy in either or both of two ways, by improving the allocation of resources in the capital goods sector and by adding to portfolio diversification opportunities, hence wealth owner's surplus. There is a counterpart to this gain in the form of capital gains to those who are licensed or first seize the chance to operate private banks: The market value of bank shares may be greater than what would be predicted from the buildings and capital equipment owned by banks because some or all banks enjoy something of a monopolistic position conferred upon them by the government. But this does not imply that bank shares should be treated as a 'monetary' asset rather than essentially as a 'real' asset that, like corporate shares, tends to keep pace roughly with advances in the price level. A meticulous analysis would need to specify the monetary events occurring with, and perhaps contributing to, the unexpected inflation under discussion.

among the poor, but probably the figure of 17 percent is not far off; it is already much higher than the estimates of investigators in the 1950s.) Remarkably, that percentage is hardly different from rough estimates of aggregate net monetary assets as a percentage of aggregate private net worth. If we divide the federal debt held by the public directly or indirectly through the Federal Reserve holdings (about $300 billion) together with state and local government debt (about $130 billion) by a rough-and-ready estimate of private net worth of $2.5 trillion, we arrive at 17 percent.

One could quarrel with the implicit assumption that the value of corporate shares (in which the nonpoor have almost the sole stake) would keep up with the price level in a period of unexpected inflation. There may be only a long-run tendency for share values to do so, and undoubtedly the matter is more complicated than that. Moreover, the data themselves are certainly shaky as their variability from source to source would suggest. Nevertheless we have learned enough to doubt that the net worth of the poor is more inflation-vulnerable than is the net worth of the nonpoor. When one considers that nonhuman net worth is a comparatively less important income source for the poor than for the nonpoor one emerges with the conclusion that the relative position of the poor is improved by unexpected inflation on this account.

Nevertheless there are always stones still left unturned (or anxiety springs eternal). It could be that some loss in comparative real income for the poor would come about through reduction of the real value of predetermined government transfer payments as a result of unexpected inflation. This is the subject of the next and final section.

5.3.6. *Real Transfer to the Poor.* There is some evidence, if any be needed, that legislators think about money transfers in real terms.[29] But, as with households and firms, they often operate on incomplete information. When, as predicted by the natural-rate hypothesis, the reduction of the unemployment rate is accompanied by a rise in the quantity of unexpected inflation, that unexpected inflation is unlikely to have been anticipated by the legislators when they determined the money amounts of income-transfers to the poor. It can be said, therefore, that the unexpected inflation reduces the real value of the previously determined transfers to the poor. If the money transfers are determined annually and if the rise of the inflation rate each year

[29] N. W. Swan, *Inflation and the Distribution of Income*, doctoral dissertation, University of Pennsylvania, 1969.

is continually underanticipated by a percentage point, the real value of the money transfers made each year will always be 1 percent less than what the legislators anticipated and what the majority of them intended.

Where the periodic review of a transfer program is less frequent or the review is occasioned only by the perception of some critical shortfall in real transfers from what had previously been intended, the real value of the predetermined money transfers will be falling at an increasing proportionate rate; for if the expected inflation rate maintains a constant distance behind the actual inflation rate but rises in adaptation to the underexpectation of each year's actual inflation rate, the actual inflation rate will be rising over time.

It is always open to the legislators to review annually the money amounts being devoted to the various transfer programs it has established. The cost of this annual review is the decision-making time it occupies of the legislators, and perhaps the uncertainty it creates for the beneficiaries of the programs. The social security program benefits have been revised every 2 or 3 years by the Congress in recent years, in 1965, 1968, and again in 1970. The successive years of unexpected inflation between 1965 and 1969 did not prevent an actual rise in the real value of the transfer payments under this program. Yet the real value of the transfers may in each year have been less than intended.[30]

It is not inevitable, however, that any loss of real transfers from what was intended by the legislators is gone forever. Legislators may exercise their powers not only to anticipate higher inflation when they find their previous predictions were too low; they may also exercise their powers to make up some or all of the previous unanticipated real income loss (for those surviving beneficiaries at any rate). This is most practical and likely where the legislators plan routinely to review the transfer program frequently in the future anyway so that no mounting future overrecoupment is implied by a decision to compensate for past losses. No doubt this is impractical where the unanticipated real losses are trivial amounts arising from slight or unperceived underanticipations; but small real losses are also of small concern.

We have been looking at the possible effects of unexpected inflation on the outlay side. There is also the receipts side. An increase of

---

[30] The increasing support for tying social security benefits to the consumer price index within the Congress might be taken as some evidence for that interpretation.

the inflation rate in excess of the expected inflation rate also brings about an unanticipated rise in tax payments, even apart from its concomitant effects upon real output and employment.

It would be hard to say how the share of the total tax revenue paid by the poor is affected by unexpected inflation. We do not have a uniformly progressive overall tax structure; the poor bear a high share of total taxes by reason of regressive state and local taxation. But it may be that the marginal tax rate for the poor is closer to their average tax rate than is the case for the nonpoor. Then the share of taxes paid by the poor would be reduced a little on this account by the unexpected inflation. The share of taxes paid by the nonpoor will also be increased by unexpected inflation through the failure of legislators to adjust corporate tax rates for the unexpected decrease in the real value of permitted depreciation allowances.

The same factors just noted suggest that unexpected inflation brings a more-than-proportionate unexpected increase of tax receipts, so that the real value of taxes collected is thereby increased, again even apart from the accompanying increase of output and real incomes. This rise of real revenue might be a temporary benefit for the poor. However, by itself this inadvertent rise of tax rates on real incomes would not have lasting effects on government expenditures and transfers. There are nevertheless some minor lasting effects of an indirect character. There results from the real revenue increase an unanticipated reduction of the budgetary deficit (or unanticipated increase of the budgetary surplus) of the consolidated public sector. This retardation (or even reduction) of government indebtedness reduces the real quantity of future tax revenues necessary to service the government debt in the future. Furthermore, the unexpected inflation brings an immediate fall in the real value of the government debt already outstanding. As a result of these two factors, legislators will estimate that tax rates can be reduced and transfers increased – without any implied change in expenditures on public goods or subsidy programs – or, if real taxes and transfers are maintained, the tax revenues added and freed by the above factors can be used to finance new expenditure programs. There might be some mild tendency for the poor to gain disproportionately on either account or both.

We come finally to the tax and transfer effects of the unemployment reduction itself. Note that while the reduction of the unemployment rate may be assumed to be unanticipated by legislatures, we can assume that they will adjust quickly to the new level (or to its most pertinent fiscal effects). As we are discussing an unemployment re-

duction that is consistent with the achievement of allocative efficiency, it is fair to assume that production and real taxable income
will thereby be increased. The net progressivity of the tax system is
probably such as to raise government tax revenues in greater proportion than real incomes, so there is at first a gain in the relative
share of resources available to the public sector. As long as it lasts,
the distributive consequences of this shift is probably favorable to
the poor. It could actually be the case that the social security transfers to the aged – in particular to the aged poor – in 1969, while less
than the Congress intended they be in real terms when payments
were revised in 1968 because of the unexpected inflation rate increase
in 1969, were greater than they would have been had the level of
employment and production been at normal levels during that period.

Ultimately we might expect, however, that tax revenues would be
returned to some normal share of national income. The equiproportionate rise of real tax revenues with the rise of production produces
an 'income effect' on the real outlay of transfer moneys to the poor;
by itself this tends roughly to increase real transfers to the poor in
proportion to real tax revenues and real production. But the distributive bias of the unemployment reduction in favor of the poor
creates a 'substitution effect', for with the poor now better off compared to the nonpoor by virtue of the unemployment reduction (on
a before-tax-and-transfer basis), there is now less incentive to maintain at its customary level the amount of redistributive transfers to
the poor as a share of national income. But the cutback of transfers
is not so large as to nullify the pretransfer comparative gain to the
poor from the unemployment reduction.

I conclude that the effects of unemployment reduction and accompanying unexpected inflation upon the real transfers received by the
poor are not sufficiently predictable or sufficiently major to doubt
that, on balance, the poor as a group are the comparative gainers
from the unemployment reduction.

6 Efficiency and Distributional Aspects of Anticipated Inflation

CHAPTERS 4 and 5 dealt with the consequences for distribution and efficiency of a change in the actual inflation rate, 'holding constant' the expected inflation rate. The subject of this chapter is the consequence for efficiency and distribution of a change in the expected inflation rate which is matched by an equal change of the actual inflation rate. It will suffice to examine, in particular, the equilibrium cases in which the actual rate of inflation is exactly equaled by the expected inflation rate. Except insofar as the government can effect a change of the expected inflation rate by announcement of its intentions or its forecasts and the like, it is of course true that the move from one equilibrium inflation rate to another will be marked by a disequilibrium transition of the sort studied in Chapters 4 and 5. Having covered disequilibrium previously, we can confine ourselves in this chapter to 'comparative statics' analysis of alternative equilibrium inflation rates.

This kind of analysis can be found in the economic literature under the heading of anticipated inflation. An inflation is said to be 'anticipated', or sometimes 'fully anticipated', if the current inflation rate is equal to the current expected inflation rate *and* if the current rate of inflation was earlier anticipated as far back in time as the age of the oldest currently existing money contracts outstanding. This year's inflation may be 'expected' this year but it may not have been anticipated in the past. Therefore an unanticipated increase of the equilibrium inflation rate, such as our comparative statics analyses will involve, will produce a wave of future price increases which will not have been anticipated. The redistributional consequences of such unanticipated losses and gains to creditors and debtors have already been covered. The distributional aspects needing attention here are only those pertaining to the rate of anticipated inflation. (We will still have to take cognizance of asset revaluations in an equilibrium shift, but for other reasons.)

After a brief introduction, the following sections discuss the consequences for allocative efficiency of the choice of the equilibrium inflation rate. The first two of these discusses the effect of inflation on the contribution of money to exchange efficiency under assumptions such that 'monetary-efficiency' is the only one of relevance. The subsequent section discusses overall monetary-fiscal efficiency in exchange from a more general and realistic point of view. The distributional consequences of the choice of the equilibrium inflation rate are taken up there. The final section brings in some other practical aspects involving the role of money as a unit of account and the associated question of the 'credibility' of the government's stabilization target when 'zero inflation' is desanctified.

6.1. *Preliminary Remarks on the Pure Theory of Money and Banking*

As is common knowledge in our society money plays four roles: as the medium of exchange, the unit of account, a store of value, and a source of anxiety.[1] Each of these roles stems from the first of these functions. Money *is* whatever has currency as the main medium of exchange. These things are well known, but a brief review may help to set the stage.

The theory of money as the principal medium of exchange, like the theory of unemployment, turns on the existence of frictions in the conduct of transactions between buyers and sellers of both goods and factor services. Fundamentally, these frictions arise from the imperfect information, and hence assurance, that each of us has that others will be able or willing to honor their credit obligations. Uncertainties about the future and the great heterogeneity of would-be borrowers and of the assets they would purchase combine to limit the amount of credit that each borrower can obtain (at terms he could afford to pay). There is a use, therefore, for some kind of money to 'keep people honest': with cash in hand, individuals can make some purchases which, while economically sound, they could not make on credit. The opportunities for trades are thus widened and markets are made less imperfect. Of course, the existence of this medium of exchange (in a limited amount) does not eliminate the extension of credit, especially to borrowers about whose credit worthiness there is good information; it may actually encourage useful extensions of credit.

---

[1] My facetious fourth function, no more obscure than that of the textbooks, calls many things to mind. The popular worry and excitement aroused by 'monetary instability' or the risk of it may indeed be a mildly productive conduit for the release of excess social tensions, or perhaps, more frequently, a counterproductive deflection of healthy social concerns. In another vein, one economist actually refers to people's concern for the safety of cash and the costs of guarding it!

It is possible to imagine, however, the development of customs in which certain liabilities (credit instruments) of some private borrowers come to be so easily exchangeable for goods at such predictable future market values that these private debts serve as money. But the prevailing wisdom for many decades has been that a laissez-faire system of private money creation 'cannot manage itself', at least not satisfactorily. What has evolved is basically a system of fiat money declared legal tender by the government and, adjoined to it, a limited system of privately created money that is guaranteed to be exchangeable at par for this fiat money and the quantity of which is limited by the central bank, that is, the Federal Reserve. There are a few credit institutions, traveler check issuers and credit card companies, whose liabilities are readily accepted as a means of payment and the quantities of which are not under government control; but the market for this private money is still sufficiently limited that these institutions do not appear to impair significantly the reliability, imperfect as it is, with which the central bank can influence the demands (money offers) of households and firms for goods.

Nevertheless there is a spectrum of private liabilities (and government obligations) that to varying degrees constitute near money. Money is what is perfectly liquid, a dollar of it being readily acceptable for an amount of a good the money price of which is quoted at a dollar. The near moneys – time deposits, some commercial and government obligations – are not perfectly liquid: a 'dollar's worth' of these near moneys cannot generally be used to buy an amount of goods the money price of which is a dollar. This is because the heterogeneous specialized nature of these assets imposes transactions costs in exchanging them for money or for one another. Finding a buyer at a specified price is risky, and if a specialist takes over that risk he charges a brokerage fee. For this same reason these near-money assets will be purchased and held by the people only if their pecuniary return is expected to be sufficiently above any pecuniary return earned by holding money to compensate for their lesser liquidity. The same is true of capital claims (equities and the rest), most of which are even less liquid. Taking for granted the convention that only money is used as payment, the demand for money to hold or the finiteness of the velocity of money is ultimately dependent, given a spread between the respective pecuniary returns, upon the presence of these transactions costs.

It is also natural that fiat money, being the most frequently traded item, should serve as the unit of account. The goods value of a unit of money is normally known with more certainty than the other-goods-value of some other good; normally the 'money price level' is more accurately estimated by people than the 'price level' of goods in general relative to some particular good that might be conceivable as a *numeraire*.

Finally, fiat money and other money exchangeable at par with it plays a role as a store of value. But the wealth represented by fiat money and other money does not necessarily make a net addition to the real value of private wealth owned by the households in the economy. The same may be said of interest-bearing public debt. It is possible that the real value of the money supply is 'backed' in part by earning assets held by the government so that the net indebtness position of the government is less than the real value of its fiat money outstanding and its interest-bearing obligations held by the public. More precisely, those assets of the government that earn user charges paid by the public (net of operating costs) or other rents paid by the private sector constitute a deduction from the addition to private wealth made by fiat money and public debt in the hands of the public in toting up net government indebtedness. Fortunately, the question of the benefit to be gained from a net contribution by the government to private wealth by debt plus fiat money creation is largely separable from the question of optimum anticipated inflation. But the extent to which money may have a comparative advantage over other assets in this function deserves some attention.

So much, by the way of preliminaries, for the theory of money in the narrow or traditional sense. We should add that in this country (as in most others) money is also involved in the theory of loan-banking and financial intermediation. The fractional reserve system on which commercial banks operate in this country places them in the role of financial intermediaries. The net amount of money created by the commercial banks has a counterpart in the loans and investments undertaken by private commercial bankers. It is widely agreed that there is some gain in the efficiency of financial allocations from the existence of some funds for the disposal of loan specialists and poolers of risk such as commercial banks.

We shall need some definitions. The three kinds of fiat money – government currency, coin, and deposits at the Federal Reserve System – sum up to what may be called the quantity of outside money. This quantity is 'outside' in the sense that it is an exogenous datum for the private sector of the economy. The deposits at the central bank are not themselves money, as they are not held directly by the public.

These deposits are held by the commercial banks and serve as the base for a quantity of demand deposits at commercial banks that is larger than the base by some multiple determined by the fractional reserve ratio. It will be harmless to follow the relatively standard practice of defining these demand deposits held by the public together with their holdings of coin and currency as the total quantity of money. Then the excess of this total over the aforementioned outside quantity may be called the quantity of inside money. This last quantity is the sum lent or invested by the commercial banks – abstracting from the other loans and investments they make in connection with their time deposit business.

I have been discussing some rudiments of the pure theory of money – or more accurately, the pure theory of *some* money. This is like the pure theory of international trade that assures us that some amount of trade can be found which is superior to no trade. Some amount of 'moneyness' or liquidity is desirable as grease to overcome the frictions of imperfect information and uncertainty in the economic machine. But how much liquidity? Specifically, how does the selection of the equilibrium or expected rate of inflation affect the contribution that money makes to economic efficiency?

I begin this inquiry under the instructive yet ultimately indefensible assumption that the 'marginal social costs' of raising tax revenues and of stabilization operations are zero. The reasons why that assumption must finally be abandoned, and the ramifications of its abandonment for the answers to the above questions, are the subject of section 6.4.

6.2. *Monetary Efficiency: The Medium of Exchange*

Here I shall abstract from banking aspects of the subject, reserving this side of the question for section 6.3. Specifically, I shall suppose that the quantity of inside money is equal to zero. One can still, if he wishes, imagine the presence of demand deposits at private commercial banks, but such banks would have to be conceived as being required to keep 100 percent reserves against those deposits, thus earning whatever profits their competition allows them only through customer charges for banking services rendered.

In this rarefied setting it is fitting enough to assume that the marginal social cost of creating money and of maintaining any given real quantity of it are zero, or are at least negligible. The emphasis here is on currency. In the next section, where commercial banking is intro-

duced, it will be important to consider various social costs of adding to the economy's liquidity.

Why should the rate of anticipated inflation have anything to do with the determination of the amount of liquidity that will prevail in macroequilibrium? The relevant concept of liquidity is the real value of the quantity of money, normalized in some way to adjust for changes in the size of the capital stock or the population of the country. If the nominal supply of money is taken as fixed, we still have to view the real value of that supply as a 'variable' in macroequilibrium with an equilibrium value corresponding to the specified macroequilibrium: then the price 'level' at any given moment of time must be such as to make the real value of that supply equal to the quantity of money demanded when expressed in real terms. If, instead, the path of the price level is taken as fixed, the supply of money must somehow be adjusted to such a level that its real value is equal to the real quantity of money demanded. In either case, macroequilibrium requires that the real quantity of money be always equal to the real quantity of money demanded. Hence, the rate of anticipated inflation, if it affects the liquidity of the economy in macroequilibrium, will do so through an effect on the real demand for money.

The principal influence of the equilibrium rate of inflation upon the real quantity of money demanded is through its effect on the opportunity cost of holding money – at least if, as asserted by the natural unemployment rate hypothesis, the volume of transactions that people would otherwise like to undertake would not be appreciably affected by the anticipated inflation rate. Given the rate of pecuniary return (if any) that is paid to holders of money, the faster the expected rate of inflation the larger each individual will perceive the opportunity cost of holding any amount of money in real terms to be. If you are holding cash and shopping now, the opportunity cost of shopping further for a better buy will be greater the more likely you think it is that those relatively better buys will be marked up in price before you find them. Under the equilibrium conditions specified here, the opportunity costs of waiting to invest in stocks or bonds will also be increased by an increase of the expected inflation rate: Share prices will on average be rising, and be expected to rise, at a rate which is increased by the same amount, and bond prices will be sufficiently down to offer a comparable increase in the nominal yields (including subsequent capital gains to maturity) expected by bond purchasers. These increased opportunity costs will induce a reduction in the real quantity of money demanded. Liquidity is thus decreased.[2]

If in fact holders of money would receive a matching increase in the pecuniary return on money when there was such an increase in the equilibrium rate of inflation, there would of course be no resulting increase in this opportunity cost of holding cash. But of course fiat money in this country pays no own-interest at all and, especially with reference to coin and currency, there are sufficient reasons why it would not be good economic policy to institute such interest payments.

One could say that the government has been somewhat exploitive, allowing itself to reap a *seigniorage* that is the difference between the zero rate, at which princes and other lucky creators of money through history have been able to 'borrow', and that at which ordinary borrowers have had to pay. Our government is not forced to pay interest on its currency or even deposits at the central bank; it has a legal monopoly on the printing of currency and it keeps the expected inflation rate low enough that no commodity money or near money can come close to rivaling its money. There are good reasons why interest ought not to be paid on at least some types of government money. It is quite impractical to make interest payments to holders of coin and currency. The costs imposed by any system of periodic registry of cash holdings with local government offices would be likely to eat up any economic gains from the resulting encouragement to greater liquidity. In addition, it is imaginable that a benevolent government might reasonably regard the nonpayment of interest on its money (or at least the underpayment) as a justifiable user tax, believing that there were more worthy uses of its scarce tax revenues. But this anticipates a portion of a subsequent section of this chapter.

We have established the notion that the smaller the anticipated inflation rate the larger, at least up to a point, the quantity of liquidity is. We have to ask now whether there exists an *ideal* quantity of liquidity and, if so, what the anticipated inflation rate must be – positive or negative, large or small – in order to achieve it in conditions of macroequilibrium.

[2] This result would at first not appear to be obtainable under the older version of the 'quantity theory of money' which makes the demand for real cash balances independent of the money rate of interest. Yet if such interest inelasticity were only the consequence of the 'income effect' of the rise in opportunity cost of liquidity, the result would still follow, because the 'compensated' demand curve for money must be negatively sloped, in the appropriate analytical setting. See Section 6.4.

Those questions can be answered meaningfully only in terms of some reasonably specific conception of the structure of the economy in question, particularly in the relevant aspects. Partly for the sake of clarity and in part because the more sophisticated analysis of the subsequent section will especially benefit by it, I shall sketch a couple of ultrasimple types of monetary economies. In these types of economies, the population is stationary as is the technology. Government expenditure (outlays of the resource-absorbing type) is confined to consumption-type goods and is also stationary over time in real terms. Taxes are imagined to be lump-sum; they are not believed by any taxpayer to be related to his taxable income and so they have no substitution effects upon the taxpayer's incentives to work or to save or to be liquid. Any transfer payments by the government, such as compensations to the disabled, are equally lump-sum in character. Thus revenue-raising and stabilization by the government are socially costless.

Throughout this section, merely to defer a complication, we exclude the government from creating money by the means of 'open-market' purchases of securities from the public. But, as the alternative to tax finance, the government can in effect print money to make its transfer and expenditure payments. In stationary equilibrium the real value of the money printed in any interval of time will be offset by equal real capital losses over that interval on existing outside money from the anticipated inflation rate corresponding to the rate of growth of the money supply.[3]

It is in this setting that the concept of the optimum rate of anticipated inflation has most often been discussed in the literature of the past decade – though, paradoxically, an optimum is somewhat less likely to exist in this situation than in the banking situation introduced in the next section. The 'optimum', here as throughout this chapter, is conceived in a static way, neglectful of any costs of

---

[3] We add some realism when we ultimately allow for the presence of government interest-bearing debt and the existence of a central bank which can buy or sell these government bonds and possible private interest-bearing liabilities or wealth claims as well. Then each stationary equilibrium will be marked by a certain constant ratio of government debt to outside money in the hands of the public. Then the budget deficit (or surplus) can more realistically be viewed as being met by government borrowing (or lending) at interest, with the central bank regularly monetizing a certain fraction of each year's government borrowing. At first we are assuming, though, that the government neither borrows nor lends at interest vis-à-vis the public directly; any budget deficit is borrowed from the central bank and any surplus is hoarded rather than invested in the private sector.

benefits accruing in the transition from one macroequilibrium (with its level of liquidity) to another macroequilibrium (with its different quantity of liquidity). In this comparative statics sense, I shall refer to the *ideal* quantity of liquidity as that degree of liquidity at which the marginal social benefit from greater liquidity equals the marginal social cost of higher liquidity. The optimum inflation rate in this idealized setting is that which produces the ideal degree of liquidity.

6.2.1. *Full Transaction Liquidity*. According to an increasingly familiar argument of recent years, there does exist such an optimum in the kind of model under discussion. In this kind of model the marginal social cost of liquidity can be taken to be zero – at least in the neighborhood where the corresponding rate of anticipated inflation imposes no calculational costs on persons of making allowances for rapidly changing trends in money wage rates and money prices. Yet there can be expected to exist a level of liquidity at which the marginal social benefit of liquidity is also zero. When liquidity has reached the point at which a further increase would not reduce further the frictional costs to individuals of exchanging goods and services with one another, the marginal social benefit of liquidity is held to be zero and there is said to be *full liquidity*. The argument is thus that, with respect to money as a medium of exchange, monetary efficiency requires that there be full liquidity.[4]

The concept of full liquidity has its origins in inventory theoretic models of the behavior and composition of an economic unit's transactions balances when, as usual, there is nonsynchronization of payments and receipts owing to the specialization of labor, the non-coincidence of wants, and so on. The periodicity of income receipts and of some expenditures causes periodic peaks in total transactions balances. These peak balances may be large enough in some households to induce them to invest a fraction in earning assets for a time when the pecuniary return on the latter, the various money rates of interest, are sufficiently above the zero pecuniary return to cash. A similar phenomenon can be expected to be found at many firms and may be quantitatively more significant. If the real yield on capital and equity claims is sufficiently large or the equilibrium rate of inflation sufficiently high, the nominal or pecuniary rates of return

---

[4] See E. S. Phelps, 'Anticipated Inflation and Economic Welfare', *Journal of Political Economy*, February 1965, and A. L. Marty, 'Money in a Theory of Finance', *Journal of Political Economy*, February 1961. Marty speaks of the satiety level of real cash balances.

available on interest-bearing assets will be large enough to encourage households to incur brokerage outlays to go in and out of earning assets, to divert their time from leisure or secondary jobs into activities such as more frequent banking to economize on cash, and to stimulate firms to divert some workers into performing financial tasks having the same purpose.

By shifting to a macroequilibrium with a sufficiently small inflation rate – perhaps a negative rate is required – the pecuniary yields on earning assets, which reflect the anticipated inflation rate, can be made small enough that there is insufficient incentive to invest any fraction of ordinary transactions balances in noncash assets. Money rates of interest on these nonmoney assets need *not* be brought to zero because of the transactions costs to each individual and firm of switching in and out of earning assets.[5] At a still lower spread in yields, the transaction demand for cash would remain at the same full-liquidity level though the quantity of cash demanded for speculative purposes would presumably be higher. Anticipated deflation is required for full liquidity if the real rates of return available on private liabilities and equity claims tend to exceed the threshold level determined by the transactions costs of switching in and out of them and by the lengths of the receipts and expenditure periods.[6]

6.2.2. *Full Precautionary Liquidity?* It is of some importance to consider the notion of ideal liquidity in terms of another motive for holding money – the precautionary motive. Cash is pictured as being held until an urgent need appears or an acceptable buying opportunity is found or presents itself. The emergence or opportunity could be a consumption act as well as an investment good.

In the above transactions demand analysis of money demand, it is

---

[5] This is depicted diagrammatically in Phelps, 'Anticipated Inflation'. A transactions model having this property is present in J. Tobin, 'The Interest-elasticity of transactions demand for cash', *REStat.* 38 (August 1956), pp. 241–247. Continuously variable models without set-up transactions costs miss this threshold feature.

[6] In a world of zero transactions costs, one might at first think of full liquidity as obtaining only at a zero spread, the anticipated deflation rate being matched to the real rate of return on capital so as to equate the real (nonpecuniary) yields on the two assets. All capital goods, fresh supplies as well as old capital goods and equity claims, would be willingly held as long as their real yields matched that of money, there never being a cost to switching freely from one asset to the other. But in that world where all nonmoney assets are themselves perfectly liquid, there would be no reason for money to exist.

the existence of privately owned capital and the various wealth claims to which it gives rise that provide to wealthowners their alternative to liquidity. Presumably much precautionary liquidity is likewise an alternative for households and firms to investing immediately in earning assets. I shall return in a moment to this source of precautionary demands for money

An important cause of demands by households for precautionary balances is their wish not to be unable to avail themselves of an attractive consumption purchase for lack of timely liquidity. It may be instructive to imagine, in the spirit of some modern researches into the foundations of monetary theory, that the economy produces only a polyglot of labor services, each man producing a heterogeneous consumption service unassisted by any tangible capital. Let us in fact at first exclude tangible capital and other tangible assets such as land. Money is the only store of value. Each 'producer' gropes his way through the imperfectly informed market looking for buyers of his service with the cash on hand to pay him the price he asks. As a 'consumer', he can accept (or, of course, reject) an offer to supply him with a consumption service if he has the necessary cash and he will accept occasional offers if the prices asked are low enough. The more liquid he can afford to become, the better are his chances as a consumer of not having to pass up extraordinarily attractive offers. Further, his liquidity serves him as a producer, for it saves him from having to make a drastic price reduction in the event of a distressing run of no sales. Hence, liquidity is a productive asset for the household and the more there is of it the larger the household's expectation is of 'real income' or consumption services received.[7]

In this quaint parable, liquidity is a capital good and it has a social as well as a private productivity. But it is not generally expectable that the typical household will individually be willing to make the 'apparent' consumption sacrifice necessary to accumulate liquidity to the point of maximum social benefit. Even without technological progress, 'pure time preference' may stand in the way of liquidity satiation, just as Schumpeter's savers of tangible capital leave some railroad track unstraightened. Yet if the marginal social cost of increasing liquidity can be taken to be zero, there would appear to be

[7] Correspondingly, other people's liquidity contributes to the individual's real income. The more liquid other people are the more easily will the individual be able to find buyers for his service who are liquid and so the higher his optimal relative price or rate of sales or both. On the other hand, the more liquid they are, .the better they will be able to hold out for higher prices from him as a buyer of their services.

a clear gain obtainable from reducing the rate of anticipated inflation so as to instill private incentives to greater liquidity. Liquidity
saturation should be sought if, unlike capital saturation, there is no
foregone consumption cost.

But is there a full-liquidity stopping place? It is not clear that any
individual would feel there to be no further private yield to greater
liquidity at any finite liquidity level. Just as there may always be
room for a little closer straightening of rail tracks, each household
may have an insatiable want for liquidity. In this case we may say
that the social benefits from liquidity are always improvable a little
by a still closer approximation of the anticipated deflation rate to the
aforementioned pure time preference rate.[8]

Let us now acknowledge that precautionary liquidity is an alternative to investing in some immediately available earning asset. Then
the precautionary demand for idle cash balances stems partly from
the wish to be temporarily liquid as a 'precaution' against being
unable to buy an especially attractive earning asset in timely fashion
for lack of liquidity. The smaller the mean pecuniary return he
expects to find available to him on earning assets, the smaller is the
expected opportunity cost of any average fraction of his wealth held
in liquid form. The individual owning a given amount of wealth will
be likely to hold a larger fraction of it in money form on the average,
amassing larger amounts of liquidity between investments and
making his investments in larger 'lots', the smaller the opportunity
cost is to him of staying liquid.

By engineering a smaller anticipated inflation rate over some range
the government can reduce the opportunity cost of precautionary
liquidity. This can be assumed to yield some social benefit by reducing
transactions costs (as in the earlier model), that is, reducing the
average rate of turnover of the representative man's portfolio: One
would expect that the typical individual would be encouraged to
omit relatively inferior investments usually held for short-term
between longer-term placements and to make the latter investments
in larger lots.[9] But the main benefit of the increased precautionary

---

[8] In these successive approximations, liquidity and the capital gains on money
would become enormous – but so would the taxes dictated by the budget surplus
necessary to shrink the money supply for realization of the deflation. Would
such a large liquidity overhang, in fact, impose a real social cost? The answer may
better be discussed under the assumption of the coexistence of tangible capital,
as in Section 6.3.1.

[9] It is not altogether clear, however, that individuals would be encouraged to
invest for longer durations, since the opportunity cost of taking cover in liquid

liquidity would be to improve the allocative effectiveness of the market for heterogeneous capital goods. If we think of the anticipated deflation rate as being successively increased in small amounts, the pecuniary rates of return to the relatively liquid types of capital goods such as inventories will, at their initial stock levels, come to be unfavorable compared to the zero pecuniary return on money. Now while macroequilibrium requires that the existing aggregate of capital be voluntarily held, there is no requirement that each kind of capital good be held in an unvarying quantity as the opportunity cost of liquidity is successively reduced. Let us stipulate that the investment sector can transmute capital goods. Then there will result successive shifts to less liquid types of capital goods as the premium on relatively liquid capital diminishes with increased money liquidity. Full liquidity, if it exists, may be characterized as having arrived when the opportunity cost of liquidity is so small that there is no liquidity premium to any type of capital good relative to another, since liquidity is no longer scarce.[10] But at any finite spread in yields, it is doubtful that there would be enough 'waiting' between investments such that no capital goods would exist which, owing to their extraordinary unfamiliarity and resulting thinness of the market for them, would promise a real rate of return somewhat above the norm. No finite quantity of liquidity can *perfect* the market for uncertain heterogeneous capital goods!

We can now take it as established, some might say overestablished, that the increase of liquidity associated with a decrease of the (algebraic) rate of anticipated inflation confers certain gains in monetary efficiency in terms of the present model. But a satisfactory understanding of the subject demands that we take up two loose threads much spun in the literature (one more than the other). One thread is the hypothesis that the anticipated inflation rate, in the process of altering the economy's liquidity, has an influence through its 'wealth effects' upon the rate of capital formation and hence ultimately upon the capital intensiveness of the economy. The other thread concerns the significance of inside money for the subject of monetary and financial efficiency. Both of these matters properly involve considering what scope the central bank may have for nulli-

money has diminished. The question of monetary 'stability' at low or negative rates of anticipated inflation will be taken up in Section 6.4. Let us attempt to abstract from this consideration here.

[10] This does not mean that there will not be *risk* premiums in rates of return.

fying or modifying certain side effects which a change of the anticipated inflation rate might otherwise have.

6.3. *Monetary Efficiency: Money, Debt, and other Stores of Value*

For centuries economists have sometimes suggested that anticipated
inflation is 'good for growth' in this way: it is an inducement to
greater thrift out of any given real income and hence it leads to some
additional capital deepening. There is a grain of truth to this; it will
be shown to be a part of a larger harvest from the more realistic
analysis given below. Here I shall try to show why this conclusion
does not necessarily follow in the present and more abstract setting
in which these matters are usually discussed. The real objective of the
present discussion is to grasp the potentialities of central bank action
in the present model, and so to learn some lessons of significance for
the more realistic analysis to follow.

6.3.1. *Liquidity and 'Growth'.* Early 'forced saving' analysts knew
that the anticipated capital losses on fiat money implied by anticipated inflation are a subtraction from consumers' spendable income:
they must set aside that much real income per unit time to maintain
their sustainable consumption stream intact, other things equal. But
the maintenance of the anticipated inflation implies that government
taxes must fall short of the budget-balancing level by such an amount
that the real value of the money freshly created by the government at
each moment is just enough to replenish the real anticipated capital
losses on the already existing real money supply. The saving 'forced'
by the latter is offset by the government's *dis*saving represented by
the former. This is for stationary equilibriums.

There now exist two modern reformulations of the old doctrine.
According to one argument, the real rate of interest (or real rate of
return on capital) at which households will hold a given amount of
capital is higher the larger the real value is of the outside money
which, when added to the value of the capital stock, constitutes
private wealth. If this is so, the monetary economist who is bent on
improving the monetary efficiency of the economy will find that, as
he engineers a lower anticipated inflation rate, the 'flight' into money
and the resulting increase in its real value engenders a decrease of
thrift, a shift of resources to consumer goods production, and thus
some rise of *real* rates of interest.[11] One would not expect this result

[11] R. A. Mundell, 'Inflation and Real Interest', *Journal of Political Economy*,
June 1963.

in an economy of infinitely lived families – or their Meadean equiva-
lents – who can be counted on to pass along all existing wealth into
the future so long as its real yield does not fall short of their pure
time preference rate. But one would expect to see this phenomenon
in a life-cycle model of household saving where not all wealth is
bequeathed in that fashion: then one would be prepared for some
displacement of private capital by the enlarged social capital that is
liquidity.

The second modern forced saving doctrine turns on the growth of
the economy in macroequilibrium. It is postulated that the economy,
if not continuously driven from macroequilibrium (i.e., from the
natural unemployment rate), will exhibit a tendency to steady geometric growth rather than toward a stationary state as assumed heretofore. For simplicity we suppose that geometric population growth
is the sole driving force; the economy's rate of output growth then
tends toward the population rate as the 'great ratios', like capital per
head, tend to level off. In this case, real money must steadily be
increased if the continuous additions to the population are to be
made as liquid as the existing population. Consequently, the real
value of the money created by the government to keep the real money
supply constant per capita (if the growth comes only from population
increase) must exceed the real capital losses on existing money from
any anticipated inflation going on by an amount equal to the level of
the real money supply multiplied by the steady growth rate. This is a
net addition to the aggregate real spendable income to be associated
with a given level of aggregate real production. One supposes that it
will add something to the demand for consumption goods. The
smaller the anticipated inflation rate selected, and hence the larger
the real money supply, the larger this addition is. Hence, as the
monetary efficiency expert 'tries' lower rates of anticipated inflation
in his quest for full liquidity, one can expect that there will tend (at
least eventually) to be an increase of consumption demand relative
to output (at macroequilibrium) and hence a tendency for capital
intensity to decline and the real rate of return to capital to find a
higher level in some new balanced-growth state.[12]

[12] J. Tobin, 'Money and Growth', *Econometrica*, January 1967. See also
D. Patinkin and D. Levhari, 'Money, Growth and Welfare', *American Economic
Review*, September 1968. It may be noted that if the level of liquidity is far from
'full', in that neighborhood the contribution that an increment of it makes to
output may for a while exceed its stimulus to consumption demand. But the
former vanishes as full liquidity is approached while it is entirely reasonable to
suppose that the latter does not.

There is an apparent conflict, therefore, between capital intensiveness as measured, for example, by the stock of capital per head (to
which the system tends) and liquidity as measured by the per capita
real money supply. But that conflict rests upon a questionable restriction: All money is outside money and all outside wealth is outside money. By outside wealth is meant the sum of outside money
and interest-bearing obligations of the government held by the
public net of any income-earning wealth or wealth claims held by the
government – all in real terms. It is the stock of outside wealth and
its increase that matter for consumption demand in the above
modern treatments, not the stock or increase of liquidity as such.
The link between the two can be broken as soon as we unleash the
central bank.

We now permit the treasury to run a budget deficit or surplus but
constrain it to cover such discrepancies with the issue (or retirement)
of interest-bearing obligations. We endow the central bank with the
control over the money supply – empowering it to 'monetize' all or
only a portion of the interest-bearing public debt and, if there is no
more of that left, perhaps to rediscount private wealth claims. If the
bank monetizes the entire public debt, no more and no less, we are
in the previous world where outside wealth equals outside money.
If it monetizes only a fraction of the public debt, outside wealth
exceeds outside money – by the amount of the interest-bearing
government debt held by the public rather than the bank. And if we
imagine the bank to monetize all the public debt and additionally to
make purchases of some private claims, outside wealth is then less
than outside money.

Variation of the fiscal tool – the budget deficit and hence ultimately the stock of public debt – together with the monetary tool –
open-market purchase and hence the supply of money – provide
enough control to achieve a change of liquidity without any concomitant change in thrift. The effect which an attainable increase in
the *real* money supply might otherwise have on capital intensiveness
or 'growth' can be neutralized by jointly compensatory fiscal-
monetary steps.[13] We can sketch an example:

Our hypothetical economy is initially in macroequilibrium at an

---

[13] The point is made geometrically (in too short-run a context) in Phelps,
'Anticipated Inflation'. An analysis of the choice of long-run paths available (in
the steady growth case) can be found in E. Burmeister and E. S. Phelps, 'Money,
Public Debt, Inflation and Real Interest', *Journal of Money, Credit and Banking*,
May 1971. Mention may also be made of some related work of a rather different
character by Foley, Sidrauski, Shell, Liviatan, and Sheshinski.

anticipated inflation rate of, for example, 5 percent per annum. It is also in a state of steady growth – real output, real public expenditure, capital, the real public debt (held by the central bank and the public), and the real money supply all growing at the same rate as population and the labor force, for example, 3 percent annually. Then the nominal public debt must be rising at 8 percent annually and the central bank must be monetizing an unchanging 'fraction' of that growing total (a fraction less or greater than one) so that the money supply is growing at the same rate. It follows that the annual real treasury deficit – the shortfall of taxes collected from expenditures, transfers, and interest payments to the public, all in real terms, that must be covered by borrowing – is equal to 8 percent of the real value of the public debt.[14]

Consider now that the government wishes to establish macro-equilibrium at 4 percent expected inflation and to do so without inducing any real-wealth effects upon thrift or consumption demand. Assume it were possible to reduce the expected inflation rate 'by announcement' without any interim of below-equilibrium employment and hence no unexpected 'drop' of the price 'level'. Immediately then the one-point reduction of the expected inflation rate will produce a rush from capital and capital claims (equities) into money; insofar as the public debt is not rolled over to pay the lower coupon rates of interest at which the public will now be willing to hold treasury obligations at par, there will be a rush into government interest-bearing obligations as well. Let us assume that treasury debt, to be held by the public, must promise the same real rate of return that is expected to be earned from equity holding. And let us further assume that the rate of money interest paid on the public debt is quickly adjusted downward by one percentage point so that government bonds do not appreciate relative to equities. There still remains an excess demand for money, its opportunity costs having been reduced by the one point fall of the expected inflation rate.

To shore up the demand for earning assets and hence the demand for goods – and thus to prevent an unexpected drop of the price level – the central bank need simply make whatever size open-market purchase of government debt from the public as is required to 'support' the money price of treasury obligations. Because the price level at 'time zero' is thus maintained and because the central bank

---

[14] The 'real deficit' is thus greater than the increase per unit time in the real value of the debt by the amount of the anticipated inflation rate times the real value of the debt.

pays a dollar for every dollar's worth of government debt purchased, the real value of outside wealth is consequently held constant. In this manner the central bank prevents a positive real-wealth effect that would stimulate consumption demand.

Note that with the time path of real outside wealth unchanged, the treasury must adjust its tax collections to reduce its annual real deficit to 7 percent of real outside wealth instead of 8 percent. But while the real deficit must be reduced by 1 percent of the unchanged real outside wealth, this does not necessitate an increase in real tax collections by that amount. The lower money interest to be paid on publicly held government debt automatically reduces the deficit by a fraction of the required amount equal to the fraction of outside wealth held in interest-bearing form. That leaves somehow to be accomplished a deficit reduction equal to 1 percent of outside wealth *not* in interest-bearing form; hence, 1 percent of outside money. But even this overestimates the tax increase by an amount equal to the interest payments the treasury makes on that amount of its debt which the central bank has purchased in the support operation, for this interest earned by the bank must be returned to the treasury.[15] So if the elasticity of the real value of the money supply with respect to the nominal rate of interest on earning assets is unity or greater (in absolute value), real taxes could be left alone or actually decreased while still meeting the requirement for a lower deficit. But so large an elasticity appears to be empirically quite unlikely, at least in the range of historically familiar money rates of interest. The likelihood that lower anticipated inflation requires higher rates of taxation if the volume of government expenditures and the willingness to accumulate wealth are to be left undisturbed will be a matter of major significance in the final assessment of the benefits and costs of increased anticipated inflation.

The proposition that emerges is that, over some range, the treasury and central bank can jointly control (after the necessary disequilibration) the rate of expected inflation and per capita real outside wealth; thus it can jointly determine liquidity and thrift. The point can be made another way which brings out a familiar point in

[15] Let C, G, Y, T, M, D, D_B, p, i, r, and x denote, respectively, real private consumption, government expenditure, income, and taxes; nominal money, government debt, and bank-held debt; money interest rate, real interest rate, and expected inflation rate. We have (1) $i - x = r$, (2) $C + G = Y$, and (3) $M = D_B$ at par values. Consumers' budget in stationary equilibrium is (4) $pC = p = pY - pT - xM + (i - x)(D - M)$. The deficit is (5) $F = pG + i(D - D_B) - pT$. Therefore, (6) $F = xD$ and (7) $pT = pG + i(D - M) - xD = pG + rD - (x + r)M$.

monetary theory which underlies it. Take the stationary case and for simplicity take the anticipated inflation rate as given; the latter determines the equal rate of growth of money and government debt outstanding. The 'levels' of money and publicly held debt at 'time zero' nevertheless remain to be determined. We know that if the levels of debt and money should each be increased equiproportionately, the macroequilibrium price 'level' will simply be increased in the same proportion, leaving real outside wealth and liquidity unaffected. If the 'level' of the money supply is increased by an open-market purchase, with no change in the existing level of the total debt, the price level must rise and so real outside wealth must fall. Liquidity in the sense of the interest spreads between earning assets is improved insofar as the decline of real outside wealth contracts

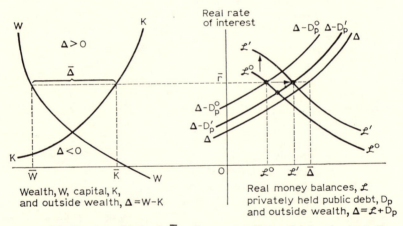

Wealth, W, capital, κ,
and outside wealth, Δ = W−K

Real money balances, £
privately held public debt, D_p
and outside wealth, $Δ = £ + D_p$

Figure 6.1 For a wealth level $\bar{W}$ and corresponding real interest rate, $\bar{r}$, the quantity of outside wealth must be $\bar{Δ}$. Of this, the public is willing to hold $£^0$ in liquid form at, for example, a zero rate of anticipated inflation. An open-market purchase, by reducing the privately held debt, for example, to D_p', would leave an excess supply of money at $\bar{r}$ and hence cause a rise of the price level which reduces $Δ$. The fall of $Δ$ would increase $£$ but only insofar as it reduced r through its stimulus to deepening of capital beyond $\bar{K}$. (The increase of $£$ thus induced will moderate the fall of r by its upward shifting of the KK schedule, which shift is abstracted from.)

An appropriate simultaneous decrease of the expected inflation rate, however, can nullify the wealth effect upon capital deepening from the open-market purchase. Such a decrease shifts upward the $££$ schedule by the amount of the decrease, since the same r then corresponds to lower money rates of interest. The induced flight into money just matches the open-market purchase, $D_p^0 - D_p'$, with the result that $£'$ is produced at the same $\bar{Δ}$ and $\bar{K}$. Without that purchase, $Δ$ would rise, forcing K down and r up.

consumption demand and thus leads to a fall in the nominal rates of return on earning assets.[16] An appropriate increase in the supply of outstanding public debt can nullify the decline of real outside wealth, but in so doing it will erase the rise in liquidity in the above sense. There is, therefore, a certain liquidity level available for each level of real outside wealth. Additional liquidity, in the sense of the term just employed, can be purchased only at the price of reduced real outside wealth and consequent additional capital deepening – *given* the constraint that the anticipated inflation rate cannot be tampered with. But if that constraint is relaxed, the attainable liquidity level that corresponds to any prescribed level of real outside wealth and hence capital intensiveness can be improved by the 'selection' of a lower rate of anticipated inflation.[17]

An interesting observation can now be made. When the central bank was excluded and the treasury issued money rather than bonds, our earlier assumption of convenience, driving down the anticipated inflation rate toward the full-liquidity point, had the consequence of driving the real value of the money supply to infinity. This was a feature of the precautionary liquidity model in which liquidity could always be increased by a further shrinkage of the private opportunity cost of being liquid. Yet this is clearly not a necessary consequence of driving the anticipated inflation rate toward the full liquidity point once we allow open market purchases by the central bank. Given that some level of real outside wealth is to be maintained and hence also the level of capital intensiveness corresponding to it, the approach to full liquidity cannot cause the real money supply to go to infinity; the reason is that the latter cannot exceed real outside wealth by more than the real value of the claims to private capital available for purchase by the central bank and there is only a finite amount of

---

[16] In a celebrated paper, L. A. Metzler deduces this without there being any interest-bearing debt and hence without any real capital loss on debt left outstanding after the open-market purchase. In his analysis, the loss of ownership of equities purchased by the bank reduces real *total* private wealth if the price level should rise in proportion to the money supply. This reduction lowers consumption, reduces the interest rate, and dampens the wealth decline. See L. A. Metzler, 'Wealth, Saving and the Rate of Interest', *Journal of Political Economy*, February 1951.

[17] It is clear now, it may be noted, that we need not view, as in the earlier example, the treasury as determining the rate of anticipated inflation and the central bank as determining real outside wealth. We could equally well view the central bank as determining the anticipated inflation rate by its selection of the rate of growth of the money supply if, accordingly, we charge the treasury with maintaining a deficit policy which keeps the real value of the public debt outstanding invariant to the money growth rate.

these (namely, the amount of capital per head that the given real outside wealth level causes to be sustained in macroequilibrium). What does go to infinity as the opportunity cost of being liquid goes to zero is the ratio of the real money supply to the capital stock *in private ownership*.

This innocent observation leads to the conclusion that (on the assumption just made of an insatiable demand for liquidity by households) full liquidity requires full intermediation by the central bank; the bank is the nation's stockholder and households hold the bank's money at a real rate of return (owing to anticipated deflation) with which equities cannot compete. It is obvious that there are strong objections to such a situation, objections involving real economic costs as well as ideological ones with which one might or might not choose to side.

We seem to have reduced the pursuit of full liquidity to a practical absurdity. In fact it will be the conclusion of this chapter that nothing like full liquidity should be sought by macroeconomic policy. But it should be understood that increases in liquidity, though not full liquidity, can be obtained by a different institutional means.

6.3.2. *'Inside' Money and Commercial Banks.* Once the anticipated inflation rate has been reduced to the point where all the public debt can be monetized without disturbing the quantity of real outside wealth, it is still possible to achieve a further increase of liquidity by the institution of private fractional reserve commercial banking. As was remarked earlier, the concept of the government-run monopoly bank in the previous setting could have been interpreted as a convenient expository device for describing the essential workings of a private banking system with 100 percent reserves under central bank control through its open-market operations. It is clearly possible for additional private assets to be monetized by reducing the fractional reserve requirement.

Assume, momentarily without questioning the assumption, that bankers are not permitted by law to pay interest on their customers' demand deposits. So there is a deposit rate ceiling at zero. It is also supposed that on the cost side there is 'free storage' of money deposits. Consequently, it is reasonable to suppose that the competition of banks with one another will prevent them from being able to 'tax' their customers' demand deposits. Then if the treasury and central bank contrive to lower the anticipated inflation rate – the operation we have been studying – there will be an increased demand for bank deposits in real terms. The private opportunity costs to households of holding bank money as well as currency will have decreased, if it is assumed that the real rate of return on earning assets is not appreciably altered. Then clearly the reduction of the fractional reserve requirement is a way that the central bank can accommodate the increased real demand for money; as before, the increase in liquidity takes place without the need for an interim period in which the price 'level' has to adjust to an inflexible money level rather than the other way around.

Now about that assumption. It is true that if the banks were permitted to pay interest and if the anticipated inflation rate were initially high enough, they would actually pay some money interest rate on money deposited with them. We might assume then that as the anticipated inflation rate is successively reduced by small amounts, this deposit rate falls by roughly the same amounts. In this case there would result no increase in the real demand for bank money, the opportunity costs of holding it not being reduced; indeed, there may be some runoff into currency. But the point is that as we are focusing in this section on ideal liquidity, we surely want to require that the opportunity costs of holding currency and holding bank money be roughly the same. This rules out achieving high liquidity in terms of bank money at the expense of currency illiquidity. Furthermore, if we are going to explore the attainment of ideal liquidity via the inside money route we can justifiably anticipate that this will entail a rate of inflation that is in the neighborhood of zero or perhaps negative. In that case, it might well be the case that the banks would not individually choose to pay interest to their depositors even if they were legally permitted to, the nominal earnings rates on their investments being so low. It is entirely appropriate in this section, therefore, to restrict ourselves to the case where deposit rates paid on bank money are zero.

We have argued that the increased demand for liquidity at a lower anticipated inflation rate can be accommodated without the necessity for central bank purchase of private liabilities or capital claims. It can be accomplished by 'inside monetization' instead of 'outside monetization'. Now the great virtue of outside monetization, developed in the previous section, is that it accommodates the increased demand for money in real terms without simultaneously allowing an increase in real outside wealth; this wealth level is the central way by which the government affects thrift and thus the room that is left, after consumption, for capital formation. So let us ask whether this inside monetization will have that same virtue.

The 'nonbank public' has sold some securities to the banks in return for an equal increase in their real holdings of bank deposits. But the owners of the banks are also people. Their assets are up in real value by the amount of the securities purchased. It is true that their liabilities are also up an equal amount, namely, by the amount of the increase in the deposits left with them. But if they do not have to pay interest on their deposits, as they do earn interest from their holdings of securities, the banks' profits are up and so is the market value of bank shares in real terms. Neglecting any increased costs from the larger scale of the banks' operations, bank shares will be increased in value by the amount of the securities purchased, which is to say by the amount of the addition to their deposits. Roughly, the real value of bank shares (in aggregate) has risen by the amount of the increase in the real money supply, and this rise in bank shares is a net addition to real private wealth.[18]

It would seem that, by the ingenious stroke of reducing the reserve requirement, the central bank has failed to accommodate the increased liquidity in such a way as to maintain the pace of capital formation. Those who were fortunate enough to own bank shares reap a windfall capital gain not matched by anyone else's capital loss, so that one would expect some increase in their consumption demand. The operation would appear to have been 'bad for growth'. This would not substantially be altered if the banks tended to compete away the increase in monopoly rents by nonprice competition for deposits that took the form of more numerous and more expensive bank branches and buildings. Capital is then diverted rather than displaced.

Yet this displacement or diversion of capital that we have deduced is a consequence of going from nothing to something. As the anticipated inflation rate is reduced further, there must come a point where bank profits fall as a result of the lower nominal interest rates earned on loans and security investments owing to the lower inflation rate. Over the range of anticipated inflation rates from 10 percent to zero, for example, it is not empirically certain whether the larger real quantity of bank-held earning assets made possible by a reduction of the anticipated inflation rate would overcome the corresponding

---

[18] If one likes, he can treat the addition to the real value of bank shares as an addition to real outside wealth on the argument that it is a rise in the capitalized value of certain government licenses.

fall of the spread between the interest rate paid on deposits and the interest rate earned on investments. It is fairly clear, I believe, that the opposition of many banks to *increased* inflation arises very largely from their unhappiness at experiencing windfall real capital losses on loans and investments contracted at nominal interest rates when the credit market was not anticipating the faster inflation. This wealth reduction is redistributive, not a net reduction.

Despite this zone of uncertainty with respect to the wealth effect, it will be instructive to finish the inside money tale. Let us first ask: If the anticipated inflation rate is further reduced toward zero and beyond, will full liquidity be approached? The accompanying decline in the nominal rates of return expected to be obtainable on earning assets will drive the public to attempt to rid themselves of an ever-larger fraction of these assets in favor of money the opportunity cost of which is correspondingly lower. This requires that reserve requirements of the commercial banks be reduced so that they can create the money deposits with which to buy these earning assets – loans, bills, and whatever other securities the banks are permitted to invest in. But like the proverbial horse led to water, the commercial banks are not thereby forced to drink down these investments. The banks themselves will have a precautionary demand for liquidity, and at a sufficiently small nominal rate of return on available earning assets the banks will prefer to hold reserves in excess of requirements. Even though the banks' depositors are insured against losses, the banks' own prudent self-interest will set a lower bound on the level to which the reserve ratio can be driven down. Because this bound is definitely above zero, full liquidity cannot be indefinitely approximated to; that is, there is some positive lower bound on the spread between the rates of return on earning assets and the zero return on money that is attributable to the incapacity of the central bank to induce the commercial banks to undertake full monetization or full intermediation.[19] Only a public agency, such as the central bank, could be so bold as to monetize the risky credit instruments and capital claims of the private sector to the point of full liquidity.

The other question we have to face is this: Are there not some

---

[19] Inevitably one is reminded of the 'liquidity trap'. This is not the same thing, at least as usually interpreted. Trap doctrine asserts that the real money supply goes to infinity as 'the' nominal interest rate is driven down to some positive figure. It is assumed here that the latter figure is zero. But the nominal interest rate is still bounded above zero because the real money supply has a finite upper bound so that one emerges with a conclusion that differs with respect to maximum liquidity but is the same with respect to the lowest attainable nominal interest rate.

differences in the benefits and costs from additional liquidity when it is provided by the inside money route as contrasted to the outside money route? If so, the selection of the anticipated inflation rate which offers maximum liquidity by the inside money route may not be the ideal choice, even in the highly abstract setting to which we are confining ourselves in this and the previous section. In particular, if there is a positive social cost attached to each addition to liquidity through the inside route, the ideal amount of liquidity is less than the full amount; it may also be less than the maximum inducible liquidity level.

We have already noticed one difference with respect to 'cost' of additional liquidity when generated the inside way. At sufficiently high anticipated inflation rates and correspondingly high reserve requirements, it is probable that a reduction of the inflation rate and corresponding reduction of the fractional reserve requirement will increase the real profitability for each bank of attracting an additional real dollar of deposits (at a given real cost of doing so). This increase in the profitability of expanding the scale of a bank's operation will intensify the bank's nonprice competition for deposits – whereas there will be no similar increase in the real profitability of investment in the private nonbank sector. Once liquidity has increased to the point of equilibrating the supply and demand for capital *in toto*, there is left an excess of the real rate of return to capital in the commercial bank sector over the real return still available in the other sector. This excess will be driven out by a diversion of real capital from the latter to the former sector. This shift of capital will take the form of additional bank branches and expansion of capital facilities generally in the bank sector. To some extent this shift of capital will come from nonbank financial intermediaries; this is the case if the deposit rates which these institutions pay fall by the amount (roughly) of the decline in the anticipated inflation rate and in nominal interest rates on earning assets. Here there is no cost insofar as the commercial banks take over the facilities of the nonbank intermediaries or the shift is a slow process in which each year the banks simply make the replacement investments and net investments that would otherwise have gone into the facilities of the intermediaries. But even from this 'timeless' viewpoint, there is definitely some social cost from the shift of capital away from the non-bank-non-intermediary sector.[20]

[20] An analytically disconcerting feature of this capital-cost aspect of increased inside money expansion is that once the anticipated inflation rate has been

At the lower anticipated inflation rate and correspondingly lower nominal interest rates on earning assets, households' demand for bank money will be greater, and it was of course the object of the reserve requirement reduction to supply this additional bank money. But the banks' depositors will naturally demand the kinds of services from the additional bank money that make holding more of it attractive when its opportunity costs are reduced. It is after all the availability of these services that will lead people to want to hold additional bank money rather than merely additional coin and currency. To provide the larger volume of services that goes with the increase in the size and number of deposits at the banks, more resources in the form of labor and capital will be required. Not all the increase in overall running costs of commercial banks constitutes a net cost to society, for the additional resources the banks employ for the purposes of their larger investment activities are partly offset by the reduction in the resources employed for the same purpose by nonbank financial intermediaries. However, it is the larger operating costs of the banks *qua* suppliers of liquidity that we have in mind. These are definitely net costs to society which must be set against the social benefit of the addition to liquidity that is obtained.[21]

The lesson to be drawn is that there are always positive social costs to additional liquidity (over the whole attainable range) when the increase in liquidity is produced via the inside money and banking route. They are not zero as in the parable of outside coin and currency only. At least to a degree, the same conclusion would hold if increases in liquidity were produced by a single publicly owned bank the manager of which, upon receiving the signal that the shadow price of liquidity had been marked up by the Lange-Lerner planning authorities, undertakes to hire more resources in order to produce more. Undoubtedly all the *optimum* ways by which liquidity

---

reduced moderately far, it may no longer be true that the banks will be keen to proliferate their facilities to attract additional deposits; they will begin to feel the risks of staying fully loaned up. In any case, there are other cost elements.

[21] Of course, it makes no difference to the amount of the net cost who pays for the banking services. The incidence of these costs does affect the demand for bank money however. If the reduction of the anticipated inflation rate produces an 'effective' reduction in the own-rate of interest paid to bank depositors on their deposits in the disguise of increases in service charges, the increase in the quantity of bank liquidity demanded that results from the reduction of the inflation rate will be less or even nil. The matter of deposit rates is discussed in a later section.

can be increased do impose some positive marginal social cost. This positive marginal social cost (over the whole attainable range) guarantees that the ideal quantity of liquidity – where marginal social benefit just covers marginal social cost – is smaller than the full liquidity level characterized by zero marginal social benefit.

This conclusion leaves open the question of whether the ideal level of liquidity is also smaller than the maximum amount of liquidity the commercial banks can be induced to create. I believe the answer is probably yes, especially if we introduce additional social costs, those involving risk. As the anticipated inflation rate is reduced toward the point where the banks are unwilling to expand their loans and investments, the nonbank public may possibly still gain from larger liquidity. But what of the people who own the banks? Because they are not forced to pay depositors a larger real rate of return on their deposits, while the real rates of return on earning assets are essentially unchanged, the bank owners will feel that their 'expected utility' is being decreased. Even if they grit their teeth and stay fully loaned up until the exact point of maximum liquidity is reached, it does not follow that the approach to maximum liquidity is producing a gain for them or even for society as a whole. If bank share prices are sharply down with the approach to maximum liquidity, this is some sign that intermediation and the reallocation of risk-bearing is being carried too far.

The above presumption would be strengthened if it could be shown (as is probably the case) that maximum liquidity imposes on banks the payment of a real rate of interest on money that exceeds what their free competition would drive them to pay. In fact, we know that there are some destructive side effects when banks' deposit rates reach only their 'competitive' level. Much of the support for ceilings on deposit rates, including Regulation D that forbids interest on demand deposits, comes from those who are apprehensive about 'overbanking'. They argue that there is a widespread temptation of the individual banks to offer ever higher interest rates in order to attract or retain funds. Then, in order to be able to pay out such rates, they tend to move into ever-riskier investments. In a world of perfect information, competitive market forces would prevent such situations from arising. But in our world, with its imperfect information on the part of depositors and imperfect information by bank portfolio examiners, price competition for deposits would probably entail more excessive risk-taking or more policing or both. So whether the real rate of return on deposits comes about from free competition or through reduction of the anticipated inflation rate, the social costs of the overbanking that results, or the social costs incurred to prevent its resulting, will be the same in either case.

The conclusion to be drawn from this section is the following: As fuller liquidity is sought via the inside money route – reduced anticipated inflation together with reduced reserve requirements on the commercial banks – some ideal level of liquidity is likely to be attained short of the maximum real money supply that could be achieved by this route. It is certainly not ideal, and might not be attainable if it were, to have the full monetization of illiquid assets by private commercial banks that full liquidity can be presumed to require. The anticipated inflation rate that is necessary for this ideal liquidity level may of course be negative, like that required for full liquidity, but it is possible that it is a little above zero and it will not be far from zero in either case. In all this analysis it must be remembered that we have been abstracting from the social costs of raising government revenue and the social costs of stabilization. Consequently what is 'ideal' in the way of liquidity may not, all things considered, turn out to be truly *optimum* in the world as we know it.[22]

6.3.3. *Ideal Public Indebtedness and Credit Structure.* The previous analysis of inside money gives the impression that fractional reserve commercial banking is to be thought of as a last resort for creating liquidity, real outside wealth constant or almost so, being a device that is turned to only when the central bank has run out of interest-bearing government debt to monetize. If that were the theory of fractional reserves on which the American government has operated for so many years, however, we would not see any interest-bearing public debt outstanding, or at least not so much of it. A large portion of this publicly held government debt could be monetized by the Federal Reserve without a net expansionary effect upon aggregate demand if reserve requirements were at the same time raised to 100 percent.

It is possible to say something in favor of the monetary efficiency of this arrangement; on the other hand, a complete defense, if one were possible, would have to include the argument that this is the arrangement that history has left us and that, in view of the social costs of changing it rapidly, it is best to let it evolve slowly in what one expects to be the right direction most of the time.

[22] The next section is somewhat academic and might better be omitted by readers who are in a hurry to reach the 'real world'.

Let us assume that the government is in debt, that is, that the quantity of real outside wealth is positive.[23] The question is then whether it is better invariably for the central bank to monetize this debt – as long as there is some of it left in the hands of the public and more liquidity is desired – or whether it might be preferable at some point for the central bank instead to reduce reserve requirements. The point was made earlier that inside money creation suffers from disadvantages as a way to produce liquidity compared to outside money creation – principally, the risks borne in holding the assets that are monetized would not be 'felt' by the managers of the central bank or appreciably felt by the taxpayer, while they would be felt by the owners of the private banks; and there would be some tendency (at least over certain ranges) for reserve requirement reductions coupled with reduced nominal earnings rates to lead to overreaching for return and overbanking in the form of nonprice competition. But there are some advantages to leaving some interest-bearing public debt outstanding rather than monetizing it all before turning to reduction of reserve requirements:

Even the interest-bearing debt of the federal government is relatively liquid compared to privately owned capital and most private obligations. Neglecting the costs of greater liquidity, which we have stressed adequately, the ideal situation would be one in which there are no liquidity premiums. Likewise, in traveling part of the way toward that goal, the most efficient route is one that monetizes the most illiquid assets left available. Thus the central bank may very well serve liquidity if at some point, being barred from monetizing private assets, it delegates commercial banks to monetize some of these high-yield low-liquidity assets. Nothing would be accomplished by this if the commercial banks simply monetized the government debt. Note that this redirection of some of the monetization will necessitate some rise in the interest rates paid on government debt relative to the yields earned on very illiquid assets.

There is a corollary to this in the area of ideal debt management. If the degree of illiquidity were the only attribute that distinguished one kind of government bond from another, the optimum mix of government debt outstanding would be that maturity structure which minimized illiquidity. Given the heterogeneity of financial needs within the population, it is unlikely that this precept would call for

---

[23] This raises the question of whether it is ideal for the government to maintain its indebtedness over time through deficits to keep up with real growth plus any inflation; this is discussed below.

nothing else but short-term bills; longer-term obligations would, in certain quantities, enjoy high liquidity in some segments of the financial markets. But there are other desiderata in debt management, some of which are suggested by the rest of the list of advantages to having some interest-bearing debt left in the hands of the public.

A second advantage is that in reducing reserve requirements the government shapes commercial banks into institutions that become specialized in extending credit to a part of the financial market. Of course, it might be asked why other financial institutions could not perform these services as well. One answer implicity 'discounts the future': we had commercial banks before we had the huge federal debt, and it may be wondered whether reassigning the banks' lending role to other institutions would be worth the transitional cost. But there are also zero-discount answers. Some institutional division of lending functions could be justified by the thought that if there were a single type of omnibus financial institution, there would be room for only a very few in each city or region and each such institution would enjoy an undesirable degree of monopoly power. Further, commercial banks probably enjoy greater stability in the size of their deposits, with or without central bank help, and so there seems to be some advantage in having this institution among those that extend credit; it is a good candidate for purchasing relatively illiquid credit instruments, such as the IOUs of small businesses.

Another advantage brings in stabilization policy (which will be considered more fully in the next section). The open-market purchase of government securities is a convenient instrument for stabilization policy. One merit is that the effect of stabilization on the cost and availability of credit to business borrowers may be more diffuse, though not different in total, if open-market operations are used instead of placing sole ar primary reliance on variations in reserve requirements. Another merit is that by insuring a steadier course of the required reserve ratio, the central bank may reduce somewhat the return to risk-bearing earned by the commercial banks, the incidence of which falls partly upon the types of borrowers who find it cheapest to borrow from the banks.

Finally, there may be some utility in having an interest rate visible when decisions are made by the government affecting the amount of federal borrowing. In this way the public and the legislators see a cost of government borrowing though the economist knows that it may be smaller, and sometimes greater, than the real cost. It might well be argued, however, that the public is in greater need of seeing the benefits of government borrowing, especially when economic activity is severly depressed but not only in these times.

This is a good point to take up another question that has been hovering in the background. If we are analyzing ideal financial and monetary arrangements, why should it be regarded as ideal that there should exist a positive amount of government indebtedness? First of all, we have in this country an amount of outside wealth that the most austere budgetary surpluses imaginable would take a decade or two to extinguish. By contrast, the kinds of changes in financial institutions that would be implied by inflation changes of the magnitude we have been discussing would not take nearly so long to complete. 'Selecting' the level of per capita outside wealth is really a longer-term process than selecting the equilibrium inflation rate if one is going to select zero public indebtedness.

However there are perfectly sound arguments for having a positive amount of government indebtedness. The superiority of outside liquidity over inside liquidity presents such an argument if the government is proscribed from monetizing private obligations. Then it must create outside *wealth* if it is going to create *outside* liquidity. The economics of this matter is always somewhat confusing because outside money *when backed* by government debt does double duty as source of wealth as well as liquidity. Yet distinctions can and should be made.

There is a case for some public indebtedness even if it is postulated that the central bank can monetize private tangible capital and tangible-capital claims without ill effect. One argument is that the public debt, whether held in interest-bearing form or in the form of money, offers an 'amenity' that might be called economic security. It offers fair assurance to the individual holding it that the income flow from it (the potential cash flow if only cash flow should be relevant to the individual) or its cash value will be somewhat statistically independent of the luck or misfortunes that strike the individual's holdings of human capital. Thus people may want marketable material wealth not solely because they want to sacrifice present consumption for the certainty of a greater future consumption but because they fear the risks of a loss of future earning power. Wealth will therefore be valued partly for that reason in order to be spent when emergency needs for it arise. Without the device of a budgetary deficit, the buildup of wealth would entail the sacrifice of present consumption; a deficit can create the wealth without that cost. In short, even if the central bank has created full liquidity, it has not thereby satiated the demand for economic security.[24]

There exist other arguments for the belief that the private sector would have a tendency to oversave if the government produced no outside wealth as an alternative to capital. Perhaps the public debt is the work of an equally invisible *political* hand. But there also exist reasons for thinking it possible that there is undersaving – it is possible that people overestimate or undervalue future economic benefits, saving or bequeathing less than they would really like to or ought to. As outside wealth is algebraically increased from some large negative figure, it would seem that at some point the balance of arguments would tip in favor of the undersaving contention. It is perfectly possible, perhaps probable, that this point occurs at some positive level of government indebtedness. One does not have to conclude that the present level of government indebtedness is just right. My guess is that it is too large, though this is not to say that there is enough economic security.

6.4. *Optimum Liquidity Where Taxation and Stabilization Are Costly*

We have been assuming up to now that the methods of taxation and of stabilization open to the government are not socially costly in the sense of imposing any 'deadweight loss' of consumer surplus. It will be the purpose of this section to show that when this assumption is dropped, it will be optimal to 'trade off' a certain amount of benefit from liquidity in return for some reduction in the deadweight costs of ordinary taxation and stabilization methods thereby made possible. It will be argued that the optimum quantity of liquidity, in view of this trade-off, is less than the ideal quantity of liquidity – the latter being optimum only in the 'ideal' world where it is assumed there is no such trade-off.

Even in the ideal world just visited, it was argued that the ideal monetization of capital claims and the government debt stops short of full monetization because at some point the most worthwhile increases in liquidity are too resource-absorbing. Even in the case most favorable to liquidity, where monetization is from the 'outside', there are still positive marginal social costs of increasing the

---

[24] These ideas make their appearance in A. C. Pigou, 'The Classical Stationary State', *Economic Journal*, September 1938. I have been led to the emphasis on economic security, and to the reinterpretation of Pigou, by an unpublished paper by Donald A. Nichols.

level of liquidity. If the monopoly central bank is to induce wealth-owners to hold a larger share of their wealth in the form of deposits (swapping some of their earning assets for deposits at the bank), it is likely that the social-cost-minimizing technique to do that includes offering more convenient physical facilities and customer services, not just a greater real rate of return on deposits that wealthowners can take advantage of only at positive resource costs to themselves.[25] More clear-cut is the cost of the larger investment department needed to make loan and investment decisions the greater is the degree of monetization to be achieved. If the most illiquid assets are, after allowance for appraisal costs, the first to be monetized, it may be conjectured that a level of liquidity will be reached such that the marginal social benefit from further monetization fails to cover the marginal social costs.[26]

The first step away from that idealized world has already been taken. There are political objections to the outside monetization of private obligations and capital claims; moreover, there may be economic advantages arising from 'decentralization' and 'competition' in allowing private firms, specifically commercial banks, to select the loans and investments to be made. If we accept as a datum the prohibition against central bank investment in private claims (whatever its merits), the optimum expansion of liquidity involves some inside monetization as well as outside monetization – for private obligations and capital claims are among the best candidates for monetization. But as monetization proceeds along this route toward the ideal liquidity level, we encounter the social costs of excessive risk-bearing by private commercial banks and the possibility of wasteful overbanking.

Having accepted commercial banks into the framework, it remains to accept the rest of the universe. The most conspicuous features to be reckoned with are the social costs of stabilization and the social costs of ordinary methods of taxation. Their bearing on the optimum level of liquidity in this nonideal world (however idealized in other respects) will now be considered.

6.4.1. *Stabilization Costs and Optimum Liquidity.* It was not so long ago that fiscal policy was the principal receptacle in which faith was

---

[25] One thinks here of post office economy and mail-order banking.

[26] Insofar as these resources which are diverted to the bank merely come from private intermediary and brokerage institutions that would otherwise have employed them, there is no net cost, but then there is presumably little or no net benefit either. I am well aware, incidentally, that the presence of positive marginal social costs does not insure against a 'corner maximum' at full monetization.

placed that the government could stabilize the economy tolerably closely around some desired equilibrium point. The central bank was assigned the more prosaic tasks of insuring orderly financial markets and desirably low nominal rates of interest. The social benefit from high liquidity is nothing new in central bank theory!

On administrative grounds and on neoclassic resource allocation grounds it came to be agreed that variations in tax rates and in the timing of certain transfer payments are preferable to variation of government expenditures and of their timing for the purposes of economic stabilization. But changes in tax rates have proven to be an inflexible instrument too. There is often legislative bickering over the distribution of the additional tax burden or tax relief. Also, legislators apparently believe that tax rates are symbols for the electorate, if not for themselves; some legislators will oppose a tax increase on the ground that it will symbolize to the executive the legislative consent to certain types of government spending; other legislators with the same antispending objectives may demand the tax increase in the hope that the wrath of the electorate will force the executive to reduce the spending.

But tax rate variations are not a perfect stabilization tool no matter how wisely they are enacted. Changes in excise tax rates often cause disturbances due to anticipatory or deferred buying (the problem of leads and lags most familiarly encountered in exchange rate and tariff rate variations). Changes in rates of income taxation, especially if believed to be temporary, may have to go so far as to produce sharp reductions in disposable incomes in order to counter the increase in employment and incomes from an expansionary disturbance, say a war or an investment boom. There is probably some zone in terms of output and the inflation rate such that the fiscal steps necessary to keep those variables inside the zone will cause more instability rather than less in terms of the success with which households are able on the average to realize their economic plans.[27]

The pendulum of opinion on methods of stabilization appears now to have swung the other way. Some economists would even give the major responsibility for economic stabilization to the monetary authorities, requiring of fiscal behavior only that major destabilizing actions be moderated where possible and that tax rates be held in reserve for use in a major disequilibrium. At the minimum, it must

[27] The implied criterion seems to be a sensible one if, and only if, it is the socially optimal equilibrium point that the stabilization policies are attempting to keep the economy averaging around.

be agreed that the best stabilization policy mix gives monetary policy an important stabilization role. This does not mean that the monetary authorities are not asked to keep one eye out on the long-run target inflation rate as they attempt to contain or to moderate exogenous disturbances of the economy away from the path to that target. In the same way it can be hoped that the use of temporary surtaxes will not deflect fiscal policy from tending toward its long-run stance of budgetary tightness or ease as desired for the realization of the 'growth' target. The ship's pilot circumnavigating iceberg flows and tropical storms ought not to forget the port he is paid to reach.

It is important therefore to consider the influence of the expected rate of inflation on the costs, reliability, and tasks of stabilization by monetary means. The first point to be made is that the establishment of an expected inflation rate so low as to bring about ideal liquidity, or something near it, may leave the central bank in the position of having shot its bolt. If a contractionary disturbance calls for easier money, hence additional monetization of earning assets, the central bank may find that its commandment of ideal liquidity has left it with no more government securities outstanding that it can purchase and has left the commercial banks in the position in which further reductions of the reserve requirement encourage only a small addition in their loans and investment if any addition at all. The prohibition against private investments by the central bank might then be lifted, but perhaps not without debate over the alternatives and a loss of time.

What if new methods of accomplishing the additional monetization were permitted? The central bank might be allowed to adopt a more relaxed position on rediscounting the bank's investments or, conceivably, even to monetize some private assets directly.[28] It must be conceded, though, that there are certain losses incurred when the central bank is driven to such actions compared with the less extreme steps that would be needed to accomplish the same increase in monetization when starting from less than the ideal amount of

[28] The possibility of a tax on the commercial banks' excess reserves at the central bank also comes to mind. If coupled with an equal tax on their holdings of currency, this could drive the banks to purchase additional earning assets to escape the tax. This is a tax on money so far as the commercial banks are concerned and one that is feasible because of the difficulty of the banks in disguising or concealing the composition of their portfolios. The feasibility of such a tax on households' money holdings is less clear. Proposals to tax money as a solution to depressions are made in A. Dahlberg, *When Capital Goes on Strike* (New York: Harper, 1938), and in S. Gesell, *The Natural Economic Order* (San Antonio, Texas: Free-Economy Publishing Co., 1934).

liquidity. These are the losses from pushing monetization beyond the ideal level. (Of course, this extreme step would be preferable to fiscal and monetary inaction that left capital and other resources idle, but that is beside the point.)

The second type of objection to the establishment of nominal interest rates low enough to secure the ideal amount of liquidity involves the reliability of monetary policy in those circumstances. This objection is often expressed by saying the demand for liquidity, when pictured as a function of the average nominal rate of interest on certain earning assets, is flatter at very low rates of interest than it is at 'medium-high' rates of interest and that, as a consequence, counter-cycle monetary policy is less 'effective' at very low rates of interest.[29]

A frequent counter is that if a given reduction of the nominal rate of interest must be engineered to reestablish equilibrium, the central bank need merely increase the money supply by a greater amount the flatter demand-for-money curve is. There are various answers to that at the most practical level. One of them is that it is fortunate if you can get the monetary authorities to increase the money supply at all when output and employment are falling. Just as the treasury has the tendency to think that the automatic rise of the budgetary deficit which accompanies the fall of incomes may itself be a sufficient stimulus to return the system quickly to equilibrium, the central bank may mistake the automatic fall of interest rates consequent upon the reduction in the demand for capital and credit as a sufficient counter-cyclical force. Another answer is that the monetary authorities may suffer from 'money interest rate illusion', thinking that it is the proportionate rate of decrease of money interest rates that matters, so that a drop from 2 percent to 1 percent appears enormous.

It is likely, however, that the most rational central bank would find its effectiveness at stabilization – for a given difficulty in the degree of instability it is confronted with – impeded by the prevalence of very low money rates of interest and high liquidity. If capital goods, equities, bonds, and money are all highly liquid, it would seem that any increase of the money supply would have a less predictable effect upon the demand for capital than would be the case if these asset types were highly complementary, held very nearly in

[29] One does not have to believe in a liquidity trap at a positive nominal rate of interest to agree with the flatness assumption. Note, however, that the demand for money function will not be convex everywhere, contrary to the usual textbook drawing if, as the nominal rate of interest is increased sufficiently, the demand for money approaches zero.

'fixed proportions'. The larger the increase in the money supply required to produce the mathematical expectation of the given reduction in the nominal interest rate which is assumed to be needed, therefore, the greater the risk is that the money increase will prove too little or too much. If deviations from the target have increasing marginal disutility, the policy-maker who maximizes the expectation of utility may choose an increase of the money supply having the expectation that it will be insufficient to reach the target but will compensate for this by reducing the risk of overshooting.[30] However admirably the monetary policy-maker responds to these risks, it is still true that his performance will be better on average the less chancy are the effects of the tools with which he has to operate.

The last objection to low nominal interest rates involves their effect on the strength of the destabilizing forces present in the economy. If the establishment of a low expected rate of inflation reduced the size of the tasks required of monetary stabilization policy, this might well compensate for the costs it tends to impose in the unreliability of the monetary tools available for stabilization. In fact, the establishment of a regime of low nominal interest rates corresponding to a small rate of expected inflation is likely to exacerbate the instability with which the monetary (and fiscal) authorities have to deal.

This contention depends on an assumption regarding the sensitivity of the money-market-clearing price 'level', at any given expected price trend, to exogenous disturbances in the demand for capital, particularly an increase in the expected nominal rate of return on capital, however this comes about. It can be argued on a couple of grounds that the price level which clears the market for money is more sensitive to disturbances, and hence more likely to permit a destabilizing process to develop, the higher the level of liquidity is, hence the lower nominal rates of interest are, at any initial level of real outside wealth. Once the ground has been laid for this critical assumption, we can turn to the details of the unstable process around the equilibrium inflation rate.

One basis for this argument appeals to the wealth effects on the quantity of goods demanded of a disturbance in the demand for goods. The larger the fraction of initial outside wealth that has been monetized, it may be argued, the larger is the initial rise of the price

---

[30] This is only one possible result of many that could occur, but it does not seem that the general point about the costs of risk will be affected by potential complexities provided the policy-maker is appropriately risk-averse. Several examples of policy-making under risk are studied in W. G. Brainard, 'Monetary Policy and Uncertainty', *American Economic Review*, May 1967.

'level' induced by an increase in the expected nominal rate of return on capital. To the extent that illiquid interest-bearing government debt is outstanding, it constitutes an extra cushion between the price level and exogenous disturbances in the demand for goods. At given nominal supplies of both money and government debt outstanding, a rise of the price level reduces the real value of both the money stock and the interest-bearing debt. But if the nominal expected return on capital has increased, interest rates will rise and the real value of the government bonds will fall further. This decline in bond prices from the rush to get into equities and physical capital itself tends to moderate the increase in the quantity of capital and consumption goods demanded and thus moderates the early rise in the price of goods. The more illiquid the outside wealth, the less liquid tinder there is to be sparked by an unanticipated increase in the attractiveness of goods as against liquidity.[31]

That thesis can be expressed in these terms: A one-point increase in the expected nominal rate of return on equities (and their close substitutes) has a larger proportionate effect on the money-market-clearing level of goods prices the more liquid is the economy – for given nominal supplies of outside money and privately held government bonds; equivalently, it results in a larger proportionate fall in the market-clearing real value of the money supply the larger the initial level of the real money supply.

Another basis for this same thesis can be built on the Keynesian liquidity effect of a rise in the expected return to capital as well as the wealth effect just examined. It is commonly believed that at very low nominal rate of interest, a given increase in the expected return on capital produces a larger proportionate decrease in the quantity of real money demanded than would be the case at moderately high money interest rates. That belief seems reasonable enough. At quite low money interest rates, monetization and intermediation have reached such heights that the demand for money is largely 'asset demand' and very volatile: Small changes in the expected nominal rates of return on capital then have large proportionate effects on the total demand for money; this compared to a situation of moderately high money interest rates.[32]

[31] This point is emphasized in D. M. Winch, 'Inflation and Resource Allocation', Queen's University Conference on Inflation and the Canadian Experience, June 22–24, 1970.

[32] Note, however, that at very high interest rates, the transaction demand for money must become highly sloped, eventually reaching the vertical zero-liquidity axis, though the asset demand is in that range nil or almost so.

There is adequate basis, therefore, for an assumption commonly made in the neo-Keynesian analysis of instability begun in the early 1950s. That assumption is that a one-point increase of the nominal rate of interest (or return on capital) produces a larger proportionate decrease in the real quantity of money balances demanded the smaller the initial level of interest rate is. The (absolute) logarithmic slope of the 'demand curve' for real money balances is greater at very low nominal interest rates than at moderately high ones. As a consequence, the proportionate early rise of the price 'level' – and hence the initial increase of the inflation rate above the equilibrium inflation rate – that results from an increase in the expected nominal return on capital is greater the larger the initial real money supply is – equivalently, the lower the equilibrium rate of inflation is (given the real rate of return on capital). The larger the sensitivity of the actual inflation rate to such a disturbance in the demand for capital, presumably, the greater the likelihood is that expectations of greater inflation thereby induced will feed back strongly on the demand for money enough to produce a potentially unstable motion from equilibrium. The gist of these stability models, as I interpret them, can be briefly sketched.[33]

We adopt the natural-unemployment rate framework according to which a *dis*equilibrium is marked by a discrepancy between the actual and expected rates of inflation with the latter chasing the former in the adaptive-expectations manner discussed in Chapter 2. We suppose that the money supply is following some predesignated path, as is any quantity of outside wealth left unmonetized. Accordingly, a decrease in the quantity of money demanded, as from an increase in the expected pecuniary rate of return from holding capital claims, increases the quantity of equities, and ultimately, goods which are demanded and thus increases the monetary rate of inflation. This effect on the inflation rate is greater the larger the (absolute) logarithmic slope of the demand for money curve is, inasmuch as that

---

[33] The kind of mathematical model under discussion originates in two remarkable papers, W. S. Vickrey, 'Stability through Inflation', in K. K. Kurihara, ed., *Post-Keynesian Economics* (New Brunswick, N.J.: Rutgers University Press, 1954), and P. H. Cagan, 'The Monetary Dynamics of Hyperinflation', in M. Friedman, ed., *Studies in the Quantity Theory of Money* (Chicago: University of Chicago Press, 1956). Similar analyses of the stability problem, usually in a growth context, have recently been made by Sidrauski, Stein, Nagatani, and Tsiang, with much the same sort of results being obtained. 'Nonmonetary' sources of instability, ones having no obvious connection with inflation expectations, have been explored in well-known papers by Kaldor, Samuelson, Hicks, and Rose, to mention a few.

determines the size of the increased demand for goods (decreased demand for money) from the given increase in the expected nominal rate of return. The momentary increase of the inflation rate would be only temporary, the system returning to equilibrium at the expected inflation rate, if the latter did not rise by some fraction of the momentary increase in the actual inflation rate. But the induced rise of the expected inflation rate raises *pro tanto* the expected pecuniary rate of return on capital claims and goods. This feeds back upon the quantity of money demanded and hence upon the actual inflation rate produced 'next period', doing so *in proportion to* the logarithmic slope of the demand curve. The expected inflation rate is consequently increased again. Its rise can be likened to the familiar 'multiplier process' in fixed-price Keynesian models. The convergence of this process to some higher but steady expected inflation rate requires that the logarithmic slope not exceed unity by so much as to swamp the 'stabilizing' tendency of the expected inflation rate to make up only a fraction of the excess of actual or expected rates plus any other frictions one might posit which make the momentary inflation rate respond only sluggishly to each decrease in the quantity of money demanded.[34]

True, the logarithmic slope of the money demand curve will become smaller and therefore more stabilizing, according to our assumption, as nominal interest rates continue their rise. It would seem at first, therefore, that the system will stabilize after all, albeit only at some high level of the inflation rate. But if the monetary authorities do not accede to the higher-inflation equilibrium, the economy must overshoot, sending employment below the natural level into a downward spiral. Once nominal interest rates hit bottom, be that zero or some positive floor, the economy will be stuck until an 'active' fiscal policy comes to the rescue, liquidity at this point being not further augmentable by central bank efforts at monetization of the usual sort.

[34] The requirement for stability is that the 'marginal propensity to inflate with respect to the expected pecuniary return to capital' (or equivalently, the expected rate of inflation) be less than unity. In the world of Cagan and Sidrausky, this propensity is the fractional adaptive-expectations coefficient *times* the absolute value of the logarithmic slope of the money demand curve. These are continuous-time models of the simplest sort. Vickrey's discrete-time model yields a more stringent condition on the largest size of the logarithmic slope consistent for stability. It is local stability that is being analyzed and these conditions are not enough, it would appear, to guarantee global stability. I judge therefore that the problem of instability is really worse than these results show it to be when it is assumed that the money supply follows an inflexible predesignated course.

There are of course grave problems of realism in any comprehensible model of economic instability. The model has left out adaptive or discretionary monetary policy. I do not believe that it would be impossible to expect of monetary and fiscal policy that it keep the expected inflation rate averaging around some very low figure. Indeed, the central bank would get the same 'score' that it would earn in the high interest rate regime *if* it were, in the former case, to make up in a reduction of the slope of its credit *supply* the increase in the slope of the *demand* for money. But there is little reason to assume such a fully compensatory response.

The above considerations convince me that the costs incurred and the errors made in the attempt to stabilize the economy will be much greater at low rates of interest than at high rates. At low rates of inflation the trials of the stabilizers are made harder and their tools made blunter and less reliable. In a world of uncertainty, a policy of moderately high inflation in order to contain liquidity somewhere below the otherwise ideal level imposes a cost which can be viewed as the premium charged for (limited!) insurance against economic instability. Moreover it is the poor and disadvantaged who could expect to receive the largest benefits from this insurance. Some positive amount of such insurance would seem to be definitely worth buying.

6.4.2. *Deadweight Costs of Ordinary Taxation.* It is a familiar proposition in the theory of taxation that there are not enough fiscal tools to permit the simultaneous attainment of the many objectives that one would like to secure from the tax system. The proposition has its origin in the observation that if poll taxes are eschewed, it is open to each household to spend its time in pleasureful or ultimately productive ways that 'escape' taxation – leisure and home production being the common examples. The avoidance of poll taxes has its root in the uncertainty about the fairness that any distribution of them over households would turn out to have. The income tax, which is really many fiscal tools, one for each income bracket, exemplifies the 'imperfection' of the fiscal tools available. While it is possible over an extensive range to achieve the desired revenue for public expenditure and at the same time, by varying the progressivity, to achieve the desired distribution of after-tax income, it leaves leisure untaxed and saving twice taxed. Even if, say, saving deserves to be taxed once more (with greater or less feeling), it will be an accident if the total tax happens to produce just the right after-tax rate of return to saving. An expenditure tax, while perhaps better on the saving front, is less adaptable to the desires for tax progressivity.[35]

I shall argue here that some positive effective tax rate on liquidity, a rate which places its private opportunity cost above the marginal social benefit of liquidity at the 'ideal' level, would improve the approximation of the tax system to its various objectives. An 'inflation tax' is a useful addition to the armory of fiscal tools, no one of them being perfect by itself or even in concert. This is not quite a trivial conclusion, for the problem of fiscal inefficiency is not a matter of the paucity of tools, but rather the deleterious side effects of each tool. If one tool is merely a linear scale replica of another in use, it cannot contribute anything to fiscal efficiency. And some tax devices when used at 'positive levels' would do more harm than good, being dominated by or at least not preferred in their results to other tools. But it is very doubtful that an inflation tax falls in that immediately excludable category.

It might seem that this contention goes against an existing presumption for pricing at marginal social cost, hence production levels at the 'ideal' output rates. But that presumption fell to the ground with the development of the 'theory of second best' in the fields of tariffs and excise rates, largely in Britain, two decades ago. In fact, this attack on marginal cost pricing was only the second wave, following earlier explorations of the optimal structure of excise tax rates by Marshall, Pigou, and Ramsey.[36] In this country, the general presumption against marginal cost pricing was clearly stated by William Vickrey, a dedicated advocate of efficient resource allocation and usually associated with that pricing injunction. After speaking of various objectives that conflict with the marginal cost rule, Vickrey says:[37]

[35] See N. Kaldor, *An Expenditure Tax* (London: George Allen & Unwin, 1955), and the references to Mill, Fisher, and other writers. The latest extensive treatment of the problem of imperfect fiscal 'controllability', this one set in a dynamic context, is K. J. Arrow and M. Kurz, *Public Investment, The Rate of Return, and Optimum Fiscal Policy* (Baltimore: Johns Hopkins Press, for Resources for the Future, 1970).

[36] Much of this literature, though far from all of it, is reviewed and extended in W. J. Baumol and D. F. Bradford, 'Optimal Departures from Marginal Cost Pricing', *American Economic Review*, June 1970. See also J. S. Chipman, 'External Economies of Scale and Competitive Equilibrium', *Quarterly Journal of Economics*, August 1970. There is also the work of Meade, Little, de Graaf, Lipsey and Lancaster, Whinston and Davis, McManus, Buchanan, and others.

[37] W. S. Vickrey, 'Some Implications of Marginal Cost Pricing for Public Utilities', *American Economic Review Papers and Proceedings*, May 1955, p. 607.

By far the most important of these considerations that conflict with the strict application of marginal cost pricing is the need for revenues. Many of the more extreme advocates of marginal cost pricing for decreasing cost industries seem tacitly to assume that the Government has some perfectly costless and neutral source of revenue that is capable of very substantial expansion without ill effects. Such a state might be approached, for example, if we had an income tax free of its multiple effects, evasion proof, with no marginal cost of administration or compliance, and including in its base not only money income but all forms of direct income in kind, including an imputed value for leisure. Needless to say, this is far from the case.

The nonideal world that Vickrey describes does not yet have a presumptive pricing rule having the same wide acceptance and comprehensibility as the old marginal cost rule. Yet the following guides appear to have been established:

In a much-studied special case in consumer preferences, all taxable goods ought to be cut back if room must be made for resource-using public expenditure – and cut back roughly in the same proportion from their ideal output levels. In the general case of preferences, if good 1 has price above marginal social cost because of the need for tax revenue and good 3 has price equal to marginal social cost, because it is untaxable, for example, then there is some tax on good 2, making its price higher by some amount than its marginal social cost, that is superior to leaving it untaxed – provided this tax permits a reduction in the other tax, revenue constant. If (and only if) good 1 is more substitutable for good 3 than is good 2 at equal *ad valorem* tax rates on goods 1 and 2, there is differential pattern with a higher tax rate on good 2 and a lower one on good 1 that is superior to equal tax rates – provided each rate is in a range such that its reduction would cause a loss of tax revenue.

In all cases, the test is essentially whether the tax change will shift resources from the good or goods of which too much is consumed into the good or goods of which too little is consumed, taxes net of any (lump-sum) transfers being held constant.[38] Good 3 might be

[38] It is therefore the 'compensated elasticity of substitution' and compensated demand curves that are relevant, meaning that the representative consumer believes it could buy the same bundle of goods after the tax rate change if it wished. See W. J. Corlett and D. C. Hague, 'Complementarity and the Excess Burden of Taxation', *Review of Economic Studies*, August 1953. These results on the critical role played by separability or its absence appear also in papers by O. A. Davis and A. H. Whinston.

home-produced goods of which there is too much, given the amount of transfers or the amount of resources employed by the government the outlays for which are to be financed. If good 2 is less substitutable for leisure activities than is good 1, taxing it (good 2) more heavily will moderate the inefficient expansion of leisure that must to some extent result from the substitution effects of the taxation required for revenue.[39]

Let us now try to say something about the optimum rate of taxation of liquidity in terms of the precautionary type of liquidity model introduced above.[40] It is supposed that a given real level of after-tax transfers is to be made to the public by the government. A flat income tax rate on the cash receipts of households is one source of tax revenue for this purpose. In the normal case, an increase in the expected rate of inflation, by increasing the deficit consistent with that real outlay of transfer payments, will permit a reduction of the tax rate; the rise of the nominal interest rate (and expected inflation rate) will outweigh the induced decline in the quantity of liquidity demanded to produce a net seigniorage gain. The normal case seems certain to prevail once we are in the range of moderate nominal interest rates, whether or not it prevails very close to the ideal liquidity level. Attention will be focused on the consequences for allocative efficiency of the employment and liquidity decisions of the representative household, neglecting the effect that a change in the after-tax real rate of interest may have on the rate of total saving.

I consider two extreme cases. In the first, each household desires liquidity only for the sake of getting bargains in the things it buys, in 'getting better purchase prices'. It therefore anticipates that the portion of its outside wealth which it decides to hold in the form of interest-less real cash balances will not affect the amount of income tax it must pay. If we assume, as a rough approximation, that the before-tax real rate of interest is insensitive to the mix of taxes chosen by the government, an increase of the expected inflation rate

[39] This is, presumably, the slim rationale for the belief that it is best to tax most heavily those goods whose (compensated) demand curves are 'least elastic', like salt. Certainly a good whose compensated demand is highly inelastic must be highly complementary with leisure and with every other good. But some demand elasticities could be large because of the substitutability with one another, not with leisure and should not escape taxation for this reason! In the good 3 case, there does not appear to be a difference between the complementarity guide and the compensated elasticity guide. With an income tax, this is about all the goods we have in aggregative terms.

[40] The following material has benefited from lengthy discussions with Kenneth Arrow, Peter Diamond, David Levhari, and Eytan Sheshinski.

will be offset by a rise in the money interest rate on the illiquid portion of the outside wealth; the inflation tax is paid therefore primarily on the amount of wealth which the household elects to hold in liquid form.

One may think of the household's utility in this setting as being a function of the leisure it takes, its liquidity and its 'measured consumption' in the sense of its cash receipts from employment deflated by the average of prices in the market. The household's liquidity and its cash receipts combine to produce the amount of 'true consumption' that it can enjoy. For the larger its liquidity, the lower on average will the prices be of the things it purchases, given the average of the prices in the market. The household buys these three goods in amounts that depend in the usual way upon their after-tax prices or after-tax private opportunity costs. If the income tax rate is 25 percent, we may say that leisure is being subsidized at a 25 percent *ad valorem* rates. Alternatively, one is free to use the money wage as *numeraire* and to say that the after-tax price of 'measured consumption' is 33 percent; leisure from this view goes untaxed – its 'price' is still the before-tax money wage rate.

How does the income tax affect the after-tax opportunity cost of liquidity in this model? Abstracting from the expected inflation rate for a moment, an increase of the income tax rate, applied equally to interest income and to wage income, must *reduce* the after-tax opportunity cost of liquidity, whereas we saw earlier that the after-tax reward to liquidity was not touched by the income tax. Assume, for the sake of the argument, that the expected inflation rate is initially such that the before-tax money rate of interest is low enough for 'ideal' liquidity. If we recognize that the maintenance of the ideal level of liquidity imposes positive marginal social costs – the instability cost if not the other costs discussed, which are more persuasive in the mixed inside-outside money case than the pure outside money case – this money interest rate figure is definitely positive. The private opportunity cost of liquidity, however, is the after-tax money rate of interest in this case; this must be lower than the before-tax money interest rate by a fraction of the latter equal to the tax rate (one-quarter in the above example).

In this case, therefore, the income tax drives the private opportunity cost of liquidity below the marginal social cost of liquidity (equals marginal social benefit at the 'ideal' liquidity level) when, in the absence of the income tax effect, the nominal rate of interest would be appropriate for 'ideal' liquidity. If we regard measured consumption as being untaxed, we may say that both liquidity and leisure are being subsidized to a degree because they are ways of escaping the income tax. Alternatively, we may say that while measured consumption is subject to an excise tax (33 percent in our example), leisure and liquidity are both untaxed.[41] The conclusion is that there is too little measured consumption, too little utility being produced by real consumption expenditure (using the average market price as the deflator), and too many resources being wasted in excessive leisure and liquidity. There is a lot of home production and a lot of shopping being done and not enough paid employment being undertaken.[42]

At a minimum it can then be argued that there would be an allocative gain from establishing some higher value of the expected inflation rate. There is some increase in the 'inflation tax' which will offset the implicit subsidy to liquidity coming from the income tax effect, so that the excess liquidity is eliminated, the 'ideal' level restored. This is a clear improvement at least in the normal case where there is a seigniorage gain obtained.

At this point, if we regard measured consumption as untaxed, there is still a subsidy to leisure while none on balance to liquidity. A small further increase of the inflation tax will produce only a small departure from the 'ideal' liquidity level. But in the normal case it will permit a lower income tax rate.[43] Hence it will 'buy' a reduction in the subsidy to leisure, which is well above the optimum level to begin with. This utility gain is of a greater order of magnitude than the utility loss from the first small step away from 'ideal' liquidity. Some small net tax on liquidity, producible from added expected inflation, is definitely preferable to no tax, inasmuch as it permits a reduction in the already large subsidy to leisure. This is a straightforward application of the presumptive guide sketched earlier, which

[41] The jth consumer maximizes his utility subject to a budget constraint whose first differential yields

$$dc^j + i(1-t)d\pounds^j + \phi_n^j \cdot (1-t)dz^j = 0$$

where t is the income tax rate, c his consumption, z his leisure time, $\pounds$ his liquidity, and ϕ_n^j his marginal product. Equivalently, writing $1 + \tau = (1-t)^{-1}$, we have

$$(1+\tau)dc^j + i \cdot dM^j + \phi_n^j \cdot dz^j = 0.$$

[42] S. B. Linder, *The Harried Leisure Class* (New York: Columbia University Press, 1969).

[43] This proposition might seem overqualified on the ground that going from a zero tax on liquidity to some positive tax *must* yield a positive rectangle of tax revenue net of social 'production' costs. But in principle, the tax could produce a cross effect that diminishes the income tax collected.

says that in the normal case no taxable good should be spared some positive tax rate.

We see now that it was quite inessential to assume, realistic though it is, that at the optimum liquidity level the corresponding nominal rate of interest is positive. If the State of California could meter people for the sunshine each absorbs, even though sunning ourselves is not resource-absorbing, some small tax on basking in the sun would be a net fiscal gain, reducing the deadweight onerousness of income and sales taxes, provided only that the smallest tax on tanning does not drive us totally into the shade. Or consider the uncongested bridge that one can travel across at zero marginal social cost. Some price on crossings in excess of zero is definitely a fiscal improvement as long as the shadow price of tax revenue collected in other ways is positive. By the same analysis, the pursuit of ideal liquidity is a luxury in a world where the other sources of tax revenue impose deadweight losses of consumer surplus.

The other reference point of interest is where the net tax on liquidity is equal on an *ad valorem* basis to the tax on measured consumption, regarding leisure as being unsubsidized. The inflation tax will have reduced the income tax rate from 25 percent in our example to, for example, 20 percent, so that the new implicit excise tax rate on measured consumption is in that case 25 percent instead of 33 percent. An equal *ad valorem* rate of tax on liquidity would place its private (after tax) opportunity cost at the same 25 percent above the marginal social cost of liquidity.[44] If the marginal social cost of transforming a dollar's worth of highly illiquid assets into real cash balances is, for example, 6 percent at the second-best fiscal optimum – considering instability, overbanking, and all the rest – the household should be made to face a private opportunity cost of choosing cash instead of the illiquid asset of 7.5 percent. If breakeven

---

[44] At this point the reader may well ask what should be done with the special case in which the marginal social cost of liquidity is everywhere zero. Then any positive tax on liquidity would imply an infinitely high *ad valorem* rate. Yet we just convinced ourselves that free goods ought not to be exempted from taxation when costless sources of tax revenue are not available. A resolution of this puzzle consists of noting that when the 'price' of liquidity is near zero, the (compensated) elasticity of substitution between liquidity and leisure is close to zero so that, in that neighborhood, the substitutability guide to the tax differential does indicate a relatively high tax *ad valorem* on this good. The polar case, however, simply warns against the applicability of formulas that divide through by zero quantities. The literature does contain formulas in terms of 'specific' rates of tax, as the previous references show.

capital gains are untaxed, this corresponds to a before-tax nominal interest rate of nearly 9.4 percent. (A triplet of round numbers is 4.5, 6.0, and 7.5, respectively.)

But it might be guessed that liquidity is much more 'complementary' with leisure than is measured consumption. Equivalently, a differential tax on liquidity, coupled by a compensating reduction in the income tax rate in the normal case, would reduce the over-stimulation of leisure. Spending liquid assets is a principal use of unpaid household time. (It is possible that households would respond oppositely, making up for the increased liquidity tax by spending more time shopping even more carefully, being able less frequently to seize good bargains just chanced upon because they are willingly illiquid more often; but this outcome would not be my guess.) Of course, the increase of the liquidity tax encourages more 'trips to the bank', hence a reduction of paid employment and measured consumption. But the reduction of the income tax rate will reduce the encouragement of such unpaid productive activities. It is the differential effect that matters.

There is another angle (that of Ramsey, Boiteux, and Samuelson) that may produce insights into our conundrum. The optimum tax differential according to that analysis reduces measured consumption and liquidity approximately in the same proportion, the approximation being better the smaller the tax revenue to be collected. If the (compensated) demand for liquidity is more inelastic than the demand for measured consumption (money income at a given price 'level'), the higher tax rate on the former is indicated if cross-elasticities are negligible. One thinks of the demand for money as highly inelastic – the importance of being 'unimportant'! In any case, there seems to be no presumption that the net rate of tax on liquidity should be less than the tax on cash receipts. And this seems especially safe to say when one considers that the supply of saving is another allocation decision for the income tax to do damage to, alongside the employment decision, like a fiscal bull in a Pareto-ideal china shop.

The above analysis has broader applicability than might at first appear. The income tax stimulus to liquidity is a standard feature of transactions demand models of money-holding. If there are brokerage costs in moving in and out of earning assets, transactions balances are more likely to be held entirely in liquid form the higher the tax rate on interest income. Even Keynes's speculative bulls may pull in their horns more frequently the higher the government's take on any capital gain. But let us turn now to the *other* extreme case of precautionary money demand.

We shall now suppose that liquid balances are held exclusively to obtain greater average cash income over time, and this income is taxed at the flat income tax rate. The household may hold liquid assets so that it can ride out periods 'between employment' and thus obtain better selling prices for its services. By staying liquid between investments it can expect to get better asset purchase prices and hence obtain a larger interest (and rental) income on average from a given amount of wealth. In this case, the rewards from being liquid are taxed like the rewards of being illiquid. Both the reward and the private opportunity cost of being a little more liquid are reduced after income tax in the same proportion. There is no strong reason in this case for believing that the income tax has any direct stimulus on the demand for money at a given average nominal rate of interest on earning assets. Consequently it cannot in this extreme case be presumed that excess liquidity is induced by the income tax when the before-tax interest rate is set at the level of the marginal social cost of liquidity at the 'ideal' level – unlike the previous model.

Let us confine our attention to this neutral case. Then a flat tax rate on income can be viewed as a subsidy to leisure alone, employment and liquidity being affected only indirectly by this subsidy.[45] The case for levying an inflation-tax on liquidity must now rest exclusively on the premise that, in lowering the income tax rate needed and hence *its* implicit subsidy to leisure, it will induce some decline of leisure.

We have now to consider in this new context the question of differential substitutability. Would an inflation tax on liquidity, accompanied by a reduction of the income tax rate to keep revenue constant, decrease leisure? There is one fresh ground for an affirmative answer, one not applicable previously. The inflation tax might reduce between-jobs precautionary unemployment, and thus stimulate employment, by *reducing* liquidity. (The reduction of the tax rate it simultaneously permits in the normal case merely reinforces the lessening of leisure.) With liquidity more costly, there may be less shopping for jobs as well as shopping for consumer goods. We have been adhering to the notion of liquidity as capital, misallocated only

---

[45] If we let $\gamma(n^j, \mathcal{L}^j)$ represent our household's cash receipts, n^j being its paid employed time, the first differential of the budget equation is

$$dc^j + (1-t)(i - \gamma_{\mathcal{L}}^j) + \gamma_n^j \cdot (1-t)dz^j = 0,$$

but the household will equate $\gamma_{\mathcal{L}}$ to i, leaving no 'subsidy' to $\mathcal{L}^j$.

if the government injudiciously misprices it above its marginal production cost. But in a less than perfectly liquid economy of certainty
and full information, people may misuse their liquidity. Insofar as
added liquidity improves the market without greater average investment of time in 'search', there is a clear net gain. But if added
liquidity is complementary with resource-using search, the matter is
less clear.

More generally, if, at a given level of real public outlays, for
whatever reasons, a higher rate of anticipated inflation produces an
increase in the macroequilibrium level of employment – miscalculation, the symbol of money wage gains, whatever – we have an
effective answer to our differential substitutability question. In that
case, up to a point, the inflation tax will prove an allocative benefit.

It seems to me to be a sporting guess therefore that even in the
case in which all the perceived private rewards from a household's
liquidity are fully taxable at the income tax rate – surely quite an
extreme case – there is an allocative gain to be obtained from an
inflation tax on top of the income tax. In addition, there is a practical
aspect of income tax revenue collection that probably clinches the
argument. We have been abstracting from the resource-using collection costs. The administrative time required to increase tax
compliance is a positive marginal social cost of income tax revenue
collected. The administrative costs of the income tax machinery are
undoubtedly small per unit of tax revenue thus collected. But it is
surely likely that the last dollar collected imposes real resource costs.
The state may very well spend more money to collect the unpaid taxes
of the orneriest taxee than the amount of taxes he owes – though only
as an object lesson to others, and if the tax collectors optimize, they
will insure that the last dollar of their costs has a net tax yield overall.

It is just this consideration that has led many economists to support the use of a heavy inflation tax in underdeveloped countries
where the marginal administrative resource cost of income tax
revenue (and other kinds of tax revenue) must be considered substantial. In one well-known study, it was assumed that an extra
dollar of tax revenue would cost amount of extra resources worth
10 cents. Even a small cost like that can lead to the optimality of an
enormous inflation tax.[46]

The appeal to this practical cost of income taxation does not mean

[46] M. J. Bailey, 'The Welfare Cost of Inflationary Finance', *Journal of Political Economy*, April 1956; reprinted, with pertinent corrections, in K. J. Arrow and T. Scitovsky, eds., *Readings in Welfare Economics* (Chicago: Irwin, for the

that we can safely discard the subtle questions of differential substitutability and elasticity. These considerations must enter into the calculation of an exactly optimal mix of taxes. But the marginal administrative cost of income taxation definitely biases upward the optimum inflation tax on liquidity. This marginal social cost, while unquestionably much smaller in this country than in many less developed nations, even if only 4 cents on the marginal income tax dollar, must substantially increase the optimum tax on liquidity and, for a given total tax revenue, decrease the optimum rate of income tax.

6.4.3. *Distribution and the Public Sector.* Only economists would couch the analysis of the optimum liquidity tax in terms of differential tax analysis, public expenditures and transfer payments being held constant. It is always possible that the public and its legislators would choose, knowingly or inadvertently, to utilize the added 'revenue' from the move to an optimal inflation tax by expanding the public sector or, instead, by allowing that tax to cut back further on private consumption demand so as to allow a larger share of resources for capital formation at macroequilibrium. There may be some who would favor a little bit of all three – lower income tax rates, larger public expenditures and transfers, and smaller private consumption. As I write, there is again talk among economists, as in the years around 1960, that the public sector and capital formation both are being squeezed for want of sufficiently high taxation. We are becoming aware that our net national product is smaller than we thought it was if we require that the environment, like the capital stock, be kept 'intact'. At the threshold of a major social innovation to help the poor, the family assistance proposal, there is hesitation and the likelihood of underfunding in any case for lack of federal revenue. There is currently some talk of a 'housing shortage'. How incredible it is, therefore, that at such a time it should be once again impressed upon us how important it is to reduce expectations of inflation, and hence repeal the inflation tax.

It was argued in Chapter 5 that windfall losses in the real value of money holdings from unexpected inflation may very well be 'progressive' in the relevant proportional sense. It may be, however, that when the inflation is expected, the well-to-do are better able than the poor to hedge against that inflation, taking advantage of compen-

---

American Economic Association, 1969). See also A. L. Marty, 'Growth and the Welfare Cost of Inflationary Finance', *Journal of Political Economy*, February 1967.

satory increases in the nominal rates of return on many earning assets. But if income and expenditure taxes are left unchanged in the move to an inflation tax, there may be an additional progressive influence. The government can then undertake an increased volume of public expenditures, public investments, and transfer payments without choking off private consumption, the inflation tax accommodating the expansion of these programs. This would be likely to benefit the poor proportionately more than the nonpoor. This is true if for no other reason than the fact that a dollar's worth of improvement in the environment, for example, is a larger proportion of the poor man's living standard than it is of the prosperous man's. Moreover, it is predominantly the poor, mostly crowded in cities, who derive the greatest absolute benefit from an expansion of public services and public investments designed to improve the facilities of modern, largely urban, living.

The other scenario has tax rates, real transfers, and public expenditures not directly dependent upon the increase of the inflation tax (where the interest on the public debt is calculated in the appropriate real terms). Then private consumption is constrained by the liquidity tax and some additional capital-deepening takes place in the way of private plant and equipment, industrial research, private education, and so on. How would this increase in the capital intensiveness of the economy influence the share of total socioeconomic benefit received by the poor? If one thinks of the poor as standing outside the economy and living on public assistance, the poor will have to count on larger transfers financed by the larger tax revenue from the larger output in order to stay even with the nonpoor. Conceivably, the volume of transfer payments to the poor is a 'luxury good' (income elastic), in which case there will be some logarithmic trickling down. The poor do earn income however and a larger share of their income, one assumes, comes from their wages than is the case with the nonpoor. But it is not clear that the rental to strong-back labor will thereby be increased.

Lastly, to reinforce the ideas of this section, consider that once an inflation tax has been established at high levels, it will inevitably be proposed that banks be allowed to pay interest on money. They would not be allowed presumably to compete indefinitely for deposits to such a point that the resource waste of overbanking become flagrant. But it might be proposed that the deposit-rate ceiling of zero be raised by the amount of the increase in nominal interest rates resulting from the inflation tax.

Obviously, the payment of the same own-rate of interest on every kind of money, including currency and coin, would simply undo the gain in moving to an optimal inflation tax rate. The effective tax on liquidity would thus be removed. But what would be the effect of a differentially lower effective tax on deposits alone? For the same tax revenue, either the income tax rate (or other ordinary rates of taxation) would have to be increased or else the effective rate of tax on currency would have to be increased. In the latter case, which seems the natural one, we are back to the standard question in differential tax analysis where initially two tax rates are equal and we are contemplating unequalizing them. I see no obvious case for such unequalizing of the two liquidity tax rates in terms of differential substitutability and elasticity.

There is, however, the point that it is deposits which are likely to exhibit the higher level of marginal social cost, not currency. It is the dangers of overintermediation, overbanking, and instability that impose some marginal social cost on liquidity, and these dangers refer more to deposits at banks than to coin and currency. This suggests that it is deposits that should present the higher private opportunity cost of holding, not currency. Nevertheless, it should be mentioned that one must not prohibit pecuniary interest on demand deposits, while at the same time permitting the banks to pay an effective interest on deposits held through the offering of free goods.

6.5. *Monetary Efficiency: The Unit of Account*

Probably the oldest objections to inflation involve its impairment of the efficiency of money as the principal unit of account. Before turning to these objections, we should consider briefly the proper measurement of inflation. This has not been until now a question requiring attention, for monetary efficiency with respect to liquidity alone involves only the plainly measurable levels of nominal or money interest rates, never a 'true' (or false) real rate of interest.

6.5.1. *Price Index Biases* There are many respects in which the goods that a household can buy with a fixed hoard of dollars become preferable to those purchasable previously that are not 'objectively' measurable. Greater commodity standardization, improved quality control and product reliability, cheaper acquisition of consumer information (for a given heterogeneity of the goods available), and a widening assortment of goods produced are all normal per se and have no implication for the rise of the cost of living. It has to do with the rate at which the means of living outstrips the cost of living, both properly measured. But if some of these concomitants of the growth process are neglected by the ordinary (and perfectly defensible) methods of measuring the cost of living, the rise of cost of living will be overestimated (and so too will the rate of growth).

Another unmeasured gain in the value of a hoarded dollar comes from quality improvements in the 'same' consumer good. It has been argued that undermeasurement of the quality improvements in each year's new models of consumer goods alone biases upward the Consumer Price Index by some 2 percent annually. The period since the war may on this count by itself be one of true deflation, though probably less than the average expected true deflation rate. There must be some merit in this contention. Few are the consumers who, with a fixed budget of cash to spend, would prefer to buy from the Gross National Catalog for 1950 at its listed prices than from today's catalog of superior goods even at today's much higher prices.[47]

The growing decline of amenities attributed to rising congestion and pollution does not affect the validity of the above proposition. These phenomena have to do with the economy's rate of *economic growth*, not with the algebraic decline in the purchasing power of a dollar. The decline in the (true) cost of living measures the improvement in the opportunities of a dollar, not with any improvement in the opportunities of people. The worsening of the environment does not erode the purchasing power of the dollar because the consumer who holds a dollar cannot buy an improvement in the environment *qua* consumer: if he buys tomorrow he will get increased smog tomorrow. The purchasing power of the consumer's hoarded dollar over the goods the consumption of which he can vary by purchase or nonpurchase with his dollar will still be improving at 2 percent.

When we discuss the efficiency of money as a unit of account, it is probably the *true* rate of inflation to which we should refer. It is of some interest to note that the exact choice of an index is not important insofar as liquidity is what is at stake. One's assumption about unmeasured gains in the purchasing power of a dollar cannot affect the size of the measured inflation rate that would be judged necessary for achieving the optimum amount of liquidity – *given* the way that

[47] The price index for a given type of good should fall by at least the decline in the price of the old model if still produced. Richard Ruggles has pointed out that this is insufficient, for the consumer's choice has been expanded since he can purchase the new model if he prefers.

inflation is measured. The real rate of return from holding a dollar is increased by the unmeasured consumption good quality improvements, given the measured ones. But the real rate of return from investment in an earning asset bearing a given nominal rate of interest will be increased by the same amount. The consumer can enjoy a superior bundle of consumer goods by waiting to consume, but money is not the only store of value available for that purpose. If the consumer hoarded for 15 years, he is able now to purchase better goods albeit at higher prices. If he invested in a government bond with 15 years to maturity and promising a nominal yield of 3 percent, he still has the option now to purchase the superior goods at the higher prices. If a nominal yield on the representative earning asset of 3 percent was deemed appropriate for optimum liquidity before it dawned on academic economists that the nation's Consumers Price Index had an upward bias, the same spread between the nominal yield on earning assets and money continues to be necessary for optimum liquidity after the scientific discovery.

The question of what *measured* trend there should be in the measured price index for the attainment of ideal liquidity would become significant only if there were an 'inspired' insight into what *true* rate of inflation would be necessary for ideal liquidity. Ordinary economists will have to decide directly what spread in rates of nominal return between money and nonmoney assets is appropriate for optimum liquidity. Given the way the consumer price index is constructed, some measured rate of inflation will correspond to optimum liquidity, but its size and algebraic sign will be of no consequence for the determination of the optimum quality of liquidity. If the construction of the consumer price index should be reformed so as to capture previously unmeasured quality improvements, the new measured inflation rate corresponding to the same optimum liquidity level will of course be algebraically smaller. But if liquidity were the single touchstone for deciding on the rate of anticipated inflation, the price index problem could simply be ignored. All that the optimum liquidity analysis required of the consumer price index used for measuring the rate of inflation is that a reduction of the rate of inflation thus measured corresponds, real wealth constant, to a reduction in the nominal rates of return expected to be earned on capital, capital claims, and other illiquid nonmoney assets.[48]

[48] This belabors the obvious to a pulp. But what is one to do with analyses of optimum liquidity that conclude in favor of zero *true* inflation as if unmeasured quality changes had something to do with liquidity?

6.5.2. *Miscalculations* It has been argued that the higher the rate of anticipated inflation, considered as a positive quantity, the greater is the effort required by people in making purchase and sale decisions. The same contention presumably applies, with some qualification in a progressive economy, to the pace of anticipated deflation.[49]

Insofar as the argument is that rising prices present 'calculational' obstacles to the comparison of buy-now and buy-later plans, there is an obvious debating point in reply. The money rate of interest, if positive, necessitates the same sort of calculation even when the general price level is steady. But it ought to be granted that while the problem is the same in a qualitative way, it is quantitatively more difficult the faster prices are rising.

A deeper and perhaps more disturbing basis for the contention rests on the imperfectness of information on current price quotations. This same non-Walrasian feature underlies much of the theory of unemployment as the first chapter sought to show. If the various prices quoted in the market can be learned, subject to some constraint on money spent, only gradually over time and soon obsolesce, then decision-makers must to some degree base their transaction decisions upon their subjective calculations of the correction necessary to place price quotations observed in the past on a current basis. As people do not carry log tables in their heads, these calculations are onerous and some errors, random or systematic, are likely to be made. The larger the trend rates of change the greater must be the time needed and the scope for error.

It might seem that this argument points to the desirability of a zero rate of anticipated inflation, at least from the point of view of time lost in making calculations. One might wish to look into the structure of product prices, however, not simply the index. If all but one kind of product displayed uniformly falling prices at zero overall inflation, one might be inclined to favor some positive inflation so as to keep most prices constant. Stabilization of the price of the product having the median long-term rate of price change might be preferable to stabilization of the mean product price.

More important, at zero anticipated inflation, money-wage rates will be trending upward in a progressive economy. Then producers must make intertemporal calculations of the normal wage trend even at zero inflation of product prices. With a constant money wage index, product prices would be falling at the rate of productivity growth.

[49] For a discussion of this matter see, for example, H. G. Johnson, 'Monetary Efficiency', *Journal of Political Economy*, December 1968.

Does the minimum-error inflation rate lie between these two rates of price change? Or does any algebraic inflation rate in between lead to the same amount of time spent and error made: more in product markets at the deflation end and more in labor markets at the other end?

The errors made can be significant causes of allocational effects from differences in the anticipated inflation rate. A carpenter estimating what his materials will cost him may accept a job having undercompounded to the present date his past observations of the costs of those materials. A woman may resist an expensive coat not appreciating to what extent her present one and alternative new coats have gone up in price. It is likely that a higher anticipated inflation rate would produce a larger labor force participation rate and a reduced frequency of idleness of some workers, despite no change of the technological factor price relationships, because households believe they are being offered high relative wages, having failed to compound sufficiently the money-wage rate data they know about from the past.

Are such stimuli to employment and saving bad? They are not ideal instruments for the purpose. It is reasonable to regard them as imposing some social costs. Yet one may find these allocative effects from increased anticipated inflation to be a convenient handle for public policy in coping with some of the underemployment arising from market imperfections discussed in Chapter 4. As a stimulus to saving, it has the fortunate effect of not reducing employment, unlike the income tax, as a tool to keep consumption down. On account of its likely 'miscalculation effects' on employment and saving alone, therefore, the technique of anticipated inflation may well deserve a place in the mixed bag of second-best weapons that should be deployed against socially excessive unemployment in macroequilibrium.

Yet there are certainly some side costs from anticipated inflation. Another aspect to the relation of the price trend to the efficiency of money as a unit of account involves the frequency of currency reforms. Prices are not free to be chosen on the 'real line' but are rather chosen to the nearest penny. If the penny is worth a lot, half-pennies and even smaller units may be used. If all prices and nominal aggregates like the money supply should eventually double, a reform of the denominations of coin and currency would then be optimal if the mix of denominations was optimal before. Centimes may die out while more valuable units of coin and currency will be needed. Even the unit of account might be desirable to alter if prices increase manyfold. The more rapid the anticipated inflation or the anticipated deflation, the more often these currency reforms will be appropriate. While this factor is not of major importance for inflation rates in the plausible range, it is a consideration that ought not to be lost sight of. It is another factor, along with the other considerations of monetary efficiency, that makes a sufficiently rapid anticipated inflation rate too costly.

6.5.3. *Confidence in the Price Trend.* There is another consideration often argued to militate against the establishment of an inflationist regime. A level price trend is said to be unique in that only the grail of price stability can enlist the public spirit of sacrifice that the monetary authority needs on occasions if it is to keep the inflation rate under control at any reasonable figure. It may indeed be easier to impress the public with the sacredness of zero inflation than with the importance of some ill-understood target rate like 5 percent – both targets expressed in terms of the official price index its constructors chose to calculate or the price of meat and subway rides, not the true inflation rate which is unmeasurable. If the central bank is construed as having to bargain with a dissatisfied and recalcitrant mob, it may prefer the credibility of zero as its last offer, when 2 percent is demanded, to having to insist on 5 percent, when the mob is demanding 7.

A similar argument has it that inflation is like an addictive drug which is eventually overused at great expense once used at all. It might be optimal to take an occasional cigarette, even three or four a day, but it takes impossible will power not to take those cigarettes sooner and ultimately oftener.

What is the conclusion drawn? Either that inflation can be stabilized only at too high a rate or at too low a rate; or that attempts to steer a middle course will be a storm-tossed navigation. All this is bleakly pessimistic about human nature and capacities, like the choice posed of anarchy or oligarchy. Perhaps a country gets the inflation rate it deserves – relative to its advantages and abilities. It may be that we do not yet have the maturity in matters of economic policy to be able to handle the task of achieving an avowed goal of inflation at some moderate rate. Nevertheless there must by now be a good chance of doing so. It seems far-fetched to think that the kinds of personality defects and misjudgments exhibited in over-smoking, for example, would produce a serious amount of over-inflation. We do not lack for highly visible nuisance costs of inflation which the layman at present magnifies a thousand times. Moreover, at a moderate inflation rate the underlying technical power of the central bank to stabilize the economy would be enhanced, and the destabilizing impulses on the inflation rate diminished. The years since the war do not disprove that moderate inflations, in many countries at least, can proceed without leading to runaway rising inflation and with little pretense that price stability must and will be sought.

But suppose the exercise of inflation control, once unleashed from dysfunctional conventions of the fiscal and monetary past, were to be less farsighted than one would wish, leading to too high a rate. That situation would not be irreversible. And, in any case, surely libertarians who support the right of a sane adult to spend his dollars on tobacco, private schooling, and the rest should grant educated citizens the right to spend their votes for more inflation (or more unemployment) if they should wish. It is the disutility of too much inflation that should be left to limit our appetite for it, not a taboo. The method of choosing public policies should by itself be a merit of a democracy, but it is not when the people are hobbled with myths. Better to suffer from rational errors than irrational ones. Getting hold of our policy-making potentialities is as much the point as the modest though valuable economic gain that should be expected to result.

PART III

The Nature of Optimal Inflation Policy

7 The Nature of Optimal Aggregate Demand Policy

THE preceding chapters have laid the ground for an analysis of the character of optimal demand policy over time. They have identified the primary sources of the gain or loss in (net) socioeconomic benefit, present and future, from a demand-induced change of the employment rate and from a change of the expected inflation rate. Associated with each time path of the employment rate and expected inflation rate is some time path of socioeconomic benefit. Of course, some employment rates and some expected inflation rates would be infeasible to attain. Nor can these variables be chosen independently. The path taken by the expected inflation rate is linked to the demand-induced employment time path in a dynamic way. Such a dynamic relationship between those two variables is specified by the natural-rate hypothesis. That relationship (or any of its variants) limits further the class of time paths that are feasible.

The task now is to introduce the concept of optimal policy toward aggregate demand and to examine how an optimal policy selects among the feasible set of benefit time paths made available by the existing structure of the economy according to people's intertemporal preferences for greater benefit over less, smoother benefit over more uneven, and, perhaps, for earlier benefit over later benefit. To head off some possible misunderstandings, it may be well to preface this analysis with some explanations:

1. The reader will not emerge with a number for the optimal rate of inflation. But the approach outlined permits the calculation of the optimal policy from correspondingly exact assumptions on the various functional relations involved. The reader can, in one transparent instance, actually solve for the optimal inflation policy by geometry. It must be acknowledged though that the quantification of the benefit paths is necessarily somewhat subjective in some aspects. Estimating people's intertemporal preferences about the timing of benefits must also be impressionistic in certain details. We can only guess at what people prefer, while the politician guesses at what people think they prefer. Even the conventionally econometric inflation adjustment curve of Figure 2.1 is not yet well estimated.

2. The optimum at any moment may be expressed in terms of the 'desired' inflation rate or desired unemployment rate – realistically, in the next 'period', following the transmission lag. In either case, the optimum is not a static one needing revision only when social preferences or the structure of the economy changes. The optimum can be described by a *time path*, and on that path neither the inflation rate nor the unemployment rate will be constant except under chance initial conditions. Equivalently, we can describe the optimum in terms of a *policy* that determines the action (monetary and fiscal steps) or its objective (for example, the current inflation rate) as a function of the current 'state' of the system (as described, for example, by the prevailing expected inflation rate). This policy function will be unchanging over time as long as preferences and the structure are constant.

Many writers who refer to the optimal rate of inflation have in mind the optimal anticipated inflation rate, and it is natural to assume that any anticipated rate would have to be a constant one. That concept corresponds, in the present analysis, most closely to the inflation rate which the optimal policy aims to achieve in the limit or (in the misplaced phrase) 'in the long run'. Because the costs of altering expectations of inflation at top speed are bound to be excessive, entailing huge serious unemployment or shortages for a short interval, an optimal policy aims to adjust expectations by degrees, not as quickly as possible. This 'gradualness' is grounded in the specified costs of inducing a change in expectations more quickly.

It is not implied, however, that no variable should change abruptly. Unless the initial policy, before optimization, happened to be optimal, the move to an optimal policy will cause a sharp change of the prevailing unemployment rate and of the inflation rate. Thus, an optimal policy may cause the inflation rate to jump at first and thereupon to move undeviatingly (i.e., monotonically) to their long-run values: it may even cause the inflation rate or the unemployment rate at first to 'overshoot' their long-run values, and thereupon to make a gradual approach to their long-run values. Whether there is overshooting or not, in this transitional phase the inflation rate and unemployment rate are adjusted promptly in order to put the economy on an optimal path.[1] But in neither case is the desire for

---

[1] If we recognize the sluggishness in the response of price decisions and employment decisions to a change of aggregate demand, the prompt change of monetary and fiscal policies will not be reflected in a sharp change in the level of employment and the rate of inflation. But such sluggishness in the levels of these

some anticipated inflation rate in the long run sought to be achieved at maximum speed.

3. The presence of exogenous disturbances is excluded here. The term *optimal demand policy*, when there are stochastic disturbances, can be employed to refer to that demand policy which produces the best 'expected' or 'forecasted' result. The risk of stochastic disturbances need not affect that optimal policy much, or at all, since every policy may run equally costly risks. It may be, however, that policies entailing relatively great present sacrifice for relatively greater promise of future gain are relatively risky – the future consequences being less predictable than the present ones. But the risk of a low future return from present sacrifice does not unambiguously argue for a reduction of present sacrifice: If the future is risky, it may deserve extra present sacrifice to insure for it. (The income effect may balance the substitution effect.) The exclusion of risk need not mislead us, and it is doubtful that it does so to any serious degree.

On the other hand, there certainly are some analytical difficulties in translating properly the optimization approach here to a world in which there is uncertainty about the current state of the economy. This topic will be taken up in Chapter 8.

4. No issue is raised by this analysis as to which agency of the federal government – the Treasury through federal tax rates, or the Federal Reserve through open-market operations principally – is best suited for the assignment of controlling aggregate demand and thus the behavior of the price level and the unemployment rate. I shall discuss the nature of an optimal demand policy under the two assignments. It so happens that I begin and dwell longest with the case in which a decision to change the equilibrium rate of inflation is implemented by variation of the budgetary deficit. In that case the central bank is occupied with the role of keeping the rate of investment on an even keel in the face of the fiscal move.[2]

---

variables does not imply any lack of firmness in the application of the instrument variables like Federal Reserve credit or federal tax rates.

[2] That method of inflation control is not implied to be infeasible even by the extreme hypothesis of some monetarists that the demand for money is perfectly interest-inelastic, at least in the long run. On that hypothesis as on weaker ones, an increase in the rate of inflation, if it is to be permanent, does require eventual ratification by the monetary authority. But that ratification through eventually faster growth of the supply of money, is the automatic outcome of the bank's objective of cushioning private investment from changes in the price level and the expected inflation rate (as well as in capital utilization rates).

5. The analysis in this chapter will exclude international considerations, for I believe it can be carried over, broadly intact, to an open economy, even to one with the special position in the world economy held by the United States. The applicability of the analysis here to a small country depends upon its adoption of a floating exchange rate, managed or not. It is likely that the United States will leave it to other countries to decide their exchange rates vis-à-vis the dollar. Whether any individual country in the rest of the world chooses to fix its rate with the dollar, to let it float freely, or to manage the rate by continuous adjustments is then up to that country. In many cases, the foreign country will find it best to fix its rate with the dollar, hence accepting ultimately and on the average over time the inflation rate desired by the United States; in that case, the social effects of its inflation decision upon the foreign country in question may be one of the factors it considers in measuring the benefits of a change in the actual and/or expected inflation rate at home. If the foreign country opts for a different inflation rate, hence operating on its exchange rate to keep its balance of payments consistent with its preferences for foreign exchange reserves, the effects upon that foreign country and on the United States of the implied rate of exchange depreciation or appreciation resulting from the United States inflation rate may become a factor in the American inflation decision. These considerations will be discussed in Chapter 9.

With these cautions and explanation in mind, we can turn to the character of optimal demand policy.

7.1. *The Nature of Optimal Inflation Policy: General Principles*

The first step in this inquiry is to compare the flow of benefit per period produced by each sustainable equilibrium state that could eventually be attained – appraising each as though the initial conditions ('state variables'), like the expected inflation rate, corresponding to each such state were immediately realizable without any transition cost, as if one could rewrite the relevant past and its heritage. Though this is only a virtual choice set at any given moment, the initial conditions in fact being historical data and not thus open immediately to choice, any optimal policy will aim the economy toward one of these equilibrium states if the underlying parameters, such as the population growth rate or the amount of friction in the labor market, are themselves stationary – or postulated to be more or less stationary for as long as it matters. I shall suppose that these

underlying parameters are stationary. This does not signify that an
optimal demand policy is meaningful only if the government refuses
to entertain advantageous opportunities to change some of these
parameters.

It is necessary for the optimizer to consider the benefit flow in each
attainable equilibrium because the optimal moves in the early stages
generally depend upon which of these is the 'rest point', the one at
which it is optimal to end up. You have to know where you want to
go. That observation is possibly too obvious. But it should be clearly
understood that if it is calculated that an optimal policy must eventually increase, reestablish, or decrease, respectively, the expected
inflation rate in relation to its present level, this rest point target
largely determines the nature of near-term policy objectives. For
example, if an optimal policy must drive the expected rate above its
present level, the present objectives of the optimal policy will be to
drive the employment rate above the equilibrium level corresponding
to the present expected inflation rate, that is, above the 'natural'
employment rate in the simplest model. Quite possibly, therefore,
an optimal policy will aim in the present to push the employment
rate to a level beyond what will be acceptable in the future as well as
beyond what would be preferable from a purely short-term point of
view.

In surveying the sustainable equilibrium states, it is natural to look
first at that state (or states) which, if attained, would give the highest
level of benefits per unit of time. Figure 6.1 illustrates the idea of the
sustainable social benefit maximizing rate of anticipated inflation.
But it would be a mistake to conclude that this sustainable benefit
maximizing state is necessarily the state of rest toward which the
optimum path heads. A discrepancy between the benefit maximizing
state (optimal from an ahistorical or statical point of view) and the
rest point state of an optimal path arises if short-term benefits can
be obtained by relinquishing that benefit maximizing state and if
society prefers to discount future benefits gained or lost in relation to
present benefits. Provided there are temporary benefits currently
obtainable from a departure from the benefit maximizing equilibrium state, the benefit maximizing equilibrium state is a nonoptimal
one to aim for, and a nonoptimal one to remain in if perchance that
is the state in which we initially find ourselves, if society wishes to
'discount' total future benefits relative to total present benefits of
the same magnitude. If there exists this positive social discounting of
late benefits as against early benefits, society will be willing to accept

a *lower* sustained level of benefit over the long-range future than could have been attained in return for extra benefits over the near-term. The same calculation leads society to refuse to make those temporary sacrifices that would be necessary to reverse the after effects of the temporary benefits. Time discounting leads the optimizing economy to a point that is a little poorer in the current benefit though a little richer in memories. The optimal rest point (when there is positive time preference) is just far enough from the benefit maximizing equilibrium state that a further widening of the distance between the two states would not yield enough temporary benefits in the early transition to be worth the continuing loss over the future.

The upshot of this for optimal inflation over time follows easily if we make two assumptions for which we have argued at length in previous chapters. Assume that the rise of the expected inflation rate is the only perfectly lasting consequence (of any significant benefit or costliness) of a temporary episode of disequilibrium in which the actual inflation rate is kept above the expected inflation rate. All other effects, however long to linger, tend to vanish from obsolescence, forgetting, and death. Only the expected inflation rate (and corresponding expected rate of money wage increase) goes on being inherited from decade to decade in the absence of new and different experience that would dislodge that expectation. People are not born to expect zero inflation (or 3 percent money-wage growth) but rather tend to expect what experience has made viable. Then the sustainable benefit maximizing expected inflation rate is the optimum inflation rate to be sought in the long run *if* there is no discounting. What if there is positive discounting of future benefits? Then we will be willing to trade some steady flow of benefit in each period of the far future in return for some extra benefit in the present. Let us assume that there is a positive net benefit in the present (or more generally, over the near future) from engineering an actual inflation rate a little above the expected inflation rate in the neighborhood of the sustainable benefit maximizing expected inflation rate. Then it follows that the optimal policy will seize the opportunity for a certain present gain at the cost of allowing the expected inflation rate to drift to some optimum point that is above the sustainable benefit maximizing rate.

Whether the display of such social time discounting is mature, healthy, or in conformance with our real ethical beliefs has been a recurring controversy in political economy and the field of economic policy for many decades. As my whimsical reference to memories may suggest, it is not unreasonable that a household with a finite time to live takes the Grand Tour early enough in life that there is plenty of time to enjoy the memories of it. But if memories of a society eventually fade with the passing parade of generations, this consideration does not create a discrepancy between the optimal rest point and the point of maximum sustainable current benefit. A more plausible defense of the introduction of positive time discounting appeals to the uncertainty of continuing human life; the discounting of future certain benefits is a shortcut to the correct optimization problem under uncertainty. Another defense of positive discounting proceeds from the observation that far-future benefits will be enjoyed only vicariously by presently living people. A society may feel benevolent toward its future generations, toward the foreign world, even the animal kingdom; but it is not customary for a nation to go so far as to treat these objects on an equal footing with its own. Even if society 'discounts the future', its optimal actions will leave the future better than the present if the present cost of doing so is small enough or if it would only spite ourselves not to do so. We had better make room for positive discounting in our analysis, though we shall emphasize the zero discount case.[3]

The remaining part of the problem is finding the optimum path of the economy from its initial state – as described by such historical (state) variables as current expectations, existing money contracts, and current information about wage and job opportunities in the labor market – to its optimal state of rest as previously determined. Some paths are nonoptimal because they would move the state of the economy (thus described) too quickly or too slowly to the optimal rest point. Of course, there are any number of other paths whose departures from the optimum path are more complex. The higher the social discount rate, the more heavily society prefers to discount future benefits relative to present ones, the more important is the transition, especially its early stage, from the initial state to the target state. But whatever the rate of time discount, optimization requires attention to the nature of the time path from the initial state to the rest point.

---

[3] If future generations are larger in population than the present one, equal treatment of each 'generation' will lead to less sacrifice of present benefits for future benefit than would the assignment of equal weight to each man. I have in mind the former meaning of zero discounting.

The kind of efficiency calculation involved in the selection of a path is familiar to economists. It involves the requirement that in no two adjacent periods is there any possibility of revising the policy in the first period in such a way that the sum of the (appropriately discounted) benefits in the two periods is greater, given an unchanged provision for the possibility of benefits in the further future. One is reminded of Irving Fisher's rule for consuming which equates the marginal rate of substitution between consumption this year and next year to the marginal terms of trade available to the chooser. If that kind of rule were followed over an indefinitely long period of time from an arbitrary initial consumption level, the decision-maker would find himself happily bringing into the long-run rest point level of consumption he wanted only by luck. More likely he would land on another equilibrium or even diverge off into the blue. For an optimum we choose the *present* level of benefits such that, in conjunction with the planned application of the efficiency rules, we can expect to find ourselves moving toward the optimal rest point.[4]

7.2. *The Optimal Inflation Path: An Illustrative Model*

For concreteness and simplicity, we appeal to the natural rate of unemployment hypothesis. The maintenance of a steady rate of inflation leads asymptotically to a rate of unemployment and a rate of idle capacity that are both invariant to the rate of inflation chosen. Nevertheless, there may be some effects on resource allocation and hence on productivity as brought out in the previous chapter.

It will be convenient to simplify the description of the 'state' of the economy, The term *state variables* refers to those current data or predetermined variables which the policy-makers must accept as historically given today but on which their policy action today will have effects in the future. The expected rate of inflation is the single state variable that we shall keep track of. This is a heroic simplification, but it is the natural choice if we limit ourselves to one. When the inflation rate is *temporarily* set well above the expected rate, the latter

---

[4] Should it happen that more than one choice of the initial level of benefits (corresponding to different present policies) will permit an approach to the optimal rest point, despite adherence to the intertemporal efficiency conditions, both paths are optimal. But the presence of diminishing returns in the structure of the economy and of diminishing marginal utility in the structure of social preferences – so-called concavity conditions – are likely to insure the uniqueness of the optimal path as well as its existence.

is perhaps the only variable that will feel a permanent effect – unless erased by subsequent disinflation – while the other effects, those on distribution, skills, and so on, may be eroded by time.

To that end, we abstract entirely from the function of unemployment as a provider of wage and job vacancy information by which it promotes a better allocation of any given employment level in the future. It is as if this information were independent of unemployment which is thus a deadweight loss in this respect. Then the past history of the unemployment rate is an unnecessary datum for describing the current state of the economy. Let us abstract too from the overhang of money contracts not yet expired so that the past history of inflation in relation to the past history of inflation expectations is irrelevant to the present distribution of wealth and thus to the social cost of the consequences for that distribution of a change of the current inflation rate. We shall abstract from the sluggishness in the responses of employment and possibly output to changes in aggregate demand so that just-past values of the unemployment rate and the rate of idle capacity are also not among the predetermined historical data necessary to describe the state of the economy as the policy-makers find it at each moment. We shall assume the rate of capital formation per worker employed and unemployed to be kept constant by means of compensatory monetary policy and further suppose that this constant level of investment per worker leaves the economy continuously in a balanced state in which capital in existence per worker is also constant over time.[5] The government's real indebtedness per worker will be supposed to affect consumption demand only through disposable income, which is under current fiscal control through income taxation, and to affect the investment demand only through the rate of interest, which is under monetary control. In principle, this variable should be kept track of in any major disequilibration of the system – even if real indebtedness is ultimately restored to its desired level with the return to equilibrium – but this detail will be ignored.

The state of the economy, in the sense used here, is thus boiled down to the prevailing wage and price expectations. These expectations will be summarized by a single variable, the expected rate of inflation. This state variable is postulated to respond only slowly to current events, adjusting gradually in the direction of the actual rate

---

[5] One can allow for technological progress at a constant geometric rate by letting investment and capital be in constant ratio to labor measured in efficiency units.

of inflation in proportion to the discrepancy between the two rates.[6]

'The' money rate of interest will be made to bear a simple relation-ship to that variable: In keeping investment per worker on an even keel, the monetary authority moves the money rate of interest point for point with moves of the expected inflation rate plus another adjustment to compensate for the change of the rate of return to investment that is induced by the change of capital utilization accom-panying any change of the unemployment rate. Because investment demand is stabilized and government expenditures are postulated to be constant per worker, changes of aggregate demand take the form of changes in consumption demand, which is controllable through 'the' tax rate, for example, the federal income tax rate.[7] We adopt only a relatively simple consumption function in which the deter-minants are output, the tax rate, and the expected inflation rate. This completes the stylized picture of the technological structure of the economy that the policy-makers confront. It determines the set of choices available to fiscal policy.

Now to the nature of the social preferences which, in interaction with the structure of the economy, determine the optimal fiscal policy. The benefits of the moment that result from the current fiscal policy have their roots in the consumption, leisure, and the distribu-tion of these goods that the policy produces. These benefits can be measured in a real dollar dimension and the benefits in any time period may be aggregated to obtain the (total) current benefit in that period. The level of current benefit in any period – the current 'rate of benefit' – is derivable from three intermediate variables: the current unemployment rate, the current money rate of interest, and the current tax rate itself. These variables determine the benefit owing to consumption and leisure; the consequences of the unemployment rate for the distribution of benefits over individuals or households give that variable a double role. If we were to view idle labor time as devoted wholly to leisure (or the nonmarket production of consump-tion goods) an increase of the unemployment rate would increase leisure per head as it decreases consumption per head; even then it can be argued (as it was in Chapter 4) that the rate of benefit does not reach a maximum where the unemployment rate is at its equi-

---

[6] I insist on fixed proportionality only in one geometrically convenient version of the model portrayed in Figure 7.1.

[7] I shall ignore the effects on *after-tax* rates of money interest and real interest of the changes in the income tax rate though they may influence the demand for money (and capital) at a given before-tax rate of nominal interest to a minor degree.

librium natural-rate value. In any case we may as well view unemployed labor time as being spent partially or wholly in search for
jobs or for better wages – though in the present model we are assuming that the time thus spent produces no important gain of information about jobs and wage rates which could produce a future social
benefit. Accordingly, we treat the current rate of benefit at any
moment as an increasing function of the current employment rate
even for values of the employment rate some distance beyond the
natural or equilibrium level. (No complication results if we allow the
rate of benefit to reach a peak somewhere beyond the natural level
and thereupon to fall with further increases of the employment rate.)
The favorable effects that a reduction of the unemployment rate have
upon the distribution of income constitute another reason for supposing that the current rate of benefit is an increasing function of the
current employment rate.

The other two variables entering the derived rate of benefit function are the money rate of interest and the tax rate. They can be
regarded as determining the amount of leisure that is available, given
the employment rate. It can be argued, as in Chapter 6, that after a
point, every increase of the money rate of interest increases the incentive of households to arrange the financing of their consumption
outlays in ways that economize on the average amount of cash
balances they hold, in order to earn more in expected capital gains
and interest on assets that are alternative to cash (such as bonds,
equities, and nonperishable consumer goods), at a cost in terms of
inconvenience or time diverted from leisurely pursuits. These incentives become highly visible when money interest rates are at levels
usually associated with hyperinflationary episodes in which a great
deal of trouble is taken to keep cash on hand to very small levels.
In much the same way, when tax rates are high, there are incentives
to decrease leisure in order to engage in home production of certain
consumption goods which go untaxed – services especially, but commodities too such as garden variety foods.

It is of course possible that both the money rate of interest and the
tax rate also influence the labor force participation rate. An increase
in either of these rates may tend to reduce a little the number of
secondary workers in the labor force. There is no strong reason for
wishing to exclude the possibility of such effects in the formal model
but it will be simpler to do so. Similarly, many of the economic costs
of a high money rate of interest and of a high income tax rate may
be incurred by the firm, rather than directly at the home, as firms

divert some of their paid labor time to tasks aimed at economizing business cash holdings and reducing business tax obligations. It will be simplest, however, to suppose that the production-function relation between employment and the output of consumption and capital goods is independent of these two rates. On these simplifications the unemployment rate bears a relation to measured consumption per head (or per household) that is independent of the interest rate and the tax rate. Thus the same rate of unemployment, for example, the natural rate of unemployment, will always correspond to the same level of investment per head, capital per head, and expected real rate of interest.

Given the expected inflation rate, the money interest rate and the tax rate are deducible from the unemployment rate. The lower the tax rate set, the smaller is the unemployment rate which results and the higher is the money interest rate the central bank has to set in order to restrain investment from increasing. So in addition to the *ceteris paribus* relation between the rate of benefit and the unemployment rate there is also the total relationship in which the money interest rate and the tax rate are implicitly tied to the unemployment rate. With respect to that total relation, the rate of utility will not in every circumstance be always increasing as the unemployment rate is successively driven below the natural rate and beyond. If the expected inflation rate is high enough, that is, if the economy is near to the brink of barter, then, at least to a point, an increase of the unemployment rate beyond the natural rate would bring an increase of the current rate of benefit because it would reduce the money interest rate from the critically high level and the gain in 'monetary' efficiency would be worth the loss in consumption per head and the loss of 'fiscal' (income tax) efficiency. At the other extreme, if the expected inflation rate is low enough, certainly if it is so low as to produce ideal liquidity in macroequilibrium, that reduction of the money interest rate would bring insufficient compensation for the increase of unemployment and the loss of fiscal efficiency resulting from the required increase of the tax rate.

Given the unemployment rate, the current rate of benefit depends implicitly upon the expected inflation rate through the implications for the money interest rate and the tax rate. The higher the expected inflation rate, the higher the money interest rate is and the lower the tax rate implied by the unemployment rate is. Let the tax rate be set so as to keep the unemployment rate at its natural level while the interest rate maintains investment. As the expected inflation rate is hypothetically increased (beginning at some low rate near full liquidity), the sustainable equilibrium rate of benefit is supposed to increase at first as the gain from the successive reductions of the required tax rate outweighs the eventual losses that arise once liquidity falls below the ideal level. Some peak is eventually reached. This peak is the maximum sustainable rate of benefit. As the expected inflation rate is further increased, the equilibrium sustainable rate of benefit is successively reduced, the loss of liquidity being dominant.

The last step in the description of preference is to suppose that the social preference as between any pair of benefit time paths can be represented by a total utility indicator that is the *sum* of the discounted utilities of the respective benefit levels in each time period over the indefinite future. There is diminishing marginal utility of current benefit in each 'period' and the rate of diminution is alike for every time period. But future utilities may be discounted by a discount factor which, like compound interest, grows geometrically with the futurity of the utility in question; this corresponds to a constant rate of discount. If, for analytical convenience, we think of time as continuous rather than as falling into equal discrete time periods, we may refer to the current rate of utility at a given moment in time; the current utility rate increases with the current rate of benefit at a diminishing rate, and it may be discounted in the same way. The optimal time path of benefit, the path which is preferred among those made feasible by the structure of the economy, is then the path which gives the highest total utility indicator, and optimization of the path then boils down to maximizing total utility. If there is no discounting, we know that the optimum path of benefit must eventually approach the maximum sustainable rate of benefit and we say in that case that the preferred path is the one the cumulative total utility of which is, after some future date, not 'overtaken' by any other path that succeeds in approaching the maximum sustainable rate of benefit.

The feature of diminishing marginal rate of utility insures that the optimum benefit path will be smooth – no feasts and famines. It is obvious too from the postulated structure of the economy that a policy which produced the maximum rate of utility at the current time or over any early interval of time will always be inconsistent with maximization of *total* utility. Maximizing the current rate of utility in the model under discussion fails to take account of the effect of the inflation rate (positive or negative) upon the expected inflation rate and hence the possibility of having high rates of utility in the future. The magnitude of the utility rates beyond the early interval that are possible even under the best of policies then available will depend upon the expectations of inflation that prevail at that time.

The policy that maximizes only the current rate of utility in effect discounts future utility rates to the vanishing point. Such a short-sighted policy would ultimately drive up the expected inflation rate until it is so high that, in equilibrium, a small decrease of the unemployment rate below the natural level would no longer produce a net current gain; the gain in current consumption would be offset by the induced rise of the money interest rate (accompanying the increase of employment) when the costs of further economizing on cash balances would be acute, the money interest rate being so high by reason of the high expected inflation rate. An optimal policy in the model here, where future utility rates are discounted according to a finite rate at most, must drive up the expected inflation rate less far and more slowly, if at all. At the expected inflation rate reached by the myopic policy, an optimal policy (under finite discounting) will push up the unemployment rate beyond the natural rate to the point at which the additional loss in the current rate of utility from an additional increase of unemployment would be just compensated by the gain thereby permitted in future utility rates by the faster reduction of the expected inflation rate.

The nature of the optimal demand policy in this model can at long last be stated. Consider first the case in which future utility rates are not discounted. Then the optimal policy gradually drives the expected inflation rate toward that rate which gives the maximum sustainable rate of benefit and (hence) rate of utility. As the latter rate is approached, the unemployment rate approaches the natural rate. In the limit, the natural rate is reached as the optimal expected inflation rate is reached. The expected inflation rate is optimally made to move unidirectionally or 'monotonically' – without any stepping back prior to stepping forward (whichever way forward may be) and without any overshooting. Hence, if the initial expected inflation rate is below the target rate, the optimal policy proceeds to manipulate demand through the tax rate so as gradually to increase the expected inflation rate over time. In this case, the optimal demand policy institutes an unemployment rate below the natural rate and, correspondingly, produces an inflation rate that exceeds the present expected inflation rate.

As the expected inflation rate rises in response to the latter discrepancy, the discrepancy itself accordingly narrows over time. The smaller the shortfall of the current expected inflation rate from the optimal expected inflation rate, the smaller is the optimal shortfall of the unemployment rate from the natural rate. If the present expected inflation rate exceeds the target rate, the reverse holds: Unemployment is driven above the natural rate and correspondingly the actual inflation rate is driven below the present expected rate in order that the expected inflation rate be driven down gradually toward the ultimate expected rate.

Of course, there is an infinity of exact paths, to make fine distinctions among them, which meet this qualitative description. The optimal path is a particular path among these. In the present nondiscount case it happens that there is a simple way to characterize the speed with which it is optimal to drive the current expected inflation rate toward its optimal equilibrium value. The basic idea is that, at the currently prevailing expected inflation rate, the optimal current unemployment rate just balances the *present loss* from a little more unemployment (or less inflation) against the *future gain* that it would produce by advancing the time schedule at which the target inflation rate is approached.

The most general formula states that the currently optimal unemployment rate at each moment is such that the expected inflation rate is algebraically falling at a pace whose 'marginal cost' to the current utility rate when multiplied by pace of the fall per unit time is just equal to the *algebraic* excess of the maximum sustainable rate of utility over the current rate of utility. Both the excess and the falling will be negative quantities if, and only if, the current expected inflation rate is *below* the target. In this formula, the marginal cost in terms of the current utility rate of an increase in the pace with which the expected inflation rate is falling originates from the implied concomitant decrease of the actual inflation rate in relation to the expected inflation rate; that effect of course is negative whenever the total effect upon the current utility rate of an increase of the actual inflation rate is positive.[8]

[8] In other words, we may think of the optimizer as hypothetically increasing the pace with which the current expected inflation rate is made to decrease until that negative change per unit of time when multiplied by the negative effect upon the current utility rate of increasing the pace marginally more just equals the positive-signed difference between the ultimate maximum sustainable rate and the current utility rate that present optimum policy allows.

[*Footnote continued overleaf.*]

There is an equivalent way to state the formula in terms of the inflation rate under a slight specialization: At each moment of time, the optimum policy may be viewed as increasing the current algebraic inflation rate up to the point where the 'marginal utility' (in terms of the current utility rate) of that inflation rate equals the excess of the maximum sustainable utility rate over the current utility rate, the excess expressed as a ratio to the (algebraic) excess of the current expected inflation over the current actual inflation rate.[9] That formula is much like one that Frank Ramsey, the philosopher and mathematician, developed in his study of optimal 'national saving' and accordingly it has a similar interpretation. The first term, the one consisting of the marginal utility term, is the extra utility that would be currently *gained* from a small increase of the current inflation rate. The second term, the one involving the ratios, expresses the summed or total extra utility that would necessarily be *lost* over the cumulated future from the small increase of the current inflation rate through its setback of the progress of the expected inflation rate toward its long-run optimal level. The currently optimal inflation rate is just large enough that the current utility *gain* is just equal to the future utility *loss* from any small change of the current inflation rate. The reader may study the constructions of Figure 7.1 to see how this formula and the various relationships combine to determine the exact optimal inflation rate and unemployment rate corresponding to each expected inflation rate.[10]

In mathematical notation, if V is the current rate of utility, x the expected inflation rate, and x' its time derivative, then x' must satisfy

$$x'V_{x'}(x, x') = \max_x V(x, 0) - V(x, x').$$

V is derivable from $V = W(x, u)$ and $x' = G(u, x)$, $G_x = 0$ in the natural-rate case.
[9] Writing f for the actual inflation rate, specializing to $x' = \beta(f - x)$, $\beta = $ const. > 0, and using $U(x, f) \equiv V(x, x')$, we have

$$\beta(f - x)(\partial V(x, \beta(x - f)]/\partial f)(-\beta^{-1}) = \max_x V(x, 0) - V(x, x')$$

or
$$(x - f)U_f(x, f) = \max_x U(x, x) - U(x, f).$$

[10] Note that while Figure 7.1 illustrates the fundamental properties of any optimal path of the inflation rate, certain properties of it are a chance happenstance of the curves drawn. Thus, the optimal inflation rate in the present need not be larger the greater the present expected inflation rate is, though this is a fair enough presumption; one could draw curves that make the optimal inflation rate schedule perfectly flat or even sloped the other way and still retain the optimality feature that, because the optimal rate is greater (smaller) than the expected inflation rate when the latter is smaller (greater) than the optimal level, the expected inflation rate is driven gradually to its optimal level.

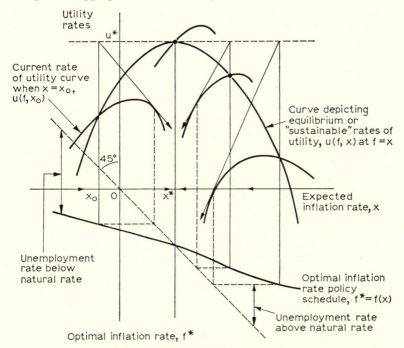

Figure 7.1 At the currently prevailing expected inflation rate, say x_0, one first finds the corresponding instantaneous current rate-of-utility function, $u(f, x_0)$, where f is the rate of inflation. At $f = x_0$ this curve gives one point on the sustainable rate-of-utility curve, $u(x, x)$ which peaks at x^*. From the corresponding point (x_0, u^*) drop a straight line down in the direction of x^* to find the tangency with the former curve. The abscissa, f_0^*, is the optimal inflation rate at x_0. By such constructions the entire optimal schedule, $f^* = f(x)$, can thus be traced out.

Before opening up the model to the many features heretofore excluded, let us briefly cover the other case in which there is a positive discount applied to future utility rates. In this case, the optimal policy for the model at hand ultimately brings the economy to equilibrium at an expected inflation rate that exceeds the expected inflation rate that would yield the maximum sustainable rate of utility, how much greater being dependent upon the size of the discount rate. If the economy should initially find itself with an expected inflation rate above this positive discount rest point rate, the optimal inflation policy drives the expected inflation rate downward, stopping at the rest point. The current costs entailed in going farther are not worth the *discounted* future benefit. If the economy should initially find itself with a smaller expected inflation rate than the rest point rate, the optimal policy carries the expected inflation rate up toward the rest point. There is no stopping short of this, say at the sustainable benefit maximizing inflation rate, because the current benefits of greater inflation outweigh the discounted future benefits of preserving the current expected inflation rate over the future. The introduction of the positive discount rate shifts downward the *schedule* or *policy function* relating the optimal current inflation rate to the current expected inflation rate (the shift not necessarily being uniform in any sense) and thus increases the equilibrium inflation rate at which the actual and expected inflation rates will come together.

An exact characterization of the rest point expected inflation rate says essentially that it is of a size such that the rate of return in terms of the (undiscounted) utility rate between a little extra inflation today and a little extra tomorrow – subject to the constraint that on the third day the expected inflation rate be left unchanged – be just equal to the discount rate.[11] (In terms of Figure 7.1, that characterization imposes a condition on the slope at which the current utility rate curve must intersect the curve depicting sustainable rates of utility.) At the rest point so determined, the marginal utility of the inflation rate is implied to be positive; only the future costs, even after discounting, of a rise of the expected inflation rate beyond its rest point value, already higher than the maximizing rate, deter the optimizing policy-maker from pushing the inflation rate beyond the expected inflation rate.[12] (The same was true of the rest point expected inflation rate in the no-discount case.)

As we assign ever larger values to the discount rate, the rest point expected inflation rate increases, reaching some large rate well short of barter in the limit as the discount rate is made to go to infinity. For any given positive discount rate, the rest point expected inflation rate depends on the magnitude of the sacrifice required to reduce the expected inflation rate via a reduction of the current inflation rate –

---

[11] At the rest point x we have, letting $\delta > 0$ denote the discount rate,

$$\delta = -V_x(x, x')/V_{x'}(x, x') = -\beta U_x(x, f)/U_f(x, f),$$

where the functions are to be evaluated at $f = x$, $x' = 0$.

[12] This follows from the absence of any point on the sustainable utility rate curve through which the latter curve is rising as a function of the expected inflation rate while the current utility rate curve is falling as a function of the actual inflation rate. If, and only if, we were to reverse our assumption that the utility rate curve peaks to the right of the expected inflation rate in the neighborhood of the top of the sustainable utility rate curve, could we find the rest point to lie on the left-hand slope of the latter curve.

unlike the zero discount rate case in which, so far as the long-run inflation rate is concerned, the steepness of the current utility rate curves are of no consequence, their role being only to influence the speed of approach to the maximum sustainable utility point that would be made possible by the reduction of the expected inflation rate by that reduction of the current inflation rate. The latter quantity is not as easy explicitly to express mathematically or diagrammatically as in the zero discount case. But it can be said that the optimal policy drives the expected inflation rate monotonically toward its rest point value, just as in the zero discount case.

7.3. *Some Extensions of the Analysis*

Some of the most notable simplifications made in the above model can be omitted without greatly complicating the description of the optimal demand policy, at least in certain key respects. On the other hand, it would be too tedious to work our way through each extended model with anything like the same attention to detail that we gave the simplest version.

7.3.1. *Inflation-dependent Equilibrium Unemployment Rates* It is conceivable that, although the Phillips-like relation between the rate of inflation and the rate of unemployment shifts upward with each increase of the expected rate of price (and wage) increase, each increase of the expected inflation rate by one percentage point shifts up the Phillips relation by *less* than a percentage point, at least over a range of low expected rates of wage and price increase if not over the whole range. The reason for this might be the difficulty people have in making compound-interest-like calculations or, possibly, the symbolic significance of maintaining one's money wage. A counterargument to the latter was discussed in Chapter 3.

Then an increase of the actual rate of inflation reduces the unemployment rate even when matched by an equal increase of the expected rate of inflation. Consequently, the equilibrium unemployment rate is smaller the larger the prevailing equilibrium rate of inflation is, over the aforementioned range. As a result, if our assumption pro tem is retained – that unemployment has no redeeming economic virtue but is merely an unfortunate by-product of demand policy that 'contains' the expected rate of inflation and hence interest rates – an increase of the equilibrium rate of inflation has an extra advantage not heretofore considered; consequently, the expected rate of inflation that maximized the sustainable utility rate in the simple ('misspecified') model is short of the maximizing rate for the model so amended, provided that the simple model would have left us in the aforementioned range. The 'qualitative' character of optimal inflation policy is not thereby changed, however: the expected inflation rate is still driven monotonically toward its rest point value, which in turn depends upon the discount rate in the way described. Indeed, Figure 7.1 and the associated formalisms remain valid for this amended model.[13]

7.3.2. *The Natural Unemployment Rate as a Band* The point was made in our first consideration of the natural-rate hypothesis that it might be a step in the direction of precision to interpret the natural-rate hypothesis as asserting the existence of a certain 'natural' bandwidth of unemployment rates. The band has the following invariance property which is the basic characteristic of the natural-rate hypothesis: A once-for-all increase of the steady rate of inflation will, if it is large enough, cause the unemployment rate temporarily to stray below the band; but the unemployment rate will gravitate toward the band's edge as expectations adapt, albeit incompletely, to the higher inflation rate. The same holds, *mutatis mutandis*, for a sufficiently large reduction of the inflation rate. Contrariwise, a small change in the inflation rate, if it leaves the discrepancy between actual and expected inflation 'less than noticeable', below some threshold quantity, will be accompanied by a small permanent change in the level of the unemployment rate within the band.

The simplest case may well be realistic enough. Assume that the low-unemployment end point of the band is still higher than would be desirable for allocative efficiency and distribution. This could not be true under conditions of hyperinflationary expectations, but assume it is true at expected inflation rate and, therefore, at smaller rates

[13] If the unemployment rate is treated as the control variable in the model, the rate of change of the expected inflation rate no longer depends upon that control variable alone but upon the current level of the expected inflation rate as well. If one treats the actual inflation rate as the control variable, it remains true that the rate of change of the expected inflation rate depends only upon the discrepancy between the actual and expected inflation rates. The rate of utility depends upon the expected inflation rate as well as upon the actual inflation rate, but this connection is not a fundamental change for the expected inflation rate already figured in the rate of utility via the money interest rate and the tax rate. The first formulation was studied in my unpublished monograph, 'Optimal Employment and Inflation Over Time' (New Haven: mimeographed, Cowles Foundation), August 1966.

of expected inflation rates in the neighborhood of the optimal rest point expected inflation rate and, therefore, at smaller rates of expected inflation as well.

The solution to the optimal inflation problem is then simple, at least in the zero discount case. Thinking before we act, we consider driving the unemployment rate down to the lower boundary of the band. If at that 'decision point' the expected inflation rate would be below the sustainable benefit maximizing rate, we would take an excursion outside the band, getting the benefits of the further temporary reduction of unemployment and securing for the future the additional net benefit to be obtained from the higher expected inflation rate that will thus be produced. If at that interim decision point the expected inflation rate would exceed the sustainable benefit maximizing rate, the optimum policy will not at first go down that road; rather it must head the opposite direction, driving the unemployment rate above the upper boundary of the band in order to reduce the expected inflation rate to the long-run target rate. When the *excess* of the expected inflation rate over the sustainable benefit maximizing rate has been purged, the optimum policy will charge back through the band to the lower boundary, thus arriving at the sustainable benefit maximizing point.

A moment of reflection will convince us that matters are complicated if there is a positive discount rate. For suppose the band is awfully wide and the current expected inflation rate is only a little above what would be regarded as the optimum rest point inflation rate appropriate to the given positive discount rate if the natural rate were a point (specifically, the lower end point) instead of a band. Then the achievement of any decrease of the expected inflation rate, however slight, will require paying the indivisible lump set-up cost of driving the unemployment rate all the way across the band – plus whatever small increase beyond that is necessary for contracting the expected inflation rate. Only if the current expected inflation exceeds the optimum rest point rate by some critical threshold amount does it pay to accept temporary purgatory outside the natural rate band as the price for eternal rest at the optimum inflation point.

In this context the zero discount man can be seen as something of a fanatic. No temporary sacrifice however large is too great to pay for the eventual attainment of maximum sustainable benefit. Any stand-pat policy that does not pay the initial cost of traversing the band can ultimately be overtaken in terms of total utility by some policy that has paid the entrance fee to bliss. At the least, we would want to be very certain that there was indeed the opportunity for an indefinitely maintainable gain in benefit before paying such a price.

It may be that the conception of a set-up cost to altering the expected rate of inflation underlies the shibboleth which says that the optimum rate of inflation at any time is simply the rate of inflation that people are expecting. That counsel is certainly not optimal in every circumstance. If the current expected inflation rate is below the sustainable benefit maximizing rate and if, at the given expected inflation rate, a reduction of the unemployment rate below the natural band would also bring a benefit, present and future benefits are both served by a demand policy that reduces unemployment and simultaneously raises the expected inflation rate. If the current expected rate is sufficiently far above the sustainable benefit maximizing rate, spending months with unemployment above the band may yet be justified by the gain in future discounted benefit. Yet the advice to stand pat contains a valuable intuition in those circumstances in which lowering the expected inflation rate would impose costs out of all proportion to the promised future benefit.

7.3.3. *Vacancy and Wage Information* The other extensions are all harder, involving an increase in the dimensions over which a discrepancy between the actual and expected inflation rate will have *future* effects. In the simple model, and in the extension of it just considered, the consequences for the future of a discrepancy in the present between actual and expected inflation rates are limited to just one effect, that upon the expected rate of inflation in the future. We know that such a discrepancy will tend to have lingering effects – or effects which can be undone only at a future cost – in other dimensions as well.

One of these dimensions is the amount of information possessed by workers of use in their choice of jobs. Some considerations discussed in Chapters 1 and 4 indicate that there may be an unemployment rate sufficiently small, yet positive, such that an aggregate demand policy which keeps the unemployment rate below that level for a time will, as the allocative effects of the resulting undersearch by the labor force build up, leave the output level corresponding to any given unemployment rate at the end of the period lower than it would have been had unemployment not been depressed. In the same way, some workers who might usefully have kept themselves idle in order to be ready for more productive work in the future will, at the end of such an episode, find themselves committed to other work; there will have built up a worsening of the match between idle workers and undone tasks corresponding to any unemployment rate at the end of the period of depressed unemployment. It is equally true, as argued in those chapters, that there may be an unemployment rate sufficiently high such that if aggregate demand policy should keep the unemployment rate higher for some interval, there will also in this case result a mounting deterioration of the output produced at any given unemployment rate because of the paucity of information being transmitted in the interval from employed workers to other employed workers and to unemployed workers.

These effects cannot properly be handled simply by correcting the rate of current utility curves for this unemployment effect, since the effect is not exclusively or even perceptibly felt in the current period but rather in the future. A proper analysis must recognize the dynamics of the process. In an abstract way, this can be done by imagining the existence of a second state variable, to be placed alongside our almost equally abstract expectations variable, namely, the average amount of job and wage information possessed by workers. This 'variable' can be supposed to seek a steady state level that depends upon the rate of unemployment that is maintained. If we postulate the natural rate of unemployment, the upshot of this extension is not significant for the sustainable benefit maximizing expected inflation rate. Any optimal policy must ultimately send the unemployment rate to its natural level so that the amount of job and wage information in the labor market is destined to level off at the quantity corresponding to the natural unemployment rate, whatever the rate of inflation that is optimal in the long run. Consequently there is no room on this postulate for job vacancy and wage information consideration to influence the relationship between the sustainable utility rate and the expected rate of inflation. In the zero discount case, accordingly, it has no influence upon the selected rest point value of the expected rate of inflation, the maximizing expected inflation rate still being the optimal one to head toward.

In the positive discount case, the consideration of labor market information will influence the rest point inflation rate selected if it modifies the overlife effect upon total utility, via its effects upon the quantity of information, of a temporary departure from the natural unemployment rate. If a period of unemployment below the natural rate produced a worsening of information, albeit a temporary worsening, the optimal long-run inflation rate would be smaller – nearer to the sustainable utility maximizing rate – than if that reduction of unemployment were viewed simply as a reduction of waste motion and fruitless effort by the otherwise unemployed workers. The reverse would be true if the temporary reduction of unemployment brought a short-lived improvement in information. As for the optimal path toward the rest point, in both the zero discount case and positive discount case, the exact path of the inflation rate (and of the corresponding unemployment path) will generally be influenced by the consideration of the information effects of alternative paths to the rest point.

If we introduce the information dimension into the amended version of the model which fails to exhibit the natural rate over the entire range of inflation rates, the long-run optimal inflation rate is more strongly influenced by considerations of information. In this case, at least over a range, an increase of the expected inflation rate brings a permanent decrease of the equilibrium unemployment rate and thus a permanent change in the quantity of job and wage information. Clearly the failure to recognize the information-producing function of unemployment (at least when unemployment is small) tends to bias downward the calculation of the equilibrium unemployment rate and bias upward the calculated expected inflation rate that gives the maximum sustainable rate of utility (Fig. 7.2).[14]

7.3.4. *The Distribution of Wealth.* Another dimension which is important to introduce is the distribution of wealth. Whether this is easy or hard, at least at the purely qualitative or conceptual level, depends as always upon how realistic one wants to be. If unemployment and inflation in the present had no effects upon the future distribution of well-being over persons – if persons out of work reduced their consumption by the whole amount of their lost wages and if every unexpected rise of the price level caused bond holders to reduce their consumption contemporaneously by enough to keep the real value of their wealth intact – we could fully allow for these distributional effects in terms of the current rate of utility; for example, the distributional effect of successive reductions of the unemployment rate would cause the rate of utility to rise more steeply and peak later, when viewed as a function of the unemployment rate (given the

---

[14] In Figure 7.2, the factor of information tends to locate the point E, around which the utility contours center, to the southeast of where it would be if unemployment were a total deadweight loss – in which case only the effect upon money interest rate from a demand policy producing a low rate of unemployment would prevent E from being some point at zero unemployment.

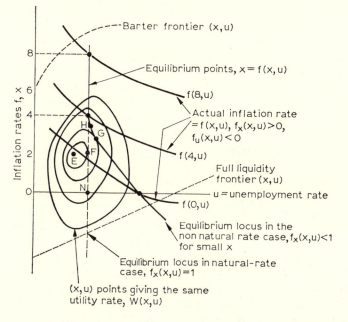

Figure 7.2 The combination of expected inflation rate and unemployment rate, (x, u), at E is not in the equilibrium choice set because $f > x$ at that point. In the natural-rate case, point F maximizes the sustainable rate of utility among all points with abscissa N, the natural rate. In the amended case of a negatively sloped equilibrium locus below $x = 4$, the maximizing equilibrium inflation rate is greater, occurring at G. Under positive discounting, an optimal policy would give up G for the present benefits of $f > x$, accepting a rest point at a lower sustainable utility rate, as at H.

expected inflation rate) to the degree that these distributional effects are stipulated to be favorable on balance.

In fact, these distributional effects are lingering. Workers draw down their net worth, dipping into savings or borrowing as long as they can do so, during their unemployment in the expectation that their loss of wages will not be permanent. (Similarly, holders of fixed money claims who suffer an unexpected increase of the cost of living adjust their consumption expenditures only fractionally, not enough to maintain their real wealth, in the expectation that the cost-of-living increase will not permanently recur.) As a consequence, when the unemployment level is increased, the distributional effect upon the 'rate of social utility' grows worse as the duration of the increased unemployment is increased, abstracting from unexpected changes of the cost of living that may be associated with the change of the unemployment level. Even if every individual worker who loses a job eventually finds a new one, there are mounting losses in the relative share of wealth owned by those, predominantly the poor, who bear a disproportional share of the increase in unemployment. It is also possible to imagine that a sustained increase of the cost of living in excess of expectations could reduce the real wealth and income of some groups to critically low levels.

How does the distributional factor affect optimal demand policy? Consider first the choice of the long-run inflation rate. In the zero discount case we want to find that rate of inflation which, in the limit, gives the largest sustained rate of utility. On the assumption of the natural rate of unemployment, the unemployment rate tends to be the same level whatever the steady inflation rate that comes to be established in the long run. In that case, the rate of expected inflation eventually selected will have no recurrent effect upon distribution.

But distributional considerations might play some role in determining the optimum inflation target if the transition of the expected inflation rate from its present value to any assigned future value left a permanent mark on the distribution of wealth. The loss of a job, even if another one as good is found later, may prevent a poor family's son from continuing in school and thus possibly to block his escape from poverty and that of his children. Increased unemployment, however temporary, may trigger suicides, family breakdowns, and mental illnesses which leave indelible marks on the children. One can also imagine that a policy which drove the expected inflation rate substantially above its present level, as compared with a policy which left it at its present level (or which drove it to a lower level), would leave a nonvanishing windfall gain in the share of wealth held by families of great wealth whose holdings of capital and equity claims comprise an unusually high proportion of – or even exceed – their net worth. These windfalls may then be bequeathed from generation to generation. The presence of such hysteresis phenomena destroys any *ahistorical* or statical relationship between the expected inflation rate and the sustainable rate of utility across alternative equilibrium states; the utility rate that a particular expected inflation rate would confer will depend upon whether the expected inflation rate would have to rise or to fall, and by how much, to reach that specified level – thus upon the present state of the expected inflation rate. In this case, then, the expected inflation rate that would in the long-run yield the greatest sustainable rate of utility will not generally be independent of the expected inflation rate existing at present. There might, for example, be some net gain obtainable on account of the distribution effect from a reduction of the expected inflation rate below its actual present level had it instead inherited a much higher expected inflation rate (and the same distribution of income).

While the great wealth of some individual families does survive from generation to generation, and the lucky breaks of some poor persons may have a lasting effect on their descendants, it may be tolerably accurate to suppose that a temporary discrepancy between the actual and expected inflation rate produces only effects upon distribution that eventually vanish. On that assumption, the relationship between the rate of utility that is sustainable over the indefinite future and the expected inflation rate across alternative equilibriums will be independent of the past history of expected inflation rate, Consequently, the expected inflation rate which maximizes the sustainable rate of utility will likewise be independent of past conditions. In the zero discount case, accordingly, the optimal inflation rate for the long run will be independent of distributional considerations.

But distributional considerations affecting the selection of the long-run inflation rate will not go away when policy is more present-minded as in the positive discount case. As in the simple model (with the natural rate), the optimal policy will settle for a rest point inflation rate that exceeds the rate maximizing the sustainable rate of utility. The distributional 'loss' which would accrue predominantly in the early future from the temporarily increased unemployment necessary to bring down the expected inflation rate is yet another reason for settling that way. If there was felt to be a net distributional benefit from the resulting fall of the cost of living relative to expectations, that distribution gain would tend of course to bias the long-run inflation rate in the opposite direction, toward the utility rate maximizing inflation rate. But because of long-term money contracts, this effect is slower-working so that it must receive less weight the greater the rate of discount is. Presumably, then, the optimal rest point inflation rate is farther above the utility maximizing rate the greater the discount rate is.

If we drop the assumption of the natural rate of unemployment, assuming instead that an increase of the expected inflation rate permits a permanent reduction of the equilibrium unemployment rate, the distributional factor imparts a stronger upward bias on the long-run optimal inflation rate. In this case, an increase of the actual inflation rate above the expected rate would bring a permanent distributional gain via the resulting permanent decline of the unemployment rate. (In terms of Figure 7.2, the distributional aspect of unemployment tends to make the utility contours steeper (refer to their right-hand sides) so that society will trade a greater increase of the expected inflation rate for a given permanent reduction of the unemployment rate in the process of locating its sustainable utility maximum.) As a corollary, the distributional aspect of the unemployment rate heightens the importance of knowing the amount of the unemployment reduction, if any, that would be obtainable permanently from an increase of the inflation rate.

Would that these remarks on the introduction of distributional effects into the optimization framework were longer than the subject deserves. Of course, governmental attention to the distributional effects of inflation policy, together with willingness to use redistributive taxes and transfers, will substantially lighten the distributional consequences of inflation policy, lessening the distributional harm when inflation policy would do harm and lessening the distributional benefit when inflation policy would do some good. Some of those techniques are tying social security payments to the cost of living (formally or informally) and offering high-percentage unemployment compensation. But substitutability is imperfect, there being no perfect tax or, if there were, a perfect government to legislate them. When there is a social cost to their erasure, distribution effects will typically not be erased, at any rate not completely; and where they are erased, one wants to keep in mind that the techniques employed for doing that may have unwanted side effects. It would not seem prudent therefore altogether to neglect distribution effects. In giving attention to distribution effects, I have been assuming that only some moderate fraction of the distributional incidence of an increase of the unemployment rate would or could be offset by compensatory use of other techniques such as unemployment insurance, income supplement tax adjustments, and variations in public employment policy.

7.3.5. *Change of Policy Assignment.* Next, I want to reconsider, with respect to the optimization model, the choice of policy instruments available for controlling aggregate demand and the matter of lags in their operation. The simple model introduced above postulated the use of federal tax policy to control demand through time, leaving the

central monetary authority with the task of keeping private investment on an even keel. It will be objected that competing demands
upon the Congress make frequent and prompt adjustment of tax
rates impossible.

It is important therefore to consider assigning to the Federal
Reserve the role of optimizing the rate of inflation – not despotically
but as one agent of a democratic government in tune with its public
policies. To bring out certain differences between the two techniques
for controlling inflation, let us follow the consequences of monetary
actions – open-market purchases of government securities that increase the money supply and stimulate the demand for goods – to
shift the economy from one equilibrium at the natural unemployment rate to another equilibrium at the natural rate with a higher
expected inflation rate. Imagine for the moment that the budgetary
deficit in real terms is left alone.

The transitional rise of employment and real incomes triggered by
the move to easier money tends to bring a present gain (an upward
movement along the current rate of utility curve) through the increased consumption induced by the increased after-tax real incomes,
whatever the direct impact upon consumption of the easier money.
But during the transition the capital stock is built up, unlike the
situation in the simple model, due to the direct impact upon private
investment demand of the open-market purchases, the subsequent
rush to invest in expectation of capital gains insofar as that is not
counteracted, and due to the inducement to invest from the increased
capital utilization rates. As employment recedes to the new equilibrium level, there is left from the transition an overhang of additional
capital per employee under the natural-rate hypothesis. Maintenance
of the new equilibrium therefore requires that the monetary authorities set expected real rates of interest at lower levels than in the earlier
equilibrium to balance the depressed real rates of return on capital
goods. Some of this bulge of the capital stock will be attenuated with
future population growth and technological progress; real rates of
return on capital will tend back toward some level consonant with
private thrift. Money interest rates will therefore be increasing for a
while. But there is some permanent effect upon capital intensity and
real interest rates from the selection of a new expected inflation rate.
Thrift will tend to be a little greater as individuals partially offset the
anticipated faster attrition of their real cash balances by reducing
their consumption.

If the government wishes to prevent the increase in the expected inflation rate from having this permanent capital-deepening effect, it must enlarge the budgetary deficit, cutting tax rates so as to divert resources from private investment activity to the production of consumption goods. The idea of using overall tax rates as a control over capital intensity (or the medium-term 'growth' of the economy) rather than as a control of short-term business conditions may still be ahead of its time. If that is the case, if it is unrealistic to assume the use of the budgetary deficit to control capital intensity, a new connection between the rate of utility and the expected rate of inflation emerges through the effect of the latter upon capital intensity; at the same time an old connection disappears, namely, the effect on fiscal efficiency of the tax-rate adjustment needed to insulate thrift and hence capital intensity from changes in the expected rate of inflation. In the model thus altered, there will still be, looking across alternative equilibrium steady-states, a maximum sustainable rate of utility and, in the absence of positive discounting, the optimal monetary policy will drive the expected inflation rate to the level corresponding to that maximum. The sustainable utility rate maximizing expected inflation rate will be greater in the revised model than in the tax-controlled model if shifting to an equilibrium with a higher expected rate of inflation would bring an increase of capital intensity that was more worthwhile (because of the consumption increase it would ultimately permit, tax rates being assumed to be unavailable for the same purpose) than the increase of fiscal efficiency which that same shift of equilibrium would bring if tax rates were reduced to offset the effect of the 'inflation tax' on consumption demand. Inflation, even anticipated inflation, is a defensible and ingenious policy for a country that lacks the fiscal capacity to finance capital-deepening primarily by ordinary taxation.

It should be mentioned that there may be relative price phenomena of importance in the course of macroeconomic control by either the monetary or fiscal means. The bulge in plant and equipment that would be created by a monetary drive that increased the rate of inflation would increase the capital stock in consumption good industries about as much as the capital stock in capital goods industries (in proportional terms). The reduction of expected real rate of interest required to eliminate the deflationary gap that this bulge in productive capacity would otherwise create, while stimulating investment demand, will not eliminate the above-equilibrium idle capacity in the consumption industries if the budgetary deficit is indeed left unchanged. Similarly, monetary measures to reduce the expected rate of inflation would leave the consumption goods sector short of capital as the new equilibrium is approached.[15]

Thus adjustments up or down in the expected rate of inflation by means of monetary controls may leave some temporary structural imbalances in their wake in the absence of fiscal jiggling. The appearance of a major structural effect upon the division of idle capacity and unemployment between the consumption and capital goods sectors, due to a major and rapid alteration of the expected inflation rate, would call for supplementary fiscal action to redress the structural imbalance. If tax rate adjustments to meet such structural effects cannot be counted on, the monetary authority will optimally move more slowly in altering the expected rate of inflation, never letting unemployment rate depart very far from its natural level so as to keep the capital structure from being markedly inappropriate to the future output mix.

7.4. *Ethical Considerations Relating to the Cost-Benefit Approach*

We could discuss the introduction of still other factors into the model, more or less carefully and explicitly, but the remainder of this chapter may be better devoted to confronting criticisms of a more fundamental nature. These are criticisms to the effect that an intertemporal cost-benefit approach to the problems of unemployment and the price level is unethical by nature, so that it will tend to produce a policy prescription that is immoral.

The gist of the objection, I believe, is that in the economist's cost-benefit analysis nothing is sacred. The gravest human costs are treated as commensurate with the most trivial costs. Essentially this is the Continuity Axiom according to which a man will risk death for another smoke (or another something) if the risk is small enough. This is enormously convenient for the economist, as it prevents him from getting into a bind of being hemmed in by too many sacreds. But if there is a contender or more for the title of sacred, the economist had better look into it.

---

[15] The consumption good we call shelter or housing is not the best example of overcapacity developing from a boom, since the rise of money interest rates accompanying the rise of the expected inflation rate (and the temporary improvement capital utilization rates) makes it difficult for the housing industry to acquire investment funds through the financial institutions that it primarily depends upon because there are ceilings on the money interest rates (or deposit rates) which those institutions are permitted to pay depositors in order to attract funds to lend.

7.4.1. *Immorality of Disinflationary Actions.* Many people feel that any economic policy which makes likely an increase of unemployment, causing presumably innocent people the frightening and crushing loss of their jobs, is ethically wrong and should therefore be inadmissible. Even a temporary swelling of unemployment, in order to bring down expectations of inflation from an excessive level, would come under this indictment. I can imagine my trial:

Revolutionist: So, professor, you say that, before the Revolution, you disliked the program of planned slump developed by the Nixon administration because you believed the costs of the unemployment were out of proportion to the future benefits?

Professor: Yes. And in view of the virtues of taut monetary control and the useful inflation tax offered by that high inflation rate, I felt there might be no future benefit at all from imposing those unemployment costs.

Revolutionist: But there is *some* inflation rate sufficiently above the one actually faced such that you would have favored 'imposing', to use your word, some joblessness in order to reduce inflationary expectations? Is that right?

Professor: Well, yes, that's an implication of the analysis, though inflation expectations which are only a little excessive would require only a little . . . [voice trailing off].

A certain amount of callousness seems to be an occupational hazard in the profession. Some pretty horrible sounding economic policies are regularly advanced by economists in the interest of free trade and economic efficiency. 'After all,' I have heard it said, 'the unemployed worker doesn't have any monopoly on suffering.' Or sometimes another horror will be conjured up to neutralize the first one: 'If wiping out those textile jobs will help shivering ill-clothed kids in Mississippi feel warmer, then I say we should do it.'

It is not callous, though, to maintain (until refuted) the acceptability of the Continuity Axiom. Suppose a popular referendum were held on the following sort of question. 'Everyone can be assured a prize of x dollars in perpetuity if everyone will vote to accept the risk that with probability p he will be thrown out of work for a duration of k months, Vote "Yes" or "No" on whether you favor exposing yourself and others to this risk for the sake of the prize.' My thought is that if p is small enough (though still positive), apart from a few crazies, everyone or nearly everyone will vote to accept the national gamble.[16]

This willingness to accept some risk over the personal distribution of a national cost or benefit comes up in various other contexts such as military conscription, dangerous highways, and the rationing of kidney machines. Of course, there are a few observers who evidently believe that this willingness to accept such risks is not really there or that, if it is, it should be disregarded as incompetent or immaterial. At any rate, there are a few who seem to favor producing however many kidney machines, spending however much money on road safety, and paying however much money for army volunteers as may be required to eliminate such individual risks.

Nevertheless the danger seems to be that the principle is recklessly applied. Thus the principle that every citizen ought to accept some risk of having to give up his life to help protect his country against aggression from some alien land inevitably smooths the way to conscription for wars with banal ends and terrible consequences. Likewise the principle that there exist inflation expectations that are sufficiently large as to warrant some rise of unemployment can be abused by being applied to situations of moderate or negligible inflations where reducing the expected inflation rate by increased unemployment would be extravagant or perverse.

Nevertheless the complaint against the insensitivity of those who would ever advocate increased unemployment, even temporarily, is still disturbing. At least economists should check to see whether there is not some alternative method to achieve the desired reduction of inflation expectations. Inevitably this brings to mind the subject of wage-price controls and, along with it, the more nebulous system called incomes policy.

It is perfectly obvious that if the expected inflation rate has a tremendous fall to make, it would be inadvisable to put all the burden of the adjustment on a disinflationary policy of slack aggregate demand. Clearly the government would want, if it used that method at all, to supplement the contrived slump, efficacious though

---

[16] The referendum has been described so as to leave room for the voter to express his altruistic feelings toward others' unemployment and others' prize money. Consider also the attitude expressed thus: 'If I have but one job separation to give, let me give it for my economy.'

it be, with a propaganda effort to persuade the public that the inflation rate will be falling rapidly. There is not necessarily anything deceptive about this. There must be some range of public predictions which would serve to reduce the errors of forecast made by the public, or at any rate not worsen them.

To my mind the use of temporary price and wage controls will under some circumstances be a preferable alternative to slackening aggregate demand. If the intention is merely to reduce the expected inflation rate, the price and wage freeze need be only temporary. Whether the step of instituting such a freeze would seem to be superior to a planned slump will largely depend upon whether the magnitude of the desired reduction in the expected inflation rate is large enough to justify incurring the initial fixed cost (or set-up cost) of establishing the freeze. If the expected inflation rate has 5 points to fall and this would take, say, 5 years of unemployment at a rate a point and a half above the natural rate via the aggregate demand route, certainly the introduction of a price and wage freeze appears to be the more attractive means to the given end. The opposite would seem to be true if only a very modest reduction of expectations is desired, so that the increase of unemployment entailed by the aggregate demand method is very slight even over a short period.

A more widely discussed approach envisions some kind of permanent government scheme for bringing about the desired wage and price behavior as a matter of social conscience. The proposal of informal public influences over individual price- and wage-setting seems to evoke very deep-seated reactions that vary with a person's view of human nature and individual obligation. There are quite a few sensitive and well-intentioned people from both ends of the political spectrum who feel the same moral distaste for attempts to persuade a person to keep his prices down as for attempts to persuade him to buy government bonds (when in both cases he would not do so without the persuasion). But since such good things as the protection of property and personal safety depend upon a good deal more than self-interest (especially these days when arrests and convictions are so rare), it is hard to see why there should be opposition in principle to the extension of the concepts of individual obligation and trust to the area of price-setting.

The question is again the standard one: of whether or not the benefits of such a system outweigh the costs, in particular the psychic costs imposed on each person of being obligated to resist the temptation to price his services relative to others at what he believes to be the level that maximizes his own self interest. For it should be clear that if a system of informal incomes policy controls is to achieve success in reducing *permanently* the unemployment rate consistent with steadiness of the inflation rate, that is, to reduce the macro-equilibrium unemployment rate, the policy must work through inducing some or all persons to seek a moderation of their relative income through a reduction of their prices relative to the expected level of others' prices; this means a continuing resistance to temptation by those who respond positively to the system. (Moreover, if some suppliers are unwilling to respond, resource allocation as between those who cooperate and those who do not may be adversely affected.)

The other empirical question about incomes policy centers on its effectiveness. Would it work? The incomes policy is likely to be ineffective, and hence fail the cost-benefit test very clearly, if there is a considerable amount of noncompliance with it. If, to take a pertinent example, price- and wage-setters in the manufacturing and service sectors of the economy are willing to cut prices and wages in relation to food prices, but suppliers of factor services in agriculture insist on maximizing profits as usual, the main effect of the incomes policy, after a *one-time* drop of the price level, is simply an alteration of relative prices and relative wages with little or no effect on the natural unemployment rate. No wonder that there is such instinctive skepticism about the efficiency of incomes policy over the long run.

7.4.2. Immorality of Proinflationary Actions. There are also many people who feel that any inflation policy is ethically wrong if it produces inflation beyond certain expectations. Two categories of expectations need to be dealt with.

In the first category, the government is a party to the expectation; there has been an implied contract between the government and the citizens, so that the disappointment of this sort of expectation is a breach of contract. Economic policies that do that, it may be argued, ought not to be admissible.

The usual example here assumes a promise, explicit or implicit, by the government to holders of its liabilities that it will protect the purchasing power of those obligations. In fact, however, it is not written on these certificates (or anywhere else, I believe) that the federal government of this country guarantees to pay a specified real interest payment to the holder. The inference might be ventured that had it been the intent of Congress to guarantee the real value of its interest-bearing obligations, it would have made arrangements to issue so-called index bonds. Indeed, the federal government may have willingly elected to pay to bondholders the premium they have demanded as compensation for the risks of unexpected inflation in order to be free of any such obligation. It is true that political parties have often campaigned on the pledge of restoring price stability but it is common knowledge that most such pledges are not redeemed, many are mutually inconsistent, and some would be injurious to carry out.

It is true though that, in a singular case, the optimality of the 'optimal inflation policy' described here depends upon a deception. That sole case is the one in which the expected inflation rate is at the sustainable benefit maximizing level and there is positive discounting. Then additional and unexpected inflation is indicated by the optimal policy for the sake of the present gain from the largely or wholly temporary reduction of unemployment that it will produce.[17] This would not be the only circumstance in which a government had ever employed secrecy or deception for the sake of an allocative or distributive social gain. A government insists that a currency devaluation will be avoided while it is planning one. A central bank forecasts that interest rates will come down in order to discourage borrowing when it does not expect to be able to reduce them. The government is always trading on the opacity of the monetary and fiscal veils in order to be able to push unemployment and inflation up or down. Honesty in public policy may sometimes compete with other high-order goods like justice, compassion, and survival.

Consider now the other class of expectations. It is sometimes argued that the government ought not to disappoint expectations in general, even when it has not helped to create some of them in the past. The suggestion is that people who have formed reasonable expectations and have carried out programs of education, job-training, investment, and saving for retirement deserve not to have those expectations frustrated by the government wherever it is feasible to satisfy them.

If expectations were mutually satisfiable, this requirement condemns economic policy to maintenance of macroequilibrium always at the prevailing distribution of wealth. Actually, expectations among

---

[17] In the zero discount case, that part of the unemployment reduction which is temporary when the expected inflation rate is driven up to the benefit maximizing rate is only a kind of side benefit but perhaps not one to be lightly thrown away by hastening the adjustment of inflation expectations through forecasts.

individuals are likely to conflict. Indeed, expectations may be inconsistent even in an individual. The man who expects price stability
may also be expecting to keep his job and have his loan paid back.
To enjoy stable prices, he may have to lose his job and see his loan
defaulted. In the revolution of expectations, people are coming to
expect good economic policies.

8 Inflation Strategy and Routine Stabilization under Uncertainty

THE purpose of this chapter is to bring together some remarks about inflation strategy in the presence of uncertainty. To this discussion is appended some fleeting remarks on the distinct problem of routine stabilization when neither the policy-making authorities nor other outside forces are altering the stochastic processes which underlie business fluctuations.

8.1 Uncertainty and Inflation Strategy

Chapter 7 charged the monetary authority (or the fiscal authority or both in a joint effort) with the task of implementing some time path of aggregate demand, with overseeing some process of adjustment to a desired equilibrium. In contrast, some observers see the monetary authority as so afflicted with hazards and uncertainties as to be unable to play that role. Certainly we have learned over the past decade that our forecasts of unemployment and inflation are much more subject to error than was supposed in the first flush of Keynesianism. The prediction of many variables, like the defense budget and farm prices, requires expertise in politics, meteorology, and other disciplines as well as economics. One thinks of scientific progress as whittling down the random component and enlarging the systematic component; but similar technological progress is constantly reforming the structure of the economy to be analyzed, so the improvement of economic forecasts is an uphill battle. At the present time there is the embarrassment of a strictly economic uncertainty over the potencies of monetary changes – roughly, changes in the composition, particularly the liquidity, of the government debt – and fiscal changes – roughly, changes in the size and rate of increase of the government debt – in influencing aggregate production and prices.

The presence of uncertainty has evoked a variety of proposals for appropriate policy response. Two notably extreme proposals for macroeconomic policy are considered here. Neither one of them seems to be tenable. Each one, in its own way, overreacts to the uncertainty to such a degree as to disregard the intertemporal complication of the inflation choice problem, making the dynamic problem into a static one. Yet it is instructive to consider their merits and demerits.

8.1.1. *The Existential Approach.* In the view of some observers, the task of monetary policy is to keep the economy afloat in turbulent waters and unpredictable currents. Intertemporal planning, even of the sequential or dynamic type, is not possible or desirable. There will seldom if ever be a time in which it will clearly be advisable deliberately to plan the disequilibration of the economy for the sake of some probable adjustment of inflation expectations in the future.

One rationale for this position asserts the costliness of stabilizing policy actions. When a war breaks out and drives unemployment below the equilibrium rate, the central bank must expand the money supply lest interest rates rise so abruptly as to precipitate a liquidity crisis (or at least an anguishing alteration of balance sheets). Thus the central bank finds itself collaborating in a rise of the expected inflation rate that it never desired. This circumstance is ultimately attributable to uncertainty: Had the bank foreseen the disturbance in ample time, it might have been able to create a cushion of real resources beforehand in anticipation of the fiscal reversal to come.[1] The upshot is that, according to this argument, the monetary authorities are best occupied with putting out fires – slowly so as not to do too much water damage – and, in view of their limitations, can ill afford to start any fires of their own.

Without agreeing that unemployment and inflation are uncontrollable, we can nevertheless draw this lesson: Optimal inflation strategy should consider the costs of rowing against the tide, for example, the costs of the liquidity squeeze from the sharply higher interest rates necessary to bring a swift reduction of the unemployment rate. Thus, in technical terms, the central bank must look, with each decision, at *two* state variables – the unemployment rate and the rate of expected inflation – the future course of which it can hope to nudge only gradually. In view of the costs associated with

---

[1] It is not clear to me that there is a forceful argument of a symmetrical character in the event of an unplanned slump. When a recession strikes, is there any positive merit in a needs-of-trade policy of sympathetic credit contraction? It is sometimes said that when credit markets are very loose, borrowers of undemonstrated credit worthiness will obtain credit, which will cause trouble later on. There is also the point that some job security may be willingly traded for the reduction in balance sheet 'capital certainty' that it permits.

pushing the unemployment rate over some short time interval, it is apparent that the central bank's optimal near-term target may be an unemployment rate that is nearly as low as the present rate, or an even lower one if exogenous forces are pushing the system that way. The bank's expectation of the rise of the expected inflation rate that will occur if the rise of the unemployment rate turns out to be as slow as it expects its policy to cause it is just the price it is willing to pay for the moderateness of its contractionary monetary steps.

The price of such policy moderation is invariably a slowing of progress in some sense. In the example we have been considering, a proper amount of moderateness may very well make it likely that things will get worse before they get better, in certain key respects at least. But while an optimally moderated policy may often be circuitous, it does not forget where it is desired to reach. An optimal policy has the mathematical expectation of ultimately reaching the long-run desired rest point target.[2] Only in rare moments of extremity is the long-run objective thrown temporarily to the wind.

The 'mathematical expectation' here is in the mind of the policy-maker. This raises the point that if he underestimates the probability of war and similarly expansionary fiscal emergencies (while making no compensating errors of other sorts), while his policy will ultimately be tending in his eyes toward the desired rest point expected inflation rate, the expected inflation rate actually achieved will tend to average around some level that is bounded above that target rate. Further, there is a distinction to be made between mean and mode. If, say, random expansionary impulses are equally probable as contractionary ones but much more intense on the average, the policy which creates the mathematical expectation of a certain asymptotical expected inflation rate will aim for a state of stochastic rest in which the expected inflation rate is a little lower 'most of the time' than the optimum mathematical expectation.

The gain from policy moderation in the above example was the avoidance of certain costs from a more aggressive tightening of money – the likelihood of bankruptcies resulting from sharply tighter credit and, possibly, some worsening of the resource allocations made by a credit market placed in temporary turmoil.[3] The risks

---

[2] More precisely, it seeks eventually to attain some stochastic rest point probability distribution of the state variables which it influences.

[3] Section 4.2.6 contains some illustrations. These financial costs are likely to be pronounced when the various financial institutions are inflexibly geared to a certain range of nominal interest rates. But here one must agree with the opponents of a highly elastic credit policy that when persistent disequilibrating

imposed in taking a large policy step are often cited as a fairly general example of the greater costs of large steps compared to small ones. The confinement of policy shifts (each month or each quarter) to some moderate range, by lessening the risks of a bad outcome, may compensate for the resulting error in the expected value of the target variable as seen in a no-risk analysis.[4] The substantive difficulty in any application is in identifying the minimum-risk policy action, in giving the appropriate content to 'abstaining from policy action'. If one measures monetary actions by the money supply normalized in some way to allow for the growth of the economy and the desired rise of the price level, zero change in this 'intensive money supply' might at first be deemed the least-risk action, whether or not the optimal one. But this policy might be relatively risky in the face of sharp fluctuations in liquidity preference.[5]

There is a concrete example of the risk-avoidance consideration that is relevant here. Assume that the current expected inflation rate is judged to exceed the figure that would be aimed for if there were no uncertainty. Assume also that the natural unemployment rate is judged to be a band, but that the extent of that band is not known for certain. The inflation planners believe that they can maintain the economy in the neighborhood of some normal unemployment rate and that by doing so they can at least insure the continuation of the present expected inflation rate. Not knowing the limits of the natural-rate band, however, they cannot be sure how much unemployment they must create in excess of this normal level in order to produce the likelihood of a fall of inflation expectations as desired. In that situation, it seems intuitively reasonable that the inflation strategists should rest content with the status quo, provided it is not critically uncomfortable. One is prepared to believe, in other words, that there is a whole range of expected inflation rates, all of which

---

forces are driving up the expected rate of inflation it only makes matters worse for the future if stiff increases in interest rates are delayed so that, as inflationary expectations gain momentum, larger increases are eventually needed. In these circumstances in which moderation is forced upon the policy-maker, promptness in taking the moderate steps is especially important, for time is working against you.

[4] See R. G. Penner, 'On the Desirability of Discretionary Policy', *Journal of Political Economy*, October 1967, and the references cited there. A related paper that emphasizes the advantages of a diversified portfolio of policy tools is W. G. Brainard, 'Monetary Policy and Uncertainty', *American Economic Review*, May 1967.

[5] The notorious *k percent rule* for increasing the money supply is the topic of the next section.

are in some sense undesirably high, having the property that they are accepted grudgingly for fear that their reduction will be found to be too expensive.

The lesson here is that there is presumably some range of expected inflation rates where the inflation planners should 'leave well enough alone'. This assumes, reasonably enough, that there is some discounting of future utilities relative to present ones. The stand-pat range is wider the larger the rate of discount. It does not appear to me, however, that it would be optimal to perpetuate every inherited expectation of the inflation rate, no matter how outsized. We have seen expectations of inflation expunged before and we can plausibly assume that the same trick can be accomplished again at some finite cost or other.

We have been discussing some ways in which various kinds of uncertainties pose costs and risks for macroeconomic policy actions in such a way as possibly to modify the appropriate inflation objective. There are also uncertainties about future structures and preferences. Even among economists, the most calculating of creatures, one sometimes detects a willingness to let the future go uncalculated, perhaps because of its nebulousness. 'It is . . . assumed that we cannot now know what we shall want later; it is safe to destroy even though one has no plans for what is to follow, because one could not now, ahead of time, know what needs we shall have. When we are in the new situation, then we shall know obviously, clearly instantly, without any bumbling uncertainty.'[6]

The optimization approach to inflation planning, it might be charged, makes the unwarranted assumption of an unchanged economic structure in the future. For example, it assumes, in the absence of any foreknowledge to the contrary, that the natural rate of unemployment (or, more generally, the equilibrium locus) will be constant over time so that an increase of unemployment over this natural level will have an essentially unchanged disutility over time (apart from regularized time discounting). Clearly any happenstance events or deliberate policy actions, now or later, which improve the functioning of the labor market, to the degree that they reduce the marginal disutility of pushing unemployment above the natural rate, would decrease the optimum *long-run* or *rest point* inflation rate (providing there is positive discounting of future benefits). Sooner

    [6] A. O. Rorty, 'The Sense of Choice and Change', unpublished draft, December 1969. The question is taken from a discussion of some contemporary student attitudes.

or later, therefore, such an alteration in the structure will make a difference for optimal inflation policy.

Because of this always present possibility that the economic structure will take a favorable turn in the future, some people believe that the intertemporal optimization approach counsels a current employment rate which errs on the low side. Their cheerful Micawberian message is that the future will take care of itself.

The economist, let us admit it, is in danger of being a fussbudget, making resource allocation so worrisome that it takes all the pleasure out of consuming.[7] But beyond that grain of truth there is not much there. Fortuitous developments which are unfavorable deserve equal weight with favorable ones.

Actually, as a technical aside, it may be remarked that a future improvement of the natural unemployment rate, and associated reduction of the long-run inflation rate, do not have unambiguous qualitative implications for the optimal inflation rate in the present. It may be that the downward adjustment of the expected rate of inflation to be accomplished ultimately will optimally be set in motion immediately, so that the rate of inflation will be a little smaller both before and after the time at which the natural rate is diminished. But it is equally plausible that the opportunity to 're-purchase' cheaply the present expected rate of inflation once the structural measures have worked their way will cause an optimal policy in the present to increase the expected inflation rate – to live on borrowed time – until the natural rate of unemployment has decreased. To my knowledge at least, there are no results available of help and little likelihood that useful answers will be easily obtainable.

For practical reasons, therefore, the optimization approach sketched above is most readily applicable to present policy-making when any major structural changes are close at hand and can be taken reliably into account or when they are very far off and heavily discounted. The introduction of future structural changes introduces a disconcerting conjectural aspect insofar as it is hard to predict how marked and how valuable the future changes will be, owing to the novelty of the actions conceived or not yet conceived. In a few years we will know better what improvements in the structure of the labor

[7] Similarly, in contrasting the romantic and heroic style with the calculated style of the economist Boulding remarks that no one should 'want his daughter to marry an economic man'. K. E. Boulding, *Economics as a Science* (New York: McGraw-Hill, 1970), p. 134.

market can be accomplished and what measures promise to be worthwhile.

8.1.2. *The Telescopical Approach.* In the mind of some other observers, the problem of macroeconomic planning is altogether different. For them it is only the long run that can be tended to. It is the short run that must be left to itself. While the former group cannot see past their thick spectacles, and must feel their way along, the latter group will not put down their telescopes, and are apt to fall down a hole. They recommend that the policy-maker content himself with choosing among policies according simply to their long-run consequences. They telescope the vast future into the present. This means that the class of eligible policies must have the property that each will promise the attainment of some (possibly stochastic) steady-state pattern. The optimal policy within this class is the one that promises the preferred long-run equilibrium steady-state (presumably taking probable transition costs into account in that preference).

The approach to policy favored by this group, like the approach discussed previously, is statical: They simplify what is in principle an intertemporal problem, one complicated by stochastic disturbances over time, into a static optimization problem and present the solution offered as suitable for the full dynamic problem.

From the telescopical viewpoint, the function of the central bank is to adhere rigidly, in all but the most extreme disequilibriums at any rate, to a predetermined course of the money supply. The belief is that such a program, if the course of the money supply is smooth enough, will tend to be more stabilizing – at least it will avoid major errors – than the efforts of the monetary authorities to adjust their actions to current observations on the state of the economy. An optimal predetermined money supply course is any one promising the appropriate long-run rate of inflation. The most famous proposal on this line is the *k percent rule* of Milton Friedman. This states that the supply of money should be made to grow regularly at *k percent* per annum – where *k* is the preferred long-run rate of inflation *plus* the projected rate of growth of real national output under conditions of macroequilibrium *less* the forecast secular rate of increase of the velocity of money correspondingly defined.[8]

Obviously there is no conflict between this rule and the optimal

[8] M. Friedman, 'A Monetary and Fiscal Framework for Economic Stability', *American Economic Review*, March 1948.

inflation policy described above when the economy is precisely in the desired rest-point equilibrium.

The conflict between the *k* percent rule and the optimal policy approach appears whenever the economy is seriously in disequilibrium *or* when the equilibrium at hand is not the desired point of rest, so that corrective disequilibration is indicated. Imagine that fine tuners and *k* percenters agree that the optimal rate of inflation for the long run is 3 percent per annum. Suppose that fine tuners at least believe that the present expected inflation rate is 6 per cent and that the unemployment rate is presently close to the natural rate. The fine tuners will bring their charts to Capitol Hill and to the Federal Reserve, saying:

> We want to aim for 5 percent inflation a year from now; if by then the expected inflation rate is down to 5.5 percent, we will recommend aiming for 4.5 percent 12 months from then. Accordingly, we recommend open-market sales followed by later purchases which, after a brief period of abnormal rediscounting, will hold the money supply constant over the next 6 months. Thereupon the real value of the money supply will be modified according to the subsequent slowdown of output as it develops. We also have to plan for various contingencies regarding the subsequent behavior of the expected inflation rate as it responds, including its feedback on the demand for money . . .

The *k* percenters would take a different position:

> Some say the expected inflation rate is now 6 per cent. They may very well be right. We don't know. We don't know what the unemployment rate is at the present time. The conflicting signals of sharp depression and mounting inflation are worrying us. In this situation we feel the best policy is to try to increase the money supply at an unchanging geometric rate of 4 percent per annum. Accordingly, we advocate buying about $30,000 of 'governments' per hour, pending the completion of new money supply data.

Clearly, the fine tuner intends a marked and early rise of unemployment followed by a gradual return to the natural rate of unemployment. The *k* percenter intends a more gradual rise of unemployment with employment probably reaching a deeper trough. With reference to inflation rates, the fine tuner intends a marked and early fall of the inflation rate. We can expect the *k* percenter to generate a more gradual fall of the inflation rate at first but one that ultimately must overshoot the 3 percent target rate.

This tendency to oscillation under the k percent rule can be understood from the observation that once the inflation rate has reached 3 percent, the real money supply will by that time be quite depressed as the price level was rising at the beginning at 6 per cent. Furthermore, at each output level, the real demand for money will be buoyed by the fall of the expected inflation rate achieved so far. Consequently, output and employment must at that point still be below their respective natural levels if the demand for money is to equal the supply. With reference only to these forecast paths, the latter k percenter path is of course not optimal from the point of view of the optimization approach in terms of a nonstochastic deterministic model. The exact nature of that nonoptimality has been shown. It is like a man who plans to tighten his belt in middle age in order to live well in his youth and in his old age.

If there is a case to be made for the k percent rule away from the desired rest point equilibrium, it must be based on some features of uncertainty in nondeterministic models. The general nature of such a case, I presume, would be that the k percent rule protects against disaster or against minor fluctuations or both better than policies which gear the money supply to current information on the economy are apt to do when the current state of the economy (and perhaps even the structure) is not precisely known – indeed, incorrectly perceived as well as incompletely perceived.

The k percent rule can perhaps be understood as a rule for operating under total ignorance. You are assigned to manage the money of an economy you know nothing about and never will *except* that it is structured like the one depicted in this book, that it is best that this economy eventually have an inflation rate of 4 percent, that its natural rate of growth is 4 percent, and that the velocity of its money rises secularly at 2 percent. Your decision is the instructions to this economy on the rate of growth this month of its money supply. Obviously, you instruct the economy to make its money supply grow at 6 percent per annum. If you knew that the economy was currently suffering hyperinflation or severe depression, you would of course choose a different growth rate of the money supply for the month. On the other hand, if you regard such data as last month's unemployment rate as so unreliable as to be worthless, you would not deviate from 6 per cent.

The k percenter thus rests his policy recommendation upon an extremely pessimistic appraisal of our knowledge of the impending state of the economy and the consequences of policy action upon it. Moreover, if the k percent rule were to be followed over a wide region of possible economic states – so that the monetary authorities would not quickly redeem the mistakes of the rule – there is some chance that the rule would be destabilizing. Downward revision of the expected inflation rate could cause the demand for real money steadily to outrun the supply of real money balances (at any fixed output level), and this gap would in turn fuel a hyperdeflation without any convergence to equilibrium.[9]

There is no danger in this day and age that we would leave the aircraft on Friedman's automatic pilot when turbulence has sent it plummeting toward earth. Something would be done. But there would be an irretrievable loss of economic welfare in the interim. Therefore, it may be more than just a marginal improvement upon the k percent rule to have an 'optimal' policy strategy available, in the face of uncertainty, for adjusting expectations of inflation to the desired level when they are out of line. Let me offer a few remarks on this topic.

The task of inflation reform, of adjusting expectations of the inflation rate, can be viewed as a problem of policy that turns up only exceptionally. Correspondingly one may cling to the view that in such episodes there are no 'laws' which describe the behavior of expectations. In any given historical setting, one may be willing to assume that expectations of the inflation rate are formed in a 'behavioral' manner that is satisfactorily described by 'adaptive expectations'. Yet, even so, we should concede that the direction and magnitude with which expectations will be revised in response to incoming data are not forecastable precisely by the analyst and policy-maker.

In this case, in which the analyst treats expectations as being formed mechanically, there are a couple of subcases worth distinguishing. In the simplest of these the analyst can forecast the expected rate of inflation (over the current period, to refer to a discrete time period analysis) subject to a random error the probability distribution of which is entirely known (and may be a known function of the policy action selected). Risk, either additive or

---

[9] For a suggestive analysis, see W. S. Vickrey, 'Stability through Inflation', in K. K. Kurihara, ed., *Post-Keynesian Economics* (New Brunswick, N.J.: Rutgers University Press, 1954). In my exposition above, I am neglecting the fact that, in the non-textbook world, share prices would fall with a decline in the expected inflation rate and thus equilibrate the money market. The outcome is nonetheless contractionary.

multiplicative, is thus introduced into the dynamic programming model in the accustomed way.

The more difficult subcase is that in which there is insufficient information each period to infer the probability distribution from which, so to speak, the expected inflation rate will be 'drawn' (for any given policy action). There is uncertainty about the state of the economy, as discussed in connection with the rationale for the k percent rule. The customary approach to problems in dynamic programming under uncertainty utilizes the Bayesian approach to statistical estimation.

Analytical difficulties multiply when we allow that the behavior of the expected inflation rate may fail to be describable in terms of the usual mechanical 'adaptive' formula. Specifically, it seems likely that a decision of the stabilization authorities to revise their long-term inflation objective, thus bringing about some change in the structure of the economy, would sooner or later engender some revision in the method by which producers and consumers form their expectations of the inflation rate. It is natural to suppose that people would begin to base their expectations of the inflation rate in part on their guesses as to the new inflation objective of the stabilization authorities. So the authorities are in the position of having to conjecture what the public is expecting it to do (and expecting it to conjecture).

I believe that the above sorts of analytical problems can be shown to have intelligible and instructive solutions. A more difficult class of problems is the one in which the parameters of the model are uncertain and in which accumulating experience gives fresh information about those parameters while presumed structural change is making old information obsolete. At some point the analyst, like someone giving instructions on how to ride a bicycle, has to say 'This is as much as I can intellectualize; now do it.'

8.2. *Routine Stabilization*

We have been discussing certain complexities confronting the policy-maker when it is desired to achieve a change in the expected rate of inflation in an optimal manner in the presence of various uncertainties. This problem is not, of course, the only task that comes to the monetary and fiscal authorities. In fact, this is not what one thinks of as the principal activity of the monetary authorities. That function is ordinarily conceived to be 'stabilization' – specifically, stabilization of output around some equilibrium trend path.

With the exception of a very few pages, it is the implication of everything written in this volume that these two tasks are somewhat conflicting. Consider only the most favorable case to a coincidence in the objectives of these two assignments; the case in which, if the system by chance finds itself at the macroequilibrium levels of output and employment, the corresponding expected inflation rate will be found to be at the desired figure. If a chance disturbance of aggregate demand should push output and employment above their respective macroequilibrium levels, and thus tend to raise the actual inflation rate, the expected inflation rate will begin to rise. According to the adaptive expectations hypothesis employed through most of this work, mere restoration of the system to macroequilibrium will not expunge the rise in the expected inflation rate. It will be necessary to send output and employment over to the other side of equilibrium – as a kind of punishment – in order to even up the forecast errors to which the expected inflation rate adapts. An illustrative sequence for the actual and expected inflation rates is as follows: (2, 2), (3, 2), (1.2, 2.2), (2, 2), . . . You need the − .8 deviation of the actual rate to erase fully the errant .2 added to the expected rate by the + 1 deviation of the actual inflation rate.

The body of Keynesian literature on stabilization seems to assume that this punishment is not required, not at any rate if stabilization policy is proceeding effectively to keep things under control. According to the received wisdom on stabilization, it is enough to enact disinflationary or counterexpansionary policy measures when output exceeds its macroequilibrium level. One wants to minimize deviations from the equilibrium level, not manufacture them out of some sense of symmetry and balance!

Evidently one or the other views of the character of appropriate stabilization policy has gone wrong at some point. I believe that the puzzle is resolved if we think of the conventional injunction to stabilize output as closely as possible around its equilibrium level as pertaining only to situations in which the disturbances are not large enough to be statistically significant; and if we think of the alternative policy formulation, which calls for balancing one disequilibrium with another, as appropriate only to situations in which cumulative stochastic disturbances have been radical enough to shake confidence in the underlying structure that each period 'throws out the numbers'.

The suggestion is that one can think of stochastic processes governing aggregate demand whose stability over time, when coupled with some successful and routine stabilization policy, gives confidence in the permanence of some particular inflation rate over the long haul by virtue of the resulting containment of whatever chance disturbances come into play. In such an enviroment, there is no longer any tendency on the part of the public to extrapolate (however provisionally) any fraction of an outsize inflation rate over the indefinite future; at most, people will expect some slowness in the decay of the 'transient' inflation rate.

The hypothesis, then, is that there exist regimes in which the normal business fluctuations, together with routine stabilization practices, do not occasion any adaption of the expected inflation rate. In a given setting, once it has become familiar, expectations become 'rational' in the sense that the conditional forecasts of each economic agent – conditional on such current data as are readily observable to him – are unbiased, that is, correct on the average in repetitions of any like set of data.[10] In such a regime it is inappropriate for the policy-maker to respond to an inadvertent bulge of output beyond the equilibrium level with a contrived slump of output below the equilibrium level. Optimal policy can content itself with cushioning or dampening the fluctuations of output around the equilibrium level (provided the corresponding expected inflation rate is the desired one).[11]

This hypothesis would be most clearly appealing if the economy did not exhibit some persistence in the random fluctuations of aggregate demand. If the policy-maker had the ability and desire to eradicate such persistence as the underlying disturbances would tend to produce without stabilization, once the policy-maker is done, the disturbances that are left would be independently disturbed from period to period. In fact such a policy would be unlikely to be optimal in view of the costliness of complete stabilization in any fairly short interval of time. This is a reiteration of the point acknowledged earlier that sharp adjustments of the policy instruments themselves impose costs so that an optimal policy rides with the punch. We can expect, therefore, that if there is serial persistence in the underlying disturbances, this will be revealed, presumably to a moderated degree, in the observable time series.

The other reason why in principle there might be no persistence, of course, is that the underlying chance impulses are themselves in-

---

[10] The classic reference is J. F. Muth, 'Rational Expectations and the Theory of Price Movements', *Econometrica*, April 1961.

[11] This will reduce the minimizing the variance of output if stabilizing actions themselves are costless.

dependently disturbed over time. Needless to say, such basic serial independence is quite implausible. If the number and scale of foreign military involvements in the present quarter-year are larger than normal, we would bet on an abnormally large involvement next quarter, though perhaps by a slackened amount. By the way, the absence of underlying persistence in the stochastic disturbances would also appear to preclude any rationale for stabilization policy.[12] If the chances are that the system will be on even keel next period, despite this period's disturbances, there is no reason to depart from the monetary and fiscal actions that would have been undertaken this period (with an eye to next period) in the absence of those disturbances. Once the expected inflation rate has been brought into conformity with public policy, the k percent rule would be apt for such a zero-persistence world – provided the appropriate k were somehow known.

But if we insist on the reality of persistence in random disturbances, we face a theoretical problem: If everyone expects some persistence of certain disturbances ('experts said they expected a continuation of the disturbances in the Middle East'), and everyone expects everyone else to expect it, what happens? Consider a situation in which previous disturbances have established expectations of larger-than-average level of aggregate demand, output, and employment in the next period. Assume that producers learn that, to some degree, the promise of good times is general; producers believe that the chances are for better than average business all round in the coming period. If every producer likes to raise his price whenever he expects an above-average level of demand for his product at his normal price, and if this is common knowledge, all producers in the situation under consideration will presumably anticipate some raise in the prices of their competitors (as well as a similar rise in the cost of living). But how is the extent of this competitive anticipatory price rise to be determinate? If each producer has come to expect some persistence in economy-wide sales, he must be presumed also to have learned to expect some associated adjustment of his competitor's prices in anticipation of just such persistence, at least if they also now recognize the bulge in the demands for their products to have been partly macroeconomic and general rather than individual or specific. Some stay-even price rise is therefore warranted for each seller on top of the

---

[12] One still has the nonlinear cycle models and other deterministic cycle models as possible motivations for stabilization policy. Yet there must be some tricky noise in the background if the agents of these economies never learn to anticipate these regular cycles. It is often said that descriptiveness of these models depends finally upon the presence of 'economic growth and structural change'.

gain he seeks in his relative price. 'I will raise my prices by 1 percent to help clear the floor of queues. But so will my competitors. So I can raise my prices by 2 percent with the same real effect? But then it must be that they also will raise their prices by 2 percent for they are like me. So I will raise by 3 . . .'

The objective of the model-builder should be to describe an economy in which (1) the policy-maker expects some persistence in the chance impulses on aggregate demand; (2) he acts so as to leave some persistence in the system; (3) the public *on average* anticipates the persistence left in as a matter of policy. A critical problem for him then is to explain why the rate at which other producers are expected to push up their prices in response to the anticipated persistence of the disturbance in aggregate demand (even after partial policy correction) does not induce sellers to attempt to match that increase on top of the price increases they would set if they did not expect their competitors to raise prices.

One possible answer points out that an upside disturbance of aggregate demand (e.g., foreign military involvements, again) coupled with an incompletely offsetting monetary tightening (speaking with reference to the predictions of the model) must leave nominal interest rates abnormally high – and expected real interest rates too. This is a transitory effect in the system but nonetheless real. It may reasonably be assumed to stimulate incentives to work longer hours and to run capital equipment more intensively. Thus the mountain may come to Mohammed: At some large enough expected real rate of (long-term) interest the quantity of aggregate output supplied is equated to the temporarily enlarged quantity of aggregate output demanded. At a highly intuitive level, one may view the matter in the following manner: When national needs for production are pressing, incentives to work and save are enhanced and both supply and demand are increased; the return to normal patterns of activity will be gradual and anticipated (in a probabilistic sense), being marked by a subsidence of the inflation rate, the money interest rate, and the expected real interest rate. At the other end, when the world market for the national export goes bust or investment opportunities run out, real interest rates are depressed and the country takes a vacation; if expectations are confirmed, business gradually returns to normal. Never in these scenarios is there any 'fundamental disequilibrium'. One has to think of equilibrium trajectories all of which lead to the natural employment level (to stick to the simplest model). Stochastic disturbances of the sort described knock the economy onto one of these remote trajectories – 'unexpectedly' to be sure – but the ensuing history is not implied to be one of systematic surprise.[13]

Another conceivable answer – and here we abandon the above assumption that the expected real interest rate differs systematically in situations of high and low aggregate demand – is this: While producers and households make unbiased forecasts, conditional on their available information at the time, of the rates at which others will raise or lower prices, their action depends upon their estimates of each others' expectations, and these may be forever biased. Precisely, businessmen may accurately forecast one another's price rises but opt not to raise their own prices beyond their competitors out of fear that their customers do not anticipate so large an increase in the going price. (One could even imagine that simultaneously the consumer is smiling because he thinks his supplier is unaware that his competitors have raised their prices as much as he has.) This does not imply, of course, that either party would bank on a continuation of the other's ignorance if the magnitude of the inflation (relative to the norm) were to continue in such a way as to raise doubts about the constancy of the underlying structure. Whatever the substantive merits of this latter answer, the theorist might well feel that it is analytically unattractive to have to keep track of *expectations of expectations* in his vision of how the economy works.

A third potential way to reconcile predictable deviations from trend with the assumption of rational expectations is to invoke the hypothesis that the idleness of resources is inversely dependent upon the quantity of liquidity in the economy. When a random impulse dictates a policy of tight money to stabilize (incompletely) the level of aggregate demand, the resulting shortage of liquidity and/or higher nominal interest rates may itself induce an increase of aggregate supply by causing producers to be willing to reduce stocks, run capital equipment more intensively, and cause households to accept job offers earlier. Inasmuch as a permanent increase of the average inflation rate that comes to be anticipated will also correspond to reduced

<hr/>

[13] In my own work on macroeconomic disequilibrium, I several times raised the concept of a nonsteady-state equilibrium path and used the term steady-state equilibrium to refer to the simpler concept. Undoubtedly Lucas and Rapping have been the heaviest users of the concept of a nonsteady equilibrium trajectory. It is doubtful, however, that such equilibrium trajectories have a comparable degree of appeal in models that abandon the assumption that prices and wage rates are market-clearing. (See the references in Chapter 1; and see also R. E. Lucas, Jr., 'Econometric Testing of the Natural Rate Hypothesis', typescript, November 1970, to be published.)

liquidity and higher money interest rates, this method of reconciliation contradicts the natural-rate hypothesis and thus complicates the model somewhat.

A fourth way out of the modeling dilemma is to appeal to the controversial hypothesis broached in Chapter 2, and cited briefly in Chapter 7, that the natural rate of unemployment is a *band*. This is especially plausible, if it ever is, when aggregate demand fluctuates. On this hypothesis, there can be systematic prediction errors, but there is a range of errors which are not noticeable.

The fifth way involves recognizing that in any month or quarter most firms are locked into their current wage rates and price lists. Thus short-lived disturbances do not get the opportunity to explode the price level.

If these or other ways of obtaining a determinate inflation rate in generally predictably perturbed situations are judged to be unsatisfactory, one may then have to fall back on some modification of the rational expectations hypothesis. After all, for many traders the problem of finding the statistical relationships involved in making unbiased forecasts is sufficiently difficult to justify the assumption that, under some conditions, the conditional forecasts of some or all economic agents are *systematically in error*.[14] This does not imply that *un*conditional forecasts are in error; everyone may be assumed to know what the average inflation rate is (or behave as if he knew that). Consequently it is not implied that the shift from one stabilization rule to another rule will offer any permanent improvement in the average output rate realized by the economy. But it is not clear, not without analysis of examples, whether there exist modifications of the rational expectations hypothesis that would not land the analyst back in the situation in which, according to the model, booms must be followed by planned slumps if the desired figure for the equilibrium inflation rate is to be maintained in the face of fluctuations.

[14] Even professional forecasters!

9 International Ramifications of American Inflation Policies

FOR the purposes of economic policy-making, much of the interest in the preceding chapters turns on the assumption that this country can make a moderate change in its inflation rate without impairing its gains from international trade and investment. While the size and diversity of the United States have left comparatively little room for gains from foreign trade and investment, a major impairment of these gains would not be a negligible consideration. Furthermore, in view of the enormous gap in living standards between this nation and the rest of the world, we ought to give heavy weight also to the economic benefits obtainable by foreign countries, both from their international and purely internal economic activities. The object of this chapter is to consider the international costs and benefits of this country's rate of inflation.

If this country were to establish a high rate of inflation domestically, 10 percent or more per annum, that would probably be disadvantageous to the rest of the world taken as a whole. It would also, even more probably, be directly disadvantageous to us. To the extent that countries abroad took measures to reduce the burdens to them of rapid inflation here, some of those measures would add significantly to the costs borne by us of the rapid inflation. But a moderate inflation rate in this country, one that would be beneficial to us in the absence of foreign repercussions, might be beneficial for the same sort of reasons to the rest of the world as a whole, provided that all the other countries of the world were to conform to it. It might be, however, that some countries would not accept this inflation rate. The steps they might take to avoid that inflation rate in their own countries might harm other countries in the world, this country, and possibly themselves. There is a complex of direct and indirect costs and benefits to us and to other countries associated with this country's inflation rate policy.

Let me begin the discussion with the help of an abstraction which, however severe, is not uncommon in present-day theorizing about the international monetary system: The system operates on the 'dollar standard': that is, the only widely held foreign monetary assets are assets paying a dollar return, typically the monetary obligations of the American government or of American firms. To begin with, let us consider that the various countries in the rest of the world are each of negligible size next to the United States and that there is no currency bloc among any of them. Later we can examine the role played by gold as an international monetary asset, the place of SDRs, and the potentiality of the development of some rival international reserve unit by some coalition of countries abroad.

9.1. *The Dollar Standard*

The key feature of the dollar standard, as a view of the international monetary system, is that American monetary assets – demand deposits, time deposits, government securities, and corporate obligations for the most part as well – enjoy a degree of international liquidity that exceeds that of their counterparts in the rest of the world. Owing to their small size and comparatively low levels of wealth, and perhaps to some extent also to the internal imperfections of their financial markets, the countries in the rest of the world face a comparatively thin market for their own monetary assets. The smaller or poorer the country, the smaller is the size of the internal market for its assets, the more likely is it that its trading mechanisms are less developed, and the greater are the foreign exchange risks of holding its assets.

In this system, foreign holders of American monetary assets on the whole pay a liquidity premium, cheerfully or not, in return for the 'services' of the international liquidity imparted by these assets. The situation is not essentially different from the standard view of a closed money economy where wealth-owners give up some interest income (or the expectation thereof) in return for the features provided by money in an amount that accords with their liquidity preference and the opportunity cost entailed. The parallels between the international economy on the dollar standard and the standard picture of the closed economy are striking. The American government can be portrayed as choosing the paths of its money supply and the quantity of its interest-bearing government debt. At any moment there corresponds to these stocks an equilibrium solution in which American nationals, foreign nationals, and foreign governments determine the 'real value' (or purchasing power) of these assets. The 'world price level', when expressed in terms of the dollar cost of buying a fixed bundle of goods, must in equilibrium be such as to cause these American monetary assets willingly to be held in some distribution or other around the world.

If everyone in the system is free of money illusion and if we can neglect debtor-creditor wealth redistributions in calculating market behavior, the door is open to a straightforward extension to the international economy of the threadworn neutrality theorem that is now standard in closed-economy monetary theory: Other things equal – such parameters as tax rates, reserve requirement ratios, the expected rate of inflation, and so on – if the total quantity of American government indebtedness (interest-bearing plus noninterest-bearing, in nominal terms) and the quantity of that debt which is monetized by the central bank were each b percent larger at the present moment, the equilibrium world price level of goods expressed in dollars would at the same moment be the same b percent larger. In the new equilibrium, no 'real magnitudes', like employment rates, interest rates or trade and capital flows, would be different from the old.

This is a comparative-statics proposition that leaves open the question of whether or not, in the event that the thought-experiment of increasing the stocks were actually carried out, the economy would tend to the new equilibrium path. Further, it is another story to say in what manner dollar prices in any foreign country would rise: A country might cause its currency to appreciate relative to the dollar, so that its domestic prices in dollars would rise without any corresponding rise in local currency prices; or it might maintain its exchange rate with the dollar, leaving its local currency prices to rise *pari passu* with prices expressed in dollars around the world; or it might allow some intermediate outcome to take place.[1]

Our concern here goes beyond the international quantity theory and corollary neutrality theorem to the question of how the international economy would be affected by a change in the dollar inflation

---

[1] The early Cambridge 'quantity theory of the price level', espoused by Marshall, Pigou, and Fisher, and revived by Metzler and Patinkin after the war, referred only to the increase in the quantity of 'outside' fiat money. In a world in which a substantial part of the total government debt is in interest-bearing form, it is important to stipulate that all outside assets increase in the same proportion in deducing the equiproportionate increase in the equilibrium price level. The same point was made in Chapter 6 concerning the nonneutral effect of an open-market purchase. For a statement of the sophisticated 'quantity theorem', see, for example, P. A. Samuelson, *Economics*, 8th ed. (New York: McGraw-Hill, 1970), pp. 326–327. Ironically, the analogous theorem for a world on the gold (or gold exchange) standard, a theorem associated with David Hume and his price-specie-flow mechanism, is inaccurate insofar as gold doubles as an industrial raw material.

rate wrought by some variation of American monetary and fiscal policy. But there is a little more to the comparative statics of the system that ought to occupy us before we turn to that question.

The evolution of the international system, even when steadfastly in equilibrium, where at least the rate of inflation is working out as expected, is certainly not invariant to the mix of fiscal and monetary policy that is selected among the set of mixes consistent with a given anticipated inflation rate. I content myself with illustrating this point in terms of a model which is both unrealistic and misleading in this respect: international discrepancies among real rates of return on earning assets tend to approach liquidity premiums which are *constants*, almost as if there were no liquidity considerations, and indeed only a small and unsatisfactory step away from that.

In such a world, each country's rate of domestic capital formation (and the various types of 'intangible' investment) is a matter of international arbitrage past the reach of the treasury of that country (except through its powers to institute distorting nonlump-sum taxes and bounties on this and that economic activity). Each country's fiscal or 'budgetary' policy governs the deficit on current account of its balance of payments, given other countries' fiscal and monetary policies. Under fixed exchange rates, a country's monetary policy determines its capital-account balance sheet.

As an exercise, consider in a 'stationary' world setting an open-market purchase by the American monetary authority. This action results in American purchases of earning assets abroad, hence a temporary one-time capital account deficit. The implied increase in the international demand for world capital entails a rise in the dollar-world-price level, though less than proportional to the increase in dollars if American interest-bearing debt has not increased likewise. (Were prices to rise equiproportionately, international liquidity would be lower than before – real money supplies would be the same but the American monetary authorities would have a larger portion of the other marketable assets – and there would result a tendency for reduced consumption demand, a reduction of the rate of return on capital assets as capital-deepening resulted, and via liquidity preference a consequent downward adjustment of price from that too-high level.) Note that by this open-market purchase the quantity of American interest-bearing wealth is of course increased. This exercise shows incidentally the power of a large country or, equally, a large region of small countries, to expropriate a portion of the world's earning assets through unanticipated credit creation.

Or consider this fiscal exercise. It is a mark of the excellence of Keynesian teaching that many Wall Street economists in the 1960s hypothesized an efflux mechanism under which a budgetary deficit of the United States, in conditions of macroequilibrium, would spill over into the balance of payments deficit of this country. Imports tend to be stimulated, exports choked off, so that the overall deficit is increased unless foreign governments pursue offsetting deficit actions or American monetary policy engineers an offsetting capital account surplus.

If we confine ourselves to policy choices consistent with expectations of the world price level, an acceleration of open-market purchase by the American authorities is only allowable insofar as there is greater fiscal austerity in the form of a larger American budgetary surplus. A temporary budget surplus would tend to improve the American current account surplus, adding to the stock of claims against foreigners though only at the cost of foregone consumption at home. The retardation of America's government indebtedness, as well as the reduction of the real return on capital goods to which it leads, necessitates an easing of American monetary policy if the price level is to continue its expected path. This operation engineers an increase in American wealth which eventually increases the volume of American imports consistent with current account balance by the amount of the increase in foreign interest and profit earnings.

Without having given a complete, not to say satisfying, account of international general equilibrium, let alone disequilibrium, it is still possible to address intelligently the various issues that appear to surround the question of the international 'incidence' of alternative American policies toward its inflation rate in the context of the dollar standard. I begin with the international consequences of alternative rates of American inflation which are expected or anticipated (the more stringent concept).

9.1.1. *Invariance of International Liquidity and Seigniorage*. There is a kind of *seigniorage* obtained by the country whose monetary assets constitute the principal international reserve, America in the case at hand. The countries of the rest of the world find themselves in the position of having exchanged claims against their wealth, or else having exchanged exportable goods, in return for these American monetary assets.

In the former case, the seigniorage gain is spread over time or annuitized; it is measured by the increase in the sustained import surplus of the United States (or a decrease of the export surplus) which is financed by the earnings from the additional wealth claims against foreign nationals *net* of any interest received by foreigners from their additional holdings of American monetary assets. Because the latter assets are comparatively liquid, for reasons discussed above, this interest differential is normally positive.

In the latter case, the seigniorage is capitalized as it were, being spent immediately and leading to a temporary import surplus of the United States. (Only a fraction of the resources made available to America by foreigners' purchases of American monetary assets needs to be invested, at home or abroad, by America in order to generate the future foreign exchange to pay any interest foreigners receive on their holdings of the American monetary assets.) When foreigners present America with a seigniorage opportunity, therefore, it shows up in the form either of a temporary deficit on capital account (the former case) or a temporary deficit on current account (the latter case), or something in between. Which configuration actually results depends upon the interactions of private propensities and national fiscal and monetary policies around the world.

When there is real economic growth generally in the world, the corresponding growth of international trade and finance produces a rising demand for real balances in the form of international dollar reserves. Unless the dollar world price level is falling offsettingly fast, therefore, foreigners will tend each year to make new purchases of liquid American monetary assets and so the United States will find itself each year with a fresh opportunity for seigniorage. Each year therefore the American balance of payments, either on current account or capital account, will tend to be in deficit.[2]

While one thinks primarily of official foreign dollar holdings in this connection, a private demand for dollars abroad of course presents the United States with the same seigniorage opportunity. To some extent foreign firms, preponderantly West European firms, have sold long-term bonds while at the same time some foreign nationals have purchased relatively liquid American monetary assets, a reflection in part of private international liquidity preference, the imperfections of foreign capital markets, and other factors.[3] Insofar

---

[2] If the American balance of payments were measured properly so that the deficit would be the increase in the *real* value of foreigners' liquid claims against America, the proviso about the price trend would be unnecessary.

[3] C. P. Kindleberger, 'Balance of Payments Deficits and the International Market for Liquidity', Essays in International Finance, No. 46 (Princeton: International Finance Section, Princeton University, 1965).

as these capital flows are matching, the United States is cast in the role of a financial intermediary for the private world financial sector; it earns seigniorage of the sort that any bank earns from the spread between deposit rate and loan rate. But it is the desire of foreign nationals to hold American monetary assets, not the attractiveness to foreign firms of selling claims for dollars to be spent on domestic capital formation, that creates the seigniorage gain for the United States. If foreign nationals do not wish to hold American monetary assets, insofar as the dollar proceeds of international capital market flotations by foreign firms end up staying abroad, the reason is ultimately because the governments (or their central banks) to whom the dollars are sold in return for local currency choose to hold those dollar assets for use as additional international reserves rather than to select fiscal, monetary, or commercial actions that would encourage their expenditure by stimulating imports, foreign investment, and so on. Official holdings of international reserves should, in other words, be viewed normally as a voluntary decision that is based upon the benefits and opportunity costs of holding those reserves.

How, if at all, does the rate of anticipated inflation in the world affect the size of the seigniorage gain of the United States in the pure dollar standard? The answer depends upon a crucial difference between the situation of countries abroad vis-à-vis the United States and the customary situation of households and firms vis-à-vis a seigniorage-gaining currency-issuing government in a closed economy. The countries abroad, excepting perhaps the very smallest, will find it economical to hold most of their international liquid assets in interest-bearing form. They will hold most or all of their reserves in government securities and time deposits which, at least in situations of macroequilibrium (the context here), bear positive real rates of return. Viewing these real rates of return as rather inflexibly linked to the real rates of return on tangible American capital, and noting that there is no necessary connection between the latter rates, on the one hand, and the anticipated inflation rate, on the other, we see that the real rates of return available to foreigners on their holdings of dollar reserves should not be presumed to deteriorate with an increase of the anticipated inflation rate. As a first approximation over the range of expected inflation rates that we might reasonably contemplate, it is only if one has a theory that a shift of American policy toward greater capital-deepening and hence lower real rates of return on American tangible capital formation would be part and parcel of a shift of American policy toward a higher inflation rate (in some new macroequilibrium) that one would presume some deterioration in the real rates of return available to foreigners on their holdings of American monetary assets as a result of the shift to higher inflation. Moreover, it would further be necessary to argue that the same shift to higher inflation would not tend to produce the same reduction in real rates of return on tangible investments abroad so that, indeed, there would be a widening of the seigniorage gain available to America from borrowing at low real rates of return.

Looking at the short-term consequences only of an increase of the expected inflation rate, there is the elementary point that the size of the capital stock and hence its average real rate of return is largely inherited and not influenced much by private and public decisions in the near term. Consequently an increase of the expected inflation rate tends to raise expected nominal rates of return on capital goods, producers' and consumers' durables both, and equities by the amount of the inflation rate increase. This tends to raise the nominal rates of return on monetary earning assets by the same amount, thus maintaining their real rates of return. The only qualification, one applicable to the long run discussed in the preceding paragraph as well as to the short run, is that insofar as the increased expected inflation rate reduces domestic liquidity, in America and abroad for that matter, there may be some tendency for the structure of nominal rates of return to be stretched between in a more uniform way between zero, the nominal yield on money, and the prospective yield on capital goods; if cash liquidity is reduced, a greater liquidity premium on those earning assets which are relatively liquid may result.

I conclude that there is little or no presumption that the seigniorage cost paid by the rest of the world for the use of dollar assets as international liquid reserves would be widened by an increase of the expected inflation rate in a pure dollar standard. Neither consequently should there be supposed to be any reduction in the level of international liquidity that would tend to prevail in the world when operating under a somewhat higher rate of anticipated inflation. If some observers of the actual international monetary system have thought that inflation was injurious to the functioning of the dollar as a reserve, for better or worse from the point of view of the system, it may be because they believe that higher inflation would heighten speculative interest in holding gold as an alternative to the dollar.

Because gold is truly otiose, bearing no interest at all unlike American monetary assets, it must be maintained by those holding this position that the increased prospect of a rise in the dollar price of gold is sufficient to offset the increase in foregone interest earnings entailed by holding gold as long as the gold price is maintained. In any case, let us defer the introduction of gold into the picture until the next section.

It is apparent that the greatest virtue of the dollar standard as against metallic standards is that the American monetary assets available as international reserves bear interest. Only if there were some commodity which, in addition to having the convenient monetary properties of divisibility and a low weight value ratio, bore some competitive physical real rate of return, like musical metal, would it be 'economical' for the world to produce that commodity reserve at a cost in scarce resources and to use it as a world money. Surely it would be the worst part of envy for foreigners to wish that the United States had to produce the monetary assets it sells abroad at a cost in human toil and foregone consumption in America. A second virtue is that the international inflation rate can be selected without the peculiar feature of a concomitant variation in the rate of commodity money production, for example, gold mining. The international paper money standard is as liberating as was the breakaway to paper money domestically, both facts disturbing to monetary conservatives.

Nevertheless to many people it seems unjust that America, the richest country in the world, should because of that very degree of economic development happen to enjoy the seigniorage from printing the world's international money. Irresistibly this reminds me of the film of Edna Ferber's novel *Saratoga Trunk*. At some point a man tells the Creole heroine, played by Ingrid Bergman, that she is very beautiful, to which she replies, 'Yes, isn't it lucky!' She exploits her beauty to serve her own tasteless and egoistic ambitions. Of course there can be no more legitimate objection to an attractive economy and to the opportunities that come naturally to it than to an attractive anatomy. What is in fact unjust in the international economic sphere is not that America so to speak grew up beautiful in certain economic respects but rather the absence of sufficient consciousness on her part of the need systematically to share some of those advantages with the economically less favored. There is the further problem of devising a suitable mechanism of international sharing of unequal economic advantages, seigniorage being just one such advantage.

Until these problems of the redistribution of seigniorage are met, it is understandable that there should be some international discontent with the rule of the dollar standard, even one alloyed with gold. What I have been arguing up to this point is simply that, so far as seigniorage and the adequacy of international liquidity are concerned, an increase or decrease of the expected dollar inflation rate brought about by American domestic policy does not significantly alter the balance of advantages and disadvantages of the dollar standard.

9.1.2. *Invariance of Foreigners' Control Over Their Balance of Payments.* A change in the expected rate of inflation of world dollar prices does not alter the 'autonomy' of any country over the structure of its balance of payments and its rate of wealth accumulation through its use of standard monetary and fiscal tools.

In any international monetary system there is some kind of constraint on a country's overall balance of payments deficit which it must heed eventually, at least when the system is operating roughly in equilibrium so that the future outcomes of present policies are being broadly foreseen. In a stationary world economy operating at a zero equilibrium inflation rate, no country can maintain indefinitely an overall balance of payments deficit. In a growing world economy, as we saw earlier, at a zero expected inflation rate the countries in the rest of the world have eventually to run an overall surplus in order to accumulate growing balances of dollar monetary assets. 'Nominally' the required surpluses are greater when the expected inflation rate is higher, and this would at first appear to be an economic loss for foreign countries. But it follows from the foregoing analysis that the additional nominal surplus is automatically provided to foreigners by the increase in nominal interest rates on their holdings of American monetary assets that necessarily accompanies the increase in the expected inflation rate, 'necessarily' as long as the countries of the world pursue the same rate of wealth accumulation so that real rates of return on earning assets around the world do not change concomitantly with the increased inflation rate.

Here we are concerned with the division of a country's overall balance of payments surplus between that on current account and that on capital account. The ordinary domestic monetary and fiscal policy tools give a country power over that division. Let us, for the moment, neglect the liquidity differences of earning assets from country to country, treating world capital markets as perfect (and thus depriving the dollar standard of its liquidity theory). Then an increase in a country's government budgetary surplus, given the budgetary positions of the other governments in the world, reduces domestic consumption demand; thus it causes an increase in that country's balance of trade and hence (at least in the short run) an increase in its surplus on current account. Its imports of consumables will fall, and resources will be released into the export industries until a new equilibrium is reached where the sum of 'foreign plus domestic aggregate demand' is enough to absorb the equilibrium rate of aggregate production. The rate of domestic capital formation proceeds at the same rate, being governed by international arbitrage. Hence the tax increase leads to a rise in the country's net foreign investment (and total investment), a rise equal to the amount of the increase in public saving (the increase in the budgetary surplus) less any (smaller) decrease of private saving that occurs insofar as private consumption is not cut back by the full amount of the tax increase.

In the world of money where goods and services are imperfectly liquid, such a fiscal shift needs to be accommodated by an easing of the country's monetary policy if there is not to be an interval (at least) of below-equilibrium resource use and prices falling below expected trends. The monetary easing would be of such a magnitude as to stimulate additional domestic capital formation at least temporarily so that the increase in national wealth induced by the fiscal tightening would not be wholly in the form of foreign earning assets. A tendency of nationals in the country experiencing the fiscal tightening to diversify their portfolio investments across borders would imply that even in the long run the increase in national wealth would be marked by an appreciable capital-deepening at home, not simply an inflow of capital claims against foreigners.

The lesson is simply that a country can use its fiscal tools to influence the rate of national wealth accumulation while its monetary policy is employed to maintain its level of economic activity in keeping with macroequilibrium. The only wrinkle that distinguishes the application of this principle to an open economy from a closed economy is that, in the former case, some part of any increase in a country's national wealth will take the form of foreign investment.

It is perhaps unnecessary to say that this power of the taxing authority of a country over its rate of national wealth accumulation is not lessened by an increase of the expected world inflation rate. Each country, acting alone, still has the fiscal power to achieve the path of national wealth it would have selected in a situation of lower expected world inflation. Indeed its fiscal powers are enhanced by an increase of the dollar inflation rate if it elects to manage its exchange rate and its central bank operations in such a way as to produce at home the same inflation rate in terms of its national currency. Since the expectation of inflation by nationals holding the local currency is a kind of tax tending to reduce their desired consumption rate at given rates of real national income, an increase of the expected inflation rate takes some strain off the country's ordinary instruments of taxation. I shall come back to this point in the next subsection, where the true costs and benefits to countries in the rest of the world of an increase of the dollar inflation rate are discussed.

What we can conclude to this point is that an increase of the expected world inflation rate in terms of dollar-expressed prices does not increase the opportunity cost to foreign governments (and foreign nationals) of international liquidity and it does decrease the cost in deadweight losses from domestic taxation of accumulating national wealth. Any disadvantage to foreign countries of an increase of the expected dollar inflation rate must be sought elsewhere.

9.1.3. *Foreign Costs and Benefits From Expected Dollar Inflation.* The true costs, and likewise the true benefits, of an increase in the expected rate of inflation of world prices measured in dollars spring from the necessity of each country abroad to choose between matching its own rate of inflation in terms of the national currency to the world dollar inflation rate or, alternatively, electing continuously to raise its exchange rate with the dollar (compared with the path it would otherwise have set for the exchange rate), or taking some middle course between these two options. Unquestionably for many countries in the world the course of adapting its own local inflation rate to the increase in the expected dollar inflation rate is the wiser one. Let us first address ourselves to the costs and benefits accruing to foreign countries which would in fact choose this option, recognizing that the net balance of gains and losses for any such country abroad will depend to some extent on what the other countries choose to do with their inflation rates.

There is some tendency to identify this 'matching' case with fixed exchange rates. It may be true that a foreign country that equates its domestic inflation rate in local currency to the dollar inflation rate in the rest of the world is less likely to have to adjust its exchange rate with the dollar than a country which adopts a greatly different domestic inflation rate. But clearly a country which elects to increase its domestic inflation rate by an amount exactly equal to the increase in the anticipated dollar inflation rate in the world is not logically implied to be keeping its exchange rate with the dollar fixed. One would suppose that if, in the absence of the increase in the dollar inflation rate, the country would have devalued its currency from time to time, then upon maintaining the difference between its domestic inflation rate and the dollar rate when the latter is increased, it will still find that it devalues from time to time, though not necessarily with the exact same frequency or amount. The postwar history of the international monetary system is largely a compendium of devaluation stories. Had the United States early after the war followed a more inflationary policy and the countries abroad followed suit, we would still have had most or all of this devaluation. We may think of the case at hand in which a foreign country matches the increase in the dollar inflation rate as one in which, in doing so, that country makes it likely that its exchange rate will follow much the same trend as it would have had the dollar inflation rate not increased; but this is hardly exact for, after all, if the increase in the expected domestic inflation rate makes a difference to the foreign country, it is possible and likely that it will affect its resource allocation and balance of payments.

The prevailing opinion among American and especially European economists appears to be that an increase of the anticipated inflation rate in America, if it did indeed increase domestic inflation rates (in local currencies) in some or all countries abroad, would be bad for those economies, as it would be bad for America, and for the same reasons, whatever they may be! Obviously this book will have been unpersuasive if the reader takes it for granted that an increase of the expected inflation rate in America – over the range of moderate inflation rates we have in mind – would indeed do 'domestic' or intra-national injury to the American economy, leaving aside feedbacks from the rest of the world. It was argued in Chapter 6 that up to some point, 5 percent is an appealing intuitive estimate, there would be a net benefit to the United States from an increase of the expected inflation rate by virtue of its contribution to monetary stability, to fiscal efficiency and, insofar as it is obtained by a disequilibrium expansion involving increased work experience, lessened job separations and all the rest, its contribution to worker attitudes, habits, and skills.

It would seem therefore to be a sin of overconfidence, if not arrogance, for anyone to make the blanket assertion than an increase of the expected inflation rate would, in leading some foreign countries to match it, do economic harm to these countries. There is obviously a parallel to be drawn here to the problem of foreign policy toward parts of the world about which we are largely ignorant. When there is little or no assurance that a policy course by America will be helpful abroad or at home it would be foolish to pay the price of adopting that policy. We cannot say with any sureness how a policy decision by us to hold down (or to reduce) the expected inflation rate in the rest of the world would affect the average level of economic well-being abroad, or which countries might be hurt and which helped, or whether the neediest groups of people in any foreign country would gain or lose. How fantastic therefore that some Chicago banker should presume to know what change of the inflation rate, up or down, would be preferable for Indian peasants, Turkish migrants, French workers, and the rest. It is hard enough to estimate the consequences of greater or less expected inflation upon the well-being of Americans and to differentiate the incidence between poor and non-poor.

Clearly it is necessary to consider the nations of the world, or the various groups of like nations, one by one, or at least by type. It is natural to assume that countries that have achieved a highly developed fiscal and financial system would benefit as much as America from an increase of the expected inflation rate up to some moderate level. This is an 'equal ignorance' assumption. I would place the burden of analysis on any who believe some other assumption is appropriate to these countries.

The situation is very different in the less developed countries of the world. I should suppose that in many Latin American countries the anticipated inflation rate there plays a significant fiscal role as an inflation tax that holds down consumption demand, thus releasing resources for government use and for private capital formation. This does not mean, of course, that still more inflation in Brazil would be still better for Brazilians, or that Brazil has never inflated too fast. But if an increase of the expected inflation rate in terms of dollars brought about by American policy were in some way to reduce the costliness to the Latin American economies of that particular method of 'taxation', it stands to reason that they would benefit by this rise in the dollar inflation rate, and benefit more on this account than countries where the inflation tax was a less crucial ingredient of the fiscal system. (Such a reduction in the costliness of expected inflation would result from an increase in American expected inflation because, at the same rate of domestic inflation, the average magnitude of exchange adjustment and the average frequency of discrete jumps in the exchange rate would be lessened, both factors probably playing some inhibiting role in the setting of the inflation rate.)

I have been discussing the benefits and costs of an increase in the expected rate of dollar inflation which accrue to foreign countries that respond by stepping up their own planned rate of inflation by an equal amount. This matching response would be expectable, though not exclusively so, from those countries that have an overriding preference for maintaining a 'fixed' exchange rate with the dollar on the ground of its convenience to traders in financial and commodity markets which do a lot of business inside a dollar exchange area of countries that likewise prefer to fix their exchange rates. Yet many countries, even some economically close to the United States, may prefer to adhere to an unvarying inflation rate policy. Countries that fall into exchange areas where there is little international trade and financial transactions with the dollar exchange area are especially unlikely to wish to match an expected increase in the dollar inflation rate with an increase of their own inflation rates.

A frequent objection to an increase in the equilibrium rate of inflation in America, hence an increase in the expected rate of world inflation in terms of dollar prices, is that it will require countries that prefer the maintenance of their own inflation rates to embark on a program of more-or-less continuous managed appreciation of their exchange rates with the dollar – with its associated costs to the conduct of international trade and finance – or, worse, to choose between a course of more frequent jumps in 'fixed' exchange rates, on the one hand, and freely fluctuating exchange rates (with official intervention in the foreign exchange market), on the other.

It has to be pointed out, in reply to this objection, that if the average inflation rate in terms of local currencies desired by countries following an independent inflation course exceeds the dollar inflation rate, then a small increase of the latter *reduces* the average rate of exchange depreciation by these countries or it *reduces* the frequency of their devaluations of their 'fixed' exchange rates. If one rejects the perhaps ethnocentric assumption of so many Continental economists that the whole world, outside of the United States at least, prefers a stable price level despite the imperfections of these countries' fiscal systems, the shoe is on the other foot: An increase of the expected inflation rate in America, by narrowing the discrepancy between the average inflation rate sought in the rest of the world and the

American target inflation rate, would tend presumably to stabilize the international exchanges.

Does not the postwar history of inflation abroad and recurrent exchange devaluations against the dollar (from which hardly any country has been excepted) in fact reveal a preference of foreign governments for a higher secular and anticipated rate of inflation – averaging over countries – than America's officially preferred inflation rate? Surely yes when it comes to the less developed countries of the world, if not because of the usefulness of inflation as a tax, then simply because of the heavy transition cost of reducing domestic expectations of inflation in those countries. In those more developed countries where the inflation rate has tended to exceed the American one, it may be on the other hand that the inflation represented unplanned deviations above official inflation targets, deviations that were larger than the corresponding deviations in America. The necessary reply is that if the foreign countries' economic situation and policies are such as to continue to produce about the same excess of inflation over what is planned, it is the actual average inflation outcome of those policies that is relevant for our purposes, not some hoped-for inflation rate.

One might interpret many of the postwar currency devaluations as springing not from a desire to correct for some inflation rate differential, planned or unplanned, but rather from a desire of the devaluing country to improve its inflow of international liquidity in a situation in which sole reliance on monetary tightening or fiscal tightening (or both), with whatever tendencies to produce economic slack that such actions might have, would have been regarded as inferior means to that same end. Insofar as such devaluations were unassisted by any fiscal or monetary tightening at all, they must have led to a compensating upward cost push of the domestic price level. One may suppose that it took one or more such experiences to convince foreign countries that the way to a stronger balance of payments surplus involves fiscal or monetary tightening, whatever the desired trend of domestic prices. For the future, therefore, one might expect rather fewer and smaller devaluations, undertaken only when the devaluing countries are prepared to undergo the fiscal belt-tightening to assure the devaluation of success in an inflow stimulating of international reserves. Some portion of the various postwar devaluations should be regarded as misguided and leading to temporary inflation beyond what the foreign countries desired. This means, at a minimum, that an increase of the expected inflation rate in dollar terms originating in America will make less of a contribution to the reduction of exchange devaluation episodes than one might suppose from looking at postwar data, there being fewer devaluations in the cards for the future than was the case in the past.

But let us give the devil his due. What of the costs from increased expected dollar inflation to those countries which, in the absence of such increased American inflation, would have been able to enjoy their own preferred inflation rate (in home currency terms, of course) at a virtually unchanging exchange rate with the dollar, devaluing if at all only very infrequently? Such countries would then find themselves having to appreciate their currencies, either occasionally by large discrete amounts or in some relatively smooth continuous manner, if they are to preserve the same equilibrium inflation rate at home.

There are perhaps three major ways by which such countries could accomplish the trend of currency appreciation. Subjecting its exchange rate to the vagaries of a fluctuating private market in foreign exchange, with little or no intervention in that market by the authorities, is one of these, though probably the least appealing. If a 'freely fluctuating' exchange rate is not attractive to a foreign country when its balance of payments situation gives promise of being consistent with a fixed exchange rate for a long time, it is not likely that the prospect of an *average* rate of exchange appreciation of, for example, 2 percent per annum will tip the balance of arguments in favour of abandoning intensive exchange rate intervention by the monetary authorities. The other two ways of coping with the need to appreciate in some manner or another over time will typically be more attractive.

One of these other ways is the familiar process of occasional adjustment of the 'fixed' exchange rate (the adjustable peg, so-called). That mode of exchange rate adjustment is obviously not without significant costs to the country concerned and to those that trade with it. As the time nears at which the exchange rate will obviously need adjusting, there arise strong speculative pressures in favor of the home currency. In large part, however, these can be accommodated by a compensating easing of internal monetary policy so that domestic liquidity (and liquidity in neighboring countries) would not be greatly disrupted. If the currency appreciations are sufficiently frequent, each appreciation need not be of momentous size nor will it be expected to be of such size in international financial markets. The problems of leads and lags in trade flows are no doubt more difficult to offset.

In countries in which these problems are indeed serious, the third option may be preferred. This is the option of relatively steady exchange appreciation in a managed way. 'In the limit', as the mathematicians say, this approach is just a trivial generalization of the policy of a 'fixed' exchange rate. What is fixed is the ratio of the country's exchange rate to the internal purchasing power of the dollar; that is, the country intervenes in the market so as to keep its dollar exchange rate within certain limits around a par value that 'improves' at a rate just equal to the difference between the rate of inflation it expects in terms of dollars in the world and the rate of inflation it expects its policies to produce at home. When disparate real forces or unplanned monetary forces have cumulated to bring a foreseeable long-term payments disequilibrium, the moving parity can be adjusted to a new trend path.

What would be the costs of a country's opting for the course of relatively smooth 'managed appreciation'? Domestic interest rates are not affected by the country's insistence on following its own inflation rate star. By itself the anticipation of appreciation of the country's currency makes the country's monetary assets more attractive and would tend to force down its interest rates in the absence of effective domestic monetary counteraction; but the increase in nominal interest rates in the faster-inflating dollar area corresponding to the increase in the expected dollar inflation rate just offsets this. The currency appreciation of the slowly inflating country obviates the need for a rise of its domestic interest rates, just as it avoids the need for an increase of its inflation rate, this being the whole point to the foreign country that will not be swayed from its inflation target by the policies elsewhere.[4] Further, since relative prices expressed in dollars are left on the same course, and nominal rate of return on international assets expressed in any *one* currency (after allowance for expected exchange rate changes) are also left the same as before, no change in the country's tax rates is called for. The principal cost to the countries in question resulting from the increase in the expected dollar inflation rate is the increased 'confusion' to international traders and financial transactors caused by the awareness of the moving exchange rate.

This is a regrettable state of affairs, but it is one which is inescap-

---

[4] Likewise if a country should embark on a decreased inflation rate program, it must reduce its domestic interest rate; but the international capital flow effect is erased by the offsetting anticipation of that country's rate of currency appreciation (or decreased rate of depreciation).

able as long as the American inflation rate lies between the lowest inflation rate sought by any foreign country and the highest rate aimed for by the most inflationist of those countries. In that case, and it is surely the realistic one, the United States cannot please every country by any move of its inflation rate, be it up or down. An increase of the rate of anticipated inflation in America must add a little to the confusion surrounding the international transactions of countries which, in order to maintain their inflation rates (in the home currencies), need to widen the rate of appreciation of their currencies with respect to the dollar; but it will also reduce the confusion surrounding international transactions in currencies that now are depreciated less rapidly because their countries wish to maintain their inflation rates.

One may say that the inflation rate around the world when all prices are expressed in terms of dollars is like a public good. An increase in that rate holds the same implications for the price trend of Peugots expressed in dollars as for Argentinian beef in the same currency units. Just as it will be rare that an increase in lighthouses will be preferred by all voters in a closed economy (without side payment compensations), it will not usually be the case that an increase of the dollar inflation rate would ever receive a unanimous negative or affirmative vote in some world-wide referendum. The opponents of a moderate increase in the expected dollar inflation rate have not even demonstrated that the foreign losers could compensate the gainers enough to cause a world-wide vote against such an increase, let alone offered any demonstration that the losers are the more disadvantaged and therefore more deserving of consideration.

9.1.4. *Foreign Burden of Unexpected Dollar Inflation Increase.* The international cost benefit calculation when it comes to an unexpected increase in the dollar inflation rate is a quite different story. When there is an unexpected rise or acceleration in the dollar price level, the real capital losses experienced by American holders of their own country's monetary assets do not add up to a net aggregate capital loss for Americans in any ordinary accounting sense, since American taxpayers and transfer recipients can receive a compensating increase in their disposable incomes; a tax cut is eventually in store if fiscal policy adheres to the same target consumption investment mix. The gains and losses of the economically relevant sort involve liquidity, deadweight effects of tax rates, together with the concomitant effects upon output, employment, and everything else of the forces which are producing the unexpected price increase or acceleration, all topics that occupied us through Chapters 4 to 6.

By contrast, even the purely accounting capital losses suffered by foreigners on their holdings of American monetary assets are economically real. This is obvious if the increase in American prices is matched by an increase in the local currency prices or an equivalent increase in the dollar cost of the local currencies of the countries in which the foreign holders of American monetary assets intend ultimately to buy goods from the proceeds of those assets when eventually sold.[5] With the United States a net borrower abroad in respect to 'fixed income' monetary obligations, the interest burden on this net obligation abroad is reduced for the United States by the increase in world prices which was unexpected at the time the lending was undertaken.

It does not follow that an unexpected increase in the American inflation rate is disadvantageous *on balance* to countries abroad, any of them or all of them. If an increase in the expected rate of inflation would be desirable for the rest of the world as a whole, say for the fiscal reasons pondered in the previous subsection (and in Chapter 6) or even desirable only for the sake of the largely or wholly temporary bulge of output and employment it would stimulate, an episode of unexpected world inflation triggered by American policy might still be of net benefit to the rest of the world despite the real capital losses suffered by foreigners on their net holdings of American monetary assets.

This is more than a 'who knows, anything is possible' remark. It might be countered that if any or all foreign countries had wanted the benefits of a dose of unexpected inflation, with its temporary or permanent effects upon employment and so on, such countries could unilaterally have undertaken the requisite fiscal and monetary policies to achieve that outcome. But that contention would miss the point that each country acting alone may be reluctant to institute such policies without the assurance that other countries will do likewise; for if it has no reason to expect that other countries will take the same actions, each country will assume that such an action on its own part will lead it into balance-of-payments disequilib-

---

[5] A real loss to those holders also occurs if their governments take steps to protect their local currency price level from the unexpected increase in the dollar price level at least in the case in which the foreign governments were 'maximizing' in the original situation.

rium with the nuisance costs and other problems that might entail.[6]
Moreover, one should be careful not to overestimate the capital
losses that unexpected inflation imposes. A one-time increase of the
steady inflation rate from the originally expected figure, say 2 percent, to 5 percent indefinitely does not imply that American monetary
assets held by foreigners will erode forever at an extra 3 percent
without compensation: If American monetary and fiscal policy,
together with the gradual adjustment of expectations to the 5 percent
figure, combine to raise nominal interest rates by the same amount,
that is, by 3 percentage points, foreigners lose only in proportion to
the maturity of their holdings and the slowness of market expectations to adjust. For example, if foreigners were invested only in 12-
month bills, a pattern of inflation of which only 1 percent was unexpected in each year would, over a 4-year period, produce an un-
compensated capital loss of only 4 percent of the real amount held.
Further, the nominal interest rates on these bills might still be large
enough to leave a positive net real rate of return on these holdings.

If in fact these real capital losses from a spell of unexpected
American inflation are a minor factor for most foreign countries,
what then is the main injury done to them by an unexpected rise of
the dollar inflation rate? It could be that in some countries abroad
the labor markets and product markets, whether they are less
'imperfect' or involve different sorts of institutional practices from
the American kind, are such that an episode of above-equilibrium
employment and capital utilization levels does more harm than good.
It could be too that many foreign countries are less well-geared than
America to revise governmental redistributive programs to adjust
for any harm done to certain low-income disadvantaged groups in
their societies. Again, the message is that they are not like us, not
exactly anyway, so we should be prepared to accept the possibility

---

[6] There is an analogy with the welfare economics of the equilibrium employment level developed in Chapter 4. How can a rise of aggregate demand, in
raising the price level and stimulating a rise of employment above the equilibrium
level, be argued to benefit workers and owners of capital? If they had wanted
greater employment and capital utilization, they would have been cutting their
prices! This *prima facie* objection overlooks the distinction between a unilateral
real wage cut by an individual not expecting a general reduction of real wage rates
on the one hand and a concerted reduction of real wage demands on the other.

In the same vein, if the United States produces an unexpected rise in dollar
prices, any individual country abroad may be hesitant to institute an immediate
currency appreciation of a size that would be exactly neutralizing in the event
that all other foreign countries follow suit if in fact it is uncertain what competing countries are going to do.

that the engineering of a certain unexpected increase in the inflation rate of a size whose transitional effects would be largely beneficial on balance to the United States might not bring the same net short-term benefit to some or all countries abroad.

Surely one of the most troubling aspects to foreign governments of an American boom with its unexpected rise of the dollar inflation rate is that it is unexpected by foreign governments as well as by private American citizens. As a consequence, whether they are happily surprised at the unexpected turn of events or sadly disappointed, foreign governments are apt to feel that they have lost a measure of control over their own economies. For example, an episode of unexpected inflation and above-equilibrium employment which is triggered by fiscal developments (planned or unplanned) would by itself tend to bring an unplanned improvement in foreign countries' trade surplus while the tendency toward higher interest rates in the United States resulting from the boom might at the same time cause an unplanned deterioration of foreign countries' balance of payments on capital account. Some countries may of course have been seeking just such a change at some deliberate pace which takes account of the costs of change. But we cannot presume that there will regularly be such a coincidence of wants, even on the average over time. Most governments most of the time will feel that the task of economic planning has been made harder for them by the ever-present possibility of some disequilibrating impulse originating in the United States. They may feel resentful if the American disequilibrium is being sanctioned to a degree, let alone conspired beforehand, by the American fiscal and monetary authorities.

It is natural therefore that some foreign governments will urge that the United States, and any other countries large enough to have an appreciable effect on the world economy, bind themselves to some sort of international agreement to forswear intentional disequilibrating monetary and fiscal moves and to accept international responsibility to deal appropriately with unplanned disequilibriums. This brings us to the subject that is sometimes called the 'rules of the game'.

The rules of the game are the 'directions' given to each country in balance of payments disequilibrium as to how to adjust its economy according to whether it is in surplus or deficit, and whether this disequilibrium is 'structural' or 'demand-side' in origin. The intent is to bring about a faster and smoother equilibration than would be obtained if each country acted unilaterally.

It will be clear that, properly expressed, the rules that are internationally appropriate when the international equilibrium inflation rate is, for example, 5 percent annually, should not be expected to differ from those rules that are appropriate to international equilibrium inflation at 2 percent. Needless to say, in the former case, no country's actual inflation at 5 percent will signify any internal disequilibrium; and the nominal surpluses of foreign countries in terms of dollars needed to 'stay even' with declining real values of monetary assets will not signify external disequilibrium.

9.2. *Gold and 'Paper Gold'*

In the international monetary system as it is, some countries like to hold a portion of their international reserves in the form of gold rather than American monetary assets. This preference would not substantially alter the workings of the dollar standard any more than the preference of some countries to hold Picassos if the dollar were preeminently liquid and the reserve commodities favored by some countries not very liquid and not widely held. The utility of such reserve commodities would depend upon their being available at prices in terms of the dollar which cleared the market for them. If America were to double its domestic price level, it would be left to foreigners to demand twice as high a dollar price for their commodity reserves, or ration them, lest those reserves be drained away into other uses.

At the other extreme is the case in which all countries' monetary assets, including dollar assets, are highly illiquid internationally as compared to gold. Then, if America would double its supplies of monetary assets, thus to double its price level, it must be prepared to double the price in terms of its own currency that it will pay for gold, lest its gold reserves be drained away.

The present system lies between these extremes, though exactly where is hard to tell. The actual system is on the gold standard in one superficial respect, that the United States at present undertakes to buy and sell gold for dollars in transactions with central banks at a price which, from appearances, is high enough that its gold stocks are not depleted and low enough that gold does not flow in, given the other parameters that determine these flows. More accurately, the system is on a gold exchange standard in which American monetary assets are widely held as international reserves in addition to gold, with dollar reserves predominating in most countries abroad.

Because both gold and American monetary assets enjoy a high degree of international liquidity and are somewhat substitutable (at some margin or other), the demand for each exhibits some elasticity with respect to an increase in the opportunity cost of holding the other asset. The United States can consequently pursue domestic policies which produce an increase in the real quantity of dollar reserves held abroad (relative to the real value of gold stocks) if its monetary policy presents an improvement in the prospective rate of return to holding dollars as against gold.

The United States has considerable latitude therefore to increase or decrease its domestic (dollar) price level relative to the (dollar) price of gold. But it does not follow, of course, that America could inflate indefinitely at any desired rate relative to a given dollar price of gold. One would think that if American dollar prices rise beyond some rate, there would come a point in time at which American monetary policy could not afford to make the dollars held abroad sufficiently attractive to those whose preference is for the shrinking real quantity of gold (in terms of its purchasing power over goods). Some positive American inflation rate might be maintainable indefinitely but only insofar as there is simultaneously occurring some attrition in the preference for gold. So it would appear that fixity of the dollar price of gold would act as a tether to the world price level expressed in dollars, and the higher the inflation rate the sooner the tether is stretched taut.

According to what seems that most likely scenario, the general anticipation of continuing inflation would heighten the speculation of gold holders that a rise in the dollar price of gold was not far off.[7] It might be that an increase of the anticipated inflation rate in terms of dollars would at first keep gold at bay. The increase in nominal interest rates on American monetary assets might match or even exceed the resulting increase in the 'expected' current rate of apprecia-

---

[7] Nevertheless it is conceivable. It seems possible, though we cannot decide the empirical matter here, that the development of a substantially higher dollar inflation rate in the world compared to what had traditionally been expected back in the days when gold was at its zenith might decisively extinguish the glitter of that metal. While the rise of nominal interest rates on American monetary assets that would presumably accompany a rise of the dollar inflation rate, once it has come to be anticipated, might not at first greatly reduce the quantity of gold demanded, it might be that several years of continuing capital losses to gold holders from the rising prices of world goods (expressed in dollars) would finally induce countries still preferring gold to give up the metal in favor of dollar assets whose interest earnings offered compensation for the upward price trend – despite the prospect of an eventual gold price rise.

tion of the dollar price of gold. But if, as the gold price rise does not take place, that price increase of gold is thought to be more and more imminent, the expected capital gain from holding onto gold must eventually predominate. In what follows, let us assume the worst, so to speak, accepting the proposition that an increase of the American inflation rate places in prospect the necessity, at some future time or other, to make some new arrangement regarding gold and the dollar. Indeed, it has been thought by many economists that even if the United States were to maintain a 'level' price trend, the growth of world trade and consequent growth (relative to gold supply) of the demand for international reserves, including gold in particular, would eventually spell a draining of America's gold stocks with the same resulting need to do something about gold. This thought lay partly behind the innovation of the Special Drawing Rights. The SDR was designed as an international reserve asset to supplement gold stocks; it can be augmented as desired by agreement of the major central banks in accordance with the growth of international trade and finance. However, let us hold off our consideration of the role that SDRs might play in the event of a shortage of gold.

9.2.1. *Gold Price Revaluation.* One possibility is that there would be an effort to restore the normal working order of the gold exchange standard by means of a substantial rise in the dollar price of gold. It is probably realistic to assume that if that were done, there would at first be no change by countries abroad in the exchange rates of their currencies in terms of the dollar. Even without such currency appreciation of their currencies, in terms of the dollar, by foreign countries, the 'ideal' outcome may very well come to pass: The increase in the real value of the gold holdings of foreign countries, in gratifying their desire for increased international liquidity, would induce them to drop their policies designed to run balance of payments surpluses. Indeed, if the gold price increase were sufficiently large, according to this prediction of the outcome, the increase in international liquidity will be so great as to lead to successive rounds of competitive easings of monetary and fiscal policies by the countries abroad which find themselves refreshingly free for a change of the worry of scarce international liquidity.

It might be contended that if even this gold price surgery is the technical success just described, occasional operations of this sort are not a satisfactory long-run solution for the patient who wants to lead a life of inflation. True, each gold price rise puts a temporary stop to expectations of an imminent gold price rise in the near future. But even if each gold price rise succeeds in staving off a drain of gold from the United States, it may be argued, gold would be enhanced as a reserve asset, the dollar would be correspondingly weakened, and there would be greater uncertainty from the prospect of future occasional gold price changes.

This is pretty long-term stuff. It is not clear what the international monetary options would be 20 or more years after an initial gold price rise, or even whether gold would continue to exist as a principal international monetary asset. But leaving that aside, it should be said first of all that the enhancement of gold implicit in the expectation of a secular rise in its price is merely compensatory, keeping it on an unchanged footing with dollar assets whose nominal rates of return would tend to be higher by the amount of the inflation (as compared to a zero inflation pattern). Similarly the rise in revenue open to gold-producing countries is better viewed as a catch-up increase rather than a windfall gain. It is hardly the fault of the United States, or any inflationary policy of that country, that some nations with the right ores in their ground benefit from the metallic preferences of some other countries.

It is primarily the prospect of successive gold price rises, with its invitation to speculation and the resulting fluctuations in international liquidity, that would be undesirable. But after a sufficient gold price rise of sufficient magnitude, in the event such a price rise was overdue to begin with, there would be breathing space enough to work out a less unsettling method of offsetting the erosion of the real value of the slow-growing gold stock. A system might be worked out under which the price of gold would be raised each year by some percentage amount called the 'dollar inflation correction'.

A different sort of objection to a gold price rise is that it involves a loss of prestige for the United States which has pledged to keep the parity of the dollar with gold at $35. Of course it is hard to know how much the average American would pay for a given increase in international prestige. But even if prestige abroad is greatly valued in this country, it may be that the alternative courses of action to ensure the feasibility of a satisfactorily high inflation rate in America would cost more in prestige.

A more serious issue is the understandable American concern for those countries which have been willing to hold dollar assets as international reserves in the trust that they will thereby not miss out on a capital gain from a gold price rise.[8] One could imagine various kinds of reparations to these countries being paid, a kind of exchange guarantee after the fact if not before; the capital gain on the gold stock owned by America would provide the bookkeeping basis for reparations to countries which were willing to forego purchasing it (or attempting to do so). But this has an impractical ring to it.

It would be better to point out to these countries that over a couple of decades of earning interest on dollars at 3 percent or more they have gotten a doubling of their wealth, and over nearly 40 years a much greater increase in their holdings than that and to point out that the dollar will continue to earn a positive real rate of interest whereas gold, however faithfully it keeps pace with the general price level, will not offer a positive real rate of pecuniary return. Besides, the interests of every foreign country, including those that have trustingly held dollars as international reserves in sizeable amounts, depend much more on the health of the American economy and the functioning of the international monetary system than upon the international distribution of windfall gains to gold holders.

Some of the antagonism that exists toward a gold price rise is due not to any outright horror at its consequences but to the belief that it is an inferior solution to the problem of insufficiently growing gold stocks in the face of increasing world trade and increasing world price level (in terms of the dollar). Accordingly let us turn our attention to the other two responses to the problem that have been widely discussed.

9.2.2. SDR Creation. The rationale of the Special Drawing Right arrangement, at least in the American version, was to provide international reserve assets supplementary to gold and dollars that would enable the international system to meet its growing demand for reserves without entailing that the United States incur a payments deficit – at least not a deficit beyond the size at which some continuing attrition of American gold stocks would accompany the deficit. The thought was that the accumulation of SDRs would add to international liquidity and thus encourage foreign countries to pursue easier monetary and fiscal policies which would have the effect of reducing their demand for additional dollar balances and, in particular, for gold. In addition, if the SDR is more substitutable

---

[8] Is a foregone revaluation gain equivalent to a true loss? Yes if the gold-holding gainers bid up dollar prices, or if, to prevent that, countries must raise interest rates and their tax rates.

for gold than for dollars, the creation of SDR would have the additional effect of reducing the ratio of gold to dollars that countries prefer to have for purposes of international reserves. On the other hand, if the SDR bore no substitutability for gold in the view of foreign countries, its creation would not help to stop the gold drain from the United States; then a dollar's worth of SDR created would simply reduce by some fraction, at most by one dollar, the increase in holdings of dollar balances (and hence, the U.S. deficit) that would otherwise have taken place. If the SDR and dollar balances bore about the same rate of interest, one could imagine that a dollar of SDR would displace about a dollar of dollar balances. In fact, the SDR bears little interest and contains a gold guarantee.

One supposes therefore that insofar as countries abroad choose to hold SDRs in their reserves, they are viewed as substitution to a degree for gold – that is, an additional dollar's worth of SDR would displace some amount of gold in the reserves of countries abroad. At present there is some question as to the powerfulness of the SDR to substitute for either gold or dollar balances – European holdings of both dollar balances and gold have increased in the face of the SDR creation in the past year. But it may well be that the SDR will come increasingly to enjoy the status of gold, gaining gold's aura by association, benefiting from increased familiarity and its gold guarantee winning greater credibility.

If we assume that the SDR will indeed come to play the role of paper gold, whether or not on a dollar for dollar basis with gold, it is open for the members of the International Monetary Fund to vote a growth of SDR each year that would be sufficient to forestall a draining of the American gold stock at the given gold parity. This would require European governments' reconciliation to continuing inflation of world goods prices in terms of dollars at least in the sense of their accepting the preferability of this course to the need to alter the arrangements between the dollar and gold. The possibility of this reconciliation seems somewhat remote at the present time. But it may be noted that the present time schedule of SDR creation was agreed upon at a time when inflation in the Western part of the world had reached a postwar high. If continuing dollar inflation presents the rest of the world with a *fait accompli* of reduced international liquidity in nondollar form, it is not unlikely that another round of SDR creation would take place which ratifies the past inflation since the last agreement. In that case, continuing American inflation might cause international liquidity creation always to be a little less than

it would have been under stable dollar prices and an American re-
solve to continue same. But the SDRs are, in a sense, for the Europeans, and they would be spiting themselves to stop short the growth
of these reserves.

To sum up: There seems to be a reasonable chance that SDR
creation will proceed at such a pace as to avert a critical shortage of
nondollar international liquidity whether or not America chooses to
pursue a course of moderate inflation. But whether or not an adequate supply of SDRs are created for this purpose, it remains open
for the United States unilaterally to increase the dollar price of gold
in order to achieve the same objective. In the long run, the latter
method would require that recurring gold price increases be more
or less continuous rather than by discrete jumps. However the details of such an orderly method of gold price increases are not of
immediate concern.

9.3. *The Possibilities of a European Bloc*

The analysis to this point has for the most part treated the 'rest of
the world' as an atomistic conglomerate in which no one country has
any significant bargaining power with the United States and in which
there are no coalitions having important bargaining power. The real
world might better be described as consisting of several intermediate-
size nationals such as Britain, France, Germany, Japan, Italy, and
so on.

This situation has at least a couple of consequences, one of which
is that a medium-size nation can exert political pressures upon the
United States designed to induce an American inflation rate more to
its liking. Between such countries and the United States there are
myriad international arrangements which depend upon a certain
amount of mutual trust and amiability. The United States would not
want to insist on having entirely its own way on inflation if that risked
jeopardizing bilateral agreements which are of importance both to
America and to the other countries concerned. Undoubtedly any
serious opposition to a given inflation rate target of the United States
would, and ought to, temper somewhat the inflation aspirations of
this country. Yet America can and should press the case for its inflation target, seeking to explain that this is not truly injurious to the
other country (if indeed it is not) and that it may be beneficial to certain other countries and to the international system as a whole (if
indeed it is). Just like a person making his way, America should act

on inflation under the reasonable assumption that its behavior will displease only a few and they may very well forgive it, especially if there is consultation and explanation.

The other consequence – really a set of consequences – from the existence of several medium-size economies arises from the conjectural interdependence among them and the resulting incentives for their coalition. Each of these medium-size countries is a significant rival of the others and each must act wondering how its three or four closest rivals will act.

This interdependence can be illustrated in terms of the familiar game-theoretic Prisoner's Dilemma. Consider that the United States has just demonetized gold in order that it can continue, it hopes, to run a balance of payments deficit with the rest of the world. If no country in the rest of the world elects to appreciate its currency relative to the dollar, each country will go on accumulating dollars, for example, beyond its wishes to do so. This outcome is bad enough. On the other hand, if the principal rivals of some country do appreciate and the country in question does not appreciate, thinking that the others will not do so, the outcome is worse for that country. Alternatively, if one of these countries appreciates by the large amount it would choose if it believed others would do the same, and those countries actually appreciate by the same amount, the outcome is good for each such country. But if the other countries do not appreciate by anything like this amount, the outcome will be worst of all for the country if it appreciates by such an amount. Faced with such speculative interdependence, each country may very well consider it prudent not to appreciate or to appreciate by less than each would prefer if assured the others would do the same. This state of affairs will leave each country with a greater inflow of dollars than it desires (at least until enough time has elapsed for the various countries to grope their way nearer to their desired position). The same sort of conjectural interdependence might operate to inhibit the countries concerned from their preferred response in the event of a rise in the dollar price of gold.[9]

There is consequently a strong incentive for some or all of the medium-size countries, together with their smaller neighbors, to decide their exchange rates with the dollar collusively. This is a motive for the establishment of a European reserve unit – at least a unit of

[9] I doubt, however, that one should expect such inhibitions against currency appreciation in a completely routinized situation of steady American inflation as discussed in the first section of this chapter.

account if not a store of value and medium of exchange – in terms of which many or all European countries would normally fix the rate of exchange of their own currency. The exchange rate of the common reserve unit with the dollar would in turn be set by the concerted decision of the collaborating countries concerned. In principle each individual country belonging to the reserve unit coalition would retain autonomy over its exchange rate with the reserve unit and hence with the dollar. But there would no doubt be felt to be advantages from maintaining fixity of the exchange rate in terms of the reserve unit under all but the most abnormal conditions.

There is also a motive for the establishment of a European reserve unit for use as a store of value and medium of exchange among European central banks. The institution of such a second nonmetallic international money would reduce the amount of international seigniorage earned by the United States. It would reduce the amount of seigniorage paid by Europeans to America and it might earn for the Europeans some seigniorage from the rest of the world.

It may be that if America pursues a policy of moderate inflation, it will be faced with the threat of the establishment of such a European reserve unit. But such a threat or prospect, if forthcoming, should not hold any terror for the United States. It may be a mixed blessing.

There would be some loss of seigniorage for the United States. But such a loss would not be of major proportions economically. There might even be some relief in the United States that we no longer found ourselves earning seigniorage from countries poorer than we to quite the same degree as we have been doing. The existence of a rival international money would not of course prevent the United States from running the payments deficit implicit in the maintenance of a given real stock of dollar balances held by foreigners when the dollar price level was rising.

Another effect would be some lessening of the liquidity of the dollar as an international money owing to the introduction of the European international money. But the United States might welcome being relieved of the position of being the sole unilateral central banker of the world.

Naturally the smooth functioning of the international system would require that the two international monies be exchangeable for one another. If America were to continue a course of inflation faster than the European bloc, there would have to be instituted some regularized program of dollar devaluation against gold or appreciation of the European unit against the dollar (and gold). What I have in mind here is a program of managed depreciation or appreciation of a more or less continuous kind. A certain amount of exchange rate adjustment would be recurrent, normal, and perhaps even automatic according to some formula.

There are some costs here, American costs especially if the onus of exchange adjustment should fall on the dollar (relative to gold, say) rather than on the European unit. Each year brings its special circumstances and, if the dollar depreciation were not automatic, each such step would be the occasion for some conflict between export (and import-competing) interests favoring greater devaluation and the interests of importers and fixed-incomists favoring less devaluation. To avert this, it would be helpful to devise some concept as a purchasing-power-parity-adjusted exchange rate between America and the rest of the world or Europe in particular. Insofar as the exchange rate adjustment process was not highly continuous (that is, quite smooth) there would also tend to result some disturbances in trade and capital flows – leads and lags – in anticipation of the next exchange rate step. This point argues for making the process of exchange rate adjustment a smooth rather than a periodic or occasional one. On the other hand, with respect to another desideratum, namely the risks of foreign trade transactions, the fact that the par value of the dollar in terms of gold and the European unit is moving over time, does not appear to present any disadvantages. If the par value is moving at a predesignated rate, corresponding to planned differences in inflation objectives between these two areas, for example, there is of course, no additional risk. And insofar as the par value is subject to automatic adjustments in keeping with ex post trends in price-level relatives, this flexibility of the exchange rate actually reduces the risks of foreign transactions in terms of the trader's home currency.

On the other hand, if the difference between the desired inflation rates of the two areas, America and Europe, were within a couple of percentage points annually, a fixed exchange rate between the two areas would be feasible. Monetary policies in the two areas could be made to accommodate the mounting disequilibriums most of the time with only occasional need for a discrete refixing of the exchange rate once the strain on monetary instruments proved too onerous.

9.4. Conclusions

As a closed-economy theorist, I feel I have walked through the fire with the exploration of the international side of the inflation question.

Can I still be reasonably confident that an inflationist program is in the economic interests of America and of the world generally?

When it comes to economic predictions, as with other empirical extrapolations, I am sure of nothing (and wish others would be as diffident). But I am less unsure of the merits on balance of moderate American inflation over the foreseeable future than I am gravely doubtful of the wisdom of a painful restoration of an approximately stable price level. To acknowledge that continuing American inflation would eventually require an adjustment of the gold price, and still later some fresh arrangement for more continuous gold price adjustments, or else the vigorous creation of a supplement to gold such as the SDRs, hardly militates strongly against adoption of such an inflationary program. What are international economists for if not to work out such matters? The day is past that we should tie our economic policies in any part to the accident of some mineral deposits. Something will have to be done about gold anyway, whether or not America inflates in the future at some moderate rate.

The other cost, duly acknowledged, arises if there is established some European currency bloc whose members choose to inflate at a slower rate than America. Then devaluations by America against gold imply some devaluation against the European unit. In such an eventuality there would be some complex decision-making to be done by the United States in arriving at a suitable method of achieving such regular currency depreciation. But while these costs should properly temper America's inflation objectives, they should not deter the United States from choosing an appropriate inflation rate target. It would be nearly as foolish to constrain ourselves to policies which are compatible with the American and European currencies trading at rigid exchange rates as to rig the production of pears and apples so as to insure that they trade with one another at a fixed price ratio for the convenience of grocers and shoppers.

But who is to say for certain that the Europeans, with or without their bloc reserve unit, would necessarily refuse to follow America in a course of moderate inflation? Ideally what the United States will do is to convince the rest of the world that a program of moderate and well-contained inflation is economically sound and internationally just among the nations of the world. With the understanding that such persuasion would bring, the problems of international adaptation to moderate dollar inflation fade into insignificance.

Index to Names

Index to Subjects

Date Due

NOV 14 '76		
MAR 8		
JUL 8 '76		
NOV 9 '76		
NOV 8		
MAY 12 '78		